"I'm in the middle of planning a big family trip to Yellowstone National Park. It's daunting! The place is beautiful, I know, but it's big and it's hard to know where to start. It's the same with the Bible. That's why a guide like Charlotte Coyle is so helpful. In *Living in The Story*, she gives us a guided tour of this amazing library, helping us see its beauty, history, and mystery too."

—BRIAN D. MCLAREN
Author of *Faith after Doubt: Why Your Beliefs*
Stopped Working and What to Do about It

"We rarely hold books in our hands anymore, let alone in our hearts. *Living in The Story* is a way to grasp the scope and breadth of the Bible in a new and profound way."

—EDD EASON
Assistant Vice President of Housing, CitySquare, Dallas

"With helpful commentary on weekly readings from across the Old and New Testaments, Charlotte Coyle invites us to fresh and faithful encounters with the God who is still speaking. These chapters will open the hearts and minds of both experienced and beginning readers of Scripture."

—D. NEWELL WILLIAMS
President and Professor of Church History, Brite Divinity School

"If you've ever wanted to explore the Bible more deeply and consistently, you will find that *Living in The Story* is written just for you. Charlotte Coyle provides a map for reading the Bible through in a year . . . Her inclusive approach to texts enables the reader to track how important ideas develop through time, and her incisive weekly commentary provides thoughtful reflection about how the Bible speaks, and how God's activity continues, for us today. This book is well worth your time, even if you decide to turn one year into two or three!"

—MARK G. TOULOUSE
Author of *God in Public: Four Ways American Christianity and Public Life Relate*

"In *Living in The Story*, Charlotte Coyle's fresh approach to biblical revelations and teachings ties together stories and lessons from one end of the Bible to the other. As a rookie theologian participating in some of her classes, I have appreciated her explanation of the themes that prevail throughout Scripture and the recognition of the very human characters who lived the story back then. By using readings from the Old Testament, Psalms, Gospels, and New Testament in each chapter of her book, Coyle clarifies what 'reading backwards' meant for the New Testament writers and for us. This book offers much to new biblical explorers and seasoned theologians."

—MARY WALKER CLARK
Author of *Landing in My Present: A Father, a Daughter, and the Singular Himalayan Journey that Reunited Them*

"*Living in The Story* adopts a highly creative, integrated methodology for engaging Bible study across the entire landscape of Scripture. For the beginner set out to come to grips with the formidable assignment of at last reading the intimidating book so long avoided, to the more experienced student of the text and its sometimes seemingly contradictory worldviews, *Living in The Story* provides a refreshing, practical approach to growth in biblical study and understanding. Perfect for private, quiet times. Motivational for group settings. Written by an insightful pastor and theologian with a proven record of highly effective congregational ministry, this volume is a must-have addition to any serious collection of Bible-study materials."

—LARRY JAMES
CEO emeritus, CitySquare

Thank you!
CVC

Living in The Story

Living in The Story

A Year to Read the Bible and Ponder
God's Story of Love and Grace

Charlotte Vaughan Coyle

Foreword by M. Eugene Boring

RESOURCE *Publications* · Eugene, Oregon

LIVING IN THE STORY
A Year to Read the Bible and Ponder God's Story of Love and Grace

Resource Publications
An Imprint of Wipf and Stock Publishers
199 W. 8th Ave., Suite 3
Eugene, OR 97401

www.wipfandstock.com

PAPERBACK ISBN: 978-1-6667-0523-2
HARDCOVER ISBN: 978-1-6667-0524-9
EBOOK ISBN: 978-1-6667-0525-6

08/13/21

To Jerry
Best Friend, Husband, and Editor par excellence
We've been living and crafting our own chapter in *The Story* of love
and grace for fifty years now and, every day, you keep showing me
what "love and grace" can actually look like.
Happy 50th Anniversary, my Love.

And to my Grandchildren
So you can know something of my story.
May you find joy living your own lives in God's Story.

Reading Guide

Foreword

"DON'T YOU STORY TO me!" These were the words of my mom to her five-year old son. It was a lot of fun in our rural neighborhood of east Tennessee to play with an abandoned truck tire, rolling it down the gravel road and through the fields around our home. The tire, as tall as I was and considerably heavier, got away from me, and left an ugly path as it rolled through the flower bed in our front lawn. When my mom discovered what had happened and called me to account, she didn't want to accuse her oldest son of lying, but I understood the thinly-disguised warning as the equivalent of placing the right hand on the Bible and raising the other hand. She wanted to know the truth, and using noun as verb, made it clear that "storying" was on the wrong side of the ledger. Through the years, I was to learn that she was not the only person in our culture who would pose the question about an issue of some consequence, "Is that true, or is that just a story." I would even hear this question in church.

Personal Story, "Bible Stories," *The* Story

Charlotte Coyle helps us better understand The Story as the vehicle of ultimate truth. Stories are not decorations or illustrations for truth established on some other basis, but the means of communicating the truth of God. We grasp and are grasped by this truth not by getting the "moral of the story," but by learning to hear "Bible stories" as little stories within the Big Story, the Story of Everything that is the one story of the Bible, Genesis to Revelation. We do not hear this story from a safe distance. The Bible wants us to understand our own stories as embraced and given meaning by living in The Story. Charlotte does not hesitate to share her own story as interwoven into the biblical story. She preaches, teaches, and writes from within this Story, sharing Paul's self-revelation that "like a nurse tenderly caring for her children, so deeply do we care for you that we are determined to share with you not only the gospel of God, but our own selves" (1 Thess 2:7–8). Like Paul, she understands that we preachers have been entrusted with the message of the gospel (1 Thess 2:4), that it's not about us, but that the gospel is heard and communicated as the encounter of our story with The Story of the gospel.

Faith Seeking Understanding

Charlotte Coyle lives and exercises her ministry under the theologian's banner from Anselm, "Faith Seeking Understanding." We live in a day of "seekers," of sincere folk who understand how the world works and are well acquainted with common sense reality, but perhaps remembering Peggy Lee and Bette Midler ask "Is that all there is?" Their invitation is not to celebrate that the Buried Treasure or Pearl of Great Price has been found, but to join in the quest for meaning and peace of mind along the road of life: join the search, not join the church. This sort of serious quest might be called "understanding seeking faith."[1] We might prefer this per-spective on what the world, life, and the meaning of things is all about to the smug bumper sticker announcing "I Found It." The real opposite of the seeker-stance, however, is not the finder-stance, but the beginning point. Christian believers define themselves neither as seekers or finders, but as those who *been* found. This is what the Lost Coin and Lost Sheep would say if they could speak to us. The Waiting Father does not kill the fatted calf and have the Welcome Home Party because the Prodigal Son finally found his way back home, but assures us we should go ahead and join the party because "This son of mine was dead and is alive again; he was lost and is found" (Luke 15:3–32). This is what we sing in John Newton's 1779 hymn "Amazing Grace:"

> "I once was lost, but now am found,
> Was blind, but now I see."

This is faith seeking understanding, and this is the task of theology, its continuing journey, discovery and being discovered.

---

1. See Leander Keck, *The Church Confident* (Nashville: Abingdon, 1993) 57–59, and the title of R. Scott *Colglazier's Finding a Faith that Makes Sense* (St. Louis: Chalice Press, 1996).

The Church is the Locus of Theology

Theology is best done in the context of the church's life and worship—congregational, denominational, and ecumenical—and by the church's pastors and teachers whose burden and joy it is to communicate the faith and deepen the understanding of "ordinary" church members (that extraordinary company of saints, salt of the earth and light of the world). The church's pastors and teachers do this not from an ivory tower, but week by week from pulpit and lectern, in conversation, blog, and email. From the Apostle Paul through Barth and Bonhoeffer, the task of preaching that bridges the biblical there-and-then with the nitty-gritty here-and-now is faith seeking understanding, not only in the mind and heart, but in the muscles, checkbook, and voting booth. This is theology. Charlotte Coyle is a theologian. She encourages her readers to be theologians. She is not writing for preachers—though fellow preachers will benefit from the form, function, and content of what she has to say. In this book, as in her sermons and congregational teaching, her writing is itself theological actualization of what she is talking about.

Week by Week, Year by Year

One of the sturdy virtues of this book is that the plumber, Walmart cashier, and bank president who want to grow in understanding their faith but can only find an hour or two each week for serious study, will all find helpful guidance for daily Bible reading and weekly help from one of the church's pastor-teachers. Every week will bring new insight, not only for the text of the week, but as seeing each text as part of the Grand Narrative of the whole Bible. At the end of the year, readers will not end up with a nice collection of fragments of stained glass, but will find themselves standing in a cathedral.

M. Eugene Boring
Fort Worth, TX
6 April 2021

Preface

Charlotte's Story

I GREW UP IMMERSED in the life and logic of the Churches of Christ, one of many "Bible-believing" denominations typical across the South. I adored my preacher father and fervently believed everything he preached from the pulpits of these small, conservative congregations.

I believed it all, that is, until I started asking questions.

The questions started the unraveling. The questions moved me away from literalist readings of the Bible because they revealed cracks and contradictions in my fundamentalist belief system. In particular, the questions about my place as a woman in a patriarchal, hierarchical church led me to dive deeply into a study of Scripture. The questions ultimately led me to seminary and into ordained ministry.

Questions saved me and, to this day, I still believe the questions are more important than the answers.

I was forty years old when I finally allowed myself to ask the crucial question: *who am I?*—both as a woman and as a Bible-believing Christian. How can I reconcile the passion I have for Scripture and ministry in the church with the limitations my denomination imposed upon me?

I was forty-three years old when I found my way to Brite Divinity School, the seminary at Texas Christian University. By that time, I had moved from fundamentalist Church of Christ to progressive Church of Christ, but my old way of reading Scripture stayed with me; I had no idea how to read the Bible any other way but literally.

My four-year journey through seminary changed everything. It took every minute of every day of those four years to discover how to "take the Bible seriously without taking it literally." Seminary turned my theological, social, and political understandings upside-down. And then inside-out. And then right-side-up.

I see now how Spirit has been calling me into ministry my entire life; I just couldn't hear. I couldn't see or fathom such a thing because of my lifelong fundamentalist evangelical paradigm. But when I emerged on the other side of that pivotal time in seminary, I finally was able to conceive of another possibility to the *who am I?* question. The answers that were coming led me to ordination with the Christian Church (Disciples of Christ) in 1997. But I also learned that the question *who am I?* was not done seeking new answers.

I was sixty years old when I went back to seminary to work on a Doctorate of Ministry degree. A preaching course I took in 2012 prompted this *Living in The Story* project, this read-through-the-Bible-in-a-year plan that invites readers to engage with the many different biblical authors across the broad sweep of the Bible's history. The reading plan lets readers see more clearly how the process of writing, editing, and compiling the Bible over several centuries allowed for *The Story's* theological and social understandings to blossom, deepen, and develop.

As a preacher, pastor, and friend, everywhere I go I encounter people who are asking questions about the Bible similar to those I have been asking for much of my life. Since most of these seekers will never have the opportunity to go to seminary as I had done, I wanted to share with the larger church the profound insights that had changed my own life. *Living in The Story* is designed for students of the Bible who want to take it seriously but, because of long held paradigms, have trouble understanding and interpreting what the Bible means. This effort is a good fit for regular people who aren't afraid of the questions and are looking for tools to help them explore Scripture deeply and honestly.

I am well aware that many people of faith are not asking the same questions some of us need to probe. I have no quarrel with them, but those folks are not necessarily my conversation partners here in *Living in The Story*. I hope all people of faith will never stop asking, seeking, and knocking for greater wisdom, but I know *Living in The Story* is not for everyone. However, for those of us who want to take the Bible seriously without taking it literally, *Living in The Story* can be a helpful resource.

After I designed the reading plan, I needed to take it for a test run, so the next phase of the project took place in the pulpit of my congregation. Some of these good folks agreed to read through the reading guide (or at least make a stab at it!) while I challenged myself to preach these weekly texts over the course of a year. Each week, I sought out connections and wrestled with contradictions, wanting to give my church a sense of the big picture of the story of God's people—a people ever on a journey of "faith seeking understanding." By the end of 2013, I had forty-eight sermons, commentary on the forty-eight weeks of the *Living in The Story* reading guide.

When I retired from church work and the pulpit, the *who am I?* question once again took on new meaning. Pretty soon, those *Living in The Story* sermons became blogs on my LivingInTheStory.com website, where a wider audience might find the reading guide and interpretation tools it offered.

In 2016, I created another series of essays that offer further insights about the connections and variations within the weekly companion texts. These additional "As You Read" blogs point out more explicitly some of the ways the biblical writers reassessed their own understandings over the years; how the prophets and the Wisdom writers, for example, critique some of the assumptions of Torah. Or how the New Testament authors read and reread the Scriptures of their ancient faith and developed fresh understandings in light of their encounter with Jesus Christ.

Another phase of *Living in The Story* grew out of my experience with my lovely little home Bible study group when we considered some of the Psalms together. This lively circle of seekers motivated me to write yet another series of essays that explored ways the psalmists and poets often challenged status quo theology with their own practical theology. During this year of *Living in The Story's* evolution, more blogs of musing and commentary were added to the mix. Now I've reread and reworked all these numerous essays and condensed them into this forty-eight week project designed to begin the first week of any calendar year and end just before the first week of Advent.

Now it's a book—my contribution to the faith of the church as we continue to "seek understanding" and to live our own stories with faith, hope, and integrity.

Acknowledgments

THE CHURCHES OF CHRIST were my spiritual home, and even though I have moved away from that stream of the larger church, I remain grateful for the ways this tradition grounded me in Scripture. Churches of Christ and (my current church home) the Christian Church (Disciples of Christ) grew from a unity movement that blossomed in the rich soil of the American frontier in the early 1800s. The sad reality, however, is that this unity movement fractured and divided several times, in large part due to the ways these good folks read the Bible. My teachers in the Churches of Christ taught me much about what the Bible *says*, but it is mostly my teachers outside that tradition who have helped me grasp more deeply what the Bible *means*. I am grateful for both.

My father filled the pulpits of my childhood, a proud heir to the unity movement we called "Restoration." He carried the name of a first-generation revival preacher, Tolbert Fanning, and he continued that passion for faithful proclamation. (Interestingly, that Tolbert was married to a Charlotte—also impassioned to teach and serve others.) I'm ever so grateful for so much about my dad—not the least of which is that he discovered amazing grace in his later years, grace that balanced the strictness of his earlier preaching. Dad died suddenly when I was a young mother and was not around to watch his daughter follow in his footsteps, but his life and passion have informed and encouraged me every step of my way.

My mother wondered at my vocational uprising and told me plainly that she believed women shouldn't be preachers. Early on, though, she attended worship with me one Mothers' Day and heard me preach. As we left the church that day, she tucked her arm in mine and admitted: "Hm. Maybe women *can* preach." Margie/Mom/Tutu lived with us for the last two years of her life and I couldn't have had a better live-in cheerleader.

Although I mostly consider myself a "progressive" Christian now, I respect Christians who think of themselves as "conservative." After all, "conservative" is who I was for so many years, and I won't disparage those who do not share my journey. Even as I moved in a different direction, most of my Church of Christ friends granted me freedom to grow and change without judgment or censure. This blessing does not always come to evangelical women who find their way into the pulpit; numerous clergywomen making this shift find themselves ostracized, condemned, and even divorced. I am grateful to have been shaped and influenced by several grace-filled Church of Christ congregations from Texas to California to Hawaii—the most significant of which was Richardson East in Richardson, Texas.

Richardson East was the seedbed where the kernel of my call into ministry took root and began to grow. The (all male) leadership provided me opportunity to explore what it could look like for a woman to lead and to serve within the church, and an amazing support group shepherded me though a yearlong internship; we all learned together through this holy process of discernment. I am grateful that the Church at Richardson East (now CARE church) was willing to walk with me through these exciting and intimidating years. I am particularly indebted to my ministers, mentors, and friends, Larry James and Edd Eason, who urged me on to this larger world and broader journey.

If the CARE church was my seedbed, the seminary at Brite Divinity School was my greenhouse. I still remember my admissions interview with Stan Hagadone, how outlandish (and how absolutely right) this next step felt for me. I still remember my first seminary course, a weekend intensive retreat learning Greek grammar and translating the Prologue in the Gospel of John with Dr. Eugene Boring. This class unlocked closed off places in my mind and my heart—places within me that, to this day, continue to fill to overflowing with questions and yearnings, with hunger and gratitude. I will forever be grateful to the amazing Brite ecosystem that nurtured me: inspiring professors and encouraging staff, not to mention fellow students who sharpened and quickened me. Many of these students were also second career seekers, and not a few were women who, like me, had heard this divine call in mid-life. I can't fully describe how invigorating it was for me to join with so many others who had experienced this mysterious divine urging. It was in no small part because of my Brite family that I found the courage to answer the call that had been growing roots within me for so much of my life, a call that finally began to bud into unimaginable new life. I'm especially grateful to my favorite teacher, mentor, and friend, Gene Boring, who has continued to inspire and encourage me—and who graciously has provided the foreword for this book.

First Christian Church in Allen, Texas welcomed me as their associate minister while I was still a seminary student. Although our time together as a congregation was fraught with some painful conversations and heartbreaking divisions, through all those challenges I felt only affirmation for my call and a deeper resolve to minister to (and alongside) the church with all its beauty and all its flaws. I am grateful to FCC, Allen for ordaining me and blessing me as one called and sent to share the good news of Jesus Christ.

I was unusually fortunate to serve six different congregations in the Dallas area while living in the same house where my family had been from the time my children were in grade school. Benjamin, Rachel, and Jacob put up with my existential angst, endured my obsessive studying, adjusted to the unexpected relationship of being "preacher's kids," and backed me in ways small and huge as our family maneuvered our new life. I'm particularly grateful that Ben, my oldest, took time to read through the *Living in The Story* reading guide several years ago and offered some valuable suggestions; he prodded me with insightful questions and conversation. I could not have made this journey without their gracious, patient support. Now they are amazing and wise adults who continue to believe in me and teach me. I am unspeakably grateful to them—and for them.

By 2010, when I returned to Brite to work on a doctorate degree, my husband and I had moved to Paris, Texas, and I'm grateful to First Christian Church Paris for allowing space for me to continue my formal education. Again, amazing professors stretched me to new insights, one of the most significant being Lance Pape, my preaching teacher. It was in his class that I created the *Living in The Story* reading guide, and it was with his help that I developed the project to include weekly sermon-commentaries. I am thankful that he shared his passion for good preaching with me; he fanned my wearying vocational flame at an important time in my life.

And how do I begin to thank my husband? We started dating in 1968 when we were freshmen at a Church of Christ community college, and we married the semester before we graduated university. Jerry and I were still children in so many ways. But the grace of having found each other when we were young is now the grace of having grown up together for all these years. It is pure grace that we grew *together* and not apart as we each asked our questions and gave each other time and space to find our own answers. Only tenacious, stubborn love allows such a relationship and only muscular, amazing grace has brought us to this place in our lives. Jerry embodies this kind of love and grace.

Jerry has lived through my obsession with *Living in the Story* for almost a decade now, and he has supported this effort every step of the way. Even after reading every essay multiple times, he still appreciates the work and the words, and he keeps offering an encouraging word whenever I need it. He always makes me better.

Here is Jerry's summary description: *Living in The Story* is the prayerful work of a Christian pastor whom the strange new world of the Bible has confronted with its life-bending judgment. This strange new world has broken down and shaken loose the complacent assumptions of a fundamentalist upbringing by compelling an ever-expanding vision of Holy Scripture that is—like Jesus Christ—both truly human and at the same time truly divine.

Originally an academic work and then a year's worth of sermons to a church she loved, *Living in The Story* seeks to convey her insights from that confrontation. Beginning with faith that the One God whom Israel and the Church confess *has* truly spoken in and through the Bible and *will* truly speak again, she has written a guidebook to this strange new world. This guidebook knocks, seeks, and asks the immense questions implicit and explicit in the Bible from its first to last words: *Who is God?* and *Who are we?* Who are we human beings, we flawed, imperfect, misunderstanding seekers after God, we enemies of God, we lovers of God? The glimmerings of answers to these questions, however partial and fragmented, appear only when we begin to hear the Bible as a whole, a story told over centuries by many voices, a grand cosmic story that draws each of our little stories into *The Story*. This is a story in which every one of us, *all* of us (no matter how we understand ourselves or how others understand us) is included and made a part of *The Story*. This guidebook to *The Story* is a lover's poem from a pastor's heart.

Abbreviations

Scripture Abbreviations

Hebrew Bible / Old Testament

Gen	Song
Exod	Isa
Lev	Jer
Num	Lam
Deut	Ezek
Josh	Dan
Judg	Hos
Ruth	Joel
1–2 Sam	Amos
1–2 Kgs	Obad
1–2 Chr	Jonah
Ezra	Mic
Neh	Nah
Esth	Hab
Job	Zeph
Ps	Hag
Prov	Zech
Eccl (or Qoh)	Mal

New Testament

Matt	John
Mark	Acts
Luke	Rom

1–2 Cor	Phlm
Gal	Heb
Eph	Jas
Phil	1–2 Pet
Col	1–2–3 John
1–2 Thess	Jude
1–2 Tim	Rev
Titus	

Other Abbreviations

Old Testament (Hebrew Scriptures) OT
New Testament NT
Before the Common Era BCE (commonly rendered BC)
Common Era CE (commonly rendered AD)

Introduction

I BELIEVE THE ONE true loving God faithfully shepherds and sustains all-that-is from its good creation to its ultimate culmination in wholeness and *shalom*. *The Story* of this Creator-Redeemer-Sustainer God is written in stars and in DNA so that each of us—with our own individual stories—shares in that overarching story of love and grace. The Bible offers the witness of a particular people to that cosmic story. I believe that—within *and* beyond the ancient words of the Bible—the Eternal Word is still speaking.

Living in The Story provides a unique opportunity to read the Bible through fresh eyes. Each week, the reading guide leads us across the sweep of *The Story* of God's faithfulness for God's people across the ages. Each week, we will read from the Old Testament and from the Psalms alongside passages from the New Testament and the Gospels. These readings follow some of the great themes of the Bible.

As most reading schedules do, the *Living in The Story* reading guide begins in Genesis and generally follows the order of the OT canon. What is different in this schedule, however, is the way the companion scriptures from the Psalms, the Gospels, and the New Testament allow readers to watch for comparisons and contrasts in these related texts. Reading across the entire Bible each week helps us see for ourselves how Scripture developed its understandings of *The Story* as it made its journey across the ages.

For example, in week 2, the stories of creation in the first two chapters of Genesis are read in tandem with several creation Psalms as well as a remarkable chapter from the Proverbs in which *Sophia*/Wisdom describes the creation event. These ancient stories from Israel are then read together with the thoughtful NT authors who reimagined the stories of creation within the context of Jesus the Christ, the one they confessed as "firstborn of all creation;" the one they now understood to be Source and Goal of all creation.

In week 4, we engage the story of Abraham while also reading Paul's explanations about how Abraham's faith offered a template for Christian faith. Abraham also shows up in readings in the Gospel of John, allowing us to consider how John (yet another brilliant first century Christian theologian) saw connections between Abraham and Jesus.

Each week as we read the Bible with the *Living in The Story* reading guide, we are invited to re-read stories we may have read before with new insights that sharpen our vision and improve our interpretive skills. Asking good and faithful questions of the Bible allows us to deepen our faith in the God who is faithful.

I talk a lot about the "stories" of Scripture, but please understand, these are not "just" stories. I think of the Bible as sacred narrative, as historical theology, or theological history. I understand these writings to be signs pointing us toward divine and human realities that are beyond anything we can name with our limited human words and concepts. These stories seek to express *The Story* as faithfully as possible—with bold confidence and honest humility.

Beside the reading plan, weekly essays offer insights about these sometimes difficult, culturally influenced, and time-bound biblical stories. These pastoral reflections, in combination with the "As You Read" teaching essays, give context and tools for readers to see connections and find meaning in sometimes odd and troubling texts.

Theology is "faith seeking understanding" (Anselm taught us), and so each week, we seek to understand more clearly how *God's Story* intersects our human story. Each week, we will begin with faith that—in some mysterious grace—God is still speaking through the Holy Scriptures of the church.

Although I originally created *Living in The Story* for the church, I have paid close attention to how the companion essays might be read by people who are not churched. I've tried to listen to the questions of my sisters and brothers who may have given up on institutional Christianity but still see themselves as "spiritual but not religious." If that spirituality might venture a renewed effort to make sense of the Christian Scriptures, then I pray *Living in The Story* might help address some of the conundrums of faith and doubt. I firmly believe doubt is an invaluable aspect of authentic faith, and that God honors our "asking, seeking, knocking"— and even our most uncomfortable questions.

Some Practical Considerations

Living in The Story can be read at any time of the year at whatever pace the reader chooses. It was designed to begin the first week in January of any given year and to end as Advent begins: forty-eight weeks. These extra four weeks in the calendar year allow readers some extra time to catch up if they have had trouble keeping up with the reading guide. (Some reading weeks have more material than others.)

Because *Living in The Story* designates the Scripture readings by the week, readers have freedom to distribute the passages over the seven days of a week depending on the demands of their own schedules. Some days may only allow enough time to read a Psalm or a gospel passage. Other days may allow more time to read entire books of the Bible or longer passages in one sitting. Occasionally *Living in The Story* will encourage the reader to make time to read a particular book in its entirety, for example the book of Jonah, Daniel, or the Revelation. Sometimes this kind of extended engagement with a text is an important way to get its deeper meaning and flavor.

Some readers may choose to use *Living in The Story* in an abbreviated fashion, engaging only the Psalms and the gospel readings, for example; or only the New Testament passages for a read-through-the-NT-in-a-year experience. Even with a shortened effort, the "As You Read" essays make connections and offer insights into the larger biblical story that can help readers discover deeper meaning.

Numerous online resources give readers a variety of options for reading. Bible Gateway is a free tool that allows readers to choose their preferred translation and search for the chapter and verse where they want to begin. Bible Gateway[2] also offers several audio options, good possibilities for keeping up with the reading schedule while doing other activities such as driving or walking. Sometimes listening to a good reader read provides insights and nuance we miss when we read the printed words ourselves. Several other online versions of the Bible are available for purchase; many provide additional tools that allow readers to research, look up words, highlight passages, or make notes as they go along.

Engaging *Living in The Story* as a congregation-wide effort would be a good way for preachers to challenge themselves and their church to spend a year going deeper with the church's Scriptures. My own effort to preach these texts was a significant opportunity for me to grow in my

2. Explore Bible Gateway at BibleGateway.com.

own ability to proclaim the gospel. Small groups of church folks might take on this *Living in The Story* project, meeting together to share their experiences as they read through the Bible. Or fellow seekers across time zones could get together in cyberspace to discuss the week's readings and ponder what they are learning. It is this kind of communal "faith seeking understanding" that has been the story of God's faithful people throughout the ages.

Thank you for joining in this effort to live in *The Story* of God's welcome and grace—a divinely beautiful story that emerges from the stumbling story of God's own people as chronicled within the pages of the Bible.

Week 1

We Begin with Faith

Deuteronomy 6–8
Psalm 119
Second Timothy 3
John 5

As You Read in Overview

WHAT IS YOUR BASIC understanding of where the Bible comes from and how it functions? How were you taught or what did you absorb as you were growing up? How have you changed your views over the years? What questions have shifted your thinking? Our first week of reading the Bible with *Living in The Story* begins by considering the nature of Scripture. Together we will ponder the question, "what kind of book is the Bible?" as we read this week.

A popular aphorism says: "We do not see things as they are. We see things as we are." I absolutely believe this. We all interpret. We all interpret everything. There is no such thing as un-interpreted awareness. We all have some lens or another through which we see the world. We all have a framework with which we make meaning. This was as true of the biblical writers as it is true of us Bible readers.

The authors of these ancient texts began with faith. They started with a confidence that God was somehow in their story and as they collected and recollected the stories of their life together as God's people, they sought to understand its meaning. The biblical writers are not, for the most part, apologists, arguing for their faith in a way that was designed to convince nonbelievers. Rather their writings were intended to confess and explore their faith within a community of faith.

As You Read the Old Testament

This week's readings from Deuteronomy are key for the self-understanding of God's ancient people, Israel. Deuteronomy is the fifth book of the Torah, traditionally and poetically called "the books of Moses." The stage of the Deuteronomy drama is set at the River Jordan as the descendants of Abraham, Isaac, and Jacob recalled their liberation from bondage in Egypt and their forty years in the wilderness. Moses is the revered leader, calling them to remember God's past faithfulness and urging them to entrust themselves to God's ongoing fidelity.

But consider that the actual historical setting of the story in Deuteronomy probably is juxtaposed within the setting of Israel's dilemma many years later, ca. 597 BCE. Most likely, during the time the book of Deuteronomy was composed, the nation once more was displaced from their homeland. God's people were seeing their past history through the lens of their current captivity in Babylon, and they recognized they were standing on a precipice. Either they will learn from this experience. Or they will be lost.

So Moses' ancient challenge to their ancestors to "hear"—to remember, recall, take heed, obey—is also a word for Israel centuries later: love God, the one God, God alone; this is everything. All the rules of the Law, all the codes and commandments and ethics and devotion, everything that is written is designed and intended to shape God's people into a community of love.

As You Read the Psalms

The ancient Hebrew tradition says God spoke to Moses in fire and cloud on the mountaintop and wrote "the ten words," the Ten Commandments, with the Divine Finger. Psalm 119 celebrates the Law of the Lord handed down from Mount Sinai and revered as God's definitive word for God's chosen people.

As you are reading this week's psalm, consider its form as well as its message. Psalm 119 is the longest chapter in the Bible and it is written as a poetic Hebrew acrostic. This hymn is shaped according to the Hebrew alphabet, the several lines of the first stanza beginning with the Hebrew letter, *aleph*, then all the lines of the second stanza starting with the second letter *bet* and so on through the alphabet.

The poets of Israel believed that in all of life—from "A" to "Z"—the Way of God is ordered and trustworthy, that creation is "good," that light and darkness exist as they were created to exist, in perfect harmony. The teachers of Israel taught that the whole of life is founded upon trust in the Law of the Lord. They believed that every challenge of life can be overcome by faithful obedience to God's Word; that true life, right life, good life comes not through simple obedience to rules, but rather through the grace and mercy of Yahweh who sustains all creation. In this methodical, disciplined form of acrostic, the singer/psalmist is able to wax eloquent about God's Law in a poetic, alphabetical cadence.

Notice how the psalmist uses several different words to describe God's way: Torah, Law, Word of the Lord, ordinances, statutes, precepts.

I would add another: the Tao. 600 years before Christ, the philosophy of the Tao developed in China. This "tao" literally means "way, path, and road" and it teaches that there is a way within the cosmos, a way of perfect balance that is the natural order of things, a way that flows from the unity of all things, a way that exists in harmony with all creation, and coincides with the core Truth that binds the universe together.

Father Richard Rohr describes this reality when he, too, speaks of The Story in which "the patterns are always true." Each of us has a personal story, most of us are a part of a group story, but transcending and including all the smaller stories of our humanity is The Story.

> The biblical tradition takes all three levels seriously: My Story, Our Story, and *The* Story. Biblical revelation is saying that the only way you dare move up to The Story and understand it with any depth is that you must walk through and take personal responsibility for *your personal* story and also for *your group* story . . .
>
> We are neither trapped inside of our little culture and group identity, or our private pain and hurts. We are people of the Big Picture . . . full of meaning, where nothing is eliminated and all is used to bring us to life.[1]

The psalmist begins with the faith that this kind of Law, Truth, Word, and Way is the foundation upon which all other just laws are founded.

---

1. Rohr, *Things Hidden*, 23–24 italics in the original. Find a summary of "The Three Domes" at the Center for Action and Contemplation website https://cac.org/the-three-domes-2021-21-24.

Think of Torah/Law/Word within this framework of The Great Way, *The Story* of Creator's way for all creation.

As You Read the New Testament

We know from Acts and Paul's undisputed letters that Timothy was a student and colleague of the apostle Paul. Probably these two letters addressed to Timothy were written in Paul's name by second-generation disciples nearly one hundred years post-Jesus as the Church mushroomed across the Roman Empire. The original Christians were all Jews, but as the movement spread, many Gentiles (non-Jews) came to claim Jesus as their Lord and Savior.

"All scripture is inspired by God," Second Timothy asserts. But consider there were no New Testament scriptures during this time; there was only the Old Testament, the ancient Hebrew Scriptures. So the exhortation for Timothy to continue in the "sacred writings" has to mean the ancient Scriptures of the Hebrew people. "All scripture is inspired by God" has to mean that God's Breath, Life, Presence, Word—somehow, in some mystery—can be encountered within very imperfect, incomplete (and even ancient) human words.

Within the Christian tradition that followed from Paul, John, and Timothy, we continue to acknowledge the wisdom of Scripture that can and does "instruct, teach, reprove, correct, train, equip." Now we Christians have the NT, our own sacred writings that have made their own journey of writing, editing, and compiling over a hundred years or so. But even as Christians revere and respect the Holy Scriptures, Christians will only worship and follow the God who is Creator-Redeemer-Sustainer, the one to whom our Bible gives witness.

As You Read the Gospel

As we read chapter five of the Gospel of John, we see John's Jesus countering religious leaders who seem to have lost the sense of this overarching way and have limited themselves to the smaller ways of codes and rituals. It appears as if they are literalist followers of the Law of Moses: toeing lines, dotting i's, crossing t's, scoring points. Jesus, however, challenges this lesser way of reading Scripture.

Writing at the close of the first century, maybe seventy years after Jesus, John offers an intriguing interpretation of God made known in Jesus Christ. In John's gospel:

- Jesus is "the Word made flesh" (1:14).

- Jesus is the holy Temple where God's glory resides (2:18–22).

- Jesus is God's Way/Truth/Life embodied (14:6).

John and the other theologians who authored the NT make an astounding claim: it is not a book, a Bible, a Scripture (no matter how holy) that is God's eternal Truth. It is a person, one particular person in history who has come into existence to perfectly embody God's Eternal Way.

Reflection: *We Begin with Faith*

When I was a girl, I didn't know how to read the Bible. The truth is sometimes I still don't know. What kind of book is it anyway? Is it a rulebook? A history book? Is it a book filled with interesting stories with moral lessons? Or maybe a collection of fantastic stories that don't seem to have much connection to our modern day world?

Was the Bible somehow dictated directly by God and given to the people of God as something to be revered? Did the Spirit speak so clearly to holy men of God that they wrote down everything perfectly whether they understood what they were writing or not? Did they write for their time? For future times? For all times? Lots of people over lots of years have asked lots of questions about the nature of this beautiful, odd, comforting, disturbing book the church calls its "Holy Scripture."

In my own journey with the Bible, it was only when I finally did the crucial work of asking hard questions and even arguing with the texts that Scripture was transformed for me into a symphony of polyphonic voices, into a masterpiece work of art that painted an alternative vision of the world, into a complex novel-like story unavoidably embedded in its own culture and time—and yet, somehow, in some mystery—able to give witness to the God beyond history who has acted (and continues to act) within history.

Sometimes when I deal with Scripture, I feel like I'm sailing a vast ocean; the wideness of it makes me suck in my breath. Then I put on my snorkel gear and plunge beneath the surface; its immense, colorful world opens up before me and I am astounded. Then I put on my scuba gear and dive even deeper; its mystery stretches endlessly before me.

Sometimes I think of Scripture as a conversation with a dear friend where I am invited to listen to the story of another. I listen respectfully to a point of view that may be different from mine. I listen carefully because we come from different places and cultures. I listen to more than just the words because often we need to listen beneath the words, beyond the words, to listen not only to what this one is saying, but to listen for what it means. And sometimes in this conversation, I argue (respectfully, of course. This is a friend, after all!) But I know I don't have to agree absolutely with every single thing I read here.

When I'm in this kind of conversation with Scripture, I find everything works better when I begin with trust. When I am able to place myself within a proper hearing distance and open my ears to hear whatever it may want to say to me; when I can open my eyes to see what it needs to show me. When we read the Bible this way—trusting that somehow God is in this event of Scripture, trusting that this really does matter, trusting that, in these ancient words, a true and eternal Word is still being spoken—then we begin with faith.

We begin as the church has always begun, trusting that "in the reading of Scripture, the Creator is at work, something is made out of nothing, the church takes form around the words of the Word."[2]

Centuries ago, the wise saint Anselm said: *credo ut intelligam*—"I believe so that I may understand." Contrary to our modern conventional wisdom that "seeing is believing," the church has long recognized that understanding, knowing, comprehending the presence of God can never be a matter of evidences or proofs. Knowing God has always been a matter of faith. It is by knowing from the heart, trusting within the spirit, placing ourselves into a listening space, and then waiting to be addressed that we can ever hope to understand the least little thing about God and God's way.

We begin with faith.

We begin by opening ourselves to the possibility that even in these often odd, time-bound, culture-bound words, the Living Word of the Living God just may show up. It is our faith (and the faith of the church across the ages) that moves us to suspend our disbelief and to let ourselves

2. Willimon, *Pastor*, 128.

trust that the eternal God just may meet us here in—and beyond—the pages of Scripture.

When I say: "we begin with faith," I don't mean we have to believe that every history-like story can be fact checked or that every miracle story has some relationship with our modern day scientific method. When I say: "we begin with faith," I don't mean we have to take every word at face value and believe that God is the literal, personal author of this book we call the Bible. When I say: "we begin with faith," I don't mean we can't disagree.

But what I do mean when I say: "we begin with faith" is that we begin by entrusting ourselves to the one whom we confess to be the Author of *The Story*, the overarching story of the cosmos. And we trust that this one has written us into that story so that, consequently, our lives matter. Our lives matter a great deal!

We begin with faith that this inscribed ancient text can be translated into contemporary human lives. We begin with faith that this story is now written not with ink but by the Holy Spirit, not on stone tablets, but now on the vast multitude of pages that are all of our very human hearts (2 Cor 3:3).

"Scripture does not just want to recreate some world of the past" (William Willimon says), "but rather wants to form a new world in the present—to recreate us!"

> We call the Bible 'inspired' because the Bible keeps reaching out to us, keeps striking us with its strange truth, keeps truthfully depicting God . . . We trust the Bible because on enough days we discover that God's Word has the power to produce the readers that it requires . . .
>
> When the authority of the Bible is challenged with: "Is the Bible true?" we are not to trot out our little arguments but rather [we are expected to trot out] our little lives. The truthfulness of Scripture is demonstrated in the true and authentic lives it is able to produce.[3]

When we stand with Israel on the banks of the Promised Land, we stand in faith that we too are living in this same story. As they were liberated from slavery in Egypt, as they were saved from Exile in Babylon—so too we acknowledge all our own exiles and recognize all our salvations. We come to understand how we too desperately need liberation from

3. Willimon, *Pastor*, 128–30.

earthly pharaohs and worldly powers that alienate, estrange, and oppress. And when we finally name our own helplessness, we hear again the call to shape our lives around the one God who is to be our only God. We hear again that the one core commandment is to love this God with all that we are and with all that we have, "with heart and soul and might" (Deut 6).

When we sing the Psalms with the passionate psalmists, we learn how to name our own passion and how to speak boldly our yearning for God's way, for God's life (Ps 119).

When we sit at the feet of Paul, Timothy, or Matthew, Mark, Luke, and John, we remember the wisdom of submitting ourselves to these sacred writings, to this holy Scripture that is inspired to teach and reprove, to correct and train, to equip and prepare God's people to do good works; to do God's work in our world (2 Tim 3).

When we stand with religious rule-followers arguing with John's Jesus, we begin to see all the ways we too misuse and abuse Scripture to prove our little points, to serve our petty agendas, to endorse the visions of our small imaginations. The living Word of the living Christ confronts us as well when we stand before this Word made flesh. When we are honest and bold to open ourselves to really hear and truly see, then (and only then) do we find life—real life, true life, eternal life that begins here and now.

"Bending our lives toward the text that is ever reaching out to us . . . the church is forever formed and reformed . . ." Willimon reminds us.[4]

During this year as we read and live in *The Story*, let us move out of the shallows and dive deeper into the vast ocean of the Word so we can marvel at the wonders hidden there for us. Let us "gather around the words of Scripture with the expectation that these words will become for us the Word of God Incarnate."[5]

And as we read, may we be created and recreated: formed, reformed, and ever transformed into the image of the Christ whose Word dwells richly within us and among us.

---

4. Willimon, *Pastor*, 126

5. Willimon, *Pastor*, 125.

Week 2

Creation

Genesis 1 and 2
Psalm 29
Psalm 33
Psalm 104
Psalm 148
Proverbs 8
Colossians
John 1–8

As You Read the Old Testament

As you read about creation this week, watch for the confession of faith that God is Creator-Redeemer-Sustainer of all-that-is. Listen for the confession both of Israel and Christianity that everything is "good."

As you read Genesis 1 and 2, watch for differences in the two creation stories: for example, see how God's name is different, the order of creation is different, and theology is different. Some students of the Bible are troubled by these seeming contradictions, but the stories are different by design and purpose. Scholars understand chapter one to have come from the historical tradition of Israel called "Priestly"—these passages refer to God as *Elohim*. Chapter two seems to come from another tradition we call "Yahwist" since these texts cite God's name as *Yahweh* (Yнwн).[1] When we read the stories

---

1. Etienne Charpentier's concise guide *How to Read the Bible* offers helpful discussions about these various historical traditions and how they became woven together into the Jewish Scriptures.

side by side, not as scientific reports but rather as theological reflections, then we recognize the beauty of the diverse poetic ways that Genesis describes how all the generations of creation were first generated. (Note the many word plays throughout both chapters. This is rich reading!)

During my earliest days of questioning *who am I?* as a woman believer who wants to take the Bible seriously, I spent months studying these two short chapters in Genesis. That deep dive completely changed my understanding of how men and women relate appropriately to one another in the home, in society, and in the church. For example, in the first story, there is no hint of patriarchy or hierarchy; the man and woman are created at the same time and given equal responsibility for the care of the creation. In the second story, man is created first then later woman is shaped from a bone taken from his side and presented to the man as "helper." This Hebrew word and the context of the story do not suggest the woman's submission; rather, both stories picture equality. It was this epiphany of biblical equality that was the genesis of my own journey into ordained ministry.

It's hard to recognize Hebrew word plays when we read chapter two in English, but seeing the puns gives the story new meaning. For example, the word *adam* is a word play that names the *adam* as coming from *adamah*: ground, soil, or earth. The human was created from the humus.

We will get to chapter three next week so don't rush to the "sin" story. This week ponder Creator's pronouncement that all this physical, material creation is "good." Spend this week considering the beauty and goodness of all created things and their balanced relationship within the broad scope of creation. Consider creation's rich, multivalent relationship with Creator.

As You Read the Psalms

As you read Psalms 33 and 104, bask in the beautiful poetry. Especially appreciate Psalm 33: "by the word of the Lord the heavens were made . . . God spoke and it came to be . . ." Psalm 104 celebrates both the creation and the Creator:

> You are wrapped in light as with a garment.
> You stretch out the heavens like a tent.
> You set the beams of your chambers on the waters.
> You make the clouds your chariot and ride on the wings of the wind . . .

As the Genesis stories affirm, the psalmist also acknowledges creation as good—the gift of a good and merciful Creator.

Both Psalm 104 and Genesis 1 picture the Creator as existing and creating from outside the cosmos. Like a poet or an artist or a sculptor, the Creator is not a part of creation but is, rather, its creative source and originator. And yet, at the same time, both Psalm 104 and Genesis 2 picture the Creator as intimately connected with all that is created. In the second Genesis story, God molds the human from the humus of the earth, breathes the breath of life into its nostrils, and walks with the man and the woman in the cool of the evening. Powerful poetic intimacy.

Psalm 104 suggests that Creator set the cosmos into motion so that the days and the seasons continue to endure. Creator shared creative power with the plants and the creatures so they continue to recreate and endlessly procreate of their own accord. And yet, also, at the same time, everything is held together by the spirit and breath of the Creator who is also its Sustainer.

The poet of the psalms sees the world as any typical ancient would have understood it, the cosmos and the earth existing in three tiers. In this cosmology, the heavens (the dome of the skies) are above, the underworld (chaotic sea) is below, while in the middle, the table of the earth is set firmly on a pillared foundation keeping it steadfast and safe. The stories of Genesis frame creation from within this ancient understanding, so as we read these psalms, we must keep in mind that none is intended to be science.

As you read Proverbs 8, enjoy the lovely Hebrew anthropomorphic poetry. Wisdom is pictured here as *Sophia*, Creator's partner from before the beginning. Hold this image together with John's image of *Logos*. Hebrew and Greek words carry a sense of gender, and I love how the "femininity" of Wisdom couples with the "masculinity" of Word. It's a kind of yin/yang wholeness portrayed in this ancient way of thinking about the meaning of creation.

As You Read the New Testament

The letter to the church at Colossae was written either by Paul or by one of his next-generation disciples who continued his ministry. The Christology of this amazing little letter is cosmic, proclaiming the Christ to be beyond and outside of creation as the one who "holds all things together" (we would call this a very "high" Christology). At the same time, Colossians also proclaims that: "in Christ, the whole fullness of deity dwells bodily . . ." By incarnation the Christ became a part of creation (Col 1:5 and 2:9). Again the language is profound, remarkable, and full of mystery. As you read Colossians, let the soaring poetry get into your soul.

As you read *Living in The Story* for week 2, remember that all these texts are steeped in poetry. The Genesis stories, the Psalms, the Proverbs, the Prologue of John, the soaring singing theology of Colossians—all these biblical works speak truth deeper and broader and larger than any historical facts, scientific formulas, or creedal interpretations. Reflect on the ways poetry speaks of unspeakably marvelous realities. The poetry of creation continues to shape even us within the rhyme and rhythm of the Creator, The Poet of *The Story*.

As You Read the Gospel

John's narrative style is quite different from the other three gospels because his way was to tell *fewer* stories and to go *deeper*. There are not many explicit quotations from the Hebrew Scriptures, but John crafts a rich and complex connection of the ancient story to the story of the life of Jesus the Christ. Theologian Richard Hays calls this connection "reading backwards."

> Even more explicitly than the other Gospel writers, John champions reading backwards as an essential strategy for illuminating Jesus' identity.
> Only by reading backwards, in light of the resurrection under the guidance of the Spirit, can we understand both Israel's Scripture and Jesus' words.[2]

Genesis, the book of beginnings, begins, "In the beginning—when God created the heavens and the earth, God said . . ." Centuries later, the Gospel according to John opened with a fresh interpretation, a rereading of the Genesis story: "In the beginning—was the Word, the *Logos*."

Reading the sacred Hebrew Scriptures through the lens of the Christ brought John to startling new insights. In his understanding, in some unfathomable mystery the eternal creative energy and wisdom of Divinity had been enfleshed in Jesus of Nazareth: "The Word became flesh and dwelt among us . . ." (John 1:14). John's theology of incarnation is another

2. Hays, *Reading Backwards*, 85–86.

clear allusion to the goodness of creation and created flesh. The confession of faith that "the Word became flesh," that the eternal principle of *Logos* became one particular human being, was and is radical Christology.

The Christian understanding of incarnation is unique among the world religions. Islam locates God's "presence" in the Koran, ancient Israel pictured God's presence ("glory") in the Temple, while Christianity proclaims God's presence in the unique life of Jesus.

As you read John's prologue in 1:1–18, notice the numerous images, symbols, and figures John incorporates into this gospel. Watch how images of word and light and life particularly hearken back to the Genesis creation stories.

Reflection: *The Cosmic Creating Christ*

One of my favorite poems is James Weldon Johnson's *The Creation*: "And God stepped out on space / And looked around and said, / 'I'm lonely /—I'll make me a world' . . ."

> Then this great God,
> Like a mammy bending over her baby,
> Kneeled down in the dust
> Toiling over a lump of clay
> Till he shaped it in is his own image;
> Then into it he blew the breath of life,
> And man became a living soul.
> Amen. Amen.[3]

I feel sorry for people who try to turn the wide, wonderful creation stories into small, sterile science texts. It's obvious to me that the stories in Genesis 1 and 2 are poetry in the very best sense of the word. This kind of poetic drama makes the story so much bigger, tells the story so much truer than some other literary forms because we find here deep, profound truth about who we are and about who God is. We discover truth about the eternal God who is outside of time but who also is ever breaking into time, ever breaking into our lives in unexpected places and unexpected ways.

The two creation stories in the first two chapters of Genesis most likely grew out of the Babylonian Exile. Before the Exile, descendants of Abraham were never actually a monotheistic people worshiping only one

---

3. Johnson, "The Creation" in *God's Trombones*, 17–20. Find a recording of James Weldon Johnson reading his wonderful poem on YouTube.

God. Again and again, in spite of the call to love and worship the one true God, the biblical histories tell about (what the prophets called) "adulteries." The stories describe a people with a double mind and a divided heart.

It was only in Babylon that Israel finally obeyed their call to love this one God who is God alone. It was during their Exile that they learned to put their hope only in *this* God. It was here in the darkness and void of Exile they finally began to trust that, even now, even here God could and would create something out of their nothingness. They held onto hope that God was at work creating a new people with new hearts and a re-newed future.

Thus the image of God as Creator became a consuming image that gave hope and purpose to these people who were, in some very real ways, disintegrating; a people whose very existence was at risk. It was in their Exile, as they told their story, that they imagined themselves, reimagined themselves to be a people created and recreated by this Creator.

Babylon had several tales of beginnings (every culture does), but in the creation stories preserved for us in Scripture we can see how Israel did not buy into the Babylonian worldview. Instead Israel reframed the conventional wisdom of their time and rewrote the story of the dominant culture in order to craft an alternative vision that gave witness to and sustained their own faith. All-that-is (the children of Abraham insisted) did not emerge from the carcass of a defeated cosmic monster. Rather all-that-is purposefully was conceived, crafted, and created within the mind of the one true God. All-that-is in the beginning was woven into matter by Wisdom, spoken into being by Word, breathed into existence by Spirit. In these creation tales, we can see the subversive way Israel stood against their enslaving culture and rejected its power to name them. They rewrote the story the world tried to impose upon them and stood firmly in their faith.

In the first creation story of chapter 1, we see Israel's testimony that God is the Transcendent One, outside of creation, speaking and willing everything into existence, while in the second creation story in chapter 2, God is the Immanent One, intimately bound to creation. God is both/and, unsearchable and yet, at the same time, known. Unreachable and also near like a friend in a garden. In this conception of a purposely-crafted creation, the biblical authors claim that we humans are God's creatures, God's desire, God's beloved—and ultimately God's responsibility. These stories remember the one who is Source, Sustainer, and Goal;

they remind who we are and why we exist. They remind us whose we are—creatures of the creation intimately bound to the Creator.

The stories remind us *who* we are and they remind us *whose* we are. The stories teach us that God is God and we are not.

This re-writing, re-telling, re-imagining became Israel's Scripture, and these creation stories continue to be foundational stories for Jews and Christians alike because they affirm that our very existence is gift and grace.

Centuries later, when John wrote his gospel, John also rewrote creation stories, but not in the same way Israel rewrote the stories of Babylon; rather John was bold to rewrite his own Scripture! "In the beginning . . . was the Word. And the Word was with God. And the Word was God." For John and the Christ followers of the first century, for these deeply spiritual people who were grounded in Israel's Scriptures, everything had changed.

How does a believer rethink everything they have believed before? How does one reimagine what once was firmly set and seemingly unalterable? For these faithful people of God, putting their faith in Jesus Christ had changed everything. Now when they looked back at the old stories, they saw them through the prism of the Christ. Now when they considered the story of God's Way in the world, they saw it was much bigger than their one particular national story. Now in Jesus Christ, their story had been broken wide open. *The Story* was now the story of every Jew and Gentile, every man and woman, rich and poor, slave and free.

Equally amazing was the recognition, the confession that this cosmic reality had been incarnated in one particular human being who "lived among us for a while." The Transcendent One who spoke creation into existence and pronounced all things "good," the Immanent One with dirty hands who shaped a human out of the humus of the earth, now this one (we confess) has entered into creation like no story before could have imagined. Jesus Christ (as Colossians says) in his fleshly body, in his death, in that reality of humility and powerlessness, in that attitude of self-giving and letting go has reconciled all creation.

This Cosmic Creating Christ, the Word who spoke all things into being, who is before all things, and in whom all things hold together—this one was the baby in the manger and the man upon the cross. And this one is now, we confess, the Risen Christ, the very Energy, Power, Wisdom, Word of God, who continues to create and recreate. The Cosmic Creating Christ continues to form, reform, and transform all us creatures of creation. This is The Cosmic Story within which all our smaller stories are written. Like Israel, retelling the story of creation within the darkness of their exile, we too can remember and reimagine that we are God's creatures, God's desire, and ultimately God's responsibility.

As we read these *Living in The Story* scriptures in the coming weeks, maybe we will find ourselves in these poems, stories, and narratives. As we read, let us trust that the Word is still speaking into our every darkness; that Wisdom is still weaving beauty into every chaos; that Spirit is still brooding, hovering, nesting over all-that-is.

As we read, may we too, like the ancestors, come to realize that we are always growing, not only in our understandings, but also in our very ability to become our fully human selves.

Week 3

Sin

Genesis 3–11
Psalm 5
Psalm 10
Psalm 53
Romans 1–3
John 9–12

Reading the Old Testament

AS YOU READ GENESIS 3–11, notice how these stories seem to be set out of time. Next week when we start with Abraham and the patriarchs, we will see more geographies and genealogies and we'll recognize that the telling of those stories is more history-like. But the opening chapters of Genesis tell us primeval mythological stories of origins.

"Mythological" is not a slur. Myth is one way to speak about things that are deeply true even if they are not factual or historical. Consider this description from Britannica:

> Myth has existed in every society. Indeed, it would seem to be a basic constituent of human culture . . .
>
> A people's myths reflect, express, and explore the people's self-image. The study of myth is thus of central importance in the study both of individual societies and of human culture as a whole.[1]

1. Bolle, "Myth," *Britannica*.

Myths are the stories we tell that help us understand where we come from and what is the meaning of our existence. All our human religions include this type of narrative as a way to point toward deep truth that is difficult to understand or explain.

Every religion is true one way or another; true, that is, when understood metaphorically. But when religion gets stuck in its own metaphors, interpreting them as facts, we get into trouble. (American Christianity has its own special challenges when it comes to getting "stuck" in metaphor.) But when we allow ourselves to get unstuck, to break free from literal, concrete thinking, then we begin to discover truth that is wider, deeper, and higher than simple facts.

As you read these fascinating stories in this section of Genesis, resist asking questions such as, "Did the serpent really talk?" or "Where did Cain get his wife?" or "How could all those animals fit into an ark?" Instead challenge yourself to ask the big questions, What does this mean? What do these stories teach us about who God is and who we are as humans?

As You Read the Psalms

"Fools say in their hearts, 'There is no God.'" The psalmist's blunt description makes us think that our poet has suffered too many fools and has had to endure the consequences of chaos that can occur when other people live their lives without wisdom. They are corrupt, they commit abominable acts, they have all fallen away, they are all alike perverse; "they eat up my people as they eat bread and do not call upon God" (Ps 53). The psalmist pictures God earnestly searching for wisdom among the humans, the Holy One calling out for righteousness. But, as in the Garden of Eden, the Creator only finds folly. "There is no one who does good; No, not one."

We modern Christians believe in the redemption Christ Jesus brought into the world, but we too still suffer fools. And we still act the fool. We remember all of us humans are both good *and* bad, right *and* wrong, wise *and* foolish. But we—like people of faith have always done—trust anyway, because this faith is an eschatological faith. That is, we live with confidence in the here–and–now because we ground ourselves in the then–and–there; we trust in the ultimate *shalom* God is bringing for all creation. This trust allows us to experience a peace that passes understanding (Phil 2) because we believe that the Christ already has brought

God's reign into the world even as we know it is not yet completed. Peace and salvation are not quite yet realized.

And so the psalmist puts his faith in God, the God of Abraham, Isaac, and Jacob, and he trusts that the Surprising God of Unfathomable Faithfulness will—one day, some how—make everything right. And like the psalmist, we too hold onto hope and continue to put our trust in the Unfathomable Faithfulness of our ever Surprising God. We too give witness to the already-and-not-yet character of the salvation the Christ has brought (and continues to bring!) into lives of *all* us both/and people.

As You Read the New Testament

Paul's thesis statement for the Letter to the Romans may well be the thesis statement for his entire life's work; Paul understood himself to be one called and sent, one saved and spent for the sake of the gospel. Paul's confidence in the gospel is grounded in the power of the one true Triune God: the eternal will of the Father, the faithfulness of the Son, and the life-giving love of the Spirit. "I am not ashamed of the gospel; it is the power of God . . ." (Rom 1:16). Paul was a deeply pious Jew immersed in the story of Israel as the chosen people of God. Drawing from the rich conceptual history within the Hebrew Scriptures, Paul proclaims that "the gospel of God" is also "the gospel concerning his Son."

The gospel is God's story, God's movement, God's purpose and grace, God's action on behalf of all creation. It is "the gospel of God," Paul insists, the good news *of, from,* and *about* the one True God permeating all creation from the very beginning. Paul's spirit-breathed brilliance was his ability to think and then rethink the meaning and mystery of God's story in light of the life–death–resurrection of Jesus Christ. The conversion of his mind, his fresh examination of previously fixed conceptions, his complete surrender to the sheer force of God's story reimagined led him to perceive and proclaim a message of God's reconciliation of *all* people. God indeed has kept covenant with Abraham and now has created one family of God from all the families of the earth. This reconciliation has happened in and through the Christ. It is God's will, determination, action, word, and act enfleshed in the life and death of Jesus that is the turning point of history.

The gospel concerning God's Son flows from the narrative story of Israel. For Paul, Jesus is herald of the good news, legitimate king in the

line of David, the anticipated Messiah, beloved of the Father, Son of God.
Paul's narrative reading of the ancient text as the story of God allowed
him to see Jesus the Christ as the continuation and climax of this ongoing
story and thus proclaim Jesus "Son of God" *as* the "gospel of God."

"Son" language in the biblical story is multivalent vocabulary, but
Paul proclaims it is *in the resurrection* that the human Jesus was shown
to be, was marked out, as the authentic expression, demonstration, and
incarnation of the one true God. As Alan Lewis said, whether "in this
Son, God had become a perfect human, or that in this human, God had
found a perfect Son,"[2] this Jesus, a son of Israel, was declared to be the
perfect Son of God.

In Romans 1–3, see how Paul is retelling the story of humanity.
Watch how he alludes to good creation and a generous Creator and then
considers how sin twisted and bent this goodness into something ugly
and hostile. As you read, consider how Genesis 3 as well as the Psalms
and the prophets hover in the background of Romans 1–3. As a faithful
Hebrew, Paul was immersed in the story from the Hebrew Scriptures, and
he wrote this letter to the church in Rome in order to explore and explain
how God, through the Christ, continues to redeem the brokenness and
hopelessness of creation. Now, because of Jesus, redemption has taken on
a whole new meaning.

Watch Paul pound the pagan Gentiles for their immoral, unethi-
cal, idolatrous culture, and then watch him pivot and pound the Jews for
their self-righteousness and hypocrisy. Then this astonishing statement,
especially astounding to the faithful, practicing Jews of his day: "There
is no distinction. All have sinned and fall short of the glory of God . . ."
(Rom 3). All of us are sinners, Paul insists, each of us individually and
all of us together. Naming, recognizing, and owning up to this hopeless
dilemma is the only way for us to truly appreciate the radical grace of the
gospel made known in Jesus Christ.

Those of us who are faithful, practicing religious folks may look at
Paul's list of evils and reassure ourselves that we are not *that* bad (we humans are very good at rationalizing and justifying ourselves). But Spirit
nudges us to see ourselves clearly and to name ourselves honestly. In order to begin to grasp the magnitude of the grace of our redemption, we
must first grasp the deep significance of our fallen-ness. So Paul's proclamation of the gospel, God's solution to the problem of sin, astounds us

---

2. Lewis, *Between Cross and Resurrection*, 121.

even more. For Jews and Gentiles alike, for the wise and for the foolish, for the good and the bad . . . there is no distinction!

> Since all have sinned and fall short of the glory of God, they are justified by his grace as a gift, through the redemption which is in Christ Jesus . . . Rom 3:21–26.

As you compare Psalms 5 and 10 to these opening chapters of Romans, you will recognize how Paul's treatise on sin echoes the psalmist's powerful descriptions. Also note that the consequences of the sins of some people will always infect and influence the lives of other people. We who are bound together within this human community live in a complex interdependent human ecosystem that has very real consequences in lives other than our own.

As You Read the Gospel

As you read John 9–12, pay special attention to the discussion Jesus and the disciples have about the topic of sin in chapter 9, "Who sinned, this man or his parents?" They assumed, as many people still do, that sickness and misfortune are the result of sin. Today, we might call this "blaming the victim."

Here's some helpful background on the gospels. Matthew, Mark, and Luke are called the "synoptic" gospels because their vision and version is similar to one another (*syn* = similar + *optic* = seeing). John's gospel, however, is quite different because it has its own unique chronology, geography, theology, and style.

As you read the Gospel according to John, notice that it has no birth narrative, no shepherds (Luke), no wise men (Matthew) and significantly, no story of a miraculous virgin birth. There is no last supper with breaking the bread and taking the wine in remembrance. John tells the story of the Christ event in his own deeply theological and poetic way.

Also as you read, understand that in the canonical chronology of our New Testament, Paul wrote his version of the good news of Jesus Christ first. His letters to congregations during the 50s and 60s proclaimed the gospel not in story, but rather in practical, lived theology. Mark probably came next, around 70 CE. Then Matthew and Luke wrote around the year 90. Finally, around the turn of the century, John wrote his gospel. These gospel writers' way of proclaiming the gospel was different from Paul's; their approach was to craft their Christology into story. It was a new and distinctive narrative theology that told the Jesus story by making connections back to the story of Israel.

Each gospel writer demonstrated his own way to reread the Hebrew Scriptures and apply a Christ hermeneutic, a way of interpreting *The Story* through the lens of the Christ. God's redemption of human sinfulness began from the foundation of the world then unfolded in divine faithfulness to Israel. God's work of grace and salvation was now seen to continue and to find its climax in the life, death, and resurrection of Jesus. Such thoughtful, prayerful reflection is the origin of Christian theology.

Reflection *Sin: the Lost Language of Salvation*

I borrowed this title from Barbara Brown Taylor's fine little book, *Speaking of Sin: The Lost Language of Salvation*. In these helpful essays, Taylor explores scriptural models and traditional Christian theology that frequently use medical or legal language to describe sin. If we think of sin as sickness then its solution is a healing. If we think of sin as crime then its solution must be a punishment. But in her effort to recover "the lost language of salvation," Taylor prefers a third way that acknowledges the core problem is broken relationship.

> In theological language, the choice to remain in wrecked relationship with God and other human beings is called sin.
> The choice to enter into the process of repair is called repentance, an often bitter medicine with the undisputed power to save lives.[3]

The powerful story of *Les Misérables* demonstrates this "bitter medicine with power to save lives" just about as well as any story I've ever read. In the years since the musical has been on the stage, more than sixty million people have experienced the *Gospel according to Victor Hugo*. While the story breaks our heart with its dark picture of human brokenness, the gospel breaks our hearts wide open with its promise of unlikely redemption and amazing grace. The 2012 movie shows Jean Valjean wrestling with his choices in a small chapel under a crucifix, an image of the body of Christ also broken by the brokenness of the world. It's a powerful scene as Valjean comes to repentance and gives himself over to redemption.

But this grace, he discovered, must be lived day-by-day, moment-by-moment, and his choice for redemption needed to be made again

---

3. Taylor, *Speaking of Sin*, 41.

and again. Valjean found that he must repeatedly reorient himself to forgiveness in order to remember who he is—a broken man made new, a lost man redeemed. Even after the priest's redemption and after his own repentance, the circumstances of his life demanded that he consistently recommit himself to stand firmly in grace in order to find the wisdom and power to truly live in redemption, in order to live as an agent of reconciliation for others.

This is not easy. We humans are naturals at self-righteousness and we have excellent skills at self-deception. Martin Luther (and Augustine before him) talked about sin as "the self curving in on itself," *Homo incurvatus in se*. This "curving" I think is part of what it means to be human, each of us individually and all of us together. The nations we build, the societies we form, even the churches that are supposed to offer a radical alternative to this universal human tendency—even the church all too often is a "self curving in on itself."

When Paul wrote his letter to the church at Rome, his description of human sinfulness was stark and startling. Something like the Genesis description of the downward spiral of humanity in the days of Noah. Something like the heart breaking cries of the psalmist. Something like the systemic brokenness of the world of Jean Valjean. Something like the ugly realities of ovens of Auschwitz, or killing fields of Cambodia, or slave ships in the Middle Passage. Something like the gut wrenching stories we keep hearing every time we open the newspaper or turn on our TV.

The human condition is shot through with a sense of separation from God, with a reality of estrangement from one another, and with a deep awareness of fragmentation within our own souls. Our bending in upon ourselves is an embedded pattern that perpetuates itself from generation to generation. Awareness of these realities can spiral us down into despair. Or it can be the soil within which grace grows roots and redemption bears fruit.

Surely Paul wrote Romans in conversation with the Adam and Eve story in Genesis 3: "Where are you," the Creator calls, walking in the garden in the cool of the evening. "Where are you? I miss you." This sad story says the humans were hiding, their eyes opened to the estrangement that had now come into existence. Their eyes opened to their new independence that felt a lot like isolation. The humans were now untethered and set adrift from the Source of their life. That's what broken relationship looks like and feels like.

These broken relationships are everywhere we turn, and they break our hearts. Or at least, I hope this breaks our heart; I daresay it breaks God's heart. Even so, I think Creator created this world knowing full well what pain was in store. I think God created this world knowing full well the cross was in view. The stories from Genesis tell us God calls out, "where are you?" and God's own people hide themselves. The prologue from John sadly agrees:

> He was in the world, and the world came into being through him; yet the world did not know him. He came to what was his own, and his own people did not accept him.

The opening chapters from Romans affirm this human reality as well:

> But even though people knew God, they would not honor God as God or give thanks . . .

The story of judgment in Genesis 3 used to trouble me until I experienced an epiphany in one bright moment several years ago. The pronouncements of judgment in this story are not necessarily a litany of arbitrary punishments imposed by a vengeful Creator. Rather, consider that this is God's heart-heavy statement of a new reality, the fact that actions have consequences. Creator didn't need to impose punishment on these hapless creatures; they themselves opened Pandora's box so that now the natural consequences of their brokenness and stubbornness began to have their way. That is not God's doing; we humans do this to ourselves. Barbara Brown Taylor says it this way:

> God's judgment is not so much some kind of extra punishment God dumps on [people] as it is God's announcement that they have abandoned the way of life.
> Like some divine jiu-jitsu master, God does not set out to hurt them. God simply spins the rejection of life around so that they can feel the full force of it for themselves.[4]

When God is our judge, God tells us the truth about ourselves. God sees and names what is real and what is deadly within us. God opens our eyes to our own nakedness, hopelessness, and alienation so that we can enter into repentance, enter into grace.

This God of Justice and Grace is the one upon whom we are called to bend ourselves so that our lives will align with that which is true and

---

4. Taylor, *Speaking of Sin*, 35.

good and right and just; so that we may be the body of Christ working God's work in the world. Like the priest who offered radical grace to Jean Valjean, we are called to be God's partners, offering new possibilities in life's impossible circumstances; called to do God's work in our broken communities, created to shine God's light into this stubborn darkness, challenged to inject grace into the vicious cycles of whatever Jean Valjeans may show up on our doorsteps.

And we don't stop. We don't stop entrusting ourselves and our families and our communities to the Creator who is still creating and recreating goodness out of our every chaos. We have a choice: we can keep on curving in upon ourselves, and die. Or we can die to ourselves, bending ourselves toward God for the sake of the world—and truly live.

Week 4
Abraham

Genesis 12–20
Psalm 23
Psalm 25
Romans 4–8
John 13–17

As You Read the Old Testament

As you read this week, you might consider the fact that Abraham was not a Jew. Is that a startling statement? The people known as "Jews" didn't come into being until much later than the time of the Patriarchs. Abraham is highly honored within the traditions of Judaism, Christianity, and Islam because all three monotheistic religions see him as one who shaped the foundational understanding of these faiths.

As you read Genesis 12–20 (and as you read all these stories about the patriarchs in Genesis), notice the numerous descriptions of ancient Middle Eastern culture within the story. For example, the practice of polygamy and of producing children with several wives, concubines, and slaves was common. Also note the cultural understanding of the role of women. Across the ages, across the globe, in countless societies, women have been subservient to men in general and to the male head of the household in particular. Even to this day in some societies, a woman's value is measured by her ability to produce sons. (In light of this, consider how unwise it is for modern societies to use the Bible as a template for so-called "biblical family values.")

Last week, in the story of Noah, we were introduced to the notion of covenant. When order was restored after the chaos of the flood, God covenanted with all creation and marked that divine promise with the sign of the rainbow. Now here in the Abraham story, we see covenant narrow as it becomes more personal and particular. God chooses, calls, guides, and protects this one man, creating covenant with him and thus with his descendants. Covenant always is God's initiative, God's choice, and God's sustaining grace.

From Abraham on, we will watch the story narrow even more. It is his son Isaac (not Ishmael) who continues this particular covenant relationship with God. It is Jacob (not Esau) who continues the story. Jacob's twelve sons become the tribal people of Israel who eventually become the political nation of Israel.

We know that there are countless other stories of other people and nations who lived during the same time as the patriarchs and Israel, but they either are not mentioned at all or are mentioned as a kind of footnote; that's because the Hebrew Scriptures are written as the story of one particular people. The Hebrew Bible is Israel's personal witness to their experience with the one who called and redeemed them. The story of Israel tells the good, the bad, and the ugly of their human experience where mistakes, misunderstandings, foolishness, and violence are documented with startling honesty. Even so, the story claims that the covenant with Abraham's descendants continues because of God's grace. Covenant is grounded in the faithfulness of the Covenant Maker.

As You Read the Psalms

As you read the Psalms this week, consider the nomadic life of Abraham and his sons, shepherds deeply committed to the well being of their flock as they navigate the land and the seasons. The image of shepherd takes center stage in our beloved Psalm 23.

This poet acknowledges the reality of "dark valleys, evil, and enemies," but even when he walks through these experiences, there is complete trust in God who is Shepherd and Protector. The psalmist believes everything that is needed for life—food, drink, rest, and right paths—comes ultimately from the hand of the God who is Shepherd and Provider. This psalm is a song of gratitude and deep confidence.

In the Hebrew Scriptures, the image of shepherd often dovetailed with the image of king. Within the ancient nation of Israel, the king was to be caretaker and protector of God's people. Sadly, a common complaint of the prophets was that the kings of Israel too often neglected their shepherding responsibilities and instead became guilty of plundering God's flock. Whenever this neglect and oppression happened, the prophets would accuse and challenge the false shepherds and promise that God would, one day once again, re-gather the scattered flock, leading them and tending to them as their ever-faithful Shepherd.

As we read through the Psalms this year, we will see other metaphors that describe our human experience with God. In the best tradition of poetry, the poems of the Psalms offer us images, metaphors, and pictures of this God who created and sustains all things. Besides shepherd and king, God is like a father, like a mother, like a judge, like eagle's wings. God is like a rock, a fortress, a shield; like water and light.

Note the ways the poets of the Psalms explore the same core questions that emerge again and again throughout all the Scriptures: *who is God?* and *who are we?* What does it mean to be God's people, the families of the patriarchs, the children of Israel, the community of the church? These questions of Scripture ponder who we are together in relationship with one another because we are in relationship with the God who created us all—Creator who is Source and Goal of all creation.

The relationship described in Psalm 23 reminds us of the parable Jesus told about the shepherd who left the ninety-nine sheep in order to go in search of the one that was lost. When he found that single sheep, he rejoiced and called on the whole community to rejoice with him (Luke 15:3–7). Each life is precious beyond measure. "The Lord is my Shepherd" and so the *hesed* of the Lord—God's goodness/mercy/compassion—follows me, pursues me, runs after me all the days of my life.

As You Read the New Testament

As you read Romans 4–8, see how the apostle Paul hearkens back to the Abraham story to make his crucial arguments for the inclusion of Gentiles within the new Christian community. Abraham is the father of all the faithful, Paul insists, not just those who are circumcised (an essential symbolic, physical, covenant act for all faithful Jewish males.) Paul asserts that now, circumcision is spiritual, not literal. "Circumcision of the heart" becomes the sign of unity within the Christian community and a person is a "Jew" who is one inwardly; real circumcision is a matter of the heart, Paul insists (2:29).

Abraham's faith was "reckoned to him as righteousness" *before* he participated in the sign and symbol of circumcision, Paul confirms (4:9–12). The timing of this divine reckoning allows him to make his core argument: obeying the Law does not produce righteousness, rather, living in faithfulness and trusting in the one who is faithful and trustworthy allows the faithful to be "reckoned as righteous." Acceptable relationship with God doesn't come about by our human efforts, rather, relationship (covenant, promise) is God's divine grace given freely to us.

Just as Abraham experienced grace—even with all his mistakes and stumbles, even with his "dead" body—so we too experience God's gift of grace in the very midst of our weaknesses, sinfulness, and estrangement.

> There is therefore now no condemnation for those who are in Christ Jesus. For the law of the Spirit of life in Christ Jesus has set you free from the law of sin and of death (8:1–2).
>
> If Christ is in you, though the body is dead because of sin, the Spirit is life because of righteousness (8:10).

As You Read the Gospel

The Gospel of John also taps into the Shepherd metaphor as it tells the Jesus story. John's Jesus says explicitly: "I Am the Good Shepherd who lays down his life for the sheep" (John 10). For John, it is Jesus who leads God's sheep, provides sustenance, offers protection, and secures salvation.

You also might want to look back at John 8 while you are reading the Abraham story this week and recall an important conversation between Jesus and "the Jews" discussing the meaning of Abraham for the people of Israel as understood by John. "I tell you, before Abraham was, *I Am*. So they picked up stones to stone him . . ." Understand how theologically brazen this *I Am* claim would be for these monotheistic Jews. It's a Christology that conflates the being of Jesus with the very essence of God. Every Jew reading John's Gospel would immediately recognize the ancient story of the burning bush in which Moses is encountered by the Voice from the flame and experienced the self-revelation of the One-Who-Is. "*I Am*," said the voice, "this is my name" (Ex 3). When we read

John's gospel, we find ourselves awash in the long story of Scripture; we find ourselves in the same story that has been flowing fresh for millennia.

As you read John's stories that seem to cast "the Jews" in negative light, please remember that just about everyone in the Gospel of John is a Jew. The phrase, "the Jews," was one way John designated those who did not accept Jesus as Messiah and so were in opposition to the new Jesus movement. We'll talk more about this later.

Reflection: *Where is All This Going?*

Several years ago, a group of friends and I walked a labyrinth together. It was interesting to do this personal spiritual practice alongside a larger spiritual community. We all started in the same place, of course, but we began at different times and progressed at different rates so we never were in the same place at the same time. We all stood in various places along the same path.

When you walk a labyrinth, at first it feels a bit like a maze with a pathway that twists and turns. But unlike a maze, in a labyrinth there is never a dead end; there always is a way forward. Sometimes we would be oh-so-near the center when the way forward would spiral around until we found ourselves almost back to where we started; our orientation would be completely readjusted.

The Christian practice of walking a prayer labyrinth developed centuries ago as a mini-experience of holy pilgrimage with Jerusalem as its goal and center. These days, many Christians who engage in this spiritual practice understand the center not so much as a geographic location but rather as an encounter with God. Walkers of this way understand that our "center" is not one particular place; rather the whole labyrinth—our entire journey of faith—is embraced within the Ground of Being.[1] Everything in all creation is enveloped and enfolded within the one who is Love-Truth-Reality, *The* Center of all-that-is.

As we read the Genesis stories this week, we will hear God's call for Abram to "go," to enter the pilgrim's life and leave behind everything familiar and comfortable. Abram is called to walk away from land, home, and family and to walk toward an unknown future in his labyrinthine way with God. (By the way, that leaving impresses me in a deep spiritual sense, but also in a very practical way. When archaeologists' describe Abram's

---

1. A phrase made popular by theologian Paul Tillich.

hometown, Ur of the Chaldeans, they say Abram may well have had running water and indoor toilets! Walking away from indoor plumbing to live as a nomad in a tent is more faithfulness than I probably could muster!)

Abraham's life of faith and faithfulness is legendary and has become the foundation of the religious faith of most of the people on our planet, the "father of many nations." His example of faith gives us a touchstone while we figure out how we too might be a blessing to the nations of the earth in which we live.

But the Abraham narratives also show us how often he stumbled in his walk with God. Abraham's journey in faith happened stage-by-stage and step-by-step; his labyrinthine walk with God happened in fits and starts, in twists and turns. When we actually read these stories for ourselves instead of hearing them in their children's version, we recognize what a mixed bag our biblical heroes really are. But even with Abram's imperfect faith, we see in him a stubborn faithfulness that helps all of us mixed-bag followers keep hoping against hope that God is more faithful than we ever can be.

Abraham and Paul

Abraham was a pivotal a figure for the apostle Paul as Paul read and re-read the ancient stories and reinterpreted the historic faith of Judaism in light of the Christ event. In his letter to the Romans, Paul draws extensively from the story of Abraham as he argues his point that—even though God has done a whole new thing in the universe in the event of Jesus Christ—still God's work of making things right in the world, of making people right with God, has been going on for a very long time.

> Hoping against hope, Abraham believed that he would become 'the father of many nations,' according to what was said: 'So numerous shall your descendants be.' He did not weaken in faith when he considered his own body, which was already as good as dead (for he was about a hundred years old), or when he considered the barrenness of Sarah's womb.
>
> No distrust made him waver concerning the promise of God, but he grew strong in his faith as he gave glory to God, being fully convinced that God was able to do what he had promised. Therefore his faith 'was reckoned to him as righteousness' (Rom 4:18–22).

NT scholars and pastors M. Eugene Boring and Fred Craddock
consider what this means in their excellent resource, *The People's New
Testament Commentary*. Here is part of their reflection:

> Paul's own faith is centered on the God who raised Jesus from
> the dead, the God who generates hope when there is no hope,
> the same God who acted in the 'dead' bodies of Abraham and
> Sarah to give new life . . . For Paul, all those such as Abraham
> who trust in God's impossible promises have resurrection
> faith—even though they may never have heard of Jesus.[2]

Now that's a hopeful interpretation! If Abraham is the father of the
faithful, then surely this is true of *all* people whose faith points them
toward the one true God—no matter what they may call the one who
is beyond all names, no matter what they might understand about how
that hope has been accomplished. Surely, even still, this is faith that God
honors and reckons.

No matter where we are on our labyrinthine journey of faith, at all
our different stages and places, any faith that holds on to God's impossible possibilities and leads us toward the Center; any faith that leads us
to love is faith that God reckons as righteousness.

Boring and Craddock observe something else helpful in this Christian reflection of the Abraham story. Consider their explanation of this
idea of reckoning. Paul's term, reckoned and counted as righteous, "has
legal connotations, but it is not a matter of a 'legal fiction,' as though the
judge treats the accused 'as if' they were not guilty." Rather, in Paul's argument, God's pronouncement of righteous "is performative language that
creates the reality it pronounces."[3]

A minister pronounces, "You are married" and something very real
comes into being. An umpire calls, "strike!" and so it is. Paul proclaims
that—because of the work of God and the Word of God made visible in
Jesus Christ—the guilty are "right" and sinners are "righteous" and so we
become what God pronounces. In God's work of justification and reckoning, an alternative reality comes into existence completely without our
participation or help. And so any faith that hopes against hope in God's
impossible possibilities, any faith that leads us toward the Center, is faith
that God "reckons as righteous."

2. Boring and Craddock, *People's New Testament Commentary*, 478–79.

3. Boring and Craddock, *People's New Testament Commentary*, 478.

Abraham and John

In the Gospel of John, we also find that the Abraham story has special relationship with John's Jesus and important theological significance. For the Christians in John's community, following Christ "in the way" meant their lives were immersed in the way of God that has been unfolding since the beginning of history; the same way Abraham was called to follow.

And yet, now Christians claim that it is in Jesus the Christ, the perfect and revealed Way of God, that all our journeys of faith are included. Like a cosmic labyrinth, God's Christ encompasses all creation—every beginning, every ending, and every step in between—"even though they may never have heard of Jesus," Boring and Craddock remind us.

Journey is and has always been a primary paradigm for the way of the people of God. Journey is an important metaphor that stands in opposition to seeing ourselves as a settled people because settled faith can become comfortable, safe, and predictable. We easily become set in our ways; we become stuck. That's why an intentional and disciplined faith journey is crucial. Even when we journey in fits and starts as Abraham did, even when we don't know where we're going or exactly what we're doing, even when we make mistakes or refuse what God is unfolding before us—even so we, like Abraham, can "hope against hope" that all this is going somewhere, somewhere good and right.

Like Abraham, who saw the fulfillment of God's promise not with human eyes but with the eyes of hope and confidence, we too entrust ourselves to the one who is our Eternal Center, the one who generates all hope. That faith reminds us why we need each other, why we need spiritual community: to encourage each other and to embody hope for one another throughout life's journey.

Whenever we see ourselves journeying with Abraham, on the move with Paul, following Christ as the Way, then we can live with confidence that in this journey of understanding, of thought, of theology, of practice, of life, then we are on the way with God. Even though we may feel sometimes like we're going around in circles, maybe what we really are doing is progressing through the spiraling path of a cosmic labyrinth God is unfolding before us.

"Where is all this going?" we may ask, but I wonder, Is that really ours to know? When we live our lives in God's labyrinth, we follow the path God opens up before us. We are called to take the next step and then the next step after that. We are called to faithfulness.

Week 5

Isaac

Genesis 21–26
Psalm 22
Psalm 34
Psalm 116
Romans 9–13
John 18–21

As You Read the Old Testament

As YOU READ THIS week, consider that, unlike the stories of origins from the first eleven chapters of Genesis that seem to be set out of time, the stories of the patriarchs are set within a historical context. These stories would have been told generation after generation as a part of the oral histories of this ancient people. They probably weren't written, however, until around the time of the Babylonian Exile some 1500 years later. The time of Exile is the era when the Genesis stories were gathered and edited, penned and preserved for posterity. Consider the meaning these ancient stories would have had for the nation of Israel as they were once again displaced and living away from their homeland.

As you read Genesis 21–26, remember that God had called Abraham and promised him descendants like the stars in the sky (Gen 15:5). In the ancient world and even among some people in some societies today, having descendants that continue beyond your lifetime is thought to be a kind of immortality. Perhaps this was a way Abraham believed his own life could live on in the lives of his children. But if Abraham followed the startling call of God to sacrifice his son, if he consented to give up the long awaited son of promise, then the future God had promised him would disappear. His life would have no meaning and Abraham himself would become as if he never had existed.

Place this story within the context of the Babylonian Exile. Once again, like Abraham, the people of Israel stood at the precipice of extinction. In Exile, they faced the very real possibility that they would be lost to history. Here is a people who have seen themselves (like Abraham) as bearers of the promise, called to be a blessing to the nations, chosen to be light for the world—but now they find themselves on the verge of non-existence.

Imagine how this tradition of the Binding of Isaac, might have helped shape their identity and their self-understanding as a people. Here in Exile are the very children of Abraham whose existence had been put at risk on the Mount of Moriah. When they read and reread this story in their own day, they could see how Father Abraham had—tenaciously, stubbornly, absurdly—trusted that God would keep the promise and preserve the people of the promise.

Surely for this threatened, exiled remnant of a people, this story offered comfort for their affliction, brought hope into their hopelessness, built confidence in their future, and steeled the faithfulness of those who had seen themselves as forsaken. The ancient story, reinterpreted for their own day, gave them a renewed challenge: how would they face their own testing? Would Israel choose to trust God with Abraham's same resurrection faith? Would they too believe that the Lord would provide?

As You Read the Psalms

"My God, my God, why have you forsaken me?" Who said this? If you are familiar with the passion stories in the gospels, undoubtedly you will answer, Jesus. But as you read, imagine Psalm 22 coming from the period of Exile as well. Imagine how forsaken this people of God must have felt: "My God, my God! Why have *you* forsaken *us*?"

You will recognize numerous allusions to this psalm from the passion stories in the gospels. Because Mark and Matthew, Luke and John lived their lives attentive to these songs and poems of Israel, they naturally mined the poetic and prophetic words of the Psalms as they took on the challenge of describing the indescribable, of explaining the inexplicable Christ event.

> They divide my clothes among themselves, and for my clothing they cast lots.

We don't know if the historical Jesus said exactly these words on the cross, but we can know, as the faithful Son, as the true and perfect embodiment of Israel, his experience of suffering and hope would have been grounded in his Holy Scriptures. The one who is the Living Word brings the words of Scripture to life.

The poet-theologians of Israel considered and reconsidered what it meant for Israel to be God's chosen people. *If God truly is our Covenant God,* (Israel may have pondered) *then won't God remain faithful to covenant promises for blessing?*

But the covenant also promised "curses," penalties, and consequences for sin. So again and again in the story of God's people Israel, painful cycles repeated themselves throughout generations. Faithfulness degenerated into unfaithfulness, passion turned to apathy, obedience became disobedience. During those repetitive cycles, the Covenant God would sometimes withdraw, leaving the people to their own devices. Thus the poets of Israel sang a painful lament:

> Why are you so far from helping me, from the words of my groaning? O my God, I cry by day, but you do not answer; and by night, but find no rest.

Some psalms sing in praise of order, beauty, and trustworthiness within the world. Songs of Creation, Songs of Torah, and the Wisdom Psalms give thanks that "the world is a well ordered, reliable, and life giving system, because God has ordained it that way and continues to preside effectively over the process."[1].

Other psalms lament the world gone wrong and things not as they ought to be. Chaos reigns instead of order. Unchecked wickedness and greed infect the world while goodness, honesty, and integrity seem foolish notions and unattainable fantasies. The poets cry out: Why? How long, O Lord? Where is mercy? Where is justice? Why don't you *do* something! Psalm 22 speaks to the confusion of seekers when the faithfulness and reliability of God are in question.

---

1 Brueggemann, *The Message of the Psalms,* 26.

Still other psalms speak of re-established order, justice, and beauty on the other side of disorientation; the poets sing with a new understanding of God's constancy during the darkness. In spite of all, through it all, God perseveres for reconciliation and redemption. The poet's fresh insights to this divine work make the song all the more joyful.

Psalm 22 sings out a beacon of hope in the midst of the depression: *And yet . . . Nevertheless . . .*

> And yet you are holy, enthroned on the praises of Israel. In you
> our ancestors trusted; they trusted, and you delivered them.

The psalmists do here what a good sermon does by naming both realities that are seen and realities that are hidden. Yes, in our human reality, we experience forsakenness, abandonment, and aloneness. *Nevertheless* there is also always persistent presence, stubborn love, and amazing grace. In all our laments, it helps to name the light even in the midst of the darkness.

As You Read the New Testament

This part of the letter to the Romans offers Paul's best understanding of the relationship of God with the people of Israel, the people of promise. For Paul, God's covenant is irrevocable and Israel still has a place in God's overarching plan. They continue to be a part of *The Story*.

As you read Romans 9–13, recall that Paul and then Mark, and later Matthew, Luke, and John all saw the church as a continuation and expansion of God's people, Israel. They all wrote in order to help a new community of Christ ground themselves in a faith that was founded upon the fact and unspeakable mystery of a crucified Messiah. Each one made sense a bit differently from the other because the mystery is too big to put into one box with neat descriptions and tidy explanations. Each understanding offered by faithful seekers contributes to the whole. Every different insight adds more light.

Especially ponder the profound words of Paul in Romans 12 and consider their meaning in your own life today.

> I appeal to you therefore, brothers and sisters, by the mercies
> of God, to present your bodies as a living sacrifice, holy and ac-
> ceptable to God, which is your spiritual worship.

> Do not be conformed to this world, but be transformed by
> the renewing of your minds, so that you may discern what is the
> will of God—what is good and acceptable and perfect.

Paul's letter to the Romans is a masterpiece of theological reflection by a master theologian. Centuries later, this epistle played a crucial role in the thinking of Martin Luther when he challenged the Roman Catholic Church in 1517. Luther's understandings of grace as articulated by the apostle Paul became a catalyst for the Protestant Reformation and changed the church and even Western society in many profound ways.

Again, four hundred years after Martin Luther, Paul's Romans masterpiece prompted another theological masterpiece by theologian, Karl Barth.[2] "The gospel is not a truth among other truths. Rather, it sets a question mark against all truths. The gospel is not the door but the hinge." Karl Barth spent his life setting question marks in the name of Christ against all manner of "truths." In the process, he did nothing less than alter the course of modern theology. Barth's treatise on Paul's Letter to the Romans continues to demand conversation with every theologian worth her salt since its publication in 1922.

As You Read the Gospel

As you read these chapters in John describing Jesus' passion, imagine Jesus of Nazareth carrying his cross to the Place of the Skull. If *The Story* means anything, then it must mean that Jesus, like Abraham, faced the very real possibility of extinction. For this Lamb of God, however, there would be no ram in the bush. Jesus put his faith, not in rescue and protection; Jesus' faith was grounded in the God who raises the dead.

Notice how John incorporates Psalm 22 into his telling of the Christ event. Note that he quotes the portion of the psalm about "dividing my garments" but leaves out the cry of abandonment, "why have you forsaken me?" In order to understand how John interprets his own Scriptures, recall John's Christology. For example, no one *takes* the life of John's Jesus, rather, John's Jesus gives himself over of his own free will: he *gives up* his spirit (19:30). This Christ is in control of the situation unto the very end.

---

2. Barth, *Epistle to the Romans*, 35.

Reflection: *The Binding of Isaac*

We've considered the faithfulness of father Abraham on his journey of faith and we've been impressed by his commitment to follow God; to trust and obey. But this? This story of the binding of Isaac stretches me beyond my comfort zone. Who is this God who would ask such a thing? Who is this father who would do such a thing? Who is this beloved son who would give himself willingly—and why?

In the Islamic tradition, it was Abraham's son Ishmael who submitted to this binding (another excellent opportunity to take the Bible seriously without taking it literally). The story is true; it tells us something deeply true about God and ourselves and our relationship to God. The story is true even if it is told differently in different traditions. The story is true even if it never actually happened in history.

In Abraham's cultural understanding, if he followed God's call it would mean he was sacrificing not only this son whom he loved, but also his hope that his own life would continue within his descendants. So here is a story that speaks to the very real possibility of complete annihilation and extinction, not only of Abraham and his descendants but also of God's own promise.

This story about Abraham's faithfulness to obey such a drastic call gives new meaning to the depth of his trust. Abraham's is a faith so grounded in the faithfulness of God that he believed God's promise could never be annulled.

I think of all the things I cling to so dearly, things that define my identity and my worth. I think of all the people who are precious to me and how very hard it is to let go of my expectations, to release control, to give myself and my beloveds over to the one who is Creator-Redeemer-Sustainer. This kind of trust/distrust was the primal temptation in the Garden of Eden, I believe. Fearfulness and hesitancy to entrust ourselves to our Creator continues to be a prime temptation for us humans throughout many of our own stories.

The testing of Abraham and Isaac is a story that gives a kind of flesh and blood reality to the abstract truth in scripture we speak too easily, "The one who would save his life will lose it; but the one who—for my sake—loses his life, will find it" (Matt 16:25, Mark 8:35, Luke 9:24, John 12:25).

Here is a story of resurrection faith.

The *Living in The Story* readings for this week juxtapose the Binding of Isaac with the Passion of Christ because this way of reading provides an important and intentional theological perspective. Consider Jesus as the beloved son, but for Jesus there was no ram in the bush; he truly died on that cross. He died as a human knowing that when people die, they stay dead.

Even so, Jesus died holding onto a tenacious, stubborn, absurd resurrection faith, a faith so grounded in the faithfulness of God he believed God's promise could never be annulled. Ever since, followers of Jesus still grapple with the mystery: What does this mean?

In recent years, my understanding of these matters has been influenced by two creative conversation partners, Jürgen Moltmann and Alan Lewis. For Moltmann, God did not orchestrate the crucifixion from a distance; rather in the incarnation, it is God who entered into the human experience. And in the cross, God—God's Own Self—entered into death itself. This is not "the death of God," Moltmann insists, but "this is death in God, since through the cross, death itself pierces the life and the heart of the very being of God."[3]

I can hardly get my head around that idea. What does that mean? Maybe, one thing it means is that even the Creator of all binds God's Own Self to the deep and eternal truth that "the one who would save his life will lose it; but the one who loses his life, will find it."

Maybe God allowed death to "pierce" Divine Immortality so that God's own life that is unstoppable and God's own love that is unconquerable could absorb and extinguish death itself. That is an unfathomable mystery of the cross. Alan Lewis says it well:

> The community of God in the Trinity takes on death and overcomes it in the overflow of love.
>
> This is the basis of our justification, the ground of new, divine possibilities for the sick and sinful, the dying and the dead. In justification we hear God's "Yes" and we become what we hear; we are redefined by the gospel's "word of the cross," which pronounces us forgiven and renewed.
>
> It is the same creative Word by which God raised the crucified Jesus from the grave that has from the beginning summoned existence out of nothing. It is a word not abstractly spoken at a distance, but a Word embodied in a fleshly act of divine identity with the god-forsaken, the judged, and the dead themselves.[4]

---

3. Moltmann, *The Crucified God*, 225.

4. Lewis, *Between Cross and Resurrection*, 256.

Who is this God who would ask such a thing of Abraham and Isaac? I daresay it is the same God who, from the foundation of the earth, is and always has been a God of divine Self-giving.

Abraham and Isaac never knew Jesus of Nazareth, but as they walked toward the Mount of Moriah they were propelled by Jesus' same resurrection faith. And what they discovered is that the one who gives, the God who loves, the Lord who provides was already there.

Week 6

Jacob

Genesis 27–36
Psalm 46
Psalm 47
Psalm 117
Romans 14–16
Mark 1–7

As You Read the Old Testament

AS YOU READ THIS week, consider the ancient theme of naming Scripture stories remind us that we humans will never completely understand *the who* and *the how* and *the why* of God. We all do the best we can to make sense, and often, in the stories, this making-sense is described as the biblical characters naming their experience.

- Abraham names his experience with Isaac and the ram in the bush and the angel who stops the knife as "The Lord provides" (Gen 22).

- Hagar, the courageous slave of Sarah, the tenacious mother of Ishmael, the cast out one who was found and nurtured by divine intervention names God as "The One who Sees" (Gen 16).

- Jacob names the place of his dream with a ladder of angels and a promise of blessing as Bethel, "the house of God" (Gen 28).

- Jacob's wives name their children in light of their relationships with Jacob, God, and their own experience (Gen 29–30).

- Jacob names the place of his wrestling Penuel, "I have seen God face to face, and yet my life is preserved" (Gen 32).

To this day, we moderns also do the best we can asking questions, probing mysteries, and naming the experiences of our own lives in ways that attempt to make sense. In this way, we are not really so different from our ancestors.

In Genesis 27–36, watch how Jacob demonstrates the pattern of God's surprising grace. Jacob's name means "supplanter or deceiver" so in our reading this week, we find Jacob on his way to make amends with his brother Esau, but because we know Jacob, we have to ask, is he once again manipulating, plotting, and planning to win Esau's approval by his elaborate orchestrations of gifts? Or is Jacob really sorry for what he did? Or is Jacob just sorry he's in trouble? And yet, it is Jacob the deceiver (not Esau) whom God called to receive the promise and continue the lineage of Abraham.

God's call is always surprising! After the long night of wrestling with God, Jacob is renamed and is given the new name of *Israel*. Hebrew Scripture understands this name as "the one who exerted himself with God and persevered," or "the one who held on against God," but another way to translate its meaning is, "May God prevail." This reading reminds me of the prayer our Lord taught us to pray, "Thy will be done on earth as it is in heaven . . ."

As You Read the Psalms

> We will not fear, though the earth should change, though the mountains shake in the heart of the sea; though its waters roar and foam, though the mountains tremble with its tumult.
> Because—God is our refuge and strength, a very present help in trouble (Ps 46).

This psalmist pictures *un-creation*, an experience where everything that has been solid and dependable trembles, shakes, and roars. I think of the terror of earthquakes, volcanoes, hurricanes, and wildfires. In an instant, whole worlds are devastated, turned upside-down-and-inside-out. How can we *not* fear in the midst of such upheaval?

It is said that the encouragement not to fear is one of the most prevalent and consistent announcements in the Bible. In the Genesis stories we hear God say to Abraham, "Do not be afraid; I am your shield . . ." (15:1), and to Jacob, "I am God, the God of your father; do not be afraid to go down to Egypt, for I will make of you a great nation there" (28:13–15). In the prophets, we hear the Word of the Lord come to God's people again and again:

> But now thus says the Lord,
> he who created you, O Jacob,
> he who formed you, O Israel:
> Do not fear, for I have redeemed you;
> I have called you by name. You are mine (Isa 43:1).

In the NT stories, angels almost always introduce themselves to humans with the words, "Don't be afraid." In the gospels, Jesus is pictured as the one who walks upon the *un-creation*, the raging sea: the one who stands above the chaos and the deep darkness.

> Jesus came towards them early in the morning, walking on the sea. He intended to pass them by. But when they saw him walking on the sea, they thought it was a ghost and cried out; for they all saw him and were terrified.
> But immediately he spoke to them and said, "Take heart, it is I; do not be afraid" (Mark 6:47–50).

"It is I," Jesus proclaims. *I Am.*

Fear as a human emotion is normal and common because our emotions are linked to our experiences. We feel fear when this happens; we feel sad when that happens; we feel happy when something else happens. We humans can't control these emotions since they come from our gut and not from the thinking, cognitive, choice-making part of our being.

But the Divine Encouragement addresses something deeper than either our intellect or our gut. Here is the life of faith, the way of trust. In the core of our being, we affirm the foundational Presence of *I Am*, the "Present Help," and we place every circumstance of our lives within the context of that Unseen Unshakable Reality. Even when we are afraid, we do not fear. This is the confidence of Psalm 46.

Scripture's testimony tells us there is only one to fear:

> So now, O Israel, what does the Lord your God require of you?
> Only to fear the Lord your God, to walk in all his ways, to love him, to serve the Lord your God with all your heart and with all your soul . . . (Deut 10:12).

The one we love and serve with heart and soul is always also the one whom we cannot fathom, the one beyond our understanding and out of our control. So the psalmist calls us to "behold the works of the LORD . . ." And the psalmist calls us to "be still." It is only in this still place in the core of our being, that we can know the foundational presence of *I Am*.

In both Psalms 46 and 47, notice the ways Israel's Hebrew poetry sometimes names God as "the God of Abraham" and sometimes as "the God of Jacob." But also notice the hint of universality in Psalm 47: "the princes of the peoples gather as the people of the God of Abraham . . ." Remember our Hebrew Bible is primarily the story of the Hebrew people, so all others were referred to as "the nations, the peoples, the Gentiles."

As You Read the New Testament

See how Paul quotes from the Hebrew Scriptures here in Romans 14–16 to make his case for the Gentiles' full inclusion in the church. "Christ has become a servant of the circumcised on behalf of the truth of God in order that he might confirm the promises given to the patriarchs, and in order that the Gentiles might glorify God for his mercy. As it is written: 'Therefore I will confess you among the Gentiles, and sing praises to your name.'" Then Paul quotes from several psalms, from Deuteronomy, and from Isaiah in order to make the argument that the inclusion of the Gentiles was a key part of the original promise. He makes his case from the full range of the Hebrew Scriptures—the Torah, the Prophets, and the Wisdom Writings. Remember most of us reading this are "Gentiles" so Paul's passion for an undivided church in large part opened the way for *our* full inclusion.

As You Read the Gospel

In these chapters in Mark 1–7, notice the miracles Jesus performs: walking on water, feeding the multitude, calming the sea, all sorts of healings, and even raising the dead. Mark's way of telling the story of the truly-human-truly-divine Christ is to pack the first half of his gospel with mighty deeds normally only attributed to God. When we move to the second half of Mark's gospel, we hear many of Jesus' teachings but only one more miracle. Most of Mark's final chapters deal with the passion of Christ.

As you read Mark's Gospel and ponder Mark's Jesus, ask yourself two questions: 1) What does this Jesus show me about who God is? and 2) How does this Jesus teach me something about what it means to be truly human? Read slowly. Take your time. Stop when something strikes you as important and just think about it for a while. Pray. Trust that God is still speaking. Trust that this God who is Creator and Sustainer, who is the Beginning and the End of *The Overarching Story* of creation is always also writing something new, wonderful, and mysterious into each one of our individual stories.

Reflection: *Wrestling with God*

I dislocated my shoulder during the week I was preparing to preach the Genesis story about Jacob's encounter with God by the river Jabbok. That entire week, I was moving slowly with a fair amount of pain; all that week I was living with my own limp, so now I have much more sympathy for Jacob than I had ever had before. As I studied Genesis 32, I kept thinking about the ways we all wrestle with God—at least the ways I know I wrestle with God.

- I struggled mightily with my call to ministry. It took me years to be able even to hear a call; then more years to know how to say "yes" to that call; then even more years to lean in wholeheartedly to God's call to ministry.

- I struggle to understand why cancer, dementia, and hopelessness continue to be epidemic; why some babies are born much too early and some people die much too soon; why violence and arrogance and divisiveness seem to be valued in our society while compassion, cooperation, and humility are scorned.

- Sometimes I struggle to forgive; I struggle with insecurity; I struggle with discouragement.

It seems like I am always living my life with a limp and I imagine you have your own list. I've come to believe that if we are human then there will always be ways we wrestle with life; ways we wrestle with God.

As I pondered the *Living in The Story* texts for this week, I particularly noticed that Jacob was not the one who initiated this wrestling match. Rather, the story very intentionally describes this wrestling as a Divine Intrusion, a Divine Interruption. Throughout his story, Jacob had done plenty of plotting, manipulating, and wrestling with nearly everyone with whom he came in contact. But in this story, we see Jacob minding his own business when out of the blue he is thrown flat on his back, looking at a world turned upside down. This was not a freak accident, not a twist of fate, and not by the hand of any other human. At the end, as he limps away from this encounter with the Instigator of this battle of wills, Jacob names the place, names his experience Penuel—"I have seen God face to face."

Scripture gives witness to a God who is ever breaking into the human experience in unexpected ways—intruding, interrupting, and instigating relationship. "Why does God wrestle with Jacob?" Terence Fretheim asks in his commentary on Genesis.

> Such struggles might be viewed as divinely initiated exercises in human becoming, of shaping and sharpening the faithfulness of the humans involved for the deep challenges to be faced.
>
> God's engagement in such moments in people's lives is always a gracious move, informed most basically by faithfulness to promises made, and in the interests of health, peace, and well being.[1]

When Jacob was brought to his knees in this divine wrestling match, Jacob held on for dear life. His determination and perseverance, even in the face of the Overwhelming Instigator, confirmed him to be the one who would continue to bear the promise given to Abraham. In this struggle of becoming more authentically human, God shaped and sharpened Jacob's faithfulness for the challenges yet to come. Jacob may have named this place but God named him, renamed him, and Jacob was transformed into Israel.

Do you know about Megan Phelps-Roper?[2] She's the granddaughter of Fred Phelps, the founder and leader of the infamously bigoted Westboro Baptist Church. For most of her earliest years, Megan had been ensconced in a world of judgment and hate. It was, literally, all she had ever known. She ate, drank, and slept in a certainty that Westboro was Right (with a capital R) and everyone else was Wrong (with a capital W). She believed beyond any doubt that her call in life was to proclaim the sin of the world and to announce its doom.

1. Fretheim, "Genesis," 568.

2. Phelps-Roper, Unfollow. See also "I grew up in the Westboro Baptist Church. Here's why I left" posted March 2017 in TED Talks.

But then, seemingly out of the blue, God met Megan at her own River Jabbok and initiated a wrestling match. It was a long, hard, painful wrestling and Megan Phelps-Roper, who was once so sure-footed, is now hobbling away from everyone she had known, everything she had ever believed. Now she is even dead to her family. How does one have the where-with-all to make such a radical change? To turn so completely? To let go of the known way and to walk—however lamely—toward the breaking of a new dawn in a whole new world?

Her wrestlings are not near over. I daresay Megan will be living with a limp for a long time. But I believe God's Divine Intrusion into her life will result in blessing—not only for her, but for many others as well.

We've been reading some of the letters of the apostle Paul alongside these Genesis stories. Paul's is another story about God initiating a wrestling match with someone who was immersed in a world of judgment and self-righteousness. When Paul wrote to the churches of Galatia (next week's reading), he confessed how violently he had persecuted the church of Jesus Christ (Gal 1:13–17).

When Paul wrote to the Romans, he acknowledged he is in the same boat with "all who have sinned" and he is in the same ark with all who encounter God's radical grace (Rom 3:21–26). When Paul wrote to the Corinthians, he described how he had received a "thorn in the flesh" so that he might better lean into God's grace (2 Cor 12:1–10). Paul's self-certainty was transformed into a deep dependence on the God who had wrestled him to the ground and raised him to a new life. Paul was given Christ's vision of the new people, a people of God who are not Jew or Gentile, slave or free, male and female, but who are all baptized into the one body of Jesus Christ (Gal 3:27–29).

This "becoming" brings many challenges—for Paul, for the congregations he pastored, and for us. Living into the vision and actually becoming one people of God, a whole people of Christ who really do live in the unity of the Spirit will always be a struggle. There are many who resist and even resent such a vision. So, even though Paul had been raised to new life, still he lived the rest of his life with a limp, needing always to lean into the God who had called and commissioned him for this work.

My dislocated shoulder, Jacob's hip, Paul's thorn, Megan's family—it seems there is always something or another that causes us to live with a limp, and so I've wondered how to interpret this, what I need to learn from this experience. These things come to mind: *I am more aware of God's presence.* I'm not willing to say God was the instigator, tripping me up in my garage and causing me to fall, but I am willing to say God is *at work* in all this, teaching me new ways to see and to be in my world.

That said there have been occasions in my life in which I am bold to name God as my Divine Intruder, as the one who interrupted what was and instigated something I never could have imagined on my own. Those times, like Jacob's, Paul's, and Megan's, are always very uncomfortable. Living by faith, walking into God's unknown, letting go of what has been, and trusting that the Creator is still creating new things in the universe, this is hard. Wherever these times of wrestling come from, we still can name them as opportunities, second chances to open our eyes anew to God's presence and God's way. We can let ourselves see life from a different perspective. We can rediscover our gifts and potential. We can get lots of practice leaning into the promise. And we remember with deep gratitude how interdependent we are on the supportive grace and wisdom of others.

I'm also more aware how important it is to stay grounded. Whenever we lose our balance, when things change and we find ourselves making all sorts of adjustments we can learn to live with intention and attention. We put one foot in front of the other, we take our time, we stay aware, we move with care. And we take time to "be still, to know that God is God" (Ps 46)—and to *let* God be God.

One more thing: *I am much more aware of the power of pain.* When things are going well, it's easy to become complacent but when we hurt, we can be reminded that pain and hardship are the reality of most people in the world most of the time, thus we can use our experiences to become more sensitive to the struggles and the wrestlings of others. I've learned that pain can either shut us down and make us smaller; or it can break us open and make us larger—more loving, more patient, more compassionate.

Like Jacob, may we hold on tenaciously to God, expecting God's blessing and trusting in God's promise even in the midst of the struggle. Like Paul, may we be empowered with new vision and passion for the people we are ever becoming, trusting that it is God who is always bringing us into being. Like Megan may we be bold to step out of what-has–been and into what–may–be. May God never cease sharpening and shaping faithfulness in each of us individually and all of us together for whatever challenges lay ahead.

Week 7

Joseph

Genesis 37–50
Psalm 55
Psalm 75
Psalm 80
Psalm 107
Galatians
Mark 8–10

As you read this week, you will be finishing up Genesis. If you have been reading all along, you also will have completed John, Romans, Colossians, 2 Timothy, Galatians and you are about to wrap up Mark. Look how easy this is! Be pleased about this discipline of Bible study you are developing and think about what this habit of reading Scripture can mean for you going forward.

As You Read the Old Testament

In these chapters in Genesis, watch for ways the stories of Joseph and Jesus parallel. Joseph is one of the few people the OT portrays with almost all positive descriptions. Even so, Joseph (like Jesus) was persecuted and betrayed, then raised up and exalted. Joseph, too, experienced "resurrection."

As You Read the Psalms

In Psalms 55, 75, and 107, the poet of Israel gives testimony to God's faithfulness even in times of hopelessness and despair just as many of us can look back and see the ways we have been sustained through hard times. Growing in faith means living in faithfulness even when we are in the midst of trouble and cannot see a way through. Counting on/trusting in/living with God's "steadfast love" even when we can't *feel* God's presence is a crucial part of our faith journey.

Psalm 107 celebrates surprising reversals: those who wandered in desert wastes found a straight way, prisoners bowed down in darkness were rescued and found their bonds broken, those sick near the gates of death were made whole, people tossed upon chaotic seas experienced the peace of still waters. These inversions and reversals of crisis and disaster weave a bright thread through the tapestry of Israel's life. The surprises of grace remind Israel that God is a God who *hears* and *acts*. The tradition of surprising reversals is an ancient one.

Next week we will read the beginning of the Exodus story where the God who is *I Am* spoke to Moses from the bush-that-burned-but-was-not consumed: "I have seen the misery of my people who are in Egypt. I have heard their cry on account of their taskmasters. Indeed, I know their sufferings, and I have come down to deliver them" (Ex 3:7–8). *I see. I hear. I know. I come.* So Psalm 107 repeats this theme in every refrain, "They cried to the Lord in their trouble . . ." and God delivered, God saved, God brought them to a safe place.

As Dr. Toni Craven says in her excellent work, *The Book of Psalms*, "Trust is born of a people's remembered experience of being heard, delivered, and sustained by a power independent of human control and larger than human understanding."[1] God is a God who hears and acts—not because any of us deserve it but solely because of "God's steadfast love that endures forever."

This lovely phrase, "steadfast love," is large and deep. The Hebrew word *hesed* (or *chesed*) comes into English in a variety of ways because the Hebrew meaning is quite multivalent. In English, the sense of the Hebrew word may be conveyed by mercy, kindness, goodness, favor, love, loving-kindness, covenant faithfulness, or steadfast love. "Let them thank the Lord for his steadfast love, for his wonderful works . . ."

---

1. Craven, *The Book of Psalms*, 78.

Psalm 107 sings like the song of those who have endured chaos, despair, and disorientation. This celebration is not naive or simple. Rather, it is appropriate praise offered from the other side of an abyss; thanksgiving offered with full knowledge of the grace that has redeemed impossibility and transformed it into ever-new possibilities. "Let the redeemed of the LORD say so."

As You Read the New Testament

Paul lays out his thesis statement in Galatians 3:27–28. "As many of you as were baptized into Christ have clothed yourselves with Christ. There is no longer Jew or Greek, there is no longer slave or free, there is no longer male and female; for all of you are one in Christ Jesus." Paul's passion and mission focused on the living unity of the whole people of God in Jesus Christ.

And so as you read, you may be startled by Paul's passionate personal attacks against his opponents. Evidently in the churches of Galatia, some teachers were insisting that these Gentile believers must first be circumcised and become (in effect) Jews before they could be authentic Christians. Paul's response is strong: "Hell No!" ("let them be cursed!")

We can understand that God's radical equality of Jews and Gentiles in this new community of Christ would have been a difficult concept for faithful Jews to embrace. But for Paul, anything less than the full inclusion of Gentile Christians was *not* the gospel and any who taught otherwise taught heresy. "For those who insist you must be circumcised, I say, let them go the whole way and castrate themselves!" Yes, it's startling, but it is Paul's way of saying these false teachers should not reproduce their heresy and propagate such confusion among the believers. "In Christ, you are all children of God through faith . . ." (By the way, these teachers with whom Paul took issue remind us of some Christian missionaries in the twentieth century who expected native peoples to become Westernized before they would be accepted as properly Christian. Unfortunately that small, tribal notion Paul condemned has indeed been replicated within too many generations of the church's life.)

As for the other part of Paul's thesis—male and female, slave and free—consider the state of the world in Paul's day. Rome enforced its national values all across its empire. Slavery fueled the economy while patriarchy stabilized society. Both institutions were widespread and deeply entrenched within the worldview of countless people. Even so,

Paul proclaimed his radical belief that, in Christ, there is no delineation between slave and free and male and female. In Christ, these differences are dissolved.

Paul was just one man with just a few years to proclaim this gospel of unity; there was no way he could have upended the culture of Rome and changed the entire world. But he *could* shape the DNA of the church. "No longer Jew and Gentile . . ." was the one part of his thesis he *could* do something about. If the church of Paul's day failed to grasp his vision, then it might have remained a small sect of Judaism, so it is Paul to whom we give credit for helping transform a small Jewish movement into a worldwide, multicultural, ongoing reality we now call the church universal.

Tradition has it that Paul was crucified by the Emperor Nero around 64 CE; that meant he had only about thirty years from the time of his Damascus Road conversion to proclaim the gospel that had turned his own life upside down and right side up. The fact that we Gentiles are fully included in the church of Jesus Christ is testimony to the success of Paul's ministry. Even so Paul died knowing that his dream of full inclusion was not yet lived out completely in the life of the church.

The church in the generations that followed Paul struggled to find its balance between the demands and pressures of the world and the demands and promise of the gospel. It's messy. It's risky. Paul did what he could in his one lifetime and then he left it up to the church of later generations to follow his lead and to continue to put into flesh-and-blood practice the truth of God's reconciling, redeeming work in Christ Jesus.

In the church, the body of Christ—of all places, of all people, in spite of our differences—we are called and created to embody the unity of reconciliation God has accomplished for us in Jesus Christ. As we the church continue the work of living out the good news of Jesus Christ, we must reject letting our differences create divisions. We may be male and female, rich and poor, gay and straight, young and old, black and brown and white and "blue and red and purple," but we are one in Christ.

Paul gave his life for this vision of the church and it's up to us to keep that gospel vision alive. It's up to us to make this vision a flesh-and-blood reality for our own time and place.

As You Read the Gospel

In these middle chapters of Mark, we watch the story turn. The second half of Mark's gospel becomes an extended passion narrative as Jesus makes his way to the cross in Jerusalem. In these three transitional chapters, three times Jesus proclaims his coming death and promises his resurrection. And still the disciples do not understand.

In Mark's theology and anthropology, no human is able to perceive the truly-human-truly-divine mystery of the Christ until he is manifested in resurrection. Mark communicates this mystery with a rhetorical device scholars call the "Messianic secret."[2] Mark's use of this literary device is seen clearly in the story where Peter proclaims Jesus as Messiah, and yet (at the same time) does not understand. Ponder Mark's way of telling the story about Peter's confession of the Christ. Here is as an excellent example of the Messianic secret: a both/and story about the pre-Easter Jesus and the post-Easter Christ woven together in a seamless cloth.

The revealing of the Christ never comes from reason, logic, or human ability to make sense and understand. Such epiphany always is an act of God, a grace from God.

Reflections: *Forgive and Forget?!*

I don't know if it's because of the Broadway musical or because of Sunday school stories long ago, but it seems like a lot of people know at least a little bit about the story of Joseph. Maybe it's his *Amazing Technicolor Dreamcoat*.[3] Maybe it's all the bad things that kept happening to this really nice person: betrayal by his jealous, callous brothers, slavery in the far away land of Egypt, betrayal again, injustice, imprisonment, hopelessness . . . how these numerous wrongs must have festered in those long dark nights of Joseph's suffering!

But then, by a series of odd circumstances, Joseph comes into the favor of the king and is raised to unimaginable prestige and power in his adopted land of Egypt. This is great story telling—a strong lead character who faces multiple challenges to his deep moral core, a panoply

---

2. William Wrede published *The Messianic Secret* in 1901 and altered significantly the way scholars understand Mark. We will talk more about this literary concept in week 42.

3. "Joseph and the Amazing Technicolor Dreamcoat" is a musical comedy with lyrics by Tim Rich and music by Andrew Lloyd Webber.

of interesting villains, unlikely plot twists, Technicolor dreams, poetic justice, reconciliation, and a happy-ever-after ending.

But one thing that comes to mind when I read Joseph's story is, how on earth was he able to forgive such injustice and betrayal? If you have ever been hurt deeply, you know it is not easy to forgive. And you know forgiveness does not happen quickly. Forgiveness is a process; it must be engaged with *intention* and *attention*. In order to truly forgive, we must begin with the willingness to even want to enter into the process of forgiveness. We first have to be willing to *want* to forgive before we can hope to make it to the actual act of forgiveness.

And it helps to enter the process of forgiveness keenly aware of how very badly we *need* to forgive; how forgiveness is *for us* as much (or more) than it is for the other person.

You have heard the old saw "forgive and forget," but I will argue that not only is it impossible, forgetting also is unwise. God may be able to forgive and forget, but that's not usually how it works for us humans. Experiences that have been seared into our souls leave indelible marks that change us in deep ways, and because we are human, those events stay with us. Some things we just cannot forget.

Besides, I think there is something biblical and wise about remembering—remembering who we are, what we have been through, and what we've learned along the way. I believe a key part of faithful and wise living *is* our remembering, remembering even past hurts. For one thing, remembering honors the pain we have borne. We shouldn't dismiss and downplay our pain because betrayal hurts deeply and the remembering of it acknowledges how damaging and deadly sin can be. In remembering we do not stuff our feelings or dismiss the hurt, rather we honor the significance of the wrong that has been done to us. We grieve the damage done to relationship: we grieve the loss of trust. We don't say it's okay, that it doesn't matter, because it *does* matter. It matters to us. It matters to the health and to the witness of the entire community. It matters to God.

For another thing, in our remembering we hold each other accountable to right behavior and Christ-like living. We don't make excuses for people who have hurt or harmed someone else or let them off the hook. Destructive behaviors need to be exposed and confronted. Healing happens in the light while toxic festering is what happens in the darkness of denial.

Have you ever been hurt by a minister? Me too. Have you ever been hurt by Christians? Me too. Have *you* ever hurt someone else and broken faith with another who trusted you? Me too. Right remembering not only recollects the wrongs done to *me*, it also remembers how easy it is for me to inflict hurt on *others*. Right remembering makes us wise and keeps us humble.

Something especially damaging happens when a community of faith breaks faith. Countless people have experienced tragic betrayal by the church and have been alienated from Christ's work of love and reconciliation because the body of Christ too often has lived not in reconciliation but in opposition to reconciliation. We Christians have much to answer for.

Un-forgiveness is also something we must answer for. Some years ago, someone hurt me and that hurt changed me. Sunday after Sunday I would pray the prayer, "Forgive us our sins as we forgive those who have sinned against us," but I had no clue how to forgive this deep wound. I did not know how to let go of this painful past. I was so badly curved in upon myself I was not even willing to begin the process of forgiveness.

For a long time, I held on to the hurt like dragon's treasure. I was closed off and pulled in. What I didn't realize is that, not only did I need to forgive, I needed to repent. Forgiveness and repentance are two sides of a coin. In repentance, we name the ways we hold on to bitterness or anger; the ways we participate in gossip or slander. We acknowledge how easily we can become a self-curved-in-on-itself. We admit how hard it is for us to bend our lives toward the one who creates and calls us.

In repentance, we own up and name our failings honestly—to God, to ourselves, and to at least one other human being. And then, having entered into repentance, we are empowered to enter into forgiveness. Having emptied ourselves of ourselves as best we are able, only then are we able to be filled up with that which is God's—amazing grace, profligate mercy, and unfailing love. Love is the key here.

A powerful little poem circulated on the Internet a few years ago with words that made themselves at home in my soul, "I wonder what would happen / if I treated everyone like I was in love with them, / whether I like them or not . . ." [4] When I think back and remember the times I have not forgiven well, it is clear to me that I have not loved well.

Paul's letter to the churches of Galatia is so profound in so many ways. Here Paul is preaching a gospel of God's radical grace that is astounding, unimaginable, unbelievable. So much so, as it turns out, that some fellow Jewish Christians (and even Peter!) pulled back from that

---

4. "I Wonder" has been attributed to Derek Tasker but not verified.

divine wide-openness. "Yes, but," Paul's critics said, there are rules to be followed, rituals to be honored, lines to be toed.

Paul's famous response is Love. "The fruit of the Spirit is love . . ." When Spirit has its way with us, love happens. When Spirit plants its life in us, love blooms. When Spirit breaks wide open our curved in little selves, there is amazing grace, profligate mercy, and unfailing love. And what does love look like? What does love act like? Much as he does in that wonderful thirteenth chapter of First Corinthians, so in Galatians 5 Paul clearly describes love as joy, peace, patience, kindness, goodness, faithfulness, gentleness, and self-control.

So how could anyone ever live in this life-giving Spirit and at the same time live in un-repentance or un-forgiveness? I don't think it's possible. When the wide-openness of God's love takes root in our lives, we can't help but grow towards the wide-openness of grace. It is the grace we have received that allows us to offer grace to others. When we have been hurt, wounded, or betrayed, it is only forgiveness that allows us to let go of the past and move into that wide-open future.

The one who has hurt us may never know, may not even care that we have forgiven them—but *we* know. We will know that we are released from the anger, freed from the bitterness, unshackled from the past, and changed forever. We may remember the hurt, we may still feel some of the pain, but overriding all that, we remember God's grace, mercy, and love.

The happy-ever-after ending of the Joseph story was possible because he was able to take all the hurt, pain, and betrayal of his life and let it be redeemed within the life giving process of forgiveness. Joseph was able to allow grace to absorb and transform everything that was ungracious, unjust, and unkind. Since he was human, I'm pretty sure that process took some time and effort because forgiveness doesn't just happen; forgiveness takes *attention* and *intention*.

Even for God, forgiveness requires work—and in the Christian understanding that work was accomplished in the life, death, and resurrection of Jesus Christ. In the *intention* and *attention* of God in Christ, we unlovely, undeserving people are forgiven. And we are invited to live within this story of forgiveness. We are invited to let Spirit break wide open our closed off, curved in little selves so that we may become large enough to enter into the hurt, pain, and betrayal that permeates our world. We are called to "take up our cross and follow" the Christ. We are called to share God's redemption and reconciliation wherever we go.

Week 8

Exodus

Exodus 1–15
Psalm 24
Psalm 90
Psalm 105
Ephesians
Mark 11–16

As You Read the Old Testament

WE ARE READING THE beginning of the Exodus story this week, a story that lies at the very heart of Jewish identity. Throughout the centuries, as the Jews have endured persecution, pogrom, and holocaust, the remembrance of God's deliverance has sustained them.

This story of Exodus also shaped the telling of the Christian story from the very beginning. Matthew's gospel sees Jesus as the new Moses. Mark's gospel characterizes the work of Jesus as deliverance. The Exodus story also creates hope for any number of communities that have experienced oppression; for example, the Liberation Theology of our own time is a direct descendant of this Exodus tradition and continues to spark a hopeful fire within oppressed peoples across the globe.

Whether the liberation from Egypt is a story that is set in time or one of those deeply true stories that transcends time, no one will ever know. There is less archeological confidence in the historicity of the stories of Exodus and Conquest than before given the growing insights of historical criticism. OT scholar Walter Brueggemann explains:

58

It is not possible to deny or affirm whatever may have been "historically" the case, though we must allow that some turn of events gave rise to the particular articulation of the miracle that we have in the biblical narrative. Given the limit of historical evidence and given the power of the narrative for the liturgical imagination of Israel, it may be best to understand this text as "paradigmatic" history . . .

When understood as "paradigmatic," the narrative is seen to make a claim of intense particularity, but a particularity that invites and permits rereading in a variety of circumstances and contexts.[1]

As you read Exodus 1–15, pay special attention to chapter 3. Here is a pivotal introduction of God/Yahweh/YHWH/*I Am*. Recall the *I Am* sayings of Jesus from the Gospel of John and consider again how radical John's Christology is.

If the odd phrase "the Lord hardened Pharaoh's heart" troubles you (as it has me), think about this within the context of the storytellers' theology. For the Hebrews of Egypt and the exiled Israelites in Babylon, God is the all-powerful Lord of all creation. Even the most powerful kings of the earth cannot resist the indomitable will of the Sovereign Lord of all lords. The storytellers frame the contest between God and the Pharaoh as an opportunity for God's glory to be seen—not just to Israel so as to build their faith, but also to the kings and kingdoms of the earth so as to demonstrate the supremacy of the one true God.

In our Passover story for this week, we read about the Passover lamb whose blood was applied to the doorways and whose body was eaten in a sacred meal. Within the Hebrew Bible, we find several traditions of animal sacrifice. For example, Leviticus 16 describes how animals were to be sacrificed in substitution for the sins of the people. The high priest killed one goat and offered it on the altar as atonement, a blood sacrifice. The other animal, a scapegoat, was symbolically burdened with all of Israel's sins, then driven out of the community and banished into the wilderness.

In Exodus 12, however, there are no hints of substitutionary death of the lamb on account of sin. Instead the Passover lamb is strength for the journey. It is the one around whom the community gathers, the sharing of whose life binds the community together. It is celebration and sustenance. This alternate tradition of sacrifice of blood and body was

---

1. Brueggemann, *Introduction to the Old Testament*, 54.

reinterpreted for the Christian tradition of communion/Eucharist, where Christ "our paschal lamb has been sacrificed" (1 Cor 5:7).

As You Read the Psalms

The Fourth Book of the Psalms begins with Psalm 90, a Prayer of Moses, the man of God. Moses is not the author of the psalm; rather Moses is the context. From the very beginning of the prayer, we think of Moses' encounter with the bush that burned but was not consumed, of his encounter on the mountaintop with the God in Fire and Cloud.

This psalm sings the eternity of the Divine One, the one who exists outside of time, the Lord/Sovereign/King/Creator who spoke the cosmos into existence. "Before the mountains were brought forth or ever you had formed the earth and the world . . . from everlasting to everlasting you are God. For a thousand years in your sight are like yesterday when it is past . . ." The setting of Moses in this psalm causes us to recall his deep submission to the Eternal One but also his argumentative relationship with God. At first Moses argued against his calling to confront Pharaoh and lead the people out of slavery. Later, Moses argued against God's threatening wrath on behalf of the Israelites' salvation. The context of this Psalm of Moses evokes the long weary forty years in the wilderness as Moses led the people from Egypt toward the Promised Land.

But while we are reading this psalm and considering the experience of Moses' homeless, wandering people, we also consider the context of Israel in Babylonian Exile hundreds of years later. Here is a prayer that likely emerged from their disorientation in Babylon as they grieved the loss of Temple, land, freedom, and home. In Babylon, God's people were once again homeless. So the affirmation that opens the Psalm of Moses proclaims Israel's faith that "home" is not a place; home is a Person. "LORD, you have been our dwelling place in all generations." The psalmist of the Exile reaches back into history when the ancestors had no land or Temple, no home. If the God of Moses was the faithful dwelling place for the wandering Israelites, then the Eternal God would remain faithful to these people also exiled from their homeland.

Then the prayer creates a contrast. The Lord-Sovereign-King-Creator may be timeless, but we humans are definitely time-bound creatures. "The days of our life are seventy years or perhaps eighty if we are strong . . . Therefore teach us to count our days that we may gain a wise heart."

Here is the key: wisdom. Wisdom to realize that God is God and we are not. Wisdom to understand that since God sees even our secret sins, acknowledgment and confession of those faults is the prudent response. Wisdom to comprehend that stubborn willfulness only alienates while humble repentance brings forgiveness, reconciliation, and hope. Wisdom to count our days.

This Psalm of Moses recalls the background of God's provisioned people gathering manna in each new morning, counting on just enough bread for each new day. When we read this psalm from a Christian context, we also remember the prayer our Lord taught us to pray, "Give us this day our daily bread." We pray for the bread of wisdom to live each day as gift and grace.

As the psalmist acknowledges God's power to "turn us back to dust," the prayer also cries out in faith for God's Own Self to turn as well. "Turn, O LORD! How long? Have compassion on your servants!" Turn back to us—we, your stubborn willful people. Turn back to us—we, your toil and trouble people. Turn back to us—not because of *us* but because of your steadfast love and covenant faithfulness.

We soon will read an intriguing story in Exodus 32 that relates a "turning" of both God and Moses. While the "stiff-necked" people caroused in sin and Moses conferred with Yahweh on the mountaintop, the Lord's wrath burned and threatened annihilation. Moses pleaded, argued, and confronted God's anger, recalling and reminding of the divine promises. In so doing, Moses "turned" the Divine Mind about the disaster that God had planned to bring on his people. Then Moses "turned" and went down from the mountain, carrying the two tablets of the covenant in his hands—tablets written on both sides, both on the front and on the back. The tablets were understood to be the work of God; the writing of God engraved upon stone tablets. The good and perfect Law was the "work of God," Exodus declares. The "work of God" is glory and power, the psalmist declares.

May the "work of our hands" also be thus: favored, blessed, just, and established by the one who established the cosmos and established the nation of Israel. May each day of our time-bound existence celebrate and participate in the eternal steadfast love of the Lord.[2]

---

2. Psalm 90 inspired the beloved hymn, *O God, Our Help in Ages Past* by Isaac Watts. Find a copy of all the original nine stanzas and see how closely they follow the Psalm of Moses.

Also this week, be sure to take time to appreciate Psalm 105 and its remembrance of these core stories of Israel. Compare this song with the psalm recorded in Exodus 15.

As You Read the New Testament

As you read Ephesians this week, revel in the powerful poetic prayers (there are several). Words have power to stir the human soul, power wielded by some to provoke fear and hatred, but power used by others to inspire us to awe and goodness. Also see again the Pauline passion for breaking down barriers between Jew and Gentile.

As you read, notice the repetition of the persistent biblical theme of God's deliverance from slavery, sin, and death. Note also the ongoing biblical theme of God's triumph over pharaohs and tyrants, named here as "rulers and authorities"—not just human powers on earth, but "the cosmic powers and spiritual forces of evil in the heavenly places . . ."

As You Read the Gospel

In Mark 11–16, see how Mark frames the last supper on the night before Jesus' crucifixion as a Passover meal. The Christian celebration of Easter always corresponds to the Jewish celebration of Passover and, even though the specific annual dates dance around each other based on the lunar calendar, their relationship is fixed.

Some Christian churches recognize this relationship by celebrating a Jewish Seder with a Christian twist. My friend Rabbi Jeffrey joined my congregation for a Seder meal one year and led my church through the traditional ritual. It became very clear to us how the meaning of Passover connected across the ages to the meaning of the Christ. It was a moving experience.

The amazing, surprising, unimagined thing about Mark's gospel is that God's promised intervention into history, God's promised redemption of creation, has happened in the human Jesus and in the scandalous crucifixion. Many of us comfortable American Christians have only a tiny grasp of this mystery; we understand only a hint of the paradox. First century Christians lived on the underside of their society and so, for them, the word of the cross brought hope for a great reversal of the status quo, a reversal that would—in God's ultimate plan—bring all those who are shamed, defeated, and forsaken into God's final victory.

But for those of us who are bearers of the status quo, the notion of God's great reversal can be disorienting. Some of us are so acculturated to the Christian voice as one of power and influence, so saturated with American Christendom that we forget the cross is at the very center of God's good news. As Lance Pape has said:

> The community that would speak the word of the cross rightly must practice it radically, for the cross in moderation is an unredeemed folly. The wager must be all or nothing, and half measures are sure to leave us beyond the conventional wisdom and comfort of one age, yet short of the divine wisdom and comfort of the next—a desert inhabited unhappily by those who are "of all people most to be pitied" (1 Cor 15:9).[3]

Reflection: *What Does This Mean?*

What does this mean, Amma?

What does what mean, dear one?

Abba says we need to kill my lamb tonight. I love this lamb. He's my friend. Why does he have to die?

Oh dear one, I know this is hard. But dying is part of living. Everything that lives dies sometime. People need to eat so we can live, and your lamb will help us live and grow strong. When we have our special supper tonight, we will give thanks for the life of your lamb.

Abba says it's a special night. Why is tonight different from any other night? What does this mean?

Come here, my child. Let me tell you a story. Long, long ago we were slaves in Egypt. It was a very bad time and many people died. Many in our family were hurting and sad and afraid. We cried out to God, and God heard our cries and rescued us. The Lord brought us out from Egypt with a strong hand and an outstretched arm; the Lord saved us with marvelous signs and wonders. Tonight we celebrate Passover. Tonight we remember.

I remember the story, Amma, but sometimes it scares me. I don't like the part about the frogs.

I know that sounds scary, dear one. But think of the story this way: the Lord our God is Creator of the entire universe and God intends for all the

3. Pape, *Scandal*, 9.

created beings to live in wholeness and shalom. So imagine how all God's creation (maybe even frogs!) joined together to fight against our oppression and to help deliver us. The Lord our God loves us and will do anything to save us. When we tell the story today all these years later, we also remember how God delivered us from captivity in Babylon. In every Passover, we remember all the ways God hears our cries and rescues us. At Passover, we remember God's past salvation and we put our hope in God's future redemption.

And remember, my little one, whenever we tell the story about the frogs and the other awful things that happened, we tell it with sadness. We will dip our finger into the cup of salvation tonight and remove one drop of wine for each plague: blood, frogs, lice, darkness, death. Our joy is less whenever we remember the suffering of others—even the suffering of our enemies. Our salvation is not completely full until all people can be free.

But Amma, my lamb! Why does this lamb have to die?

He is the Passover lamb, dear one. When we share this meal your lamb will provide for us, we will share life together. We will remember that we are one family, one people of God. When our ancestors put the lamb's blood on their doorposts, they were marked as God's people who had placed themselves under God's care. Just as the Lord our God made a covenant with our fathers—Abraham, Isaac, and Jacob—now God has made a covenant with us—an entire people. God has bound us together as family, bound us together with blood. In his death, the Passover Lamb gives us life.

Abba took me to Jerusalem today and I saw a man. He looked at me. I think he likes me. But we heard some people say he has to die. Amma, what does this mean?

Dr. Lance Pape teaches preaching at Brite Divinity School and often speaks and writes about the process of remembering. A good preacher, he would say, helps God's people remember. He points out how, for Israel, remembering the significance of the Exodus is "interwoven with the telling of the event itself" and the faithful reenactment of the event is opportunity to "remember rightly." [4]

Whether the liberation from Egypt is a story set in time or one of those deeply true stories that transcends time, the power of the story continues to give life and hope to oppressed people in every age. Oppression of any kind (the story suggests) is never God's will. Rather God's way is liberation, freedom, wholeness, life—and God is ever at work in the

---

4. Pape, unpublished lecture, my notes from 2015.

world bringing life. This call to "remember rightly" includes the call to remember the wrongs done by and to the human family and to stand in opposition (as Moses did) to any abusive power, to stand against all the pharaohs of the earth.

The call to "remember rightly" includes the memory of the Passover lamb, a strong tradition of community and covenant that weaves throughout the biblical texts. Abraham killed the fatted calf to welcome his angelic guests. The father killed the fatted calf to welcome home his prodigal son. Jesus ate with tax collectors and sinners, signifying them as part of his kinship community.

The Passover lamb represented the covenant God initiated with an unlikely people. Dr. Pape further developed this theme in his lecture where he framed the Lord's Supper as a "re-imagining of the Passover meal." Much as Passover helped Israel "remember rightly" the events of the Exodus, so Christians are called to remember rightly the events of the cross, acknowledging *our* slavery to sin and brokenness.

"On the night he was betrayed . . ." begin the words of institution as many churches prepare for the Eucharist. Whenever we recall these words in our own ritual reenactments, we remember it was Jesus' own friends who betrayed and denied him. When we remember rightly, we understand we share in that same failure—still betraying, denying, and abandoning the one who feeds us and transfuses us with his own life.

This image of Passover reimagined, this mystery of the-Lamb-that-was-slaughtered reigning now and forever as Lord of all; this picture of God creating a community of redeemed and reconciled people with broken bread and blood of the covenant; this invitation by the Crucified and Risen Christ, beckoning all of us wounded and scarred people with his own nail-scarred hands—all this draws us to the Table. And Christ's Table is open to all.

Week 9

Law

Exodus 16–24
Psalm 19
Psalm 37
Psalm 91
Psalm 101
First Corinthians 1–9
Matthew 1–7

As You Read the Old Testament

As you read Exodus 16–24, you will find the famous story of Moses receiving the Ten Commandments. Read the story carefully. Are there any surprises? Many of us may not realize how much we have been influenced by Hollywood's version of this story. It may be helpful for you to name the influences that are working on your interpretation as you read this week; see how well you can approach these stories with a neutral lens and an open mind.

As Exodus continues, there are more ordinances and regulations detailed in the following chapters, rules about selling one's daughter, for example, as well as a list of capital crimes: cursing or striking one's parents or killing another person (but note, there was no death penalty for killing an enslaved person). There are rules about recompense when an ox injures another person, and rules about bribery and perverting justice. This part of the Law focuses on human relationships, ethics, and morality.

Of course there is other law in the Torah as well, not just the moral code. Much of the Mosaic Law is ceremonial law that details the particulars of worship, rules for the priesthood, and rules for the sacrificial system. (We will see more of this in Leviticus.) Fundamentally, the Law from Sinai teaches the covenant people of Israel how to be in relationship with Yahweh through ceremonial worship and also with one another in fairness and justice.

Some of the laws are grounded in a specific culture, time, and place; law contingent on the particular circumstances of a particular people in a particular age. But as people and events changed throughout history, portions of the Law are now understood to have been temporary. For example, Jewish communities in 2021 do not stone rebellious children or maintain slaves, and Jews since the devastation of the Second Temple have not practiced the commandments of the ancient sacrificial system.

However, faithful Jews throughout the centuries *have* continued to be faithful to the Law's eternal decrees of love and justice. All religions evolve. All viewpoints change. Healthy faith grows and always is "seeking understanding."

As You Read the Psalms

In the ancient wisdom literature, Psalm 19 sings a song of praise for God's law that governs the universe and for the beauty and mystery of creation. It's a compelling psalm written in melodic couplets.

Psalm 19 seems to be a companion to Psalm 90. In both, the Lord is celebrated as refuge-fortress-shelter-dwelling place-home. In both psalms, this God is *my* God. Yahweh is personal. While Psalm 90 comes to this conclusion after some bold challenges demanding that God keep faith as promised, Psalm 91 begins with unquestioning trust in God's unfailing faithfulness.

I have struggled with the confidence of this song, and I'm not the only one. Some people have misread it so completely that they consider this psalm as a kind of magic assurance that they will be protected from any sort of harm. "A thousand may fall at your side, ten thousand at your right hand, but it will not come near you . . ." No, these words are not guarantees of safety. Rather, they are confessions of the deep faith of someone who has been to hell and back. This is a song that remembers the very real disorientation of crisis and yet has moved on to a new orientation that is confident and calm. This psalmist is anything but naïve; instead, he lives life in the Big Picture, trusting in the ultimate faithfulness of the Author of *The Story*.

Notice that in the temptation stories in this week's reading in the gospel of Matthew, the devil offered one of these promises with just such magical thinking.

> God will command his angels concerning you to guard you in all your ways. On their hands they will bear you up, so that you will not dash your foot against a stone.
> So therefore, "if you are the Son of God, throw yourself down from the pinnacle of this Temple . . ." (Matt 4:5–7).

Twisting Scripture is nothing new, and Jesus reminds us that responsible biblical interpretation is crucial to faithful living. "It is written, 'Do not put the Lord your God to the test.'" The life and witness of our Lord himself teaches us that, sometimes, bad things happen to good people; that God does not wave a magic wand and make dangers go away; that people of faith are called to encounter life's challenges with wisdom and courage.

When we read Psalm 91 through the lens of the deep confidence of Jesus, we too can trust in faith's *nevertheless*. No matter what happens to me or mine—God is our shelter-fortress-refuge-home. No matter what happens to me or mine—God will never leave us or forsake us.

In a bit of an unusual shift, Psalm 91 finishes with a Divine Response. The psalmist hears the word of the Lord answering the questions of Psalm 90 with a prophetic reassurance for Israel in Exile. Many individuals will not return to their homeland, but God's beloved Israel can count on *ultimate* deliverance and *eternal* faithfulness for the whole people of God.

> Those who love me, I will deliver;
> I will protect those who know my name.
> When they call to me, I will answer them;
> I will be with them in trouble,
> I will rescue them and honor them.
> With long life I will satisfy them,
> and show them my salvation (91:14–16).

God's people in all times, in all places can live with this same kind of confidence that no matter what, whatever, *nevertheless*—in God's ultimate *shalom*—the Lord is our salvation.

As You Read the New Testament

In these various letters of Paul, notice how Paul was answering specific questions. Remember, we don't know the questions; we only have Paul's answers. (Think of that game show where the contestants are given the answer and then must guess the question.) Biblical scholars pay attention to this kind of literary dynamic and work to discern what might have been going on in the context of the original epistles.

As a budding theologian, you too are learning to pay attention. *Don't be afraid to question.* Much as the Law of Moses was a law grounded in a specific culture, time, and place, so the rules Paul offers to churches in the first century can also be understood as contingent on the particular circumstances of a particular people in a particular day and age. As in ancient Israel, as in the first century communities of Christ, so we twenty-first century Christians must ponder matters of ethics, morality, and ceremony with careful and prayerful discernment with and within our own communities of faith, always beginning with faith that God is still speaking.

As you read the opening verses of the first letter to the Corinthian church, see how quickly Paul launches into admonitions for unity. There is significant division, Paul complains. The witness to the reconciliation and grace of the gospel of Jesus Christ is compromised, Paul insists. "For the message about the cross is foolishness to those who are perishing, but to us who are being saved it is the power of God . . ." (1 Cor 1). The message, the word, the *logos* of the cross is "foolishness" for some, Paul insists, because this word of God is spoken in the language of death, annihilation, and godforsaken-ness. The word is "foolish" (*moria* in the Greek—"moronic") because the *Logos* of the cosmos is spoken in the grammar of shame and defeat. Nevertheless, for Christians this word is the wisdom and power of God.

In Richard Hays' analysis of the phrase "Christ crucified", Hays points out that the Greek word for "crucified" is a perfect passive participle so it describes actions completed in the past whose effects continue into the present. (We sing a perfect passive participle in the beloved Christmas carol, *Joy to the World! The Lord is Come!*)

> When Paul summarized the gospel as *Christ crucified*, he identified Jesus Christ as the one whose identity continues to be stamped by the cross. The cross has not been canceled out by

the resurrection; rather, to know even the risen Jesus is to know
him precisely as the Crucified One.

Any other account of his identity is not the gospel.[1]

Even in resurrection and glorification, the humanity of God's Son
is affirmed.

As You Read the Gospel

"An account of the genealogy of Jesus, the Messiah, the son of David, the
son of Abraham . . ." (Matt 1:1). From its opening words, Matthew places
Jesus squarely within the story of their Jewish tradition. Jesus is *Messiah,
Christ, Anointed* by God to speak and act definitively in God's name. Jesus is son of David the king, and son of Abraham the father of all nations.
From the opening to the close of Matthew's story, Jesus is the faithful Jew
who perfectly followed Torah and completely submitted to God's will.

Besides placing Jesus within the tradition of Abraham and David,
Matthew also fixes Jesus firmly in the line of Moses. Throughout Matthew's gospel, we see numerous comparisons between Moses the Lawgiver and Jesus—the one who fulfills, affirms, and accomplishes the Law.

Just as there are five books in the Pentateuch (the Books of Moses)
so there are five major discourses of Jesus in Matthew. Just as Moses experienced significant events on mountaintops, so Jesus is pictured on the
mountain of the great sermon, on the mountain of transfiguration, and
on the mountain of his farewell in the final verses of Matthew's story.
The coupling of Jesus and Moses offers a telling insight about Matthew's
Christology, his understanding of the Christ.

It's interesting to read the Gospel according to Matthew alongside
the book of the Exodus, because this helps us see numerous comparisons
and contrasts between Jesus and Moses.

- The pharaoh in Egypt and the king in Jerusalem both seek to kill the
  male infants who threaten their power.

- "Out of Egypt I have called my son," Matthew says of Jesus while in
  the background he also sees God's "son" Israel escaping the dangers
  and persecution of Egypt.

---

1. Hays, *First Corinthians*, 35.

- Jesus is baptized in the Jordan River, passing through the waters (like the Red Sea) and then entering into a wilderness forty days and forty nights where he (like Israel) is tempted to test God.

But again and again, unlike God's son Israel (or any of the rest of us sons and daughters), Jesus is the only one who faithfully and perfectly submitted himself to the God who calls, who saves, and who provides.

Besides seeing Jesus as the one who fulfills the Law, Matthew also pictures Jesus' whole life as fulfilling the whole of Scripture. Some sixty-one times in twenty-eight chapters, Matthew quotes the Hebrew Scriptures directly. Numerous other times, he paraphrases and alludes to sayings and images that come from the Old Testament. Matthew is steeped in Judaism so, as he reflects on the life of Jesus and the meaning of the Christ event in light of his ancient Scriptures, he cannot help but see connections across the entire story.

Matthew's is a story beautifully told. The fact that this gospel is placed first within the canon of the NT says something about the way it was honored by the early Christian community, maybe because of the way the Gospel according to Matthew bridges the gap between the Hebrew Scriptures and the Christian Scriptures. Matthew introduces Jesus as the one who continues the tradition of Abraham, Moses, and David while at the same time transforming the tradition, opening it up to non-Jews. Now the call for Abraham's descendants to become a "blessing for the nations" has become—in Jesus Christ—a reality.[2]

Reflection: *The Law of the Lord*

Some years ago, a young man came to my pastor's office looking for a new church. When we talked for a while, I learned the story of his struggle with alcohol addiction. He was already active in an Alcoholics Anonymous group but he believed a church community might also help him turn his life around. I called the pastor at a nearby church to find out more about their recovery program and it sounded like a good fit for this man who was living life on survival mode. We stayed in touch for several months; I often wonder how he is doing now.

Sometimes some people need rules, structure, and clear definitions. This makes sense to us when we are raising our children; independence

2. Much of what I write here has been informed by Boring's commentary, "Matthew."

and healthy self-sufficiency can come only through a process of growing through stages and practicing living within some kind of protected environment. This makes sense to us when we remember our own journey toward maturity.

You may occasionally hear the people of Moses referred to as "the children of Israel." The term "children" isn't meant as a contrast to the concept of "adult;" it's mostly the KJV's way to describe this people's family tree and to identify them as the descendants of Abraham, Isaac, and Jacob. But maybe, in another way, "children" can also serve as a kind of archetypal description of humanity's development that can be seen in all of our various cultures and societies throughout the ages.

Without thinking of Israel as any more childish than any of the rest of us, consider how their story as chronicled in the Hebrew Scriptures might give insight to how all of us—individuals as well as societies—grow through stages toward healthy maturity. In the remarkable story of exodus and deliverance in the second book of the Hebrew Scriptures, the people emerge from the confining womb of slavery through the birth waters of the Red Sea. They emerge into a wide, new world where there is bread (manna), water, and even fresh meat. But again and again, like all us self-centered humans, they test the patience of Moses; they also test the faithfulness of the God who calls, saves, and provides.

As the story unfolds, God calls Moses to the mountaintop where he is immersed in fire and cloud and sapphired glory for forty days and forty nights. When he returns to the camp in the valley, Moses comes with the Ten Commandments, a summary of the larger Law that teaches Israel how to live in relationship with God and with one another. The two tablets represent the two aspects of this living in relationship. The first four commandments (traditionally pictured on the first tablet) address Israel's proper worshipful attention to the one who rescued them from Egypt. The last six of the Ten Words summarize what it looks like to live together in honorable community.

Then numerous laws, commandments, and precepts offer great detail about nearly every aspect of their life together in community. This includes very clear warning about the treatment of foreigners, "You shall not oppress a resident alien; you know the heart of an alien, for you were aliens in the land of Egypt . . ." (Ex 23:9). Then there is this strange promise:

> You shall worship the LORD your God, and I will bless your
> bread and your water; and I will take sickness away from among
> you. No one shall miscarry or be barren in your land; I will fulfill
> the number of your days (Ex 23:25).

Within the Hebrew Scriptures, we see this understanding repeated
again and again: "*If* you worship and obey God, *then* I will bless you . . ."
Scholars refer to this as the Deuteronomic tradition, its influence seen
in many of the OT writings. (Next week, when we look at Covenant, we
will think about some exceptions to this typical, karmic way of understanding God.)

Matthew's gospel shaped the story of the Christ from within this
paradigm of the Moses story where Moses was the first Lawgiver and
Jesus, Messiah, is the ultimate Lawgiver. Matthew claims that Jesus did
not abolish the Law but rather fulfilled it. M. Eugene Boring explains:

> This messianic fulfillment does not nullify or make obsolete
> the Law and the Prophets, but confirms them. The incorpora-
> tion of the Law in the more comprehensive history of salvation
> centered in the Christ event is an affirmation of the Law, not its
> rejection.
>
> But this affirmation, by being fulfilled by Christ, does not
> always mean a mere repetition or continuation of the original
> Law. Fulfillment may mean transcendence as well (cf. 12:1–14).[3]

Matthew's Jesus honors the Mosaic Law but makes it clear that some
parts of the Law are weightier than others (see 9:13; 12:7).

In these chapters, Matthew offers a fascinating comparison between the Law of Moses delivered from Mount Sinai and the Sermon on
the Mount delivered by Jesus, "You have heard it said . . . But I say . . ."
(5:27–48). It's not *just* about adultery or murder or divorce, Jesus says, it's
about respecting relationship and honoring commitments. It's not *just*
about how you treat your friends, Jesus says, it's about living together in
humility and integrity (even with your enemies!). It's not *just* about rules,
it's about how we all live together in this inside-out-and-right-side-up
kingdom of heaven.

Of course pious Jews already knew this. Remember Psalm 19: "The
law of the Lord is perfect, reviving the soul. The decrees of the Lord
are sure, making wise the simple . . ." The psalmist honors the Law of
Moses in these beautiful words, while he also acknowledges that before

3. Boring, "Matthew," 186.

there was the Torah, there was the cosmos. "The heavens are telling the glory of God; and the firmament proclaims his handiwork . . ." Many of the psalmists chronicle the deep wisdom of God's way present from the beginning of creation—scriptural acknowledgment and celebration of God's law of the universe, God's way in the cosmos, God's will for all creation. Creator's law, decrees, commandments, and ordinances give structure to the universe and are knitted into the very fabric of the world. Creator's will and way are part of nature's DNA, giving order and meaning to everything that exists.

According to Matthew's (very high!) Christology, Jesus the Messiah speaks for God. In Matthew's understanding, the Law is foundational but not ultimate. Rather for Matthew, it is the one to whom the law and the prophets point—the Messiah, the Christ—who is ultimate, who amplifies and completes the Law.

- It is in Jesus Christ that the Law is both affirmed and fulfilled.

- It is in Jesus Christ that the Law is both validated and transcended.

- It is Jesus Christ who is *God with us*, the one who embodies the ultimate, definitive will of God.

- It is Jesus Christ who is the final authority.

Matthew teaches that the life and work of Christ has fulfilled the Law of Moses and now brought all humanity within the cosmic law/way/will of God that is right for *all* people in *all* times and places.

The newly formed people of Israel who received the Law at Mount Sinai continued to grow in their understandings of what it means to be in relationship to God—especially during these years in Matthew's time, a time of massive disruption of Judaism's fundamental religious, social, and political structures. Over the years, our Jewish siblings have adapted their understandings of the Law, but the faithful always and ever return to their core: "I am the LORD your God, who brought you out of the land of Egypt, out of the house of slavery; you shall have no other gods before me" (Ex 20:2–3).

Matthew's community of Messiah followers also continued to grow and go deeper in their reinterpretations of the ancient faith. When a questioner pressed Jesus to identify "which commandment in the law is the greatest," the very Jewish Jesus also returned to the core: "love God" and "love your neighbor as yourself," he reaffirmed. "On these two commandments hang all the law and the prophets" (Matt 22:34–40). In other words, when we do these fundamental things; when we live in harmony with these central relationships, then every other rule and commandment fall into place.

Authentic Christians in every age have sought to take these teachings seriously even if they have not always taken them literally by returning again and again to the eternal questions, *Who is God?* and *Who are we?* Faithful interpretation must always become faithful re-interpretation. This is the way of authentic faith.

Week 10

Covenant

Exodus 25–34
Psalm 81
Psalm 106
Psalm 114
First Corinthians 10–16
Matthew 8–13

As You Read the Old Testament

As you read this week, remember earlier covenants we have seen throughout our Genesis readings.

- First the Noahic Covenant after the great flood—a covenant with all creation; the sign of the covenant is a rainbow.

- Then the Abrahamic Covenant—a covenant with one man and his descendants; the sign of that covenant is circumcision.

- Now in the Exodus readings, we experience the Mosaic Covenant—a covenant with the whole people of Israel; the sign of this covenant is Sabbath.

Covenant making and Law giving are closely related in the Exodus story. As you read this week, you will see Moses return from the mountaintop with the Ten Commandments, but then he encounters the people breaking the Law by building a golden calf.

The back and forth conversation between Yahweh and Moses shows their remarkable intimacy, but it also demonstrates the fragility of this new people of God. This obstinate, double-minded, too-often-faithless people are brought into relationship with the God who is jealous for their fidelity, single minded in commitment, and faithful to covenant love, no matter the heart and acts of God's people.

As You Read the Psalms

In the Psalms, we see how the oral history of this people is incorporated into their hymns in order to continue to communicate the meaning of their life together as a people; their life together with their God. Watch how the stories of the patriarchs and the stories of Exodus are deeply intertwined in the identity of Israel. Remember that ancient peoples were excellent storytellers, teaching the generations about the meaning of who they were and where they had come from by telling their stories. See how all praise, worship, and thanksgiving is grounded in the name, in the being, in the character of God.

God's judgment is just. God's justice is righteous. God's way is grace. And so the psalmist proclaims the reality, the state of being for all those who walk in this way as *happy/blessed*. "Happy" is how the NRSV translates the Hebrew word, while some other translations use the word "blessed." Whichever word you read here, always hear something much deeper and richer than mere feeling; this "happiness" is a state of being rather than a short-lived emotion. People who live according to God's way, God's justice, God's righteousness are in turn (and in fact) living in a state of blessedness.

However, our psalmist admits, "we have committed iniquity, we have done wickedly." Both we and our ancestors have sinned, he acknowledges. One of the prayers of confession found in some of the liturgies of the Episcopal Church puts it this way: "forgive us for the evil we have done and the evil done on our behalf." That confession gets me every time. "The evil done on my behalf" runs deep and wide throughout history and on to the current day.

Have you ever heard people complain that slavery was not their fault? Such a statement implies that because they did not personally enslave another human being, they don't need to feel responsible for the systemic racism that has plagued the United States. This attitude differs from the repentance of the psalmist. Even though he may not have been personally guilty of the sins of Israel, he accepted personal and communal responsibility. As a part of the whole people of God, we are *responsible* even when we are not to *blame*.

Also as part of the whole people of God, we are recipients of grace even when we do not deserve it.

> Many times God delivered them, but they were rebellious in their purposes, and were brought low through their iniquity. Nevertheless he regarded their distress when he heard their cry. For their sake he remembered his covenant, and showed compassion according to the abundance of his steadfast love (Ps 106:44).

God's great *nevertheless*. In spite of iniquities and rebelliousness, God remains faithful to covenant. There surely will be consequences of misery and distress for a season, but there also will be abundance of mercy, compassion, forgiveness, and steadfast love to the "thousandth generation." In other words: *forever*.

Psalm 106 completes the Third Book of the Psalms, and as with each conclusion for each of the five books, we sing a doxology. "Blessed be the LORD, the God of Israel, from everlasting to everlasting. And let all the people say: Amen. Praise the LORD!"

As You Read the New Testament

When we read through First Corinthians, we can't help but see the (all too familiar) struggles of these long ago brothers and sisters guilty of division and competition, pettiness and self-centeredness. And we can't miss how Paul addresses this problem, warning them by retelling the story of Israel's unfaithfulness to the covenant.

> Now these things happened as examples for us, so that we would not crave evil things as they also craved. Do not be idolaters, as some of them were; as it is written, "The people sat down to eat and drink, and stood up to play."

Paul is steeped in *The Story* and sees countless connections between the ancients and his own people. Paul is a master at rereading and retelling the story of Israel in light of a new covenant God has made through the faithfulness of Jesus. Now we who are "in Christ" are incorporated into that unbreakable covenant of love.

In chapters 11–14, Paul deals with a variety of issues that distracted the church's focus on their mission and threatened their witness to the gospel. Most of this section addresses issues of worship. Consider Paul's instructions about women's behavior in public worship in the same context as his words for several other groups. Remember we don't know what the original questions were; we don't know what issues were going on that were causing some sort of conflict, for example, women wearing veils or not and women speaking in a public gathering. Paul's statements about these women in this context should not be taken as eternal truth about all women in all situations; these teachings were culturally specific for those people in first century Corinth. Drawing conclusions from any of these texts about eternal truths for all people in all places *always* demands prayerful and careful interpretive approaches.

Sometimes Paul takes an approach of law: do this, don't do that. But in chapter 13, Paul describes an undergirding powerful reality; he describes what it looks like when people who have been covenanted by love actually live according to that covenant. When love happens, the character of the God-Who-Is-Love is reproduced within those who love. It's telling that this famous chapter is the centerpiece for Paul's teaching on how to get along as a worshiping community since, historically, matters of worship (actually matters of personal preference about worship!) have contributed to many of our church splits and denominational divides. Read First Corinthians 13 again and consider Paul's words on covenant love in light of how we are to treat one another within our worshiping communities.

As You Read the Gospel

Matthew probably wrote his gospel about sixty years after Jesus. Have you ever thought about what happened during those six decades that may have shaped Matthew's gospel? None of us knows for sure, of course, but scholars do a good job of uncovering clues and offering helpful theories about how the writings of Scripture were composed and edited and placed together to form the Christian Canon. Here are some very broad brushstrokes.

Jesus walked, talked, lived, and died as a Jew in Palestine around the year 30 CE, and even while he was alive, stories about him began to circulate. After his death, Jesus' people were passionate to continue to tell the stories and share their faith that this Jesus was, in fact, the one whom God had sent, the Messiah, the Christ. Some of these faithful Jews told stories of his teachings, some talked about his miracles, some people repeated his parables, and some made sure the story of his martyrdom was known near and far.

It was probably around the year 35 that Saul the Pharisee was encountered by the Risen Christ on a road to Damascus. Then Saul-turned-Paul began a significant and far-flung mission to non-Jews, the Gentiles. Paul traveled extensively and wrote letters that reflected his understanding of the meaning of the Christ event from his perspective in his relationship with the Resurrected Christ.

Around the year 70, Mark wrote the first gospel. Mark, writing for and with his community of believers, may well have created this genre; this type of writing that communicated the good news about the Christ in narrative form. This gospel was different from both the isolated stories within the oral tradition and the letters from the Pauline tradition. Mark gathered together many of the various stories of miracles, parables, and teachings and wove them into a chronological narrative.

Also around the year 70, the Jewish people in Palestine were embroiled in a war with Rome. After a long siege, the land was devastated, Jerusalem was leveled, and the Temple was destroyed. Because of the destruction of the Temple, Judaism was in turmoil. The Temple sect (the Sadducees, previous movers and shakers of Israel) lost power and the Pharisees stepped into the leadership void. Much like the massive readjustments after Babylon, first century Judaism had to reinvent itself after the loss of the Temple; those reformations continued for at least another 100–150 years.

Around the year 90, Matthew and his community likely continued many Jewish practices as they accepted Jesus as their promised Messiah. Fellow Jews who did not believe Jesus was Messiah were increasingly in tension with their Jewish sisters and brothers who accepted Jesus as the Christ. In some cases, Jewish Christians were ousted from their synagogues and the bitterness grew. (We'll see this family feud again in John.)

Matthew took Mark's gospel with its basic outline and chronology and then added more Jesus stories from various other oral traditions. There is a birth narrative and a Sermon on the Mount, for example (both rendered quite differently between Matthew and Luke, by the way). You may recognize some of the miracle stories we already have encountered in Mark, but notice how Matthew changes some of the details. As you read, you also will watch Matthew explore the meaning of "the kingdom" by offering a variety of parables with a mix of impressions about what

God's kingdom could look like. I love this little summary of Jesus' ministry and mission:

> Then Jesus went about all the cities and villages, teaching in their synagogues, and proclaiming the good news of the kingdom, and curing every disease and every sickness.
>
> When he saw the crowds, he had compassion for them, because they were harassed and helpless, like sheep without a shepherd (9:35–36).

Also, as you read Matthew, don't miss the little story about Jesus' confrontation with the Pharisees on the Sabbath day. Remember how Sabbath-keeping was a core sign of the covenant with Israel, so consider how heretical it must seem for these passionately observant Jews to hear Matthew's Jesus claim to be "Lord of the Sabbath." Here is an important turn in the story as Matthew tells it, "the Pharisees went out and conspired against him, as to how they might destroy him." Matthew is not just talking about what happened in the life of the 30 CE Jesus rather, he describes the dilemma of the entire Jewish community as they grappled with their fundamental identity. What did it mean to be a Jew without the Temple? Who is an authentic Jew? And who has the authority to say? For Matthew's Jewish-Christian community, it was clear: Jesus Messiah gets to say. Jesus is "Lord of the Sabbath."

Reflection: *Covenant*

The Ten Commandments are the corner stone of the ancient Law with its 613 *mitzvot* (rules or commandments). In the Decalogue, the first four commandments spell out human responsibility in our relationship with the God who created and called us, while the other six commandments expand on what relationship with God looks like in the flesh as it spells out our human responsibility to one another.

The rules and regulations, the do's and don'ts of the Law were set in place to help form Israel into the people God had created and called them to be. The goal of law is not to hold us back or to keep us as small-minded rule followers. Rather the purpose of law is to lead us forward into maturity and freedom, bringing God's people into larger, deeper relationship with the Creator of love who yearns for the responsive love of us human creatures.

But the Law is *not* the covenant; there is an important difference in the way the Bible talks about the Law and how it describes the covenant. There is a crucial difference in meaning and function.

When we read through Exodus, after we read about the giving of the Law, we come to a passage in chapter 34 with a remarkable little story picturing an intersection between heaven and earth, a mysterious "thin place" where the God in Cloud and Fire comes to meet Moses and other leaders of Israel. Note how God is the one who is coming, God is the one inviting, the one initiating covenant with a people who did nothing whatsoever to cause or deserve this relationship.

Fifty six times throughout the OT, God says this is "*my* covenant." The language never talks about *our* covenant, rather covenant is what *God* has done, breaking into the human experience and creating relationship. M. Eugene Boring says:

> In the Bible, the divine [covenant] is an event, not an ideal or principle. The covenant is the gracious act of God, taken at the divine initiative for the benefit of humanity. It is often associated with deliverance, validation of life and security, total well-being and peace, *shalom*, that is, it is a *saving* act.[1]

This God who initiates covenant is the self-giving God, merciful, gracious, and faithful, the God who keeps steadfast love to the thousandth generation. This covenant, this event—this saving, redeeming, transforming love—is the covenant to which Israel understood itself to be called. And this is the same basic covenant to which we also are invited.

When the apostle Paul wrote to the church at Corinth, he did not use much "covenant" language. Perhaps this is because that may not have been common vocabulary among Gentiles in first century Corinth (much as it is not a common word for us modern day Americans). But Paul's understanding of the covenant is clear: God's saving, redeeming, transforming act of love has been—once and for all—accomplished in the cross and resurrection of Jesus Christ.

When Paul talks about the covenant, he calls it the *gospel*. To the Corinthians, Paul recites the words he was taught from the tradition he had received, words that came from the earliest days of the church and continue around the Table to this day. "Jesus took the cup after supper saying, 'This cup is the new covenant in my blood. Do this, as often as you drink it, in remembrance of me'" (1 Cor 11:25). "The new covenant

---

1. Boring, *Introduction to the New Testament*, 2.

in my blood," the Christ claims. "The blood"—through the life-death-resurrection of Jesus, the life of God who is merciful, gracious, faithful, and abounding in steadfast love—has now been transfused into the life of the covenant people.

"The new covenant in my blood," the Christ proclaims. "New" in the sense that the "old" has been re-newed. "New" in the sense that "what-was" is now what it was always intended to be. And the new covenant, this event that has broken into our world by the gracious act of God, this once and for all divine intersection has birthed a new creation in the covenant people of God. Now all of us who have been brought into the new covenant by the grace and mercy of the faithful God who keeps covenant, all of us have been made into the covenant people that God intended from the beginning.

Yes. But . . . we know all too well the already-and-not-yet character of this new creation. The new covenant *is* and at the same time is *not yet.* Those of us who say "yes" to this covenant mystery still have much growing, maturing, and becoming to do. We know full well we are in process as we are being transformed into the image of this Christ by whose life we live. Just as Israel stumbled repeatedly in their journey with God, just as the Corinthians struggled to live faithfully, so we too recognize our own inability to keep covenant and be the people we are intended to be.

Even so, the covenant remains. Even so, the gospel, this event, this gracious act of God has been accomplished and now endures to all generations. Even so, this gracious act of God will find its ultimate accomplishment when all creation is brought to final culmination. Again, Dr. Boring says:

> God's covenant is unilateral, and cannot be nullified from the human side . . . This can be done only by the covenant's Maker.
>
> The covenant people can ignore the covenant or refuse to live by the responsibilities to which it calls them, but they cannot "break" the covenant.
>
> The faithfulness of God calls for a human response, but is not conditional on it.[2]

We can refuse or resist living in relationship with this God of mercy, grace, and faithful love. We might (like Israel and the Corinthians sometimes did) keep on trying to live by our own rules, our own law, but whenever we choose to live that way, we inevitably perpetuate ancient cycles of "the sins of the fathers . . ."

---

2. Boring, *Introduction to the New Testament*, 3.

An important part of our maturing and growing is learning how to expose these patterns of brokenness within us even though they may be invisible to us. An important part of growing is finding the courage and wisdom to change destructive patterns, to stop cycles of brokenness that continue to damage future generations. This is why the words from Paul in First Corinthians 13 are so crucial, because here Paul gives us the key to break those crippling cycles and thus live into the new creation God has implanted within us.

This also is why it is so crucial to stay connected to a covenant community. A people who are covenanted together within God's covenant of love can lovingly help each other break vicious cycles and live more faithfully into the transformed image of Christ.

The God who is merciful, patient, gracious, the God who "bears all things, believes all things, hopes all things, endures all things . . ." causes us to become like this as well. Not because we try hard, but because we have been incorporated into the very life of God—because we become participants in the life of God whose love never ends.

The divine covenant, the gospel, is an event, a saving act, taken at the divine initiative for the benefit of all humanity accomplished once and for all by the God who keeps covenant. At the same time, covenant is an ever-present, ongoing, continuous event in the lives of God's covenant people. Every moment of every day, God's steadfast love is at work transforming hearts, clearing vision, opening minds, and permeating lives.

Week 11

Tabernacle

Exodus 35–40
Psalm 27
Psalm 65
Psalm 84
Second Corinthians 1–5
Matthew 14–20

As You Read the Old Testament

As you read this week's scriptures, watch how several important stories and themes intertwine with one another. See the people of Israel filled with passion to give extravagantly to create the Tabernacle, a holy place for God's Glory to "dwell." See the passion of the God who had created them, called them, rescued them, and brought them on eagles' wings to God's own self. Then see Peter on the Mount of Transfiguration filled with passion for the vision of glory he was allowed to witness. See also the passion of the Christ who—when he left that glorious mountaintop experience—walked resolutely toward the paradoxical glory of the cross. Consider connections back to the ancient Exodus stories alluded to by the brilliant storyteller, Matthew.

Relax and enjoy these stories just the way they are told. Let the words create pictures in your imagination. Don't over analyze. This week, just let the beauty and generosity wash over you.

As You Read the Psalms

Psalm 27 hearkens back to Psalm 23. ". . . and I will dwell in the house of
the LORD all the days of my life" (or "forever" in the KJV). "One thing I
asked of the LORD, that will I seek after: to live in the house of the LORD
all the days of my life, to behold the beauty of the LORD, and to inquire
in his temple." This phrase doesn't suggest life after death as much as it
connotes a life immersed in God's own life; a life lived constantly and
consistently within the Presence of the Holy.

> Hear, O LORD, when I cry aloud,
> be gracious to me and answer me!
> "Come," my heart says, "seek [God's] face!"
> Your face, LORD, do I seek.
> Do not hide your face from me (27:7–9).

The psalmist shapes his request in light of the ancient blessing found
in Numbers 6. "Thus you shall bless the Israelites. You shall say to them:
'The LORD bless you and keep you; the LORD make his face to shine upon
you, and be gracious to you; the LORD lift up his countenance upon you,
and give you peace.'" And yet the psalmist also knew the enigmatic story
of the hiding of God's face from Moses.

> You cannot see my face, for no one shall see me and live. So I will
> put you in the cleft of the rock and I will cover you with my hand
> until I have passed by; then I will take away my hand and you
> shall see my back. But my face shall not be seen (Ex 33).

As you read, notice the celebration of God's "dwelling place." Probably these particular psalms came from the period of the first Temple, but
they hearken back to the ancient tradition of the Tabernacle. There was a
deep sense that the one true God who is not bound by time or space, still,
in some mystery, "dwelt" above the cherubim of the Ark of the Covenant.
The stories from Exodus speak of the Glory descending upon the Tent of
Meetings and filling it with cloud and light.

"The LORD is my light and my salvation; whom shall I fear? The LORD
is the stronghold of my life; of whom shall I be afraid?" Walter Brueggemann says the stated premise of Psalm 27 insists that "nothing . . . is severe enough to shake confidence in Yahweh who is light, salvation, and
stronghold."[1] We Christians will hear in the background the similar con-

---

1. Brueggemann, *The Message of the Psalms*, 152.

fidence of St. Paul who assured ". . . nothing in all creation will be able to separate us from the love of God in Christ Jesus our Lord" (Rom 8:38–39).

Do you see the couplets and the parallelisms in this psalm? Repeating and reinforcing an idea is a characteristic of poetry and we often see it in the poetry of the psalms. Repetition offers a bold message of deep confidence, and while this psalmist may have been besieged by troubles before, now he has experienced the unfailing faithfulness of Yahweh.

> Though an army encamp against me, my heart shall not fear;
> though war rise up against me, yet I will be confident.

Say it once and say it again. Here again is God's great *nevertheless*. Even though disasters are looming; even though real danger threatens; even though life may be collapsing all around me—*Yet, Nevertheless*—I will trust.

So our psalmist, trusting in this stated reality, places his plea at the center of his praise. His confidence is real but evidently so is some new trouble; therefore this pray-er bends God's ear and *expects* God to hear, listen, attend, answer, and resolve this problem as God has in the past.

But the psalmist also knows (as we all must realize)—God is not our puppet. God is not our personal butler jumping to meet our every need in order to rescue us from any discomfort. No, Creator-Redeemer-Sustainer God knows what we truly need and knows when we truly need it. The Lord will respond in God's own way in God's own good time. Our job is to trust. Thus the poet of Psalm 27 concludes with a call to hope and courage. "Wait for the LORD! Be strong, and let your heart take courage; wait for the LORD!"

As You Read the New Testament

The apostle Paul had his own way of understanding the significance of the Christ event and the subsequent transition from the requirements of law to the freedoms and responsibilities of grace. Reading between Matthew and Paul, it seems clear there was some tension among the NT theologians about how best to reread and reinterpret their own Scriptures. NT writers were all faithful Jews who honored their tradition and grounded their lives in the Law. For all of them, it was with deep prayer and care that they pondered new understandings of the Law in light of the Christ. Even so, as faithful and conscientious as they were, they inevitably saw some things differently, and so the Christian churches they planted emerged with some different understandings, traditions, and practices. (This is much like our own experience of ecumenical diversity within the broad Christian tradition of our own day.)

See the rich images Paul taps into from the Exodus stories, and watch for his rereading and reinterpretation of the stone tablets, the covenant, light and glory, and Moses' veiled face.

> All of us, with unveiled faces, seeing the glory of the Lord as through a mirror, are being transformed into the same image from one degree of glory to another (2 Cor 3:1, 8).

Then in chapter 5, there is an intriguing discussion of "tents." Our earthly tents, Paul says, (our mortal bodies, our human experiences) are temporary, but in heaven, God has prepared a "building" which is "eternal in the heavens." Again, Paul taps into the ancient story and alludes to ultimate meanings of Tabernacle and Temple.

Reading across the Bible with *Living in The Story* gives us insight into some of the ways the meaning of the stories evolved and deepened throughout the centuries. Even for modern day Bible students, meaning and understanding continue to grow because the Divine Presence also continues to dwell among us "in glory."

> It is God who said: "Let light shine out of darkness," who has shone in our hearts to give the light of the knowledge of the glory of God in the face of Jesus Christ.
>
> But we have this treasure in clay jars, so that it may be made clear that this extraordinary power belongs to God and does not come from us (2 Cor 4:6–7).

I love this image! "Treasure in clay jars" describes Paul, you, me, and even Scripture itself. This is brilliant, profound poetry indeed!

As You Read the Gospel

Matthew is our most most "churchly" gospel. Mark, Luke, and John say nothing about the *ekklesia*, the "called-out" community that came to be known as "church," but Matthew uses the word twice. Of course all the gospel writers are telling the story to their various congregations from within their various traditions, but it's interesting to see the way Matthew places the later reality of his church community *within* the story of Jesus a generation earlier. This is a good reminder that all of the gospels are written with a kind of dual vision; both the pre-Easter Jesus and the post-Easter Jesus can be recognized in the telling of these stories. The Jesus of the gospels is always *both* the 30 CE Jesus *and* the Crucified, Resurrected, Eternal Christ.

It's also a good reminder that none of these gospels offers objective history. Matthew's gospel and the other writings of the Bible are confessions of faith, written *by* believers *for* believers. Instead of objective history, think of them as theological history, or maybe historical theology. When we understand canonical sacred storytelling in this way—whether some of these events happened in time and space or not—the stories still speak deep and profound truth. The stories tell us something immensely true about the God made known in Jesus the Christ and something very true about ourselves.

Notice how many times Jesus teaches about his upcoming suffering, death, and resurrection (chapters 16, 17, 20). As in Mark, Matthew places these affirmations of the passion in a cluster, setting up the coming events in Jerusalem. Here in chapter 16 we see again a pivotal story repeated in all the synoptic gospels: the confession of Peter that Jesus is the Messiah. But note how Peter immediately shows his misunderstanding of what it means to be "Messiah." This is the unfolding gospel told by all four evangelists, God's way of fulfilling ancient promises of salvation is unexpected and unimagined.

Chapter 17 of Matthew gives us another classic story, the transfiguration in which our friend Moses meets Jesus on the mountaintop in cloud and light. Here is the dazzling glory of heaven descending to "dwell" on earth. Peter's offer to build three tabernacles is a poetic rereading of God's ancient people creating holy space and inviting the one who is not bound by time or space to dwell among them.

Sound familiar? We have considered previously how the gospel writers tell the story of the Christ event so that Jesus is always both the truly-human-truly-divine one. However, in this story of transfiguration, in this mysterious vision, heaven and earth intersect with unique meaning. The descriptions of Jesus come from descriptions in Exodus as well as from the apocalyptic visions of Daniel and Ezekiel. At the same time, in another layer, the transfiguration story may well reflect the visionary experience of those who encountered the glory of the resurrected Christ.

Reflection: *When Hearts are Stirred*

Years ago, we took our children to Washington DC for a Spring Break trip and while we were there we visited the National Cathedral. It's a beautiful, moving structure: high vaulted ceilings and elaborate stained glass in large lovely windows. Even the smallest detail seems carefully planned and wrought for grandeur.

This was quite different from my family's previous experience of church buildings; those structures never included towering arches and stained glass artwork. The denomination within which we were raised preferred simple buildings, functional and utilitarian. When I was growing up, we didn't even call the sanctuary a sanctuary; for us it was an "auditorium." So as we walked through the National Cathedral, our fourth grader stared with wide-eyed wonder. "Why did they make it so big and fancy?" she wondered.

Her question took me aback for a moment; I wasn't sure how to answer since the extravagance of the architecture was new and different for me as well. But then I had an insight, an important perspective for my journey into a bigger world of faith. I answered, "Because they believe God is worth it. They want to build something so very beautiful and majestic and large because God is beautiful and majestic and huge. And because God deserves the very best we can give."

"Hm . . ." she pondered. "I think I agree."

Surely something similar was going on when Israel built the Tabernacle. This story in the final chapters of Exodus describes the people paying attention to every detail; crafting beauty with every turn of their lathe and twist of their spindle. This traveling sanctuary was completely utilitarian, but everything was built with such care and passion and attention to beauty that it must have been breathtaking.

The Tabernacle sounds extravagant to me. The word "extravagant" has gotten a bad rap, I think, but the way I use it here describes an understandable outpouring of *passionate* generosity. So I've been wondering about passion: Where does passion, this *pathos*, come from? How does that happen? Like the mystery of springtime, what is it that stirs a soul and quickens life? And, conversely, what happens that may cause a lack of passion?

A wise mentor once taught me that the opposite of love is not hate; the opposite of love is apathy. *A–pathos*, lack of passion. When we don't care, when our hearts cannot be moved, when we are content to sit in our small complacency—this is dangerous and insidious because apathy is sin. The self curves in on itself so that the heart begins to lose its ability to expand and to be moved with *com*-passion for the other. The self begins to lose its ability to open itself to God.

But the Tabernacle story is a good example of hearts wide open with extravagant generosity. For all the stories we hear about Israel whining, complaining, and resisting, here is one lovely story about when they got it really right.

I've been thinking about passion and I've pondered what God's people of old might teach us modern folks about the extravagance of generosity. For one thing, the story tells us that it was God who raised up leaders and gifted them with creativity and competence. "They had been given skill by the Lord," the text says. They were called by God and by Moses to motivate and demonstrate excellence. These inspired, visionary leaders led with passion.

Another thing this story tells us is that the entire community created a culture of generosity. There are plenty of stories that describe the complaints of the Israelites as if it were some sort of epidemic. Someone starts criticizing and then before you know it, everyone around her is infected. Pretty soon the whole community is grumbling about one thing and then another. It's as if the ethos of an entire community becomes a culture of complaining.

But in *this* story, the culture the Israelites created was one of gratitude, goodness, and generosity. The hearts of some people were stirred, then pretty soon, there was an epidemic that infected the entire community with joy and generosity; they were fevered with enthusiasm.

I like the way Exodus describes all the different skills and offerings and gifts. Planning and organizing, carving and weaving, working with metal, wood, fabrics, and precious gems—everyone had something to do. Everyone had something to give. The people understood that each one of them had something significant to offer and they truly believed that what they were doing together was important.

This effort *was* important; this work they did together as a people really mattered. Working together on this hugely significant Tabernacle project helped form them as a people and define who they were as a community of faith. It also reminded them *whose* they were. In the building of the Tabernacle, they came to understand themselves as a people who worshiped this one true God who had called them into being; who had called them into relationship.

Naming relationship is foundational for the entire Law. Remember the very first words of the Ten Commandments: "*I Am* the Lord your God who brought you out of the land of Egypt, the house of slavery . . ." (Ex 20:2). The people's hearts were stirred because of this key relationship. They were moved and motivated by their gratitude to the living Lord. Their actions were a response to the self-giving God who had rescued them from Egypt.

Do you remember when you were madly in love? Can you recall when you wanted to give, give, give to your beloved and how that giving gave you such joy? Remember how your extravagance simply reminded you how precious this relationship is; how giving only made you wish you could give more? When we are truly in love, our hearts are stirred.

As I've been thinking about passion, I wonder, how do we lose it? How is it that our love can become so conservative, so careful, so cool? How does insidious apathy creep in so that the culture of an entire relationship becomes small-minded and hardhearted?

If you've been reading through Matthew this week, you've recognized the abundant extravagance of Jesus. When Jesus reinterpreted the Law, he called for an extravagant generosity, grace, and welcome among brothers and sisters for the stranger among us, and even for the enemy. When Jesus described the kingdom of heaven, he used extravagant images of God's grace breaking into the world and permeating everything like yeast in dough. When Jesus went about healing, he created extravagant outpourings of God's wholeness and *shalom* within lives that were broken and fragmented. There is no hint of apathy in Matthew's Jesus. His passionate and compassionate heart was constantly stirred to extravagant generosity.

Even in the wonderful little story of the Transfiguration in chapter 17, there is a vision of extravagant glory that tore open the mundane settledness of the disciples' world and poured into their lives as they stared with wide-eyed wonder. And did you hear Peter's response? Surely this was an extravagant response, building three tabernacles—not just one! But the Divine Voice is clear: *This is the Son, the Beloved. Listen to him!* This is the one who has been sent to show us how beautiful and majestic, how large and extravagant is God's love for us.

And this is the one who continues to show us God's glory today. Even now the Transfigured Christ is ever seeking to transfigure us; the Spirit of the Risen Christ still moves to transform us "from one degree of glory to another" (2 Cor 3:18). When hearts are stirred and transformed into the image of this Christ, then extravagant self-giving becomes the mark and the sign, the culture and the calling of the people of Christ.

Week 12

Esther

Esther
Psalm 1
Psalm 8
Psalm 76
Second Corinthians 6–11
Matthew 21–25

As You Read the Old Testament

As YOU READ THE fascinating books of Esther and Jonah, read them as within the genre of short stories or novellas. Watch the way the storyteller sets the plot and develops the characters. Listen for the historical context since they both are told within the real history of Israel. Try to make time to read the entire book in one sitting. As you read, consider how these stories address the core eternal questions we have named before: *who is God?* and *who are we as God's people?*

The story of Esther and her uncle Mordecai are tales from the Diaspora. After the Exile, many of those who had been forced to leave their homes in Palestine built new lives in foreign lands all over the world—the setting of Esther and her Jewish community. During the time of Jesus, because of the Diaspora, there probably were more Jews living in Alexandria Egypt than there were living in Jerusalem. And remember the stories you've heard about the Jewish people Paul encountered on his missionary journeys; Jews were well-established citizens in cities all across the Roman Empire.

In spite of this widespread presence and the good intentions of Jews to be good citizens in their adopted nations, history (as well as current events) documents repeated pogroms and periods of persecution against the Jews. A popular Jewish saying even in our day is *"They tried to kill us. We survived. Let's eat."* That's the Esther story in a nutshell.

Most scholars place the book of Esther in the category of Wisdom literature. Unlike the Proverbs or Ecclesiastes that recite proverbial wise sayings, this is story, another narrative that embodies the lived wisdom of Jewish understanding.

I love the way the Hebrew Scriptures offer several stories of strong women from the tradition of the Jewish people.

As You Read the Psalms

When our children were young, my husband created a lively tune for Psalm 1 so we could all memorize it. They are in their 40s now and still can sing this Revised Standard Version of this, the anchor psalm of the psalter. I call it the "anchor psalm" because the editors of Israel's hymnal organized the 150 psalms quite meticulously into five books, each with their own internal theology. The creators of Israel's hymnbook understood that Psalm 1 sets the tone not only for Book One but also for the entire collection of poems that sing the life of Israel.

Plenty of the psalms lament the sad reality that—all too often—the world is not as it should be. But Psalm 1 boldly states the ideal: it sings Israel's faith that God is *for* the righteous and God will judge the wicked. *There are two ways*, the faith of Israel insisted, *righteousness or wickedness*. We humans must choose our path even as God oversees the consequences of those choices.

When we moderns read this, it's important to read the words "righteous" and "wicked" within their ancient context. See the synonyms our poet uses for wicked: "sinners" and "scoffers." *Scoffers* is the most telling because it describes someone who does more than make a mistake or miss the mark; a scoffer intentionally rejects the instruction of the law/the Torah/the teachings. Since the precepts of the Lord are designed to bring happiness/blessedness to God's people, those who ignore this way will consequently experience unhappiness.

Ironically, this rejection of instruction, this "I-did-it-my-way" way is highly valued in our modern day society. Autonomy is considered to be a positive characteristic, a strength in Western culture. But when we look closely at this word "autonomy," it gives us a clue what is really going on. "*Nomos*" is the Greek word for law/instruction/teaching while "auto" describes the self. Thus the original meaning of "auto-nomy" is people living their lives as a law to themselves.

In contrast, within the other way—according to the wisdom of Israel—"righteous" describes those who submit to the instruction of Torah, those who trust and obey. Righteousness in biblical language never means perfect or sinless. Here as well as in the NT (especially the letters of Paul), those who are considered to be righteous are those whom God has *made* right. Here is a person who is the opposite of autonomous, a person who instead lives life open to teaching of Scripture and to the wisdom of the universe. A person grounded (like a tree by a stream) but ever growing and becoming.

Modern definitions of righteousness are mostly descriptions of *self-righteousness*. We tend to think from a human perspective and depend upon our own understandings of morality and rule following. We think of "happiness" in terms of what satisfies us and makes us feel good. All this self-centeredness is entirely different from the orientation of the Psalms where God is center; where righteousness and blessedness are gifts given by Creator to the never quite perfect creature. This core theology of Psalm 1 is woven throughout the entire psalter of Israel. Even in the laments, when the faithful complain that the wicked prosper while the righteous suffer, the core faith remains: there are two ways.

Faith says that in God's good time, because of God's faithfulness, justice, and righteousness, the wicked will never find authentic happiness; wickedness will indeed perish. Faith affirms that the Lord knows/sees/protects/blesses the way of the righteous, and it is only within this way that we humans find true prosperity and happiness.

As You Read the New Testament

Our *Living in The Story* reading guide brings First and Second Corinthians into the reading mix during the season of Lent and then Easter. In Paul's first letter to the church at Corinth, we hear Paul speak of the same wisdom demonstrated by Esther and by Jesus, wisdom that motivates self-sacrifice on behalf on another. Wisdom that looks like foolishness and maybe even recklessness to the world, the "foolish" wisdom of the cross.

In Paul's second letter, we continue to hear Paul's description of what it means to live life with the upside-down and right-side-up values of the kingdom of heaven. "If I must boast, I will boast of the things that show my weakness" (2 Cor 11:30). The gospel according to Paul challenges our human tendency to try to fix ourselves, remodel ourselves, save ourselves by ourselves. Salvation is not our work; it belongs to God. God's work in the world is to bring all creation together in grace and redemption, justice and right-making, and all this work is for the purpose of realigning and recreating humanity so that humanity might truly reflect the image of God in whose image we are created.

We theologians are called to do the wise work of discerning eternal truths that transcend our cultural limitations, and we do this crucial work with humility and prayer. We must always read and then reread these ancient texts, our Holy Scriptures, with open minds and open hearts.

As You Read the Gospel

During Holy Week, Christians follow the way of Jesus from the highs of hosannas through the horrors of the cross. We see Jesus' faithfulness to his own destiny that drove him forward because whatever happened to him personally, it was the covenant—the promise—that mattered.

As we read this week, we recognize how the lived wisdom of Esther is lived in Jesus as well. "If I perish, I perish" is not fatalism, rather, it is deep cosmic wisdom. The upside-down-right-side-up wisdom of God gives unceasingly, loves unconditionally, and saves unendingly. This God is "the source of our life in Jesus Christ" (1 Cor 1:30).

Matthew ends his story on yet another mountaintop with the resurrected Jesus giving final instructions to his disciples.

> All authority in heaven and on earth has been given to me. Go therefore and make disciples of all nations, baptizing them in the name of the Father and of the Son and of the Holy Spirit, and teaching them to obey everything that I have commanded you.
>
> And remember, I am with you always, to the end of the age.

Matthew has been claiming all along that Jesus speaks for God. Now—because of the cross and resurrection—this Jesus who perfectly fulfilled the Law is explicitly named the final authority in heaven and earth. The Jesus who emerged from a particular people and a specific tradition is now Christ for all the nations. The Jesus who died is now

living with us *always* to the end of the world. For Matthew, the Spirit of
the Risen Christ continues to speak *within* and *to* the church.

Reflection: *If I Perish, I Perish*

Several years ago, my husband and I attended Purim services at the synagogue of our friend Rabbi Jeffery. Purim celebrates and commemorates
the story of Esther, and the synagogue service we attended was truly a
hoot. I normally don't describe worship services as a "hoot," but that was
before I participated in Purim. The children dressed in costumes, most of
the girls as Esther, many of the boys as the king or as Mordecai. Even some
of the adults got into the fun; one couple came as Groucho and Harpo!

The Scripture was cantored, that is, sung in a disciplined singsong
as is typical in most Jewish worship services. All the reading was done
in its original language, Hebrew, but even so, even those of us who did
not understand Hebrew still recognized the name of the hated Haman.
Whenever his name was mentioned, we booed and hissed and rattled our
noisemakers, trying to drown out the sound of his name.

Afterwards, when we gathered for refreshments in the community
room, the favorite cookie was called "Haman's Ear" (another reason why
I say it was a hoot). Jewish worshipers really get into Purim. They "get
into it" by thoroughly enjoying themselves and having fun with the story,
but they also get into it by making it personal. As at every Passover Seder
meal, Jewish worshipers affirm, "God delivered *us* from the land of Egypt,
from the house of slavery," so at Purim and other times as they remember
their history, they confess, "*We* were saved from disaster."

In 2014, around the season of Purim, yet another hater of the Jews
sought to wreak havoc and destroy. At the Jewish Community Center in
Overland Park, Kansas, an angry, shriveled up, antisemitic soul attacked
the center and killed three people. In a strange and tragic twist, none of
the victims was Jewish.

Mindy Corporon arrived just after the shooting had occurred and
found her own father and her teenaged son as they lay dying. At the community prayer vigil that evening, Mindy spoke and even as she grieved,
she celebrated their life and love. "We were all having life," she said as she
described what they were doing the day before the shooting.[1] "And I want

---

1. Find a video of Ms. Corporon's remarks at https://www.nytimes.com/video/
us/100000002825384/family-of-shooting-victims-speaks-out.html

you to know, we will all keep having life. I encourage you to have more life also." *Having life.* This is personal. We are all in this together.

Even though Esther is the only book in the Bible that does not mention the name of God, the story offers powerful testimony to multiple ways the hidden God keeps promises and continues to work on behalf of the divine covenant. It is also about how God's people participate in covenant.

> The Book of Esther, with its tale of suffering, crisis and eventual triumph, testifies that we are not trapped helplessly in a destructive global fate . . . With bold faith, Esther took events into [her] own hands to secure the future of the covenant. Her story shines as an example of the human side of covenant responsibility . . . Esther, read through the prism of Christ, points us beyond fatalism toward the hope of the earth.[2]

It is bold faith indeed that Queen Esther demonstrates. "If I perish, I perish," she said. Esther gave herself over to the salvation and redemption of her people, risking her own life in the process—the "human side of covenant responsibility." This self-giving may seem like foolishness to some but, in fact, this is deeply lived wisdom.

The book of Esther is a story of high drama, filled with ironic turns of fortune and karmic twists of fate. Esther and Mordecai acknowledge that she has been put here in this place "for such a time as this." Her destiny drives her forward because whatever happens to her personally, it is the covenant that matters. She is committed to participate in the way of God in the world because she knows it is the future of God's people that matters. This is this wisdom that is the "hope of the earth."

The NT continues to confirm themes of God's covenant. Experiences of our living can turn our attention to God's faithfulness and teach us how to live wisely.

> The unity of Scripture lies in the central theme of covenant that runs through every book of the Bible from Genesis to Revelation . . .
> Sub-themes of the covenant—experiences of pilgrimage and promise, bondage and freedom, duty and blessing, famine and plenty, barrenness and fertility—weave their way through both testaments."[3]

2. Hambrick-Stowe, "Esther the New Moses," *The Christian Century*, 1134.

3. Hambrick-Stowe, "Esther the New Moses," 1132.

I'm often amazed when I read and reread stories about Jesus' own keen wisdom for living. He always seemed to have just the right balance in everything: self-sufficient while at the same time completely selfless and self-sacrificing, always in control and yet ever in the service of others, proactive and assertive while still being totally responsive to God's leading. For example, Matthew's gospel shows us dilemmas that constantly challenged Jesus with adversaries on every side, companions who were often clueless, and inconstant crowds. And yet the gospels (also functioning as a kind of Wisdom literature) show us how Jesus perfectly embodied wisdom as he participated in the covenant. Jesus Christ embodied the covenant, has *become* the gospel, and now has enacted the salvation that is the gracious act of God—validating life and accomplishing *shalom*.

When we follow in the way and wisdom of Esther, we discover what happens on the other side of threat only by walking right into the danger with bold faith. When we follow in the way and wisdom of Jesus, we learn what happens on the other side of death only by dying to ourselves and giving ourselves over to God's promise of resurrection. Dying to ourselves is the deeply lived wisdom that allows us to participate in the covenant and to live in the Christ, the hope of the earth and the life of the world.

Week 13

Jonah

Jonah
Psalm 18
Psalm 66
Psalm 69
Second Corinthians 12–13
Matthew 26–28

As You Read the Old Testament

THE STORY OF JONAH and the Big Fish is *supposed* to make you smile. It's an odd little novella filled with satire and tongue-in-cheek humor; with keep-you-reading plot twists and with characters that make you wonder who are the "bad guys" and who are the "good guys?" Jonah is a dark hero in his role as reluctant prophet, but his place among the prophets of Israel is extremely important because the book of Jonah is an unusual voice, a minority opinion in the multi-voice witness of Scripture.

Occasionally, Scripture describes some of "the nations" favorably. Certainly some individuals from among the Gentiles stand out in some of our favorite stories (the wonderful story of Ruth comes to mind). But generally the historical stories and the prophetic warnings portray the nations as irredeemably wicked and inherently dangerous to the spiritual and physical well being of Israel. Assyria in particular was the historical nation that conquered and destroyed the Northern Kingdom; those Ten Lost Tribes of Israel were lost to history.

But in the Jonah story, the brutal empire of Assyria is redeemed by a God who is "a gracious God and merciful, slow to anger, and abounding in steadfast love, and ready to relent from punishing" (Jonah's burning accusation in 4:2!) This amazing grace is portrayed as unacceptable to the character Jonah, but the overall prophetic witness of the book claims that God's steadfast love is for *all* people, not just for Israel. For any people who see themselves as "chosen" and "favored," this really is an astounding counterclaim. It's tempting to see those who are "other" as inherently outside God's favor, but the startling, stubborn message of Jonah is that the Creator is, always has been, and ever will be concerned for *all* creatures of the creation.

Abraham and his descendants were called to be "blessing" for the nations of the earth (Gen 22:18). Part of the purpose of chosen-ness was for Abraham's family to live lives of witness to the reality of the one true God. But Jonah is portrayed as one whose life turned inward; as one who forgot to live his life as a witness to God's grace.

In the story, God called Jonah to preach repentance to his mortal enemies (not at all a pleasing assignment), so Jonah promptly boarded a ship headed in exactly the opposite direction. When a great storm rose up out of the chaos of the sea and threatened to swallow the ship and everyone on it, Jonah realized he had not been very successful hiding from God, so he convinced the sailors to toss him overboard that they might save themselves. Sure enough, the sea immediately grew calm while Jonah sank into its depths.

There, God had a surprise, a mixed blessing, waiting for him because a great sea creature was ready to gulp him down and save him from drowning. So here is Jonah—in the belly of the beast—for three long days and three long nights. We hear Jonah's prayer from the deep darkness.

> Out of the belly of *Sheol* I cried and the LORD heard my voice . . .
> The waters closed in over me; the deep surrounded me, weeds were wrapped around my head at the roots of the mountains.
>   And yet you brought up my life from the Pit, O LORD my God (2:1–6).

When Jonah finally was able to die to himself, to give over his own plans and schemes; when he admitted he couldn't save himself; when he recognized his helplessness and gave himself over to the Source of all life, then the Lord spoke to the sea monster, and it regurgitated Jonah onto the dry land.

The prophetic witness of the book Jonah still speaks to us today because the prejudices and presuppositions of the character Jonah confront us all and call us to search our own hearts in order to unearth our own biases. The fascinating books of Esther and Jonah challenge us to consider anew the eternal questions, *who is God?* and *who are we?*

As You Read the Psalms

Psalm 69 is the longest and most complex of the laments. In all the psalms (as in all of life), there is juxtaposition of complaint and praise, of pain and confidence. This both/and archetype of crucifixion and resurrection reminds us that faith endures and sustains because of the eschatological hope for God's promised redemption.

> Save me, O God, for the waters have come up to my neck. I sink
> in deep mire where there is no foothold; I have come into deep
> waters, and the flood sweeps over me (69:1-2).

The images of this psalm are vivid as they describe the flood of overwhelming persecution. In the psalmist's understanding, the tortures he must endure are unjustified and unjust, but he remains faithful in the midst of the faithlessness of his tormentors and argues that his own troubles have come to him *because of* his trust in God. Even though this shameful treatment overwhelms the poet, what truly drives his life is his consuming passion for Yahweh.

> It is for your sake that I have borne reproach,
> that shame has covered my face.
> I have become a stranger to my kindred,
> an alien to my mother's children.
> It is zeal for your house that has consumed me;
> the insults of those who insult you have fallen on me (69:7-9).

You may recognize this phrase "zeal for your house has consumed me." John used this phrase from this psalm when he told the story of Jesus driving the moneychangers from the Temple. In John (unlike the synoptic writers) this brazen, prophetic act happened at the beginning of his ministry rather than towards the end, allowing the story to function as an introduction to Jesus' ministry. John employs the phrase as a summary of Jesus' consuming passion for God, a consuming passion that will lead Jesus to the cross and consume him.

When the psalmist's prayer turns (as the laments most always do), he contrasts the unfaithfulness of humans with the steadfastness of the Lord. He even confesses his own faults, knowing all too well the ambiguity of the human condition. The poet puts his faith squarely in divine faithfulness, steadfast love, and mercy. "Answer me, O LORD, for your steadfast love is good; according to your abundant mercy, turn to me . . . Draw near to me, redeem me, and set me free because of my enemies" (69:16–18). His plea calls God to action based on God's own promises: *answer me, draw near to me, redeem me, set me free.* People of faith wait in faith and live in hope. This is what faith is, this is what hope does, because faith and hope are eschatological, counting on God's ultimate redemption.

"I looked for pity, but there was none; and for comforters, but I found none. They gave me poison for food, and for my thirst they gave me vinegar to drink" (69:20–21). You may recognize this "vinegar to drink" phrase as well. Peppered throughout this lament are numerous phrases that allowed Christians to see within the life of the psalmist similar experiences of isolation, estrangement, and animosity in the life and death of Jesus. Not that the biblical writers of Israel were able to see into the future and predict details of Jesus' life; rather Jesus lived out the full range of human experience to which the Scriptures bear witness. Like every mortal, Jesus lived cycles of pain and hope, sorrow and joy, death and resurrection.

"Let their table be a trap for them, a snare for their allies. Let their eyes be darkened so that they cannot see, and make their loins tremble continually" (69:22–23). As the psalmist seeks vindication, tit-for-tat sounds like justice to him. *Repay what they have done to me. Give them back what they gave me.* It's a karmic understanding of justice, a human way of making sense. But who knows how Creator/Redeemer/Sustainer is making right the wrongs of the universe? It is mystery.

Within the Christian understanding, we acknowledge this mystery while at the same time we put our faith in the cross. We believe God acted within the life-death-resurrection of Jesus the Christ in order to make right the wrongs of the universe, to accomplish ultimate justice for all creation. Justice and rightness *have been* accomplished already, and justice and righteousness *will be* finally, completely fulfilled one of these days when Creator brings all things together within the eschatological *shalom.* Justice is a both/and, already-and-not-yet mystery. Therefore we sing:

I will praise the name of God with a song; I will magnify God with thanksgiving . . . Let the oppressed see it and be glad; you who seek God, let your hearts revive. For the LORD hears the needy and does not despise his own that are in bonds (69:30, 32).

And so within this already-and-not-yet-reality, we wait. People of faith wait in faith and live in hope. Because this is what faith is. This is what hope does.

As You Read the New Testament

These two chapters in Second Corinthians complete Paul's complicated correspondence to the troubled church in Corinth. Paul planted this congregation of Jesus followers and felt special responsibility for them. Throughout these two letters, he grieves the division that threatens their spiritual health and their gospel witness. He also claims his position as parent and urges them to accept his authority and heed his counsel.

It is important for us to remember that we only have one side of this story and that is Paul's side. Even the apostle's words we have here come down to us in a bit of a jumble, because quite a few scholars think there were at least three letters from Paul. As the Scriptures were being gathered and organized, three letters may have been edited and combined into two so we don't know what we've missed in the back and forth correspondence. We do the best we can to reconstruct an ancient situation and long ago relationships. That said, *Living in The Story* begins and continues with the faith that Spirit is still speaking a faithful word to us today even through such age-old, culture-bound words.

This week, take time to ponder Paul's famous "thorn in the flesh" statement:

> To keep me from being too elated, a thorn was given me in the flesh, a messenger of Satan to torment me, to keep me from being too elated. Three times I appealed to the Lord about this, that it would leave me, but he said to me, "My grace is sufficient for you, for power is made perfect in weakness."
>
> So, I will boast all the more gladly of my weaknesses, so that the power of Christ may dwell in me. Therefore I am content with weaknesses, insults, hardships, persecutions, and calamities for the sake of Christ; for whenever I am weak, then I am strong (12:7–10).

Consider his deep wisdom here and see how Spirit may speak to your own heart through Paul's personal experience.

Also ponder connections between this message of Paul we have been reading and the story of Jonah. Christ and his followers after him also are called to give witness to the reality and grace of the God who is "a gracious God and merciful, slow to anger, and abounding in steadfast love, and ready to relent from punishing" (Jon 4:2).

> So if anyone is in Christ, there is a new creation: everything old has passed away; see, everything has become new! All this is from God, who reconciled us to himself through Christ, and has given us the ministry of reconciliation; that is, in Christ God was reconciling the world to himself, not counting their trespasses against them, and entrusting the message of reconciliation to us.
> So we are ambassadors for Christ, since God is making his appeal through us (2 Cor 5:17–20).

Sadly, the history of the Christian church too often tells another story, one that is similar to the story of the reluctant prophet Jonah. Instead of welcoming all those whom God welcomes, Christians too often are judgmental and exclusivist. Instead of rejoicing in the wild and wide diversity of those whom God is calling and crafting into a people, Christians too often are fearful and resentful of those who are not like us. The inclusive gospel preached by Paul shows us a larger, more grace-filled way that we modern day Christians would be wise to follow.

As You Read the Gospel

Living in The Story offers these passages from Jonah and Matthew around the time of Holy Week and Easter Sunday. It's a powerful juxtaposition, and the power endures whenever these scriptures are read together. Matthew's Jesus makes explicit connection between his own passion and the story of Jonah, and we want to pay close attention to what this insightful NT theologian does as he tells the Jesus story in his particular way.

Reflection: *Three Days in the Belly*

On many an Easter morning, we wipe tears of joy as we share in the baptism of some of God's precious children. Easter is a perfect time to celebrate baptism because, for us Christians, it pictures death and resurrection. That's what this life with Christ is all about: dying to ourselves, admitting we can't save ourselves, recognizing our own helplessness, giving ourselves over to the Source of all life—the life that burst from the tomb on that Easter morn long ago so that, in our own dying we too trust we will find new life. Baptism gathers up all this multitude of meaning and symbolizes all this mystery: *death* and *resurrection*.

We see hints of it even in the little story of Jonah tucked away in our OT. It's a wonderful story, a kind of parable about human folly and divine mercy. Then in Matthew, there is an odd exchange between Jesus and some religious folks who wanted Jesus to prove he was the Messiah. "Give us a sign. Give us proof that you are the Anointed One of God," they demanded. But Jesus answered them, "No sign will be given except the sign of the prophet Jonah. For just as Jonah was three days and three nights in the belly of the sea monster, so for three days and three nights the Son of Man will be in the heart of the earth" (Matt 12:39–40). The sign Jesus offers is an odd one, don't you think? Jonah in the belly for three days; Jonah in the depths of the sea, at the roots of the mountains, with the seaweed wrapped around his head. This is a *good* sign? How can the sign Jesus offers as hope be something that comes from our most hopeless situations?

I'm guessing most of us live much of our lives in the belly of some monster or another. Disease that swallows all our energy and sucks us dry; broken relationships that break our hearts and overwhelm us with grief, anger, or loneliness; a job that sometimes feels like a black hole with no glimmer of light and air; financial worries that flood us with fear and anxiety; death itself—the death of those whom we have loved, hands we have held, lips we have kissed—sunken into the dark places of the earth. But it's there, right there in the despair that we find God at work.

And sometimes we discover (like Jonah did) that the belly of the beast actually saves us, keeps us, preserves us for a time and gives us a chance to see life from a different perspective.

It is good for us to stare death in the face, to acknowledge our finitude, to recognize the fragile and temporal nature of our living. It is good for us to be challenged to turn away from putting our trust in our own selves and to turn toward God—depending on God's strength, God's wisdom, God's power for our living. It is good to remember that God is God and we are not.

And it is good to remember that God is constantly at work creating life out of death. Sometimes we take life for granted. It's hard to see God working on behalf of life when we are living well and we think we have everything under control, but when we find ourselves in the belly of a monster, we know what dying feels like. We remember how hopelessness can wash over us like mighty waters as we sink deeper and deeper into despair. That's when we hold on to the sign of Jonah because if we are watching for the signs and signals Spirit is weaving into every hopeless situation, we will be able to see God's glimmer of light in our every darkness; we will be able to hold on to hope.

Jonah's sign also reminds us that our own "three days" in the belly of the beast will not go on forever. In the language symbols of the Bible, "three days" means, "*whenever* the time is right." Whenever the soil and the seed discern it's time for the sprout to push up towards the sun. Whenever the womb and the baby discern it's time for labor to begin. Whenever the Spirit moves. Whatever it may mean that God's time is "right," that's when one thing passes and another comes into being. It's good to remember that our days in the belly are not forever. We can trust this because life itself teaches us that winter passes and spring always comes; because the flowers bloom again and the frogs sing again; because the darkest night will always fade into the bright light of a new day.

But there is yet another reason we trust, believe, and hold onto hope, because the story of Scripture confesses that there was a time in human history when God broke in and disrupted the normal cycles of living and dying. There was a time when the Spirit of Life reached into the tomb after three days in the belly of the monster of death and defeated its power. There was a time when—in the power of the resurrected life of Jesus Christ—death died.

And so hope lives. And so we are Easter people. Whatever the belly of darkness and hopelessness that swallows us or engulfs those whom we love, still we hold onto this hope: that the God of Life is constantly at work creating life out of every death. *Christ is risen. Christ is risen indeed.*

Week 14

Re-Reading the Law

Leviticus 1–16
Psalm 2
Psalm 48
Psalm 95
Psalm 100
Psalm 110
Hebrews 1–5
Luke 1

As You Read the Old Testament

I HAVE A FRIEND from seminary who once tried to write a paper for a class that explored how Leviticus is the Word of God. He couldn't write it. He worked on it for weeks and never could figure out how to understand this odd, ancient book as "the word of the Lord."

My friend is not the only one. Many of us struggle to understand these kinds of strange passages from the Church's sacred texts. Just how could it be "the word of the Lord" that people with various disabilities should be excluded from worship? How could it be that people who are born a certain way should be excluded from the ministry of the priesthood?

I believe it is not possible for Christian readers of the OT to make sense of Leviticus without reading it through the lens of Jesus Christ. And that's exactly what the writer of the Letter to the Hebrews did two millennia ago; he reread and reinterpreted Leviticus through his understanding of the Christ event. This is why *Living in The Story* juxtaposes

Leviticus and Hebrews as we read during weeks 14 and 15. Reading the Bible in this way allows us to learn from this ancient Hebrew Christian theologian. We are introduced to one more faithful interpretive approach to the OT as he helps us reread our Christian Scriptures in our own day.

As I do the important work of biblical interpretation, I try to stay faithful to the tradition and open to the Spirit while I'm doing it. One principle that's really important is to value the unity of Scripture. There are lots of ways parts of the Bible don't make much sense if they are taken piecemeal. It is Scripture as a whole that gives appropriate witness to the mighty acts of God throughout history. We can't separate Leviticus from the Psalms or the Prophets or the Wisdom literature. We need all of it together in order for our faith to have any real understanding.

The Bible is like a symphony with a variety of melodies, some very different from the other, played in movements within the complex score that is our Holy Scripture. Awareness, comprehension, and appreciation emerge only as the various strains and themes and rhythms of this fascinating masterpiece are brought together into a polyphonic unity.

Leviticus stands at the center of the Five Books of Torah. The Pentateuch ("Five Books") contains the story of the Law that we so often talk about, the Ten Commandments given (poetically, symbolically) from the mouth of Yahweh and written into stone by the finger of God. Then other laws, rules, and ordinances were given to Moses for the people's life with God and with one another. These five books are crucial to the self-understanding of Israel.

Leviticus in particular defines and describes what it means to be the holy people of a Holy Lord. "Holiness" (i.e., otherness, set-apartness) is a key theme in this book. You will see this word repeated over and over, and we can understand its importance to Israel in this summary statement: "You shall be holy, for I the Lord your God am holy" (Lev 19:2).

Hang in there with these readings over the next few weeks. The Torah may seem a strange world for us moderns but it is crucial reading as we seek to understand our own faith grounded in the ancient faith of our ancestors.

As You Read the Psalms

Psalm 110 sings confidence that Israel's God upholds Israel's king. This royal psalm celebrates the king as the one anointed to rule and empowered to vanquish Israel's enemies. This famous psalm also seeds the tradition that understands God's anointed one to be "prophet, priest, and king." Psalm 110 is the most widely quoted psalm within our NT. "The LORD says to my lord, "Sit at my right hand until I make your enemies your footstool." This royal psalm celebrates the king of Israel—an earthly lord who embodied the presence and will of the Sovereign Lord within the nation of Israel. Not only did the king represent God's presence on earth but Jerusalem and the Temple represented God's holy dwelling. The king was understood to be the "anointed of God" ruling from Zion, the "city of God."

More than likely, this psalm originated during the time of the Davidic monarchy, and parts of it may have been sung at coronations (consequently categorized as an "enthronement" psalm). But probably by the time Psalm 110 was gathered into the psalter, Israel was in Exile. The land, the Temple, and the monarchy would have been gone by that time; thus the scholars of Israel were challenged to look back at their story and reinterpret its meaning for a tragic new time. Consequently, within the psalter itself we see theological rereadings and readjustments of Israel's understandings and expectations. If the Davidic kings were no more, then (Jewish teachers pondered because of the Exile) this hope of God's reign throughout the earth must be assigned to another "anointed one." Thus the hope for the Jewish messiah was born.

Psalm 110 assumes and affirms what Psalm 2 proclaims, "The LORD said to me: 'You are my son; today I have begotten you.'" The king of Israel was considered to be the "begotten" son of God, but long before the kings, the tribal people of God thought of *themselves* as God's "son." After the loss of the monarchy, the whole people of God once again considered themselves to be the beloved sons of God: Israel as God's son.

By the time we get to the gospels, we can see how these theologians extended traditional understandings of the psalmists' notions of "son" and added one more layer. Because of the Christ event, they proclaim that it is Jesus who is the ultimate, unique, one and "only" Son of God (John 1:18, 3:16). As heir to the throne of David, as the ideal Israelite, and as the completely faithful one, Jesus fulfilled and completed what it meant to be "Son of God." This new notion of "son" was a theological reinterpretation crucial to the way the gospels tell the Jesus story.

- Out of Egypt, I have called my son . . . Matt 2:15

- You are my son, the beloved . . . Mark 1:11, Luke 9:35

- The only son has made the Father known . . . John 1:18

You may recognize another aspect of this highly quoted Psalm 110 where our psalmist interpreted a passage from Genesis. "The LORD has sworn and will not change his mind: 'You are a priest forever according to the order of Melchizedek.'" The psalmist alluded to the Abraham story in Genesis 14, where the patriarch met the mysterious king-priest Melchizedek near Salem (years later, Jeru-Salem/*salam*/*shalom*). "And King Melchizedek of Salem brought out bread and wine; he was priest of God Most High" (Gen 14:18–19). The psalmist of 110 added a twist to the kingly tradition and now sees the anointed one of Israel as both king *and* priest, one who, in God's authority, both rules and serves. The king *ruled* the people and the priest *served* the people.

As NT theologians developed this theme, they came to understand Jesus the Christ as the ultimate ruler within the already-and-not-yet reign of God. But not only "king" and ruler, they also saw Jesus as intercessor and priest for the people before the throne of the Sovereign Lord. For Christians, Jesus the Christ is king *and* priest. Psalms scholar Clinton McCann writes:

> Psalm 110 is no mere artifact of ancient political propaganda. Rather, in relation to Jesus Messiah, it is a world-transforming challenge to every form of politics and power that does not begin with submission of the self to God's claim. Jesus, messiah and priest, guarantees all people access to God.
>
> Those who would deny such grace and its claims set themselves up as enemies of the reign of God.
>
> The exalted will be humbled. Persons who accept such grace and submit to its claims open themselves to abundant life; the humble will be exalted.[1]

As You Read the New Testament

It was not a given that our Christian Bible would contain both a New Testament and an Old Testament, but in historical fact the earliest Christians were Jews who incorporated their Jewish Scriptures into the Christian Bible. This is not "appropriation" in the sense of inappropriate use of another people's cultural symbols. Rather, these early Jewish-Christian

---

1. McCann, "Psalms," 1131.

thinkers understood themselves to be part of the same story, the ancient, ongoing, and overarching story of God in relationship to God's people.

These NT theologians saw the importance and the wisdom of interpreting their newfound faith within the context of the traditional faith of their ancestors. They sought to frame their current experience with God in light of the experiences and witness of God's people throughout the ages—hereby reframing their faith. As these faithful theologians read and reread their ancient Scriptures, they found there strains, themes, melodies, and rhythms that came together into a stunning new Christ movement of *The Story*.

This rereading of their own Scriptures is particularly evident as we read the Letter to the Hebrews over the next few weeks. Hebrews demonstrates another important principle for the process of Christian biblical interpretation, that is, to believe the unity of Scripture is centered in Jesus Christ. I can't read the OT except as a Christian because I am a Christian and for Christians everything coheres around the Christ. Because I see the world through this Christ prism, I make sense of all reality by this central Christ truth.

Notice also how this creative NT theologian works from both Psalm 110 and from the ancient story of Melchizedek. Hebrews 7 offers a brilliant argument that weaves both the Genesis/Melchizedek story and Psalm 110's interpretation/reinterpretation into a seamless confession of faith. The Hebrews writer confesses it is Jesus who has now embodied—in concrete, incarnational ways—the presence of God. It is Jesus, the Anointed One of God, the promised Messiah who fills this heavenly, eternal role of priest and king.

As You Read the Gospel

Luke 1 is such a rich narrative! As you read, let this marvelous storytelling fill you with hope and beauty. As you read Luke's gospel these next few weeks, enjoy how Luke's revelation of who this Jesus is comes quietly, artfully. As in any good story, Luke lays clues like breadcrumbs.

Notice the service Zechariah offers as a priest in the Temple. The story is set before the destruction of the Second Temple by the Romans even though Luke wrote his gospel years after the devastation of Jerusalem. In this little story, we catch a glimpse of Temple worship as it had been performed since it had been reinstituted after Israel's return from Exile.

Also notice the promise of the angel, Gabriel, to the astonished young woman, Mary.

> Do not be afraid, Mary, for you have found favor with God. And now, you will conceive in your womb and bear a son, and you will name him Jesus.
>
> He will be great, and will be called the Son of the Most High, and the Lord God will give to him the throne of his ancestor David. He will reign over the house of Jacob forever, and of his kingdom there will be no end (see 1:26–38).

This Jesus will be called "Son of the Most High." Luke's understanding of Jesus as "son" is completely compatible with the christological understandings of the other gospel writers as well as the author of Hebrews.

Reflection: *Re-Reading the Law*

As you read through Leviticus you surely will notice what an odd book it is. In Leviticus you will read detailed accounts of which animals were considered "clean" and could be eaten in contrast to which animals were considered "unclean" and should not even be touched. You'll read specific instructions about which parts of the sacrificed animal are to be disintegrated into smoke and which parts are to be roasted and served to the priests and their families for dinner. You'll read the descriptions of the High Priest's ceremonial clothing (even his linen underwear)! And you'll read lots and lots about blood.

Why on earth does the church of the twenty-first century read this odd and ancient text? How on earth is this the "Word of the Lord" for us moderns? I imagine the NT church asked similar questions in their day. Certainly NT theologians grappled with the challenge to understand the connections between their ancient faith from Israel and their newfound faith, informed now and changed forever by the life, death, and resurrection of Jesus Christ. Especially after the loss of the Temple and the priesthood at the end of the first century, Leviticus must have seemed out of date and out of place. Their ancient faith demanded renewal; their faith sought understanding within these a new circumstances. So today, here our Christian faith still seeks to understand, continues to ask, *what does this mean?*

The Leviticus rituals offer witness to God's atoning work on behalf of God's beloved people. The rituals tell a story of a people in process, a people whose faith was constantly seeking deeper understanding. The practices and pronouncements of Leviticus sound strange to our ears but for this ancient people, many of the images intended to picture (in some way or another) God's presence and saving grace. Now we Christians can ponder those images to see how they picture for us the presence and saving grace of Jesus the Christ.

The Hebrews theologian certainly did this kind of reimagining. When we read the Letter to the Hebrews, we notice how he taps into Greek philosophy and Platonic notions of substance and shadow, of type and prototype, of sketches and reality. Everything on earth, this theologian would say, is a shadow of some reality in the heavens. Everything on earth is patterned according to something in the beyond. The faith of this Christian community of the Hebrews (as it sought understanding) saw the Christ patterned everywhere they looked within the ancient Hebrew Scriptures.

- Christ is the perfect sacrifice offered on behalf of humanity; a blood sacrifice for sin (Lev 16:15 and Heb 9:26).

- Christ is sacrificed "outside the gate;" the one who carries sin away from the community; the scapegoat (Lev 16:10 and Heb 13:12).

- Christ is the high priest who presents the sacrifice and enters the holy place to make atonement for the people (Lev 16:3 and Heb 2:17).

Christ is multivalent, polyphonic reality.

As these Jewish Christians read and reread their Scriptures, they interpreted and reinterpreted the ancient priestly system, sacrificial system, and tabernacle system as signs that pointed beyond themselves; signs that bring to light God's saving work that finally had reached its climax in Jesus the Messiah. Through faith, these Hebrew Christians came to understand that God's work of atonement had been completed and fulfilled in Jesus the Christ.

A similar process of reinterpreting also happens within the Jewish community of our own day. For example, every autumn, our Jewish siblings observe Rosh Hashanah and Yom Kippur. During this holy season, both the devout and the secular will gather and hearken back to this very portion of Leviticus we consider in week 15. They too will hear again the ancient summons to share in the Day of Atonement. Worshipers dressed in white will confess their sins and recommit themselves to good deeds and repair of the world. As their parents, grandparents, and great-great-great grandparents did, they will hear the deep, piercing call of the shofar, the ram's horn trumpet (see Lev 23:23–32).

These modern worshipers will participate in this ancient ritual, but now without sacrifices, without priests, and without a Temple. And that's all right. Because they understand (as I believe their ancestors understood) that it is "impossible for the blood of bulls and goats to take away sins" (Heb 10:4). Rather it is—it always has been—God's work of saving grace that redeems God's people. These modern Jewish worshipers understand it is not some incantation at the Ark of the Covenant Mercy Seat that makes a difference. Rather it is—it always has been—mercy firmly seated in God's Own Being that has the power to change a human life.

I think all true worshipers have always understood it is not external rites and rituals that effect reconciliation, rather it is what God is doing—renewing, recreating, transforming the human heart, mind, and conscience. This always has been the grace of God's covenant with God's people, and this continues to be the grace of the renewed covenant made new in Jesus Christ.

So may our own Christian faith continue to seek understanding, a deep existential understanding and a profound awareness of God's remarkable love, acceptance, and welcome. And so because of this experience of unimaginable grace, may our faith continue to move us to offer similar love, acceptance, and welcome to everyone we encounter.

Week 15

Leviticus

Leviticus 17–27
Psalm 40
Psalm 99
Psalm 123
Hebrews 6–10
Luke 2

As You Read the Old Testament

RECALL AGAIN THE HERMENEUTICAL principle we considered last week that it is not possible to make sense of Leviticus without also listening to the Wisdom literature and to the prophetic writings. We should remember this important principle as we interpret any Scripture but especially these ancient texts in Leviticus. We must hear alternative voices and see the counter vision that developed within Israel's own tradition, glimpses of a future time when *all* people would be welcomed and included in the reconciling, redeeming work of God. Listen to this word of the prophet Isaiah, how different it sounds from Leviticus:

> I am about to do a new thing, [says the LORD] now it springs forth, do you not perceive it?
> For the foreigners and the eunuchs and the outcasts, [says the LORD]; for all those who hold fast my covenant—these I will bring to my holy mountain and make them joyful in my house of prayer . . . for my house shall be called a house of prayer for all peoples (Isaiah 43 and 56).

Israel's own tradition saw the rules of Leviticus as one part of the whole. Israel's own tradition saw the visions of the prophets as an equally valid voice, rereading and reframing Israel's social and ceremonial laws.

The ancient understanding of holiness with all its rules and expectations may seem odd to us, but we moderns could probably learn some good lessons from Leviticus about what it means to acknowledge and honor the mystery of the wholly otherness of this Holy God.

As You Read the Psalms

Psalm 99 makes peace with the loss of the Davidic monarchy that occurred along with the destruction of Jerusalem. Never again will Israel look to a human king for leadership; rather it is Yahweh God, the Lord alone who is king of all the earth. Israel will forever more acknowledge only *this* Sovereign who sits enthroned in the heavens. "The LORD is king; let the peoples tremble! The LORD sits enthroned upon the cherubim; let the earth quake!"

The *Shema*, the ancient and ongoing prayer of Israel proclaims, "Hear O Israel: the LORD is One, the LORD our God." But for too many of God's people, for too many centuries, it was not true that they worshiped one God. Among the ancient people, the God of Israel may have been the *highest* God but not necessarily the *only* God. It was finally during the Exile that this people became thoroughly, radically, and stubbornly monotheistic.

"Extol the LORD our God; worship at his footstool. Holy is [the LORD]!" The biblical concept of holiness acknowledges an *otherness*, a separateness that marks a clear and deep difference between God and humans. The old stories of God in fire and cloud causing the mountain at Sinai to tremble speak of this *otherness*. God is not like us. God is God and we are not.

Yahweh King loves *justice* and establishes *equity* for God's people. *Because* the King of the earth is ever at work executing *justice* and righteousness. Notice again the parallel where "justice" functions as a synonym for "equity."

Sometimes we think of justice as pay back, retribution, a karmic kind of poetic justice where bad people get what they give. But for the ancient poets and prophets of Israel, God's justice is about creating and maintaining equity, fairness, and rightness/righteousness for all God's people. This is not the same as "equality," because nothing in Scripture suggests that everyone is the same. However, biblical justice does assume that every one of us should be treated fairly and rightly by our societies and by one another; humans should treat one another with equity because this is how God's own justice works.

Holiness is a theme in the prophets as well as the psalmists. Isaiah crumpled in a heap when he was encountered by a vision of the heavenly King who is *holy, holy, holy.* John of the Revelation likewise was overwhelmed by a vision of the one seated on the throne of the heavens, the one who is praised through all eternity as *holy, holy, holy.*

In English grammar, we designate something as big, bigger, biggest or good, better, best. Biblical grammar does something similar but with poetic repetition. These poets wouldn't say, "holy, holier, holiest;" rather, this God who is limitlessly, ultimately, perfectly holy is *"holy, holy, holy."* We Christians continue this song of the psalmists and the prophets even today, but we describe our radical monotheism in the language of Trinity. We worship one God: Father-Son-Spirit. One God: Creator-Redeemer-Sustainer. And who of us doesn't know and love the old hymn, "Holy, Holy, Holy! Merciful and Mighty! God in Three Persons, blessed Trinity!"[1]

OT theologians glimpsed the mystery of the transcendent God who is immanent, but it was the NT theologians who understood Jesus as the unique one who *embodied* God's justice and holiness in an unrepeatable way. Incarnation, we call it—justice, equity, and holiness became flesh and dwelt among us.

As You Read the New Testament

In our Hebrews text we read about the ancient curtain within the Tabernacle—a thick, impenetrable curtain that separated God from the people and the Ark of the Covenant from the rest of the world; the holy from the mundane. But the Hebrews theologian (most certainly a Jewish theologian living in the first century) understood that that separation now has been eliminated; the curtain is disintegrated in Jesus Christ. This powerful reinterpretation understands that Christ's own life-death-and-resurrected-life has removed the barrier to the holy and has opened a new and living way. In the mysterious movement of God, because of the faithful work of Jesus Christ we all have access to the holy.

---

1. Reginald Heber, an Anglican bishop, penned this hymn in the early 1800s.

As You Read the Gospel

For Luke and the other gospels, Jesus is the unique one who weaves together all the other stories of their sacred scriptures; it is Jesus who reveals something brand new in the universe. Luke presents Jesus as one who fulfills the Scripture, and Luke paints larger-than-life characters to set the stage.

- Zechariah and Elizabeth's son, John, was "filled with the spirit and power of Elijah" from conception;

- Mary was told her son, Jesus, would receive the throne of his ancestor King David;

- Mary's *Magnificat* celebrates the God who continues to be faithful to the promise made to Abraham;

- the devout man Simeon recognized in the infant Jesus "the consolation of Israel";

- the prophet Anna named the infant Jesus as the one Israel had been looking for—the redeemer of Jerusalem.

In his book, *Reading Backwards*, Richard Hays calls this Luke's "intertextuality." Although Luke the narrator does not often announce (as Matthew does) that such and such happened "in order to fulfill what was spoken in the Scriptures," Luke's characters clearly are acting in the same grand drama that Israel has been enacting from the time of Abraham.

> Many of the Old Testament echoes in Luke do not function as direct typological pre-figurations of events in the life of Jesus. Still less do they function as proof texts.
> Rather, they create a broader and subtler effect: they create a narrative world thick with scriptural memory.[2]

Luke weaves delicate threads of the ancient story into the fabric of his own story of Jesus so that a perceptive reader can see the same God of Israel, the same Spirit of the prophets, the same work of rescue and redemption revealed now in the life of Jesus of Nazareth. Luke "creates a narrative world."

The angel announced to Mary, "The Holy Spirit will come upon you, and the power of the Most High will overshadow you, therefore the child to be born will be holy; he will be called Son of God" (Luke 1:35). Gospel

---

2. Hays, *Reading Backwards*, 59.

Christology says there is something distinctive about Jesus as "son," and so here we see Luke (and also Matthew) seeking to express that mystery in their stories of a virgin birth. These stories need not be interpreted as anatomical or physiological; rather these stories are meant to be theological. The virgin birth is a metaphorical way to talk about mystery beyond our understanding. This is a method of communicating the church's confession that this Jesus is "truly God and truly man."[3]

All the gospel writers referred to Jesus as "son of God," but Luke is the only one who regularly uses "Lord" as a title for Jesus. In the Hebrew Scriptures, the Tetragrammaton is the four-letter "name" for God, YHWH. It was considered to be so holy that ancient writers in the Hebrew Scriptures substituted the title *Adonai*/LORD for the name *Yahweh*/YHWH. Whenever you see the word "LORD" printed in your Bible with small caps, recognize that particular font as an indication of the original word derived from the ancient Tetragrammaton of Yahweh.

Luke proclaims Jesus of Nazareth as "Lord" and continues this tradition of naming and titling. "Why has the mother of my Lord come to me?" Elizabeth asked the newly pregnant Mary in Luke 1. "Do not be afraid; for see—I am bringing you good news of great joy for all the people: to you is born this day in the city of David a Savior, who is the Messiah, the Lord," the angels proclaimed to the shepherds in Luke 2. Luke skillfully tells the Jesus story with gentle intersections of the Hebrew story and intimations that the God of Israel and Lord of all creation is embodied in this one, *Son of God* and *Lord*.

Reflection: *A New and Living Way*

I have to warn you, this passage from Leviticus 21 is startling:

> The LORD spoke to Moses, saying: Speak to Aaron, [the High Priest] and say . . . no one who has a blemish shall draw near, one who is blind or lame, or one who has a mutilated face or a limb too long, or one who has a broken foot or a broken hand, or a hunchback, or a dwarf, or a man with a blemish in his eyes or an itching disease or scabs or crushed testicles.
>
> He shall not come near the curtain or approach the altar, because he has a blemish, that he may not profane my sanctuaries; for I am the LORD; I sanctify them . . .

---

3. Chalcedonian Creed, 451 CE.

Dare we say in response to this reading: *The Word of the Lord?*
Thanks be to God?

Whenever we read through Leviticus, we see a picture of an ancient
time and place and how the culture of Israel shaped their expectations.
Listen to these other startling words from Leviticus:

> Speak to the people of Israel and say to them: You shall not do
> as they do in the land of Egypt, where you lived, and you shall
> not do as they do in the land of Canaan, to which I am bringing
> you . . . (18:1–3).
>
> You shall not eat anything with its blood. You shall not
> round off the hair on your temples or mar the edges of your
> beard. You shall not make any tattoo marks upon you: I am the
> LORD (19:27–28).
>
> The priests shall not make bald spots on their head or shave
> off the edges of their beard. They shall not marry a divorced
> woman. They shall be holy to their God, and not profane the
> name of their God (21:5–6).
>
> You shall not sow your field with two kinds of seed; you
> shall not put on a garment made of two different kinds of ma-
> terials (19:19); you shall not lie with a male as with a woman
> (20:13); all who curse father or mother shall be put to death. I
> am the LORD (20:9).
>
> You shall not hate in your heart anyone of your kin . . . you
> shall not take vengeance or bear a grudge, but you shall love
> your neighbor as yourself: I am the LORD (19:17–18).

So I'm wondering how many of you have tattoos. How many of your
children or grandchildren have tattoos? Leviticus is pretty clear about
tattoos. I'm wondering how many of you like your steak rare; if any of
you have been divorced; if any of you plant different kinds of seeds too
close together in your gardens. I'm wondering if anybody reading this
book right now might be wearing a combination of cotton and polyester.

Some current day biblical interpreters try to use passages like these
from Leviticus to define what attitudes and practices are appropriate for
living in our modern world, but the discipline of reading Leviticus as a
whole and then reading the whole of Leviticus within the larger picture of
Scripture discloses how these kinds of interpreters do a lot of unfaithful
picking and choosing.

Those who would use these verses from Leviticus to condemn same
sex intimacy, for example, must also condemn tattoos and many other
things we take for granted these days. (Actually, a few of these folks do

attempt to be consistent; in some very scary comments a few years ago, a candidate for the Oklahoma State House suggested that stoning gay people would be appropriate "justice" based on these verses in Leviticus!) The method and the process we use to read the Bible is vitally important. It always has been important, of course, but responsible biblical interpretation is even more significant a task in our current day when perverted understandings of Scripture foster perverse politics in our civic life and fester animosity and even violence in our social life.

So whenever we try to make sense of texts like these, we must insist on faithful, sensible, and mature interpretive methods in order to unpack the historical situation and understand the cultural practices that shaped the writings of the original community. For example, it would be important for us to understand that, in this ancient day, within the experience of Israel living among the nations, the worship of idols was commonplace. Some of the rites that developed around those god and goddess cults included elaborate tattoos, male and female prostitution, and the ritual drinking of blood. Consequently, when Israel was discerning how they would behave and how they would worship, they developed very specific taboos against many of the practices of the nations around them.

Furthermore, with the cultural understandings that were typical for that age, the priests who served at the holy altar were expected to epitomize physical excellence as a way to represent holiness. The priests were to be as perfect as possible: whole, healthy, clean, and (it goes without saying in that patriarchal society) male! So when we read Leviticus, we should be very careful about bringing any of those cultural assumptions from another world and a different time forward into our own day. Faulty and unfaithful interpretations of the Bible and misapplications of some of these very obscure verses in Leviticus have been used again and again in the church to exclude and condemn people whom God is calling into relationship.

"Therefore, my friends . . ." the Hebrew writer begins our current NT passage in chapter 6. (Here is another tip for good biblical interpretation: whenever you see the word "therefore," always look back to see what the word is *there for*!) These verses provide a hinge, a pivot, and a crux in the Hebrews writer's argument. Every idea and theological reflection that has been developed in this letter-sermon up to this point, now turns. It turns from theory to practice. It turns from thinking to acting. "Therefore, my friends, since we have confidence to enter the sanctuary by the blood of Jesus, by the new and living way that he opened for us through the curtain . . ." (Heb 10:19–22). The letter has been building to this climax: the barrier has been removed. The definitions have broadened. Everything has changed. The curtain is wide open. In a famous sermon, theologian Paul Tillich rejoiced:

> You are accepted. You are accepted, accepted by that which is greater than you . . . Simply accept the fact that you are accepted![4]

No matter who you are, no matter what you've done, whatever has happened in the past, Jesus Christ has opened—and continues to open—this new way, this living way so that now *all* who approach the Holy God are accepted and are made holy.

In this theological reflection by the Hebrews author, in this image of Christ opening the curtain to the Holy of Holies, the work of the Christ has sanctified everything. Whatever was considered to be imperfect, unholy, inadequate, impure, unacceptable, all has been made perfect and holy and acceptable by the perfect work of God in Jesus Christ.

So now we are called to be who we are, to be the people God has made us to be. We are called to behave in ways that are congruent with our identity as holy people of God. Not as "holier than thou" people, but rather as people who are astounded at the grace and humbled by the mystery.

Hebrews gives us ways to do that by urging us to 1) Draw near to God in *faith*; 2) Hold on to the *hope* we confess; 3) Encourage each other toward *love* and good deeds. Faith, hope, and love are the actions and behaviors of a people who are being transformed into the image of Christ. Faith, hope, and love are the characteristics of a holy people. So if the whole church of God is really going to be a people of this new way (this living way that is the way of the Christ) then we will actively and proactively welcome all kinds of people into our Christian community—those with tattoos, those who are divorced, those who are bald, or hairy, or blind, or stubborn, or lame, or stumbling, or old, or young, or male, or female, or gay, or straight, or rich, or poor, or any other human reality.

There are still too many Christians, too many denominations, too many local congregations that have not yet figured out how to be this kind of inclusive community. All around us, all kinds of people who have been shunned and excluded and made to feel unholy and unacceptable are yearning for a place of welcome, where the curtain truly is opened wide. So here and now, in our time, in our place, let us live boldly, let us go forward with confidence in this new and living way the Christ has opened up for *all* of us.

4. Tillich sermon "You Are Accepted."

Week 16

Faith

Numbers 1–16
Psalm 54
Psalm 98
Hebrews 11–13
Luke 3–4

As You Read the Old Testament

NUMBERS DOES WHAT IT says: it names and numbers Israel. Numbers is another origins document naming the original members of this newly called out tribal people, a people who eventually will become the nation and kingdom of Israel.

As it opens, Numbers is set at the holy mountain Sinai (or Horeb as it is sometimes named), and its first ten chapters complete the Exodus story about the giving of the Law. Exodus 19:1 to Numbers 10:10 describe how this rescued people were issued into a formal covenant of relationship with the God who brought them out of Egypt. Here they received instructions about how to live within this covenantal relationship.

But always keep in mind that most of the material in these five books of the Pentateuch was written, edited, or complied centuries after the events they record. The basic shape of the Hebrew Scriptures as we know them came into being either during Israel's time in Babylon or not long afterwards.

As You Read the Psalm

Psalm 98 recollects the salvation of the Exodus and offers hope for every impossible possibility. *Remember*: the song sings. *Remember* the times in our history when we had no hope and then—completely unexpected—something new and marvelous came into being. *Remember!*

Thus Psalm 98 offers hope for Israel as they wait in Exile. Along with the prophets of the Exile, this prophetic poet holds out hope for vindication and salvation (see the similarities of encouragement in Isaiah 52). Just as God "remembers" steadfast love and faithfulness, so God's people must remember God's faithfulness and hold on to hope. Do you see the parallels in these verses?

> The LORD made known his *victory*.
> The LORD revealed his *vindication*.
> God's *vindication* is revealed in the sight of the nations.
> All the ends of the earth have seen God's *victory*.

Poetry often taps into synonyms and parallels and the psalms are a perfect example of that intensive form.

The NIV uses the term "salvation" instead of "victory" as in the NRSV, but both are good choices and demonstrate a range of appropriate translations. For example, Exodus 15 sings the Song of Moses and of Miriam as they praise the victory of God over their enemy Egypt. "Victory" and "salvation" both describe the defining event of Israel: the Exodus from slavery and journey into freedom. Centuries later in Babylon, God's victory and salvation hold out hope for those who are exiled. Looking back, exiled Israel puts their faith in the steadfast love and faithfulness of the God who brings freedom. Then more centuries later (for the NT theologians) God's victory and salvation are made concrete in the one Jesus the Christ. Jesus the Christ: God's victory over powers of darkness. Jesus the Christ: God's salvation for all the earth.

Notice how Psalm 98 is a cosmic song, an eschatological hymn. *All* nations will experience God's righteous and equitable judgment. *All* the ends of the earth will recognize God's victory and salvation. *All* creation will sing together for joy at the coming of the Lord. Psalms scholar Clinton McCann points out:

The Good News is that God rules the universe with faithfulness and love. The ecumenical, ecological, economic, social and political implications of this message are profound.[1]

Profound indeed. The psalmists and the prophets looked forward in hope while we Jesus people look backwards in confidence, trusting that something very new has happened in the cosmos. And yet—at the same time—we also look forward with all God's people across the ages towards God's ultimate newness of all creation, God's final eschatological victory and salvation.

As You Read the New Testament

We finish Hebrews this week with the famous "hall of fame" chapter in Hebrews 11. How many of these OT characters do you recognize from your Bible reading so far this year?

When we read this chapter in Hebrews, we can't miss how active real human faith really is. This chapter is chock full of verbs, the faith of our fathers and mothers that "conquered kingdoms, administered justice, obtained promises, shut the mouths of lions, quenched raging fire, escaped the edge of the sword, won strength out of weakness, put enemies to flight." The faith of the martyrs who "suffered mocking and flogging and imprisonment, who went about persecuted and tormented."

The Hebrews writer teaches us that faith is a verb. The Letter to the Hebrews pictures faithful living in one particularly powerful image with a decidedly active verb when it imagines faith "as a race that is run with perseverance." Hebrews envisions us faithful "runners" cheered on by a "cloud of witnesses," and presumes we do not run this race alone, on our own power, stamina, and know-how but rather, encircled by eternal encouragers, we run with Jesus, "the Pioneer and Perfecter of our faith."

As You Read the Gospel

Luke wrote his gospel twenty years or so after Mark, possibly with a copy of Mark's narrative sitting in front of him as he composed his own theological narrative of the Christ event. You may notice how much of Mark is quoted verbatim in Luke (and in Matthew). We also can see how Mark's

---

1. McCann, "Psalms," 1073.

basic chronology of the life of Jesus of Nazareth is recreated in Luke. But Luke had his own sources as well—and he had his own purposes.

How does one tell a story so remarkable? How does one find words and images that give credence to something so unbelievable—and yet believed and trusted by more and more people throughout the Roman Empire as Luke wrote his account of the Christ event? Luke says clearly he was not an eyewitness but rather gathered stories of those who had encountered Jesus. Luke incorporated those various written and oral sources and crafted a narrative from his particular theological perspective. (See Luke 1:1–3.)

Since he was telling the Jesus story perhaps sixty years after the life and death of Jesus, Luke had the advantage of time. Such distance can offer the gift of a bigger picture; it can provide a sense of how various chapters of *The Story* build upon one another. Luke definitely understood Jesus to be crux and climax of the story of God's grace-full, redeeming work in Israel, but he also understood that story to be ongoing. Through those past six decades, Judaism had been shaken to its roots and the infant Christian faith had mushroomed. Luke looked back over the long sweep of the history of Israel as he also looked outward over the dramatically altered cultural realities that offered both opportunity and challenge for the church's mission of witness and service.

Reflection: *Faith is a Verb*

You can write that down. Used to, I thought faith was believing right things in correct ways. Even though I've always been a part of a non-creedal Christianity, I still thought one had to assent to certain belief statements about church, God, Christ, Spirit, the Bible. I thought faith was about ideas.

Now I believe faith is a verb. For me, it's more about my *doing* faithful things, *acting* in faithful ways, and *behaving* with faithful intentions. Faith is about change and transformation, about personal commitment and the reorientation of a life. Faith is about my counting on the faithfulness of a God who creates and informs and sustains the faithfulness of my own faith. It's about entrusting myself to the faithfulness of the God who covers for me even when I believe incorrectly and behave unfaithfully. It's about letting the whole of my life flow from the life of the God who is the ultimate Verb, the one who is ever the *I Am*, always present tense, always acting on behalf of all humanity for the sake of the promise.

Sometimes the verbs of our lives are less active and describe our efforts to endure fixed realities, to wait out whatever challenges come our way. Other times the verbs of our lives are more active with the power to change our world; verbs of faith that can make things happen and transform an existing reality.

And yet, of course, faith also is a noun. There are some facts, some realities that we must assent to before we can act. Hebrews says we must first and foremost believe that God *is* then we can believe that God *acts*. Like air, even when we can't see God, faith assents to this Divine Fact of our lives. It is the grounding of ourselves in this unprovable fact that moves us and motivates *us* to act as well. Believing *that* God *is* gives us confidence to entrust ourselves to the one who is the Ultimate Verb of eternal, always-present Being. As Hebrews says, God "rewards" and responds; God acts and interacts with everyone in the life long process of our seeking.

Faith is not abstract; rather *faithing* embodies hope. Faith makes hope tangible and reveals invisible realities. *Faithing* is stepping up, and then going beyond what we can see or what we think is possible.

A few years ago, a moving interfaith worship service at the National Cathedral honored those who were wounded and killed at the Boston Marathon bombings in 2013. When I heard President Obama use words from Hebrews as a way to comfort the Boston Marathon runners and the cloud of witnesses at the finish line who had been so traumatized on that terrible Monday, my spine tingled. It was an especially powerful image in that setting: running the race with endurance and fortitude then rising again to run again in spite of the traumas life brings.

Running the race has long been an appropriate image of faith, a metaphor that pictures the patient, enduring persistence so necessary in this marathon of living. But there is another profound image of running that speaks to us today, another image of running that makes my spine tingle: the picture of people running, not away from danger and disaster, but running right *into* it.

We've seen this kind of faith and faithfulness race to confront heartbreaking, gut-wrenching pain over and over again. Wherever there is tragedy, faith and faithfulness will rush in. Faithful people will always step up, step out, and go beyond what they know is possible. Their *faithing* will always embody invisible realities of hope, compassion, and perseverance. These are people who live their lives chock full of verbs.

Then, on the other hand, there is still another kind of story, a little story about the paralysis and stagnation of unfaithfulness in Numbers 13 and 14. When Israel walked away from slavery in Egypt, they were walking in the direction of the Promised Land. The Red Sea opened up before them; a pillar of cloud and fire went ahead to guide them and followed behind to protect them; bread fell from the sky and water flowed from a rock.

Time and time again, God's people saw evidence of God's faithfulness and they experienced the *I Am* who is ever acting on behalf of humanity for the sake of the promise. But when the people sent their scouts into the land of promise to spy it out, the reports they received made them quake with fear. *It's too hard. We're too small. The challenges are overwhelming. Our resources are limited. The obstacles are like giants. We are like grasshoppers. We can't. We won't.*

Instead of running the race set before them; instead of running into the challenges that, yes, were big; instead of facing the apparent impossibilities with the faithfulness of faith, these people turned their backs on their future. As the story goes, because of this faith-less-ness, they ended up running around in circles; they wandered in a wilderness of hopelessness for forty years. "Forty years" (in Bible-speak) = a very long time.

You probably noticed the Hebrews author did not include this little story from Numbers in the Hall of Fame chapter. The "pilgrims" and "sojourners" he praises weren't wandering around in circles. They might not have known exactly where they were going, they may not have known just how to get there, but Hebrews describes how these pilgrims of faith managed to see what was invisible. He describes how they greeted God's promises from a distance, how they could imagine a city whose builder, whose architect was God. Even when they did not know where they were going, they knew they were going somewhere.

If not in their own lifetime, they entrusted themselves and their children and their great-great-grandchildren to God's faithfulness. They trusted enough to continue to live faithfully even if they didn't see the promise come true for themselves; they were content to live *toward* the promises. Consequently in the midst of all their unknowing, they still were able to live with focus, direction, and confidence.

So there is first, running with *perseverance* the race that is set before us. Then second, running with *courage* right into the challenges that come to us. And now third, running *toward* God's promises. "Faith, the assurance of things hoped for. Faith, the conviction of things not seen." Anthony Thiselton says:

> Like all God's pilgrim people of faith . . . we need forward look-ing faith which will appropriate and act on God's promises concerning the future purposes . . . Like Abraham, we must "venture forth."
>
> We need fresh vision, fresh courage, fresh perseverance, fresh heart in the face of stagnation and a desire to shelter with-in old securities. Hence we are urged: "Let us run with patience the race that is set before us, looking to Jesus the pioneer and perfecter of our faith."[2]

You and I have the same choices God's people have always had. We can let the challenges overwhelm us, paralyze us, cause us to wander around in circles. Or we can run the race that is set before us. We can wait around, wishing that God might send something more than manna (like say a global positioning system!) so we can know exactly where we are supposed to go and how we are supposed to get there. This way we don't have to depend on faith.

Or we can step out and step up *before* we know, *faithing* into our future, putting our faith and trust and hope in the one who promises to accomplish amazing, good, and impossible things *in* us and *through* us. We can pull inward inside our comfortable lives and protect ourselves. Or we can let our lives be broken bread and poured out wine, sacraments of mercy and blessing for others. We can embody hopelessness or we can embody faithfulness.

I vote for faithfulness. So may our faith, so may our lives, always be chock full of verbs.

---

2. Thiselton, *New Horizons in Hermeneutics*, 265.

Week 17

Numbers

Numbers 17–36
Psalm 39
Psalm 97
First and Second Peter
Luke 5–7

As You Read the Old Testament

LIKE MANY ANCIENT PEOPLES, the story of Israel was preserved first by their storytellers. Genealogies and oral histories of events and were handed down from generation to generation until they finally were written down. This founding story of the Exodus from slavery and the covenant with Yahweh became Israel's Scripture during another painful time centuries later, a time of exile in Babylon and alienation from their God.

The exiled people knew full well they had broken covenant and had brought this tragedy upon themselves. As they recounted and retold the stories of their ancestors, surely they recognized Israel's faithlessness in light of the covenant faithfulness of the one who had called them. Israel told the old, old stories with a stubborn hope that the God of Covenant would keep the covenant and rescue them once again. As you read, consider the implications of Israel retelling these ancient stories through the lens of their current estrangement as Exiles in Babylon. It makes these stories all the more poignant.

As You Read the Psalms

Psalm 39 is said to be written by/to/for David, but we almost can hear David's descendants singing these same words in exile in Babylon as a mournful, hopeful prayer, "LORD, let me know my end, and what is the measure of my days; let me know how fleeting my life is. You have made my days a few handbreadths, and my lifetime is as nothing in your sight. Surely everyone stands as a mere breath. *Selah.* And now, O LORD, what do I wait for? My hope is in you."

Every once in awhile, a particular period in my life, or some particular experience will remind me of my mortality. Too many days I don't think about endings; I act as if what is will always be. This is a sad delusion. The Psalms are especially good at reminding us that life is fragile; that fortunes can change; that futures can turn on a dime. The Psalms provide crucial reminders that we humans are not in control; we are "a mere breath."

Even so, our lives matter; they matter deeply. Each of us goes about enfleshing our own chapter in *The Story* of God's ongoing relationship with all creatures, great and small. Each of our lives reverberates in the lives of every other life we touch.

The poet of Psalm 39 ponders the mysteries of transgression and redemption. He wonders what he should speak and how he should refrain from speech—especially, I think, the presumption of self-defense and self-justification. What we do matters. What we say matters. Maybe we should all ponder more carefully the ripples we create with our actions and our words, ripples that continue cycles of beauty and terror in the lives of those we love. Given the fact of our own mortality, may God grant us wisdom to speak words of wisdom and hope when needed, and may God give us courage to be quiet and to shut our mouths when our words would not be helpful.

As You Read the New Testament

Notice how the author of First Peter sees the church as the continuation and enlargement of the heritage of Israel. First Peter addresses its Christian readers as heirs of Israel, "God's own people," and those who have "received mercy." First Peter understands that its Gentile (non-Jewish) readers have been incorporated into the continuing people of God.

The final word is one of divine initiative and mercy. The readers' identity is established not by their own deed, but by God's choice and effective call.[1]

This is remarkable, non-Jews sharing in the promises and blessings of the chosen people of Israel. Peter's one-time-pagan-now-turned-Jesus-people surely were remembering what life was like before Christ and what their lives had become since Christ. Dr. Boring again: First Peter sees the church as . . .

> a "chosen race" and a "holy nation" not on the basis of nature, genetics, or social standing but by the act of God, so their testimony to the world is not a matter of general truths or principles, but the declaration of God's saving acts in history, from creation to eschaton.[2]

Eschaton: creation's completion and culmination.

The testimony and witness of God's own people is that—from the very beginning of time to the end of history—God is ever acting on behalf of the promises, redeeming all kinds of people, and creating a cosmic community grounded in hope and grace. "Once you were not a people, but now you are God's own people" (2:10; see also Hos 1:8–10).

Remarkable. Who could have imagined such a thing?

As you Read the Gospel

Probably the most well known version of the beatitudes is from Matthew 5, but Luke also offers its own version of a blessed life.

> Blessed are you who are poor for yours is the kingdom of God. Blessed are you who are hungry now for you will be filled. Blessed are you who weep now for you will laugh. Blessed are you when people hate you, and when they exclude you, revile you, and defame you on account of the Son of Man.
>
> Rejoice in that day and leap for joy, for surely your reward is great in heaven, for that is what their ancestors did to the prophets (6:20–22).

Luke also contrasts blessings with woes.

---

1. Boring, *First Peter*, 100.

2. Boring, *First Peter*, 102.

But woe to you who are rich, for you have received your consolation. Woe to you who are full now, for you will be hungry.
Woe to you who are laughing now, for you will mourn and weep
(6:24–25).

These words are good reminders for believers in our own day when
the rich and the powerful seem to rule the world. In today's America,
the wealth gap is growing into a chasm, and I find myself asking, *when
will the poor be lifted up? How long, O Lord!* The wisdom writings of
Scripture remind us of the eternal sweep of God's work in the world and
reassure us that God's will *"will* be done on earth as it is in heaven"—in
God's good time.

Reflection: *A Chosen People*

When I was in elementary school, I was lousy at kick ball. During recess,
whenever the teams were chosen, I always was the very last one anybody
wanted on their team. When I was a senior in high school, I lost the elec-
tion for class president by just a few votes. When I was newly ordained, I
submitted my resume for senior minister at a church that I really, really
wanted; I was not chosen. I guess we all know what it feels like not to be
chosen. Most of us have some experience with being left out, excluded,
or dismissed.

Actually though, I have much less experience with exclusion than
a lot of people in the world. Generally I have lived my life with so much
grace that (I admit) sometimes I think I did something to deserve all the
privilege that surrounds me.

In these *Living in The Story* journeys, we have seen a lot of grace.
We've been walking with the tribal people of God: Abraham, Isaac, Jacob,
and their descendants, enslaved and then liberated, following the pillars
of fire and cloud toward their Promised Land. We've been watching how
Yahweh interrupted their lives and called them into covenant relationship as God's own people, chosen and beloved.

When we move to the NT, we still see the ancient story of Israel continuing and evolving and we will see this notion of an expanded people
clearly expressed in the two letters of Peter. "You are a chosen race," (Peter
says) "a royal priesthood, a holy nation, God's own people, in order that
you may proclaim the mighty acts of him who called you out of darkness
into his marvelous light."

> Like the Israel of the Bible and of history, the church is called
> into being not for its own sake, but as an expression of the divine
> mission to the world.
>
> The church is charged with God's mission; the gift becomes
> a responsibility.[3]

The church is all of us together, the community of Christ, the heritage of God. The church goes far beyond the boundaries that we tend to set up in our little congregations and denominations. The church is about (or at least ought to be about) what God has done.

Peter sees what God has done in Jesus Christ as the perfection of what God did for Israel in the Exodus story. In Peter, images about the life of Israel from the OT are applied directly to the church. For Peter, and for us Christians, this is *our* story.

All believers have been incorporated into mercy in this decidedly corporate, community, communal understanding. Relationship with God is bound up in relationship with God's people; again and again in Scripture, these two relationships are inseparable. In the community God creates, we are not rugged individualists; we are "a people."

But the Christian witness has taken a beating lately. Every day I see articles about people who have become disenchanted with the church. "Spiritual but not religious" is the fastest growing demographic category, researchers tell us. Some call themselves the "Nones" and others call themselves the "Dones." Every where we turn, people who have been left out, who recognize that they are "not chosen" by insider religious types, have said, "thanks but no thanks." Especially young adults—when they see the institutional church being exclusive instead of inclusive, judgmental instead of graceful—too many of our young people are questioning the authenticity of our so-called Christian message.

As I write this in 2021, Christian Nationalism has infected some streams of American Christianity and the church's witness has suffered even more as some misguided people conflate "American" with "Christian."[4] The church of Jesus Christ is *not* national. Authentic church transcends every boundary and border; reaches across every difference and

3. Boring, *First Peter*, 101.

4. If you are interested in learning more about this complex and troubling aspect of American history, I recommend these books by these Christian historians. Richard Hughes, especially, *Myths America Lives By*. (Internet searches should also help you find several recent blogs, articles, and essays by Dr. Hughes.) Also consider Mark Toulouse, *God in Public*.

divide. Faithful Christian witness gives testimony to the now expanded community of God called into being as "a chosen race, a royal priesthood, a holy nation, God's own people." Not just for people like *me* and *my* tribe, God's amazing grace and mercy is for *everyone*.

Each one of us individually and all of us together must offer testimony to the mercy of a God who—in Jesus Christ—has created a community where *all* are chosen, where *all* are welcomed, where *all* are loved. The witness of the church must be loud and clear: We *all* have been incorporated into mercy and it is God who has done this. Who could have ever imagined!

Week 18

Love

Deuteronomy 1–16
Psalm 96
Psalm 146
First John
Luke 8–10

As You Read the Old Testament

IN DEUTERONOMY, THE SCENE is set on the far side of the Jordan River, looking across into the Promised Land. From this perspective, Moses recounts the story of rescue from Egypt; he retells Yahweh's presence at Sinai; he reminds of the Ten Commandments and the Law; and he prepares them for the years ahead, when Moses will have passed on the mantle of leadership to Joshua. When we read Deuteronomy, we remember how the people of Israel were slaves in Egypt who went from being no people to being God's own people. The Hebrew Scriptures tell Israel's story—and it is shot through with amazement.

Of course there are plenty of sub-themes of arrogance as well as amazement. Whenever any people begins to think of *chosen-ness* as something that is earned; when people think their inclusion requires someone else's exclusion; when people start thinking that being chosen means they can kick back and take it easy, then know there is some deep misunderstanding of the concept of chosen-ness as it is used in Scripture. Those mistaken attitudes surely can (and often do) foster pride, self-importance, and complacency.

Deuteronomy sounds a deep warning against such tempting comfort. *If* Israel does not keep the covenant God has given them, *then* they will suffer the consequences.

> When you have had children and children's children, and become complacent in the land, if you act corruptly by making an idol in the form of anything, thus doing what is evil in the sight of the LORD your God, and provoking him to anger, I call heaven and earth to witness against you today that you will soon utterly perish from the land that you are crossing the Jordan to occupy; you will not live long on it, but will be utterly destroyed.
>
> The LORD will scatter you among the peoples; only a few of you will be left among the nations where the LORD will lead you. There you will serve other gods made by human hands, objects of wood and stone that neither see, nor hear, nor eat, nor smell (4:24–28).

Here we see the theology of the Deuteronomist, the author/community whose theology is woven throughout the Hebrew Scriptures. This is an understanding articulated especially clearly in the book of Deuteronomy, a belief that God's covenant contains conditions: that God will remain faithful as God's people continue faithfully.

But even as this warning of conditional protection is given at the leading edge of the Promised Land, Israel also, at the same time, receives the hope of unconditional grace. This promise is what sustains them and calls them back into relationship again and again. Even if an entire generation dies in the wilderness (as Deuteronomy relates), the covenant with the whole people of God will continue. "Because the LORD your God is a merciful God, he will neither abandon you nor destroy you. God will not forget the covenant with your ancestors that he swore to them" (4:31).

In Deuteronomy 4 the people have a sense of astonishment at this relationship. They had been given a vision of the one true God who is full of steadfast love, mercy, and compassion; amazement that they had been given the gift and the responsibility to bear witness to the nations concerning this vision of God. And then, on top of all that, there is also the wonder that God will hang in there with them even when they fail so badly.

As You Read the Psalm

Psalm 146 sings of the rightness of creation with the Creator reigning as Lord and Sovereign. "Praise the LORD, O my soul! I will praise the LORD as long as I live. Do not put your trust in princes, in mortals, in whom there is no help." During the time of Exile, the Davidic monarchy ended. The experience of Israel in Babylon reminded them that blindly trusting in any human (even the king) is bound to bring disappointment and even despair. There is only one who is truly faithful within all creation: the Creator.

"Happy are those whose help is the God of Jacob, whose hope is in the LORD their God, who made heaven and earth, the sea, and all that is in them" (146:5–6). Israel's God is the one who called and chose Jacob and then called Jacob's descendants to be God's own people. For Israel in exile, struggling to hold on to hope and faith, it is God alone, "the LORD who keeps faith forever!"

So what does this divine "keeping faith" look like? Our psalmist is quite specific.

> The LORD executes justice for the oppressed, gives food to the hungry, sets the prisoners free, opens the eyes of the blind, lifts up those who are bowed down, loves the righteous, watches over the strangers, upholds the orphan and the widow . . . (146:7–9).

These concrete acts of justice are what the psalmist means by "keeping faith." This proactive divine initiative on behalf of the oppressed, the hungry, the prisoners, and the righteous brings hope. Hope that, no matter the machinations of kings and empires, the Lord of all empires is ever at work lifting up the lowly.

This divine initiative is the core tenet of Liberation Theology, a theological understanding that insists the Lord of all maintains a "preferential option for the poor." The theological understanding of Liberation Theology insists that we—as followers of the liberating God—also are called to work on behalf of the oppressed, the hungry, the prisoners, the blind, and the bowed down. We too should be protecting the strangers and immigrants, the orphans and the widows. Our human value system turns upside-down and right-side-up when we realize who among us actually carries divine privilege.

Liberation Theology and one of its prime proponents, Gustavo Gutierrez, have influenced me and many other students of theology over the years. John Dear ponders the paradox of liberation as articulated by Gutierrez:

> "Clearly the gratuitousness of God's love challenges the patterns we have become used to," Gutierrez writes. "The Bartimaeuses of this world have stopped being at the side of the road. They

have jumped up and come to the Lord, their lifelong friend. Their presence may upset the old followers of Jesus, who spontaneously, and with the best reasons in the world, begin to defend their privileges."

Those of us who are privileged First World North Americans may bristle at this theology that asks them to let go of their privileges, make that option for the poor and seek Christ in their struggle for justice. But Gutierrez assures us that this movement of the Spirit among us not only hastens God's reign of justice and peace, beginning with those in extreme poverty, it leads to new blessings. This is good news. We, too, are being liberated! [1]

The Lord's "keeping faith" employs another dimension according to the psalmist. Not only is God actively *for* the poor, the psalmist declares God is actively *against* the "wicked" because wickedness is the antithesis to God's own way. This *way of the wicked* is opposed to the way of the right-working design of the cosmos and all creation. The way of the Lord assumes and expects people to care for one another as Creator cares for creation, working for justice on behalf of the oppressed, the hungry, the prisoners, the blind, and the bowed down.

"The LORD will reign forever . . . for all generations . . . Hallelu-Yah! [Praise Yah!] Praise the LORD!" As Yahweh, the Sovereign of the cosmos, continues to reign and bring all creation into perfect harmony and unity, we put our hope in God's eschatological—ultimate and final—peace and balance.

In the meantime, our call as God's people is to work in alignment with God's own way of justice and compassion within and among all people. To work while we wait and to trust that it is the Creator who will, finally and ultimately, bring all creation into perfect *shalom*.

As You Read the New Testament

Listen to what First John has to say:

> God's love was revealed among us in this way: God sent his only Son into the world so that we might live through him. In this is love, not that we loved God but that God loved us and sent his Son to be the atoning sacrifice for our sins.

1. Dear, "Gustavo Gutierrez," November 2011.

> Beloved, since God loved us so much, we also ought to love
> one another. No one has ever seen God; if we love one another,
> God lives in us, and his love is perfected in us (1 John 4:9–12).

Authentic love is always active. Because God loves us and lives in us, *therefore* we can love one another. When we make even a fledgling effort to love one another, God's own life grows in us, God's own love becomes more and more complete within us. Because (as John teaches us) "God *is* love."

For the author of First John, the good news was much more than an *announcement*. Within this unparalleled new thing the power and presence of the one true God has become effective and operative in this one Jesus Christ. As Karl Barth has said:

> The new thing consists in the fact that someone comes with
> authority to declare that it has dawned, and that it does actually
> dawn with his declaration . . . [2]

The gospel is the Word turning darkness into light, the Word embodied in fragile flesh, the Word transforming human hearts. The gospel is Spirit brooding over emptiness, the Wind blowing where it will, Breath breathing resurrection life. The gospel is unreasonable Love, incalculable giving, unstoppable Life. The gospel is transformation, reconciliation, restoration, and resurrection.

It is against all reason that Divine Presence should be concealed in human flesh and activated by defeat. Yet it is this death that actually brings into effect a power great enough to destroy death and to defeat destruction from the inside out. That paradox is the biblical witness again and again.

God's essence is love, God's mode of being is love, God's motive and method is love. In the pit of death, in the despair of defeat, right there the power of God's self-giving love is made real.

As You Read the Gospel

This week, we hear again Luke's famous story about a lawyer who came to Jesus seeking eternal life. I'm not sure what "eternal life" meant to him exactly, how a first century Jew might have thought about it, but Jesus' answer is pretty clear: *Love.* The way to life is love. Love God. Love one

---

2. Barth, *The Doctrine of Reconciliation*, 196.

another. Love the neighbor. Love the stranger. Love the enemy, the un-lovely, and the unlovable.

"But who is my neighbor?" the lawyer negotiates for specific rules and clear guidelines. I fear we have heard this story of the Good Samari-tan so often that we may yawn at its telling. But when Jesus told it, surely there were gasps of shock. Maybe there were mutterings of disapproval. Probably there were plenty of folks shaking their heads in disbelief at Jesus' surprising reversal that cast the despised Samaritan as the merciful hero of the story.

Amy-Jill Levine is a Jewish theologian who teaches New Testament studies at Vanderbilt University. She looks at this little story of Jews and Samaritans and sees the ongoing distrust between the Israelis and the Palestinians still all these centuries later. Will this never end? Dr. Levine offers this insight:

> To understand this parable in theological terms, we need to be able to see the image of God in everyone, not just members of our group.
>
> To hear this parable in contemporary terms, we should think of ourselves as the person in the ditch, and then ask, "Is there anyone, from any group, about whom we'd rather die than acknowledge, 'She offered help,' or 'He showed compassion?'" More, is there any group whose members might rather die than help us?[3]

Will we ever learn to see the image of God in everyone? The only way we truly are able to love is for God to love *in* us and *through* us. Our love is *response* to God's love.

Anthony Thiselton talks about the way we humans love each other and how that profound experience of love can completely reorient all our priorities. Thiselton says love takes our *self*-interest and "re-groups it, re-ranks it" until the self of the other becomes the center of our pri-orities.[4] We begin to see things through their eyes and we come to know something about what it means to walk in their shoes. We want them to be completely free to be who they are and we encourage them to speak and live their own truth. We spend time really getting to know them, their passions and fears, their hopes and their dreams. Love disorients and then reorients.

3. Levine, *The Misunderstood Jew*, 148–49.
4. Thiselton, *New Horizons in Hermeneutics*, 609.

Reflection: *Love is a Verb*

Love is a verb. You can write that down. This statement may sound familiar to you because just a few weeks ago, I said faith is a verb. So now here I am claiming that love is a verb.

Sometimes we think we can love in the abstract—warm, fuzzy feelings for people in general. But no, love is not so much a feeling as it is a verb, active, face-to-face, hand-to-hand—and messy. We all are real, less-than-perfect people in relationship with other real, less-than-perfect people. So the only way we are truly *able* to love is because *God* loves; God loves *in* us and loves *through* us.

We are quite good at judging others, aren't we? It is easy to see in another what we *want* to see or what we have *always* seen instead of truly accepting them as they are. It is easy to lump people into groups and categories so we can lull ourselves into thinking we actually know something about them. It is tempting to assign labels to others so we can keep them safely at arm's length. Why are we humans so good at this? And why are we Christians (of all people!) still so inclined to our own prejudices and presumptions about our neighbor instead of being more inclined to love?

The startling reversal in Jesus' story about the Good Samaritan is that *there*—right there in the messy life of that uncomfortable person—God's own presence exists. *There*—right there in the lives of "those people"—God's own purposes are at work. *There*—right there in one whom we might distrust, disrespect, and maybe even hate—love can be embodied.

I have claimed that love is not a feeling; love is a verb. And yes it is. But of course love also is deep emotion. There is a saying you may have heard: "act as if . . ." Act as if something is true, and it may actually become true. Act as if you love someone, act with proactive loving acts, then, lo and behold, pretty soon the reality of love grows, not just in our acting but also in our thinking and in our feeling as well.

What would happen if Christians actually fell head over heels in love with all the people whom God loves? How would that change our world? What would happen if our personal preferences were "rearranged and re-shaped" in light of the desires and needs of the other? When love of God becomes our center, everything is transformed! Surely this truth provides context for the foundational text from Deuteronomy 6:4. "Hear, O Israel: The LORD is our God, the LORD alone. You shall love the LORD your God with all your heart, and with all your soul, and with all your might." For people of God, loving God provides the ground and center for everything we are and everything we do with our lives.

When we love God with heart, soul, and might, God's own life grows within us; God's own love becomes more and more complete within us. As we lean into God's love and offer wholehearted love back to God (as wholehearted as we can manage), we also find more ability to love the neighbor—and even the enemy. It's a cycle of life and a circle of love.

> The out-going love from the heart of God to the creation becomes a force and motivation that transforms believers into the image of Christ.
> It is this love that allows us to see the world through the eyes and interests of God's purposes for the world.[5]

Love is "a force and motivation" that shapes how we spend our time, how we spend our money, how we spend our energy. When the love of God motivates us and transforms us, our priorities are readjusted. We grow to care about what God cares about, and we learn to love the people whom God loves.

"Who is my neighbor?" asked the lawyer. Jesus' startling reversal reorders the question: to whom will *we* be the neighbor? Whom shall *we* love? Jesus makes it abundantly clear that the way to life is love. Loving God. Loving one another. Loving the stranger. Loving the enemy. Loving the neighbor. For God *is* love.

5. Thiselton, *New Horizons*, 609.

Week 19

Deuteronomy

Deuteronomy 17–35
Psalm 4
Psalm 15
Psalm 109
Psalm 144
Second and Third John
Luke 11–13

As You Read the Old Testament

As WE COMPLETE OUR reading of Deuteronomy, we hear Moses handing down wisdom to the next generation. Recall how Deuteronomy's stage is set with the people standing on the edge of their Promised Land and Moses as the patriarch saying farewell to his children, reminding them who they are and reiterating core truths that bind them together. The generation of people who had been enslaved in Egypt was buried in the wilderness, and now a new generation of nomads is poised to enter into the land, to accept the challenges of growing into the life God has called them to.

Listen to the common sense warnings in some of Moses' words:

> Cursed be anyone who dishonors father or mother or who moves a neighbor's boundary marker or who misleads a blind person on the road or who deprives the alien, the orphan, and the widow of justice (Deut 27:16–19).

Moses' warnings/curses caution against doing anything that damages covenant—the covenant God made with Israel that claimed them as God's own people, but also the covenant of relationship that connected them together as a community. The sanctions and catalog of consequences we read here can sound severe, but it's not so much God dishing out a list of arbitrary rules and expecting people to obey unquestioningly "just because I said so." It's more like the cosmic wisdom that says "actions have consequences."

In the biblical way of thinking, a curse is pronounced as a lament or as a judgment. What we see here in Deuteronomy demonstrates a typical form for international treaties in the ancient Near East. At the end of those treaty agreements, there often was included a list of sanctions, a catalog of repercussions if one side or the other was found guilty of breaking the treaty. In Deuteronomy, God is portrayed as stating (in no uncertain terms) the dangers of ignoring the divine covenant, of breaking the "treaty."

Here in Deuteronomy, Israel is called to remember that—in pure grace—God called them into relationship, God was calling them to God's own purposes. Deuteronomy gives witness to the faithfulness of the Lord their God and the people stand amazed that they have been incorporated into such mercy. And so—even in Exile as Israel remembered these stories again—Israel dares to hope that the God of Abraham, Isaac, and Jacob will continue to keep covenant even when they did not. They hold on to hope that Yahweh will turn to them in mercy and that their own hearts will turn back to the One Who Rescues.

As You Read the Psalms

The words of Psalm 144 echo words and sentiments from other psalms, especially Psalm 18 and Psalm 8.

> The LORD is my Rock, my Fortress, my Stronghold, my Deliverer, my Shield . . . But humans are like a breath or a passing shadow . . .

It's as if our psalmist has been reading the earlier songs in Book One and now is rereading, reinterpreting, and renewing those long ago praises for his own time and place.

Even after returning home from exile in Babylon, the restored people of Israel were surrounded by adversaries, and they must have felt as if they were drowning in a sea of infidelity by those whose "right hands are false." This psalmist of Israel struggles against uncertainty and against the unreliability of their betrayers. No wonder this vision of the Savior is strong and solid and substantial. No wonder the poet imagines this Redeemer "bowing your heavens to come down; touching the mountains so they smoke; making the lightning flash and sending out arrows; stretching out your hand to rescue me from the mighty waters" (144:5–7). See here how this psalm alludes to the miracles of judgment against the oppressors of Egypt, how the song celebrates the ancient and reassuring story of rescue through the waters of the Red Sea. Ancient history for this people is not the boring stuff of textbooks; rather history is story, *our* story. This is us!

The beautiful poetry of Psalm 144 continues as our psalmist yearns for the assurance of a solid legacy, a future populated with his descendants who will carry his existence forward so that he is not forgotten. After years of deprivation and destruction, he yearns for the surety of abundance and for the safety of his people.

> May our sons in their youth be like plants full grown; our daughters like corner pillars cut for the building of a palace. May our barns be filled and may our cattle be heavy with young. May there be no breach in the walls, no exile, and no cry of distress in our streets (144:12–14).

Theologian and pastor, Clinton McCann, explains:

> Psalm 144 is an invitation to treat the Psalms not as historical artifacts but as living words which can continue both to address us with God's claim upon our lives and our world and to express our hopes and fears, our praises and prayer.[1]

It's interesting to see what an Internet search of Psalm 144 turns up. I find it disturbing that some people use this psalm to justify a belief that violence is inevitable. Do you remember the sniper character in the movie *Saving Private Ryan*? Every time he took aim, Private Jackson whispered this psalm to himself in order to steady his hand. "Blessed be the Lord who trains my hands for war and my fingers for battle."

The earliest Christians were pacifists, rejecting all violence, choosing instead to "turn the other cheek." Conscientious objectors to this day take literally the teachings of Christ and let Jesus' example of peace

---

1. McCann, "Psalms," 1256.

override the ancient example of war. So here is one more reminder that appropriate interpretation of biblical texts across the centuries must be done carefully and prayerfully.

As You Read the New Testament

John the Elder writes with deep passion for love and truth. As I write this, I am sensitive to the recent and ongoing turmoil within our nation concerning truth. "Fake news" and "alternative facts" served as more than hash tags within our society; a seismic convolution upended traditional norms and has been threatening core notions about what is true. For the Elder, truth and love are inextricably bound together. There is no authentic truth without love, and there can be no real love without truth. If something is "true," then it will exude love, grace, mercy, and peace. If something is not true, then inevitably it will ooze rancor, resentment, bedlam, and hate. How do we know what is true and what is lie? Watch for the fruit. Judge the results. Goodness, humility, harmony, and justice always will be signs that truth is speaking, that truth is growing. "I have no greater joy than this, to hear that my children are walking in the truth" (3 John 1:4). Indeed. More of this, please.

As You Read the Gospel

As we read Moses' warnings to God's people, so in these chapters in Luke, we also hear some of Jesus' own warnings. "Your eye is the lamp of your body. If your eye is healthy, your whole body is full of light; but if it is not healthy, your body is full of darkness" (Luke 11:34). Or in the way The Message paraphrases Jesus' wisdom, "If you live wide-eyed in wonder and belief, your whole life fills up with light. If you live squinty-eyed in greed and distrust, your life is a dank cellar" (MSG).

"Woe to you [when] you tithe herbs of all kinds, but you neglect justice and the love of God," Jesus warned. "Woe when you clean the outside of the cup, but inside you are full of greed and wickedness." The curses and woes caution that actions have consequences in our relationships with other people, in our relationship with God, and within our own character.

Reflection: *Warnings and Blessings*

"If you can't say anything nice, don't say anything at all." Our mothers warned us about the power of words. They cautioned us to use words that are positive and helpful and healing. "Don't judge another person until you have walked a mile in her shoes." Our mothers warned us about using our own limited experience to criticize the experiences and actions of another. And then we grew up and often were surprised to find our mamas' words coming out of our own mouths. But even as we hand on some of this age-old advice to the next generation, we still can hear our mothers' voices in our heads reminding all of us to "practice what we preach."

I know the curses and the woes we read in the Bible sound harsh. They *are* harsh sometimes; they don't mince words. But when we think of them as warnings, we see how they startle us in order to get our attention. They wake us up and (hopefully) keep us from sleepwalking and stumbling through our lives. When we think we know but we actually are mistaken, then we *need* for someone to warn us. When we think we are enlightened but the light within us is really darkness, then we *need* someone to point that out.

Recall Barbara Brown Taylor's take on this as she envisions God as a kind of divine jiu-jitsu master. God doesn't create all this bad stuff, she says; *we* are the ones who generate the negative energy and God simply spins it back around so that we experience its effect.[2]

But then there is this whole other thing, the blessing. In the biblical way of thinking, a blessing is pronounced in order to cause something good to come into being. God's blessings are not good wishes; they are more like announcements. Biblical blessings are performative language: words of blessing that have power to speak something into existence.

We understand performative language. For example, whenever we say the words "I'm sorry," we change something negative into something positive. Whenever we say, "I forgive you," we alter reality and cause a new aspect of a relationship to come into being. Whenever we speak words of affirmation, "I'm grateful for you, I appreciate your thoughtfulness," a new confidence and hope may come to life in the deep, quiet places of another. Whenever we speak words of encouragement, "you can do it, hang in there, you're not alone," something shifts, both in the one who receives encouragement and in the one who gives it. Something real really happens.

2. See the original discussion in week 3: *Sin—The Lost Language of Salvation*.

Life is full of all kinds of hard things, but the power of blessing is always stronger than any hard thing. Pronouncing, enacting, and enabling blessing to become real in the life of another can help counteract the effects of the curse of hurt and hopelessness.

Earlier we read Deuteronomy's charge to "love God with heart and soul and strength." We heard Luke's reminder that "loving our neighbor as ourselves" is not just a feeling but must function as a proactive verb.

> Surely, this commandment that I am commanding you is not too hard for you. It is not in heaven . . . neither is it beyond the sea . . .
>
> No, the word is very near you; it is in your mouth, it is in your heart . . . If you obey the commandments . . . that I am commanding you, loving the LORD your God and walking in his ways . . . then you shall live.
>
> I call heaven and earth to witness today that I have set before you life and death, blessings and curses. Choose life so that you *(and others!)* . . . may live (Deut 30:11–20).

Both Deuteronomy and Luke demonstrate what happens whenever we sin against love. Deuteronomy and Luke remind us what can happen whenever we actually practice active loving. Deuteronomy and Luke both teach us that love is more powerful than hate.

Week 20

Joshua

Joshua 1–12
Psalm 16
Psalm 103
Psalm 132
Acts 1–2
Luke 14–15

As You Read the Old Testament

WHEN JOSHUA AND THE army of Israel marched around the city of Jericho, when the priests blew the trumpets, when the walls of Jericho came tumbling down, the text says Joshua said:

> Shout! For the LORD has given you the city. The city and all that is in it shall be devoted to the LORD for destruction . . . Then they devoted to destruction by the edge of the sword everything in the city—men and women, young and old, oxen, sheep, and donkeys . . . (Josh 6:15–21).

I don't know about you, but I have trouble saying "The Word of the Lord. Thanks be to God" whenever I read something like this. It's hard for me to stomach that this proactive violence is part of our Holy Scripture. When we read these stories in the church's Scriptures, we are forced to deal with troubling aspects of this narrated violence; especially troublesome is that violence is said to be sanctioned by, even commanded by, God.

Here are some helpful insights I've gained as I've pondered these difficult passages in the Bible; maybe they will help you as well.

One, the stories are retrospective. The stories written down and pre-served (especially in writings like Joshua and Judges) most likely look back on Israel's story from the distance of several centuries. Many of these stories as they are found in Scripture reflect on their past from the perspective of their experience in Exile.

God's people nearly lost themselves in this experience, and so their soul searching was intense. As they pondered what had happened to them and pondered why they had lost their promised land, some inter-preted their reality within a Deuteronomic frame that actions have con-sequences. As they retold the stories from their past, they told them in such a way that taught their children this fundamental lesson: *when we obeyed God, we were wildly successful. When we disobeyed God, we were soundly defeated.* It is a way to give God credit for their successes and to hold themselves accountable for their failures.

So when they told the stories saying, "God said this" and "God did that," it was one way of acknowledging God's power and sovereignty. It was a way to frame the story within the big picture of God's overarching will.

Two, we humans keep doing this. Tragic cycles of human history repeat, in part, because of misguided misapplications of sacred stories. Joshua and Judges portray a nation committed to conquer their Promised Land, convinced that God had given them license for genocide against the current occupants. Thousands of years later, some in the state of Israel hold on to the promise of the land as justification for oppression of the Palestinian people. Some adherents of Islam justify violence against Israel based on their interpretation of their own Holy Scriptures that see Mus-lims as the rightful heirs of the land. During the Middle Ages, Crusaders slashed and hacked their way through the Holy Land, believing God had called them to eradicate the Jewish and Muslim people from the land.

Some early Americans were so convinced God had given them this new continent as a new kind of promised land that they claimed it was God's will that they should subjugate Native Americans. Slave owners sometimes quoted scriptures about submission as they whipped, beat, and humiliated enslaved people. Men and women across the globe con-tinue to justify mistreatment of women and girls because they think their religion allows and even demands it. These stories in *The Story* are still our story too. This is why faithful, appropriate biblical interpretation matters. It matters desperately.

Three, Jesus the Christ has transformed The Story. Jesus embodied God's way of peace and has shown humanity the way through and out of violence. By entering into the violence of the cross, by submitting to death, Jesus defeated its power. God did not ordain crucifixion and violent death; that evil is on us humans. Instead, as death did its best to defeat love and *shalom*, God-in-Jesus spun its deadly energy into life— eternal life.

Although Christians have all too often rejected the authentic way of the Christ, every day offers new opportunities to change inadequate attitudes and actions and submit ourselves to the way of life

As You Read the Psalms

"Bless the LORD, O my soul! And all that is within me, bless God's holy name. Bless the LORD, O my soul and do not forget all his benefits." Psalm 103 then proceeds to list some of those benefits: forgiveness, healing, redemption, steadfast love, mercy, compassion, goodness, vindication, and justice.

Our psalmist believes that the God who liberated Israel from slavery in Egypt is the very same God who would be faithful to Israel in Babylon. As this exiled people faced the future without their land, their Temple, and their kings, the poet reminded them of a time long before they came into the land, built their Temple, or established their monarchy. He reminds them that during the time of Moses, God alone was Home and Temple and King.

"God made known his ways to Moses, his acts to the people of Israel. The LORD is merciful and gracious, slow to anger and abounding in steadfast love . . ." (103:8). This beautiful formulaic description of the character and nature of Yahweh also hearkens back to the stories from Exodus. God's self-revelation to Moses communicated this understanding of God's essence; God's very nature is mercy, compassion, grace, patience, and steadfast eternal love.

> God does not deal with us according to our sins, nor repay us according to our iniquities. For as the heavens are high above the earth, so great is his steadfast love toward those who fear him; as far as the east is from the west, so far he removes our transgressions from us (Ps 103:12).

In our human ways of thinking, justice could suggest a tit-for-tat repayment for wrongs. It is true that "an eye for an eye, a tooth for a tooth" kind of justice was one approach incorporated into ancient Hebrew law, but Psalm 103 proclaims Creator is entitled to practice mercy and to offer compassion instead of always meting out consequences.

"As a father has compassion for his children, so the LORD has compassion for those who fear him. For he knows how we were made; he remembers that we are dust . . . our days are like grass" (103:13–15). We mortals are time bound and our lives are fleeting, "but the steadfast love of the LORD is from everlasting to everlasting and his righteousness to our children's children." God's eternal and steadfast love transcends mortal life spans and stretches on endlessly throughout all the generations—and beyond. Any who claim the God of the Old Testament is a god who only judges and condemns would do well to read again the grace and mercy sung within Psalm 103.

As You Read the New Testament

While we are still reading Luke's gospel, we now add Luke's second volume, The Acts of the Apostles, to our readings. In Acts, we encounter the Resurrected Christ and the Spirit of the Risen Christ moving in astounding ways, expanding what it means to be a chosen people, what it means to be a part of the covenant.

The story told in Acts 2 is the story of the ancient feast of Pentecost celebrated fifty days after Passover. For over a thousand years, Pentecost (*Shavuot*) had been the designated occasion for giving thanks for the early harvest with all of its refreshing renewal, the mystery of life, the reminder of abundance, and the promise of new beginnings. As was typical on Pentecost, worshipers gathered in Jerusalem for their annual celebration, but this year, the followers of the Resurrected and Ascended Jesus were wondering *what's real, what's true, what's next?*

It was this little group of Messianic believers that experienced the iconic wind of Pentecost. The doors of their small lives were blown off their hinges. The safely shuttered windows of their preconceptions were whooshed wide open. The walls of all their Jerichos came tumbling down.

You will notice the Pentecost wind Acts describes is not a gentle breeze. Sometimes, of course, God's way is a soothing breath of fresh air. Sometimes God's way is the way of cocoons and apple seeds and gradually greening fields in the patient springtime. But sometimes God's way is to blow the roof off our small settled lives, and when the Holy Spirit rushes like a mighty wind, God may well intend to blow away every insecure, inadequate thing upon which we ground our lives. This is because God's Pentecost wind is *supposed* to drive us toward new possibilities and new directions.

Whenever that shift starts happening, it most always will be uncomfortable and disorienting. But even if we are blown into new places, even if new people come gusting into our lives, even if old familiar ideas give way to new challenging insights, so what? What do we have to fear? When we are willing to live as God's Pentecost people, then we will allow our coifed and structured lives to be tousled by the Spirit's wind that is ever fresh and new.

As You Read the Gospel

Luke's Jesus stands squarely in the lineage of Abraham and the tradition of Moses. He is a son of Israel, or as Christian theology sometimes says Jesus is *the* Son of Israel, the perfect Son. Jesus was the one who lived his life in perfect obedience to Torah, loving God and loving neighbor as no one had done before or since.

When Jesus entered his public ministry within his Jewish community, he came with one primary message that "the reign of God is here. The kingdom of God is coming. The presence of God is not out there; it's here, among you" (see Luke 17:20–21). The people who heard that message didn't really know what to make of it, especially since Jesus' idea of kingdom, power, and privilege was very different from their notions. His notion was, in fact, upside-down from their own perceptions.

Jesus ate with anyone who sought him out. "Now all the tax collectors and sinners were coming near to listen to him. And the Pharisees and the scribes were grumbling and saying, 'This fellow welcomes sinners and eats with them'" (Luke 15:1–2). Jesus sought out people whom others isolated and taught his followers to do the same. "When you give a banquet, invite the poor, the crippled, the lame, and the blind . . ." (Luke 14:13). Jesus shepherded lost sheep, sought after lost coins, embraced lost sons. Jesus washed feet and broke bread.

And then Jesus took up his cross and carried it straight into the worst violence the world of his day could muster. Indeed, Jesus' "kingdom, power, and glory forever and ever" continue to be upside-down from all human understandings of power and privilege.

Reflection: *Pentecost People*

During our *Living in The Story* effort, we've been following the story of one biblical family, Abraham to Isaac to Jacob to Joseph to Moses and now Joshua, Moses' heir and Israel's new leader. As the story goes, after forty years of wandering in the wilderness, the people of Israel finally crossed the Jordan River under Joshua's leadership and moved into the land God had promised to their ancestors.

So how fitting it was that the Jewish festival of Pentecost became the occasion for this small like-minded kinship group to begin exploding into an expansive and diverse people! Because of that Pentecost morning, that small group of Jesus disciples has multiplied into a multitudinous community of Christ made up of people from every nation and every language and every walk of life.

Some of those early disciples were not comfortable with that new reality. Some of us still today are not comfortable with it. But if Pentecost means anything, it means that the wind of the Spirit is continuing to blow away barriers, to break down walls, and to breathe a new people of God into existence. The Holy Spirit keeps expanding boundaries and enlarging the territory of God's reign so that now, all kinds of people are being gathered into God's expansive community. When we live as Pentecost people, differences don't divide us because Pentecost people recognize that God's kingdom, God's reign includes all of us. We understand we have become part of God's multicultural, multifaceted, multitudinous people.

"Be strong and courageous," Joshua's God proclaimed to the people standing on the edge of a new future. "Everywhere your foot will trod, there (right there) I will be with you wherever you go" (see Josh 1:1–5). Every time we move away from established security and imagined safety, there, right there—"I will be with you." Every time we step up and step out into a bold journey of faith, there, right there—"I will be with you." Every time we act like God's reign actually *has* come into our lives, into our relationships, into our work, into our world, there, right there—"I will be with you."

By the way, "be with" is my favorite prayer whenever the lives of my loved ones are turned inside-out and upside-down. When I have no clue what they need or how to help, I count on this "be with" prayer, trusting that God knows and God acts. As a Spirit-breathed Pentecost person, I breathe this prayer in and out with the names of my beloveds. I breathe and pray that God will be with them, trusting that the Spirit of the Risen Christ still breathes the mystery of life, the reminder of abundance, and the promise of new beginnings.

Week 21

Cornerstone

Joshua 13–24
Psalm 9
Psalm 118
Acts 3–5
Luke 16–18

As You Read the Old Testament

WHEN WE READ BOOKS like Joshua and Judges, we read horrific stories of
war and violence. OT scholar Walter Brueggemann says:

> There is no question more troubling for theological interpreta-
> tion of the Old Testament than the undercurrent of violence that
> runs through a good bit of the text . . .
> There is, moreover, no part of the textual tradition that is more
> permeated with violence than the conquest traditions of Joshua.
> While the land is *promised* in the ancestral traditions of Genesis,
> that same land in the implementation of the promise is *taken* by
> the characteristic of any military operation and is perhaps espe-
> cially characteristic of the ancient practices of the Near East.[1]

And so (we may well ask) why on earth are we reading these ancient
stories that offend our modern, civilized sensibilities? What do these
stories of Joshua and the defeat of the city of Jericho, of Deborah, of the
taking of the land of Canaan, have to do with us?

---

1. Brueggemann, *Introduction to the Old Testament*, 116–17.

For one thing, these stories cause us to remember that this is our shared human story. Violence is a part of who we are; atrocity is what all us humans are capable of. We must remember that basic tragic truth and we must not forget how tempting it is for every one of us humans to sin against *shalom*. Brian McLaren has reflected and written about these biblical stories of violence and tales of conquest.

> Many religious scholars have assumed that because the Bible makes these claims [that God commands violence], we must defend them as true and good.
>
> That approach, however, is morally unacceptable for growing numbers of us, and fortunately, we have another option.[2]

McLaren goes on to name some of those other options. He explains that we can:

- acknowledge that the originators of the stories truly believed God directed their actions;

- acknowledge that in the worldview of this people, divine involvement in the wars of humans was typical and expected;

- allow that people very often find comfort in a God who will take their side and avenge their oppressors;

- admit that if we had walked in their sandals, we likely would have held similar attitudes and done similar things.

Again, none of this explains away the reality of the ugliness of some of these stories from our past, but it does challenge people of faith to rethink how we will reread these texts and how we can rethink and repent our human bent for violence. The Christian confession proclaims that the resurrection of Jesus has already overcome both human and cosmic violence—even though this victory is not yet complete. Whatever our vicious patterns have been in the past, the empty cross empowers us to embrace peace for our shared future.

As You Read the Psalms

Psalm 118 begins and ends as several praise psalms do, alluding to the formulaic understanding of Yahweh's steadfast love.

---

2. McLaren, *We Make the Road by Walking*, 47–48.

O give thanks to the LORD, for the LORD is good;
God's steadfast love endures forever!
Let Israel say, "His steadfast love endures forever."
Let the house of Aaron say, "His steadfast love endures forever."
Let those who fear the LORD say, "His steadfast love endures forever."

This affirmation of God's steadfastness is followed by several stanzas recalling times of trouble, perilous times, and events in which Yahweh intervened and "became my salvation." Here is a prayer of praise and confidence that, no matter what, God is at work in the world; God is in love with God's people.

Notice in this psalm and throughout the Scriptures the frequent references to the right hand. "There are glad songs of victory in the tents of the righteous: the right hand of the LORD does valiantly" (118:15). In Middle Eastern culture from ancient times and continuing today, the right hand is the hand of favor; this is both symbolic and practical. Within this cultural practice, the left is the hand that performs all the unclean acts required for the body while the right hand remains clean and unsoiled. Offering someone your left hand would be offensive while offering the right hand shows favor and acceptance.

Psalm 118 overflows with familiar phrases that have been quoted and reproduced within the NT. For example, "I thank you that you have answered me and have become my salvation. The stone that the builders rejected has become the chief cornerstone. This is the LORD's doing; it is marvelous in our eyes" (118:21–23). The cornerstone, capstone provides foundation and support for an entire structure and is highly prized. From rejection by others to a chosen and favored role by Yahweh, the poet rejoices in this impossible possibility. The psalmist celebrates the happy reversal God has accomplished.

As You Read the New Testament

Acts continues Luke's gospel by telling the story of the Spirit of the Risen Christ let loose in the church and in the world. Throughout this second volume, Luke tells story after story of the church's experience with the Holy Spirit and of these Christians' faithful witness to the gospel, the good news of God's saving work of grace and redemption that has been made available for all.

Since we are reading both Luke and Acts at the same time in our *Living in The Story* effort, we are hearing quite a bit about Peter. Very soon in the gospel of Luke, we will read about Peter's great shame: his denial of Jesus, his betrayal of love, his fear, cowardice, and desertion. But when Luke describes Peter here in Acts, we see what a miraculous work of transformation has been accomplished in his life by the power of Pentecost Spirit; we see Peter's uncompromising boldness for the gospel. After the healing of a lame man in Acts 4, Peter quotes Psalm 118 when he proclaims, "This man has been healed, has been saved by the name of Jesus Christ of Nazareth, whom you crucified, whom God raised from the dead. This Jesus is 'the stone that was rejected by you, the builders; it has become the cornerstone'" (4:10–11).

Besides these stories of Peter that Luke has given us, there is another witness of Peter in our NT, the two letters of Peter we read recently. Probably it was not Peter the fisherman-turned-apostle who wrote these letters with his own hand; more likely it was a disciple, continuing Peter's teaching and writing these letters in his name. But the thing that is significant for us in this conversation is the author's same use of the same quotation of the same Psalm.

> It stands in scripture: "See, I am laying in Zion a stone, a cornerstone chosen and precious; whoever believes in him will not be put to shame."
> Then to you who believe, he is precious; but for those who do not believe, "The stone that the builders rejected has become the very head of the corner," and "a stone that makes them stumble and a rock that makes them fall" (1 Pet 2:4–8).

These passages demonstrate how theologians have always read and reread, interpreted and reinterpreted the Scriptures. Here is another example. "Blessed is the one who comes in the name of the LORD. We bless you from the house of the LORD . . . Bind the festal procession with branches up to the horns of the altar" (Ps 118:26–27). Christians from a variety of liturgical traditions recite this first line nearly every Sunday, and most Christians will read about this "festal procession with branches" and recollect Jesus' Palm Sunday parade. Different from the psalmist, the church's traditional confession is that it is Jesus the Christ who "comes in the name of the LORD."

Theologian Richard Hays explores this kind of theological interpretation as a way to "read backwards." He reflects on ways the first century theologians reread their own Scriptures and found within them "figures" or "pre-figures" of Christ. They began with the Christ event and then read backwards through the Hebrew Scriptures to make sense of this never before imagined event.

What is taking place in the gospels is not so much *prediction* as it is *recognition* of divine patterns in God's interaction with humans and our human endeavor to understand this divine interaction. It's not so much about how the original texts were produced as it is about how the texts are received in any subsequent age. Hays explains:

> There is consequently a significant difference between *prediction* and *prefiguration*. Figural reading need not presume that the OT authors—or the characters they narrate—were conscious of predicting or anticipating Christ. Rather, the discernment of a figural correspondence is necessarily retrospective rather than prospective . . .
>
> Because the two poles of a figure are events within "the flowing stream" of time, the correspondence can be discerned only after the second event has occurred and imparted a new pattern of significance to the first. But once the pattern of correspondence has been grasped, the semantic force of the figure flows both ways, as the second event receives deeper significance from the first.[3]

As twenty-first century theologians, we too ponder carefully and prayerfully how we receive the texts in our own age. Disaster, despair, and death may be our human pattern, but the divine pattern displayed by death's reversal in the resurrection of Jesus Christ is a pattern that will never cease to amaze us.

As You Read the Gospel

Like both Mark and Matthew, Luke also affirms that the event of suffering-death-resurrection was necessary.

> Then he took the twelve aside and said to them, "See, we are going up to Jerusalem, and everything that is written about the Son of Man by the prophets will be accomplished. For he will be handed over to the Gentiles; and he will be mocked and insulted and spat upon. After they have flogged him, they will kill him, and on the third day he will rise again."

3. Hays. *Reading Backwards*, 2–3.

> But they understood nothing about all these things; in fact, what he said was hidden from them, and they did not grasp what was said (Luke 18:31–34).

The disciples were not stupid in their misunderstanding. Rather, in the way the gospel writers tell the story, the disciples were not capable of comprehending the meaning of Jesus before the cross. The Christ event could *only* be understood through the lens of the resurrection and the disciples could *only* make meaning and understand when their eyes and minds had been "opened" by the Crucified and Resurrected Christ. "Then the Risen Jesus said to the astonished disciples, 'These are my words that I spoke to you while I was still with you—that everything written about me in the law of Moses, the prophets, and the psalms must be fulfilled.' Then he opened their minds to understand the scriptures . . ." (Luke 24:44–48).

Reflection: *The Cosmic Cornerstone*

The thread of "cornerstone" is woven throughout the Psalms, the Prophets, through Luke and Peter. This image challenges us to ask what it means to us that the Christ is the cornerstone. M. Eugene Boring points out, "In its original context, the rejected stone of Psalm 118 was Israel, rejected by the nations but accepted by God. First Peter understands the rejected-but-vindicated stone to be both Christ and Christians." This is another example of the NT rereading the OT. It is a new way of seeing and perceiving God's work in the world through the lens of the Christ event. Dr. Boring goes on to say:

> Christ is pictured as a building stone placed in the path of humanity in general, so that one is either incorporated into the holy temple of God with Christ as the cornerstone, or one does not recognize it and stumbles over it.
>
> Since the Christ event is the definitive event of the world and of personal history, there can be no neutral stance toward it.[4]

God-through-Christ is doing a bigger work that is larger than the people of Israel. Now, in the spirit of Pentecost, all humanity is being called into relationship with the Christ of God—the one whom God has sent into the world; the one who embodies the image, presence, essence, and being of the invisible God. This understanding sees all creation as

---

4. Boring, *First Peter*, 97–98.

interrelated to the Christ who is foundation and cornerstone. Thus, it is only by the mind of Christ, only with insight of Holy Spirit that we are able to see and perceive how all things are connected and intersected in heaven and earth, from beginning to end.

Peter's sermon offers an altar call when he asserts "there is salvation in no one else, for there is no other name under heaven given among mortals by which we must be saved" (4:12). What does this mean? Is Jesus the Christ for some but not for others? Is Jesus Christ "salvation" only for those who claim and confess him? Let's unpack this statement a bit.

In *The People's New Testament Commentary*, Boring and Craddock consider how some Christians use this verse as a proof text to claim that only baptized Christians will be saved. They note that:

> For Luke and the New Testament generally, as there is only one God, there is only one way of salvation provided by God: the grace of God manifested in Jesus Christ . . .
>
> On the basis of this text, Christians ought to say neither that only Christians shall ultimately be saved nor that people can be saved through a variety of saviors.
>
> Christians should confess their faith that the God revealed in Christ is the only Savior, without claiming that only those who respond in faith will be saved.[5]

Faithful witness confesses that the Christ is the one way God has provided to save and heal all creation—whether a person knows, understands, and pronounces that reality or not. Faithful confession proclaims that God-in-Christ is the unifying force at work in the cosmos bringing everything to wholeness and *shalom*—whether one names and claims that truth or not. Faithful interpretation of this text allows us to trust in this salvation (which comes from "no one else")—even while we trust in this savior to offer salvation however and to whomever God-in-Christ chooses. Matthew's Jesus says this well in the Sermon on the Mount.

> Love your enemies and pray for those who persecute you, so that you may be sons of your Father who is in heaven; for he makes his sun rise on the evil and on the good, and sends rain on the just and on the unjust (Matt 5:44–45).

That said, the psalmist and the prophets, Luke and Peter all speak of those who "stumble" over this stone, and they grieve the disturbing rejection of this foundation of creation, this foundation for living. I grieve as

---

5. Boring and Craddock, *The People's New Testament Commentary*, 378.

well. There are and always have been those who choose to live for, from, and unto themselves. There always have been those who spend their time and energy seeking pleasure and power, prestige and privilege. Loving God and loving neighbor are foolish to them; self-sacrifice and service seem weak.

These are a people turned in upon themselves in such convulsion that God only knows if they ever will find their way to healing and wholeness in this life. This rejection of God, this stumbling over the Christ, this resistance to the Spirit, this turning away from life surely breaks the heart of God, the God of life. It makes for miserable living. Even so, God-in-Christ is their savior too.

But there is another aspect to this "stumbling" that grieves my heart. I think many modern day people stumble over a stone that is a small, false christ. Too often the Christ to whom the church gives witness is a christ just for me and for my little group, a christ who condemns you and your little group. This is false. And whenever this false christ is proclaimed, countless seekers are tripped up and reject—not the true Christ of God—but rather the christ of our own small imaginations.

In a cultural climate such as ours, rife with separation, alienation, and condemnation, living in love, unity, and *shalom* is countercultural. Even so, this countercultural living is God's call to us who ground our faith in the life of the cosmic cornerstone. Those of us who presume to wear the name of the Christ, who claim this name which is like "no other name," and can entrust ourselves to the salvation that is only God's to give.

Consider the challenging words of Luke's Jesus as we seek to apply them to our own day and our own witness. "Occasions for stumbling are bound to come, but woe to anyone by whom they come! It would be better for you if a millstone were hung around your neck and you were thrown into the sea than for you to cause one of these little ones to stumble" (17:1–2). As followers of this Christ, may we entrust ourselves to the truth which is grounded in God's unity, wholeness, and welcome. May we live within this foundational cornerstone.

Week 22

War and Violence

Judges 1–13
Psalm 28
Psalm 36
Psalm 94
Psalm 140
Acts 6–7
Luke 19–21

As You Read the Old Testament

ACROSS THE AGES, ACROSS the globe, people have used and misused Scripture to justify all kinds of sins against *shalom*. This is why our read-through-the-Bible effort challenges some previous understandings of what this story means and how to apply its truth to our current day. This challenge to reread, reconsider, and reinterpret what the Bible means is a good and crucial effort.

I don't have an adequate way of explaining the biblical stories of violence. I want to count on the scholars' help here, but many of them seem to be as puzzled as I am. I remember how I hoped author, pastor, and theologian William Willimon would explain the violence in Scripture at a preacher's workshop I attended a few years ago, but no—he simply cautioned us preachers to resist the temptation of justifying, defending, or explaining *away* these hard stories. He challenged us to admit that *The Story* is what it is: messy, confusing, and contradictory (just as we humans are messy, confusing, and contradictory. Here is a reminder that the texts of scripture are *always* human, even as we claim that somehow God's Own Word addresses and confronts us through them.) Phyllis Trible says in her classic book, *Texts of Terror*:

> To take to heart these ancient stories is to confess its present reality. But beyond confession, we must take counsel to say: "Never again!"
>
> Yet this counsel will not be effective unless we direct our hearts to that most uncompromising of all biblical commands, speaking the word not to others, but to ourselves: "Repent! Repent!"[1]

As You Read the Psalms

To their credit, the psalmists' appeals to divine justice do not presume to take vengeance and retribution into their own hands. These passionate people of faith express their grief and despair freely even as they trust in the faithfulness of God to make right what has been wronged.

In the Psalms, we learn how to pray, how to express our thanksgiving, and how to ask for what we need. Here we also learn how to name our doubts and anger and to give language to our disappointment and grief. Here in the Psalms, we learn that—while we can and should work and pray unceasingly for justice—vengeance is best left in the hands of the Holy One who is both just and gracious.

As You Read the New Testament

Acts 6–7 relates the powerful witness of deacon Stephen who summarized the history of Israel as a critique of some religious people who continued to harass the new Jesus movement. It also gives us a powerful tale about religiously motivated violence.

> Then they dragged [Stephen] out of the city and began to stone him; and the witnesses laid their coats at the feet of a young man named Saul . . . And Saul approved of their killing him (7:58—8:1).

---

1. Trible, *Texts of Terror*, 87.

Unfortunately this is nothing new, and it hasn't gone away. Throughout the centuries, religion has motivated all sorts of violent attitudes and actions.

I notice two important things about this story. First, all the characters are Jews, so recall the tension that existed within the Jewish community as some accepted and others rejected Jesus as Messiah. Who gets to say what it means to be authentically Jewish, aligned with the Torah and tradition? Who gets to interpret the story of Israel? These Jewish brothers of Stephen made the judgment that he was misrepresenting the story and maligning the Holy Name. In their minds, Stephen was guilty of blasphemy.

Secondly, the Law they followed *did* justify stoning when one was found guilty of blasphemy. The problem is, however, these legalists made a similar mistake as my seminary friend when he tried to read Leviticus and understand it as the "word of the Lord." They forgot to reread Leviticus in light of the Wisdom teachings and in conversation with their prophets. They forgot to read the requirements in Torah with the heart of the *Lord* of the Torah: the one who is "merciful and gracious, slow to anger, and abounding in steadfast love and faithfulness . . ." (Ex 34:6–7). The word of the Lord is always a word *both* of judgment/justice *and* mercy/compassion. Whenever people use religion to justify violence against any of God's creatures the result will be especially lethal.

As you read through Acts, notice how Luke develops a theme of witness. The Greek word for witness (*martus*) became our English word "martyr," so Luke's description of "the witnesses" laying their coats at the feet of the young Saul intrigues us. These witnesses/martyrs helped murder the first martyr of the church. Luke is a powerful storyteller and witness.

As You Read the Gospel

These chapters in Luke 19–21 contain what we sometimes refer to as the "Little Apocalypse." Luke's Jesus speaks of the destruction of the Temple, the desolation of Jerusalem, and the persecution of the faithful as if he is predicting a coming future violence. Remember, though, Luke was writing with and for a community of believers who lived on the other side of this devastation; Luke describes what had already come to pass.

Apocalyptic writings are a multilayered, multifaceted genre that speaks to more than simple history. "Apocalypse" means to "unveil," to pull back a curtain and catch sight of what is going on behind the scenes. The prophets of Israel frequently used otherworldly images as they wrote about divine mysteries. The most famous Christian writer who did this was John of Patmos when he recorded the vision he received in our NT book, Revelation.

Luke's Little Apocalypse offers brutal descriptions of political violence and startling visions of cosmic upheavals. Even so, Luke allows us to glimpse God's faithfulness at work behind chaotic scenes. The core message Luke's Jesus offers to believers of every age is this: *do not fear.* God's purposes will not be thwarted, therefore trust and endure. We will look more closely at apocalyptic writings when we read the prophets and the Revelation in later weeks.

Next week we will read Luke's passion narrative, yet another depiction of the horrendous violence humans are capable of visiting upon one another. However, in Christian theology, the cross also represents quintessential *cosmic* violence as it symbolizes demonic forces converging to do battle against heavenly realities. The battle is cosmic but earth and humanity are its battleground.

Will violence defeat *shalom*? Is hate stronger than love? Ultimate questions begged answers and, for three long days, the darkness seemed to overpower the light. But the Christian story proclaims that—in the cross—violence was met with divine self-giving and death was overwhelmed. "As Dietrich Bonheoffer wrote, 'God allows himself to be edged out of the world and onto the cross.' Here we have not the renunciation of divine sovereignty but its redefinition."[2] Divine sovereignty is demonstrated not in mighty acts of power but through the power of self-giving, self-sacrificing love.

Reflection: *Jesus Wept*

As my husband and I watched the powerful movie *Lincoln*, we were particularly moved by one scene in which President Abraham Lincoln rides slowly through a still smoldering battlefield. Everywhere he looks, the bodies of soldiers are tumbled together, a horrific grey and blue sculpture of death and destruction. I wept.

2. Boring and Craddock, *The People's New Testament Commentary*, 56.

Not many years after the Civil War, the commemoration of Memorial Day was instituted because people wanted to honor the fallen soldiers. This kind of remembering also should challenge us to admit our warring madness—that in those few years, over 600,000 fellow Americans killed one another.

Around this same time in American history, Julia Ward Howe initiated a Mother's Peace Day observance. Too many mothers, too many grandmothers had lowered their bright, brave sons into graves. Too many mothers had wept in the night and still ached with each morning's light. "Enough is enough," they said. Julia Howe's call for peace is now our annual Mothers' Day celebration but it began in 1870 as a way to remember the weeping of mothers and the waste of war.

On the day Jesus rode into Jerusalem, in the days before he carried his old rugged cross up the hillside, Jesus wept—not for himself but for all those who turned their backs on the peace he offered. Instead of peace, people turned to violence. Jesus saw clearly how this sin against *shalom* destroys the soul of a person. And so, Jesus took up his cross and walked right into the violence, bearing its burden and thus breaking its power by his own self-giving.

Even though the texts of Joshua and Judges represent an understanding of God-ordained, God-ordered violence, there is and always has been an alternative biblical vision of who God is and, therefore, who the people of God should be. Countercultural witness woven throughout Scripture tells another story of the God who is "merciful and gracious, slow to anger, and abounding in steadfast love and faithfulness" (Ex 34, Neh 9, Ps 86, 103, 145). A countercultural witness embedded in Scripture calls upon the people of God to turn away from violence and to live in harmony. It is only when we read Scripture through this kind of alternative lens that we can reread, reframe, reconsider what is truly true for our believing and for our living today.

Brian McLaren admits (as we must) that even though throughout history, people of faith have perpetuated violence in God's name, Jesus Christ created a new way by showing us God's way of peace. "In God's name Jesus would undergo violence, and in so doing, overcome it. That was why . . . Jesus spoke of suffering, death, and resurrection as a different kind of strategy for a different kind of victory." Because of Jesus we have tangible insight into the nature of God and the essence of community. McLaren continues:

Since the beginning, Jesus has taught that the nonviolent will inherit the earth. Violence cannot defeat violence. Hate cannot defeat hate. Fear cannot defeat fear. Domination cannot defeat domination. God's way is different. God must achieve victory through defeat, glory through shame, strength through weakness, leadership through servanthood, and life through death.[3]

When we read the Old Testament in light of the New, we recognize we are not obligated to antiquated understandings. When we read the Old Testament in light of Jesus Christ, we are freed up to be the people of the Christ because it is in Christ that we see God's will truly *done on earth as it is in heaven*. It is in Christ that we see God's authentic character demonstrated and embodied. The divine demonstration of Jesus the Christ looks like this (and teaches all people of God to live like this): self-giving, turning the other cheek, doing unto others as we would have them do unto us, dying to ourselves, and living in the peace of *shalom*.

My alma mater, Brite Divinity School, hosts an important work called *Soul Repair*, a ministry which serves to support solders' recovery from moral injury. Moral injury is different from post-traumatic stress disorder, different from psychological injury. Moral injury is a spiritual wound; it is violence done to a person's deeply held values; it is the breaking of personal promises, the betrayal of strong convictions.

"War is hell," they say and those who have borne the battle have surely lived for a while in hell. They have seen and heard and experienced horrors most of us cannot fathom. They have had to do things they never imagined they could do. They have been forced to make choices they can scarcely believe they have made. The souls of our soldiers are violated by this our perpetual human violence against *shalom*. *Soul Repair* seeks their healing.

Far too many people perpetuate violence and do not recognize the saving, healing work of God. Far too many people continue to reject nonviolence and refuse to recognize the things that make for peace. Abraham Lincoln urged us in his second inaugural address:

> With malice toward none, with charity for all, with firmness in the right as God gives us to see the right, let us strive on to finish the work we are in, to bind up the nation's wounds, to care for him who shall have borne the battle and for his widow and his orphan, to do all which may achieve and cherish a just and lasting peace among ourselves and with all nations.[4]

3. McLaren, *We Make the Road by Walking*, 118–19.
4. Lincoln, Second Inaugural Address, April 1865.

These words make me weep—not just because they are so beautiful but because we have not yet learned how to achieve and cherish just and lasting peace. There is so much injury, so much misery in our human family. Mothers have lost their sons, soldiers have lost their limbs, too many have lost their way. Surely God Almighty weeps. Jesus wept. May we weep as well.

And may we repent and take counsel together to say, *Never again!* Let us repent of the ways we turn away because of our own complacency and refusal to change the culture and economy of war. Let us repent of the violence that destroys God's children and desecrates God's peace. Let us repent of the ways we imagine God is on our side instead of beseeching God to bring us to God's side, to the work of the Holy One.

Let us repent of our lack of compassion for the brokenness of those who have borne the battle, and for our failure to care for their widows and orphans. Let us repent of our warring madness and admit that we too have been complicit in sinning against *shalom*.

And may we repair. May we be bold and courageous to take up our own cross and—following Jesus—walk courageously into the brokenness of the world. May we be a part of binding up the wounds of God's people so that each of us individually and all of us together become part of "the things that make for peace."

Week 23

Samson

Judges 14–21
Psalm 6
Psalm 31
Psalm 85
Psalm 143
Acts 8–9
Luke 22–23

As You Read the Old Testament

THE BOOK OF JUDGES flows with stories of unlikely heroes who, in the developing plot, attempted to intervene in Israel's downward spiral away from covenant faithfulness and into societal chaos. It didn't work; these judges could not stop the cycles of disobedience even though their work sometimes delayed the inevitable apostasy and disintegration.

Samson's story says that in his youth, "the spirit of the Lord began to stir him . . ." Astute *Living in The Story* readers likely will notice numerous biblical themes coming together in the story of Samson.

- An angel visits a barren couple and promises a son (like Abraham and Sarah, Elizabeth and Zechariah).

- The father asks the angel's name (like Jacob wrestling, like Zechariah's encounter).

- The father "sees" God in the angel and fears he will die (like Moses).

- The son is consecrated from birth and marked by acts of ritual purity (like John the Baptist).

- The son is destined to deliver God's people but in the end he is betrayed. With his last breath and his arms outstretched, he defeats the enemy with a surprising reversal (like Jesus).

Again and again the Samson story testifies to God's unexpected and undeserved mercy and faithfulness. The portrayal of Samson's dubious moral character and foolish hot-headedness underscore God's mysterious way of choosing and using unlikely people for ministry.

As You Read the Psalms

Psalm 6 struggles with what may be some physical illness and so speaks to those of us who have languished in the pain, fear, or misery of our body's *un*-health and *dis*-ease. "Be gracious to me, O LORD, for I am languishing! O LORD, heal me, for my bones are shaking with terror—how long?" Ever since our earliest history, we humans have wondered if negative physical circumstances could be the result of some failure to please the gods. Does the drought or the flood come because of our sin? Did the cancer or heart failure happen because of something we did wrong? Are we being punished? Or disciplined?

The psalmist seems to think so. "O LORD, do not rebuke me in your anger or discipline me in your wrath." So probably a faithful response to this dilemma may be "maybe." Or "yes" and "no." Or "both/and."

We moderns now understand the power of the psyche and its influence over the physical. The word "psychosomatic" expresses how thoughts, feelings, and emotions can create physical realities. We moderns have seen how our own patterns of exercise, eating, and drinking can contribute to deadly physical conditions. We moderns recognize how stress, grief, anger, or fear can damage heart muscles, intestinal tracts, and blood vessels.

And we have come to understand the consequences of our actions within our environment. Polluted water, soil, and air can create cancers and way too many other diseases. So "no"—I don't think God reaches out from heaven and zaps us with depression, diabetes, or asbestos poisoning as punishment for our wrongs. But "yes," our actions have consequences. And yes, we may have opportunity to learn some important lessons from the discipline life's challenges can bring so that we may change our ways for the future.

That said, no matter what caused the sickness, disease, or unhealthiness, the psalmist stands firm in the promises of God's covenant. No matter what foolishness I have engaged in; no matter what recklessness someone else may have inflicted upon me—even so, *nevertheless*—we count on God for faithfulness, salvation, and healing. Not because we deserve it, not because *we* are faithful enough but rather because God is always faithful enough.

> Turn, O LORD, save my life; deliver me for the sake of your steadfast love. For in death there is no remembrance of you; in *Sheol* who can give you praise? (6:4–5)

For the sake of steadfast love. For the sake of the cosmic witness and testimony to God's steadfast love and faithfulness. "Turn, O Lord." In other words, "repent."

In biblical language, repenting doesn't mean feeling badly, feeling sorry, or even feeling ashamed of what we have done. Repentance doesn't have much of anything to do with feelings; rather, repentance is action. Repentance is a reversal, a turning. Stopping one way of acting and beginning another different action. The psalmist entreats God to turn, to cease the inactive waiting and begin to do something: to begin the healing, redeeming, saving that is God's nature and work.

"I am weary with my moaning; every night I flood my bed with tears . . ." (6:6). Who else has been here? Who else has flooded your pillow with tears and stared into space with paralyzing self-pity? Once again, the psalmists articulate the human condition and remind us that we are not alone in our suffering.

When I used to pastor in local churches, I always tried to affirm negative emotions as completely normal, a logical response to unfair, unsettling, or uncomfortable circumstances. Sometimes when I would pray with them, we would pray these psalms and name the cancer or other diseases as "the enemy." Not that I think of them as something like demons that are able to inflict tragedy upon innocents, but I do think of these conditions as part of the "evil" and brokenness of our complicated world. Something malevolent that exists even though God did not (and does not) intend this brokenness for the human family.

There are some believers, however, who would not agree with me. Some religious folks are so concerned to assign all power to God that they insist everything that comes in life must come directly from the hand of God. If God is all-powerful, then everything that happens must be happening by the will and agency of God, they argue. In other versions of religious thinking, there are some who claim that illness, poverty, or tragedy is proof that such an afflicted person lacks faith. They teach that sickness or distress can be eliminated if a person prays hard enough or has a strong enough faith—suggesting that "enough faith" will protect people from negative experiences. This kind of magical thinking imagines faith (and maybe "enough" financial donations!) as a sort of talisman against evil. (Critics call this "prosperity gospel"; I call it heresy.)

But even as our psalmist's faith assures him that the Lord has heard his weeping, acknowledged his supplication, and accepted his prayer, he recognizes his circumstances may not magically change. So he commits himself to wait on the Lord, trusting that God knows, sees, cares, and that God will act in God's own time. "Depart from me, all you workers of evil, for the LORD has heard the sound of my weeping. The LORD has heard my supplication; the LORD accepts my prayer" (6:8–9). And so in the midst of the weeping, we too can trust and rest and wait.

As You Read the New Testament

We have two versions of Paul's come-to-Jesus meeting in our NT: one from the Acts of the Apostles and the other from Paul himself. Initially, adversary-Saul-transformed-to-apostle-Paul resisted the Jesus followers' proclamation that this crucified Jesus was the Messiah Israel had been awaiting. First, it was preposterous to believe that God's Messiah would have died in such shame. Second, Paul's Jewish commitment was to the *one* God, the *true* God—therefore any suggestion that somehow immortal God had become human must have offended his monotheistic piety.

Paul's Damascus Road experience and his vision of the Resurrected Christ turned him and his entire belief system upside-down-and-inside-out-and-right-side-up. Paul rarely referred to the earthly Jesus in his writings because Paul's Jesus was always the Crucified and Exalted One.

We may think of Paul's Damascus Road experience as a story of conversion, but Paul was not actually converted, changing from one religion to another or turning from no-faith to faith. As a matter of fact, you couldn't have found a more devout, authentic, passionate man of God in all of Israel. No, this isn't a conversion story; I think what happened

to Paul is "call." His life was redirected, reoriented, refocused, and rein-
vented for a whole new life and a bold new work.

As for these people he went to Damascus to attack, these people
Paul was so sure were blaspheming the one true God by claiming Jesus
as Messiah, these people of the Way—Ananias and his community were
the very ones who welcomed him who had been their enemy, loving him,
supporting him, and empowering him to live out this startling divine call.

As You Read the Gospel

This week, we read the story of Jesus' passion as told by Luke. It is a powerful narrative following Luke's ongoing theme of naming Jesus as Son of
Man and Son of God. Watch how Luke uses these titles at Jesus' trial among
the religious leaders when they said, "If you are the Messiah, tell us."

> Jesus replied, "If I tell you, you will not believe; and if I question
> you, you will not answer. But from now on the Son of Man will
> be seated at the right hand of the power of God."
> All of them asked, "Are you, then, the Son of God?"
> He said to them, "You say that *I Am*."
> Then they said, "What further testimony do we need? We
> have heard it ourselves from his own lips!" (22:67–71)

As you read, see how Luke paints a painful scene of abandonment
and betrayal, of humiliation and crucifixion. This week's reading ends in
the tomb and darkness of the three days. As on Good Friday, we must
stay for a while in the darkness. We must wait for God's good time.

Reflection: *Damascus Roads*

Some of us have had our cataracts removed and we can still remember
our amazement when the doctor removed the eye patches. It's a sudden
and startling reversal. "I once was blind but now I see" were the words
that came to my mind at the time. It was as if "something like scales" had
fallen from my eyes.

I love this story about Saul of Tarsus who becomes for us Paul the
Apostle. I love the startling reversal, the U-turn in his life. I love the way
the story is told, folding in so many other biblical images from so many
other stories: the split open sky, visions into the heavens, a blinding light,
three days of darkness. Three days like Jonah in the belly of the whale.

Three days like Jesus in the tomb. Three days of darkness that initiated light, enlightenment, and call.

Luke tells this story of Saul of Tarsus' Damascus Road experience as yet another story of God's unlikely, unexpected, unpredictable grace. M. Eugene Boring and Fred Craddock say:

> The whole story is not about Saul's successful quest for God, but about the grace of God that transforms a persecutor into a missionary.
>
> Readers are called not to admire Saul, but to rejoice that they belong to a church whose mission is empowered and directed by such a God.[1]

Paul's vision, Paul's epiphany—this moment of coming to awareness, this "ah hah!" moment, this "now I get it" moment—is a resurrection story. Paul is turned from death to life, from darkness to light, from dead end to new possibilities; he once was lost but now he's found, once blind but now he sees.

- Once smugly self-righteous, now Paul is brought to his knees.
- Once blissfully ignorant, now Paul is shown what is really real and truly true.
- Once arrogantly judgmental, now Paul is confronted and challenged, called and sent by the Risen Lord himself.

The Holy split open the heavens and intersected his life, nothing will ever be the same again, and all of it is God's doing. Here is the unlikely Pharisee, Saul, chosen and called by God for ministry.

Countless unlikely people have experienced these kinds of holy interruptions, For example, Sara Miles was raised in a thoroughly secular environment by parents who had rejected the Christianity of their childhood. Religions were "superstitions," they taught their own children, and Sara completely agreed. So there is no plausible explanation why Sara found herself mysteriously drawn to the little Episcopal Church in her neighborhood. As she tells the story, she had never in her life heard the Gospel, never said the Lord's Prayer, never even mentioned the name of Jesus except as a casual expletive.

But for some reason, on this Sunday morning she found herself sitting in a pew, standing for the hymns and then, amazingly, coming to

---

1. Boring and Craddock, *The People's New Testament Commentary*, 398.

the Communion Table to receive the bread and the wine. "The body and blood of Christ," the woman in the long white robe told Sara. And she took. And she ate. And Sara Miles was changed forever. "Jesus happened to me," she says.

Sara recites how confused she was over this unexpected, unsought event. Maybe she was hyper-suggestible to this new environment. Maybe she was overly emotional, like being caught up in a particularly glorious concert or a natural wonder. Maybe she was crying because of her pent up grief. But the word "Jesus" remained lodged within her and wouldn't let her go. In the introduction to her book, *Take This Bread*, Miles says:

> I was . . . hungering and thirsting for righteousness. I found it at the eternal and material core of Christianity: body, blood, bread, wine, poured out freely, shared by all.
>
> I discovered a religion rooted in the most ordinary yet subversive practice: a dinner table where everyone is welcome, where the despised and the outcasts are honored . . .
>
> In this book, I look at the Gospel that moved me, the bread that changed me, and the work that saved me, to begin a spiritual and an actual communion across the divides.[2]

Her ministry became a local food pantry in San Francisco where healthy food is offered generously and abundantly for any and all. And for Sara, the most logical place in the world to host such a food pantry was right there at the Lord's Table, where she had received bread of life offered generously and abundantly. Hers is another fascinating Damascus Road story, another story of God's unlikely, unexpected, unpredictable grace.

But all stories of call, conversion, and transformation are not so suddenly dramatic as Paul's or Sara's. My own story was a long process. It was like I had spiritual cataracts, something like scales that limited my vision and kept me from recognizing my call. Thankfully, the Spirit of the Risen Christ has never given up on chipping away at my blindness. Thankfully God has placed a whole lot of Ananiases in my path as I have made my journey.

Some of you are also on a journey to a whole new way of being and seeing; it can feel like a very long "three days," can't it? Whether the reversal is sudden or slow, it still startles. To change our mind about some of the things we had come to believe; to change the direction of a life; to change our assumptions, our habits, our motivations; to be changed from

2. Miles, *Take This Bread*, xv.

living as people who enjoy being served into people who love to serve others; to be open and obedient to God's work of transformation; to be willing to let Jesus happen to us—all stunning reversals.

I believe each one of us is called by God into some kind of ministry. Maybe we are Ananiases, supporting others who are on the journey and encouraging God's work of transformation in their lives. Maybe we are Pauls, offering courageous public witness. Maybe we are Saras, welcoming, loving, and feeding others in humble, welcoming ways.

U-turns and reorientations often come from the work of the Resurrected Christ pouring out resurrection life into the world, life that is oriented and reoriented toward God allowing us to keep our priorities aligned properly. Power and pleasure find their proper place and appropriate balance. Pride and privilege lose their appeal; they seem like small and foolish motivations in light of a passion to follow in the way of the Christ.

Whatever our call to love and serve this Lord, wherever our Damascus Road leads us, may Jesus keep happening to us in all sorts of unexpected and unpredictable places.

Week 24
Job

Job
Psalm 112
Psalm 43
Psalm 30
Psalm 82
Acts 10–12
Luke 24

As You Read the Old Testament

NOT MANY STORIES ARE as powerful as the drama of Job. Notice how his story is not told within the context of the Abraham/Isaac/Jacob tradition, nor is it understood within the circumstance of Moses and the Exodus. The story of Job is set apart from the lineage of Israel. Job's tale is its own, set outside of time. "There once was a man in the land of Uz . . ."

A righteous man, blameless, and upright, "no one like him on the earth." And then his loves, his living, and his life were all placed in jeopardy by an odd divine wager that unleashed mountains of troubles, oceans of despair, and miserable comforters. We hear blessing and cursing and eloquent searching. We listen to assertions of innocence and guilt. We recognize calls for judgment and justice.

Job is part of the Wisdom Tradition of Israel and (as is true of many stories that ponder life's mysteries) it leaves us with more questions than answers. Notice how the Creator who speaks to Job from the whirlwind does not answer Job's questions and explain *why* Job has been required to endure this suffering. But the God of the Whirlwind *does* honor Job's struggle by revealing his place in the big picture of heaven and earth. Job discovers that he is part of the wild unfathomable mystery of life, and finding his appropriate place—both humbled and esteemed—is enough.

I remember, growing up, the conventional wisdom from my childhood praised the "patience of Job." But when I read the story for myself instead of just hearing the Sunday school version (a *very* important phase in the growing up process!), I realized Job wasn't at all "patient." Like some of the psalmists, Job doubts, complains, criticizes, argues, proclaims his righteousness, and challenges God to a contest of integrity.

What a relief for me to discover that doubt is a crucial part of faith! Arguing with God is a time honored biblical tradition, and Job's example shows us what faithful, honest, passionate engagement with the Divine can look like. Rather than describing Job's faith as "patient," it's more accurate to say his faith was "enduring." It is the endurance of Job that places him on our lists of biblical heroes.

As You Read the Psalms

The Psalms for this week demonstrate the paradigm scholar Walter Brueggemann[1] articulates when he describes three fundamental aspects of living: states of Orientation (i.e., Ps 112), Disorientation (Ps 43), and New Orientation (Ps 30). In our *Living in The Story* readings, these psalms are coupled with the story of Job as his prosperity (orientation) was plunged into lengthy devastation (disorientation) before he was restored to well being (new orientation). These cycles are our shared human experience, Brueggemann believes, and the Psalms (as well as the book of Job) speak to those back and forth, up and down phases of confidence and confusion.

When tragic circumstances crushed Job, his pitiful counselors piously reiterated the conventional wisdom of orientation, insisting that bad things only happen to bad people. Since he was in trouble (they argued), his troubles must be his own fault. This understanding of how the world works has clear precedent in the Hebrew Scriptures since Deuteronomic expectations for Israel are woven throughout Torah: obey and you will be blessed, disobey and you will be cursed.

---

1. Brueggemann, *The Message of the Psalms*, 19–23.

Job, however, takes issue. For him, real life contradicts this too-neat philosophy, and he protests in the manner of the psalmists: "Vindicate me, O God, and defend my cause, against an ungodly people; from those who are deceitful and unjust, deliver me! For you are the God in whom I take refuge; why have you cast me off?" (Ps 43:1–2) Job cries in lament that, no, sometimes, bad things happen to good people. Job insists on his righteousness and challenges God's betrayal.

Psalm 30 sings some of our favorite phrases of hope and redemption, songs of New Orientation.

> Weeping may linger for the night but joy comes with the morning. You have turned my mourning into dancing.
> As for me, I said in my prosperity, "I shall never be moved." By your favor, O LORD, you had established me as a strong mountain (30:5–6).

Note how this psalmist confesses a common human hubris: "I said in my prosperity, I shall never be moved." Isn't that a typical miscalculation? When things are going well, we take the goodness for granted and forget to live in gratitude. We forget that every day, every breath is grace.

> O LORD my God, I cried to you for help, and you have healed me. You brought up my soul from *Sheol* and restored me to life from among those gone down to the Pit (30:2–3).

This story is the cosmic story of resurrection—life, death, and new life.

A counselor friend once taught me that everyone is somewhere on a spectrum, either in the midst of a crisis, just getting over a crisis, or unaware that a crisis is on its way, maybe just around the next corner. Crisis is part of our normal human experience. Other philosophers (both spiritual and secular) have described our human cycles of experience similarly. Richard Rohr calls these cycles Order, Disorder, and Reorder.[2] Brian McLaren names stages of faith as Simplicity, Complexity, Perplexity, and Harmony.[3] All of us who point out these cycles/stages remind our readers that this kind of life movement does not often happen in a smooth once-for-all-time progression; it's better to think of these experiences as spirals that loop back and forth as we encounter the circumstances of our lives, both internal and external.

---

2. Rohr, *The Wisdom Pattern: Order, Chaos, Reorder*, 8.

3. McLaren, *Faith After Doubt*, 93–95.

Life always has included all these cycles; even people of faith go through dark times because faith never protects anyone from life's common problems. The difference is that people of faith have opportunity to perceive a bigger picture, to recognize a paradigm of meaning that allows us to stand firm with both confidence and humility. People of faith can give credit to God: thanks when things are going well, hope when things are not going well, and praise when things open up into new possibilities.

This doesn't mean that it is unfaithful to grouse when we're going through hard times. Surely Job and the psalmists teach us that complaint and lament can be a healthy part of faith. It also doesn't mean that God moves humans about like chess pieces (even though the story of Job does sound like it, doesn't it?). Rather, in the cosmic mystery, we hold onto the hope that Creator holds everything together and is always working for goodness and wholeness. Even when normal human cycles bring crisis and confusion, people of faith can trust that Spirit constantly breathes hope and new possibilities. "You have taken off my sackcloth and clothed me with joy, so that my soul may praise you and not be silent. O LORD my God, I will give thanks to you forever" (30:11–12).

As You Read the New Testament

Cornelius was a Roman Centurion from Italy stationed for military duty in Palestine. Evidently, he was not the stereotypical brutal occupier in the conventional practice of empires. Instead this man had a sense of responsibility to others: the poor, the unfortunate, and the under privileged who lived all around him. And for some reason, Cornelius had a sense of Someone Bigger than himself. The anthropomorphic gods of the Roman Empire were small and petty; Cornelius hungered for Something More. He didn't know what that "More" might look like, but he entrusted himself to the asking/seeking/knocking/yearning/waiting that is so often required of faith. His piety was gentle and humble, demonstrated with both private prayer and social practice.

The Cornelius story in Acts is intriguing and, like Job, is another story of a faithful Gentile. Watch how God honors this Roman's faithfulness by sending a Jewish Christian to proclaim the good news of God's redeeming love made known in Jesus Christ. And watch how God teaches Peter some important lessons in the process.

Peter had been eyewitness to the radical, inclusive welcome Jesus offered to the unwelcomed, the outsiders, and the dispossessed. It was Peter who had proclaimed in his Pentecost sermon that God was doing a new thing, an unconventional and surprising thing. Even so, it still took Peter a while to comprehend just how unconventional and surprising this new work of God actually was. Jesus the Messiah had already upended Peter's previously settled religion but now Spirit was calling him to embrace an even larger world of faith—a community of Christ that included Gentiles.

Within Peter's understanding of the Hebrew Scriptures there was an unbridgeable chasm between Jews and Gentiles, but Scripture also gives witness to an evolving faith and faithfulness within the people of God. So when Peter had opportunity to spend time in the company of real people who also had been touched, changed, and redeemed by God's Spirit, he finally was able to see what the prophets of Scripture had always envisioned, the emerging *shalom*/wholeness/unity of all God's creatures within all God's creation. ("Anthropology challenges theology," a friend likes to remind me.) While the story tells us of Cornelius' conversion, Peter and the early Jewish Christian church needed continued conversion as well.

As You Read the Gospel

The Hebrew Scriptures give witness to Messiah, and in the Christian understanding, this Christ was Jesus of Nazareth. In his parting gift to his disciples, Luke's Jesus said, "everything written about me in the Law of Moses, the prophets, and the psalms must be fulfilled.' Then he opened their minds to understand the scriptures . . ." (Luke 24:44). This explicit connection between Torah, Psalms, Prophets, and Jesus is the prayerful, careful interpretive work of our earliest Christian theologians.

I think many Christians don't understand the significance of the hermeneutic of reading the Christ into the OT because this particular interpretive approach was not a given. Early Christian communities pondered deeply how the faith that had been handed down to them from Israel might now connect and collaborate with their newfound faith in Jesus. Discovering, discerning, and describing the compatibilities was the work of this faithful people. Interpretation and reinterpretation of the Holy Scriptures was a sacred undertaking and ever continues to be holy work.

Luke 24 is one of my favorite chapters in the Bible. I love what Luke tells us here and I love the way he tells it. If you have time, read it more than once and ponder how profound and beautiful this part of the story is. "Were not our hearts burning within us while he was talking to us on the road, while he was opening the scriptures to us?" Cleopas and his companion acknowledged with awe. (I like to think of his partner here as Mrs. Cleopas!) Whenever some new insight into the words of Scripture points me to the Living Word, I often feel my heart burn as well.

Reflection: *Righteous Gentiles*

The ancient Greeks thought of themselves as the only truly civilized people; anyone who was not Greek was considered to be "barbarian." The Israelites described those who were not a part of their tribe as "people of the nations," *ethnos*, Gentiles. Defining who is in and who is out has been happening for much of human history and our cultural stories always include tales of people who are "other." A surprising number of those stories describe outsiders whose character and courage upended "insider" expectations. For example, the Good Samaritan or "the hooker with a heart of gold" or the wisdom that comes from the mouth of babes. Scripture contains numerous stories about these kinds of people, "outsiders" in the eyes of their society but beloved of God and included nonetheless.

Peter's experience in this story reminds me of some current realities with too many Christians in our own day. When any of us think we've learned all we need to learn and grown all we need to grow, when we settle into our beliefs and set them in stone, then we can miss the enlightening, enlivening, and invigorating movement of Spirit. Today's church needs to better embrace ongoing conversion because God surely is not done creating newness among us.

I wish God's people (of all people!) would be the first to welcome this newness, but I find the staid and settled institutional church too often to be among the last to change. Instead, it is frequently the "outsiders" who reveal God's ongoing work of mercy and justice to us "insiders."

Like Cornelius, there are many unchurched people who are "spiritual but not religious." These sisters and brothers function like "faithful Gentiles" living faithfully, albeit outside the parameters of the institutional church. As with the condescending certainty of Job's comforters, too often modern day church folks shut down seekers, judge doubters, and criticize questioners; thus the spiritual but not religious folks are walking away in droves. Even so, within many of these honest, thoughtful, unchurched people, there is a deep spirituality that, in its own way, also is asking/seeking/knocking. Sometimes they are Cornelius; sometimes they are Job. Always they are precious to God and they ought to be precious to the church.

Peter finally understood what today's church needs to understand, that the community of Christ, this new family of God is boundless, embracing *all* whom God is calling and redeeming. In Christ, the divides are gone, the barriers are removed, the distinctions between holy and profane are blurred, the differences between Jew and Gentile, male and female, gay and straight, rich and poor, black and white and brown and "blue and red" become pointless. Only when our churches figure out how to become this kind of diverse, loving, welcoming fellowship will we have any chance whatsoever of enticing "faithful Gentiles" to show up and share in the community of Christ.

Job's friends remind us that conventional wisdom and easy answers are miserable comfort because efforts to define God or defend God are useless and even detrimental to faith and witness. Job reminds us that faithfulness does not always come with a pretty, peaceful piety; sometimes, authentic faith demands questions, arguments, and fierce honesty. Cornelius reminds us that God honors every act of faithfulness and graciousness; God will respond to even the slightest breath of hope and glimmer of faith. And Peter reminds us that understanding and awareness grow gradually, often one person at a time, one personal encounter at a time. *Anthropology challenges theology.*

Peter, Job, Cornelius, and all the faithful Gentiles among us remind that we should never be surprised at the people God is bringing together in order to create *shalom*—in God's own good time and in God's own mysterious way.

Week 25

Ruth

First Samuel 1–3
Ruth
Psalm 41
Psalm 86
Psalm 113
Acts 13–15
John 1

As You Read the Old Testament

OUR *LIVING IN THE Story* texts this week look at the lives of two fascinating OT women, Hannah and Ruth. These two women come from very different circumstances but both demonstrate God's way of startling reversal. I admire them both for their persistent faithfulness.

Hannah is one in a long line of biblical characters who experienced surprising abundance that interrupted her barrenness—a major theme woven into many of the biblical stories. In the cultural expectations of their world (and in too many societies still today) a woman's value was judged by her role as the bearer of children, particularly male children. When a woman was childless, she suffered cultural shame and the entire family lost standing.

Hannah was the second wife of a good man, but even the affection of an unusually tender husband was no comfort for the emptiness of her womb; Hannah was barren and she was heartbroken. As the story goes, during a visit to the sacred tent of meeting in Shiloh, Hannah wept and prayed so fervently that the priest, Eli, accused her of being drunk. (Don't get me started on this insensitivity!) As Hannah begged and prayed through her tears, she promised God that, if she could have a son, she would offer him back to God. In other words, Hannah "tithed" her firstborn son.

The priest, to his credit, listened to Hannah's pain and sent her home with a blessing, with hope for the Lord's intervention on her behalf. Her prayer was answered and she became pregnant within the year. After her time of waiting with tears, now Hannah waited in joy for the delivery of God's promise. Hannah was pregnant with the confidence that God was doing a remarkable, new thing in her life—and in the life of all Israel.

> The bows of the mighty are broken, but the feeble gird on strength . . .
> The Lord makes poor and makes rich; he brings low and also exalts.
> The barren has borne seven but she who has many children is forlorn.
> He raises up the poor from the dust and lifts up the needy from the ash heap . . . (1 Sam 2).

Hannah sings this song of praise, this psalm of redemption, this prophetic refrain of amazing grace in the midst of the startling reversal of her life. Hannah's barrenness is transformed into abundance as she becomes the mother of Samuel, one of the greatest leaders Israel would ever know. Hannah is one of the faithful, timeless heroes within the biblical tradition.

I also love the story of Ruth and Naomi. Each woman is a strong, important character and each one reminds us God always has been about the business of bringing unlikely people together, redeeming impossible situations, and creating startling reversals.

Naomi was a daughter of Israel and also barren. Earlier in her life she had been a wife and a mother but now she is a woman alone who has buried her husband and both her sons. She has been full but now she is empty. "Do not call me Naomi anymore," she says to her kinsfolk. "Call me Mara now for my life has turned to bitterness" (1:20–21). But she does have Ruth, a faithful daughter-in-law who refuses to leave the mother of her heart. Ruth is another woman who understands grief and emptiness and who clings to this one she loves, refusing to be parted. (Naomi's proffered blessing that the Lord deal "kindly" to these daughters as they had dealt "kindly" to her family comes from the Hebrew word *hesed*—a strong word of steadfast love and compassion often used to describe God.)

Ruth is a faithful Gentile, but some Israelites would always consider Ruth the Moabite to be an outsider, even an enemy of Israel. (Moabites were banned from the assembly of the Lord because of their ancestors' sins, and several biblical references indicate that Israelites held Ruth's people and her culture in contempt.)

When Naomi and Ruth encountered Boaz, they found a man of privilege and power who, in a risky act of grace, became protector and provider for these two vulnerable women. Out of the fullness of his fields, they found food. Out of the fullness of his character, they found respect. Out of the fullness of his commitment, they found a new home where their emptiness was transformed into abundance. Even in this strongly patriarchal society, here is a beautiful story of the tenacious faithfulness of women, the strong goodness of men, and the mysterious work of God weaving grace into the torn fabric of a life, God's way of startling reversals.

There is one fascinating twist in the plot of the story of Ruth that most of us modern readers miss because of the English translations of the Hebrew language. Listen to this advice of the mother-in-law to her daughter-in-law:

> Naomi her mother-in-law said to her: "My daughter, I need to seek some security for you, so that it may be well with you.
>
> Now here is our kinsman Boaz . . . See he is winnowing barley tonight at the threshing floor. Now wash and anoint yourself, and put on your best clothes and go down to the threshing floor; but do not make yourself known to the man until he has finished eating and drinking.
>
> When he lies down, observe the place where he lies; then, go and uncover his feet and lie down; and he will tell you what to do."
>
> Ruth said to Naomi: "All that you tell me, I will do" (3:1–5).

"Uncovering the feet" is a euphemism for uncovering a man's genitals, so this story suggests Ruth made herself sexually available to Boaz in a daring entreaty for his commitment and protection.[1] Naomi and Ruth manipulated Boaz, not necessarily in a harmful way, but in one of the few ways women of their day were able to get what they needed. (Women's employment of their sexuality in the service of their needs, their families, or their very survival continues to this very day in too many societies.)

1. Robertson-Farmer, "The Book of Ruth." See the lengthy discussion on page 926.

So Boaz married Ruth, Ruth bore a son, Naomi became a grand-mother, and David, the greatest king Israel would ever know, emerged from this unlikely heritage: redemption all around. Kathleen Robertson-Farmer points out that the book of Ruth is eighty-five verses long, but the words "redeem" and/or "redemption" are used some twenty-three times. God's way of doing business is to redeem every situation, every person, every community of people and to bring all things into the fullness and *shalom* of God's ultimate purposes for creation.

As You Read the Psalms

Psalm 41 completes Book One of the Psalms and begins much as Psalm 1 begins, with beatitude. "Happy are those who consider the poor; the LORD delivers them in the day of trouble. The LORD protects them and keeps them alive; they are called happy in the land." The psalmist affirms once again a crucial theme of the first book of the Psalms, that is, the gracious and compassionate God remains particularly committed to the poor and afflicted, to the humble, meek, and oppressed. This refrain is reproduced within Liberation theologies, explaining that when we commit ourselves to deliver those who struggle, we are behaving the way God behaves. Thus we too are blessed as we emulate the compassion of Creator-Redeemer-Sustainer.

Then our psalmist/poet details some of the treacherous acts done by his enemies, and he pleads for God's intervention and salvation. "Even my close friend whom I trusted—who ate my bread—has lifted up his heel against me" (41:9). The treachery of a close friend, a person who has shared bread and trust—this kind of "enemy" brings especial grief and sorrow. Evidently the psalmist encountered such a traitor and cries out for vindication and confirmation of his integrity in the face of false accusations. Usually the psalmists ask that God pay back the evil, but this psalmist seems to want that job himself. "Raise me up that I may repay them . . ." This request may be an expression of revenge but more likely, the one who began this psalm with a beatitude is seeking justice.

"Liberation for the oppressed means judgment upon their oppressors," Clinton McCann observes,[2] not just for personal vindictiveness, but also for God's own reputation. The psalmists cry out for justice not only for their own reputation, but also as a way to vindicate God's holy name.

2. McCann, "Psalms," 848.

When John tells the story of Jesus' passion, he frames Judas' betrayal of Jesus as a fulfillment of Psalm 41. When Jesus shares the final meal with his disciples, he says one of them would betray him, and then Jesus wraps a towel around his waist and kneels to wash their feet—even and significantly—the feet of his betrayer.

> I do not speak of all of you. I know the ones I have chosen. But it is so that the Scripture may be fulfilled: "He who eats my bread has lifted up his heel against me."
>
> From now on I am telling you before it comes to pass, so that when it does occur, you may believe that I am he (John 13:18–19).

For John, Jesus' act of humility and death demonstrated God's holiness. God did not take revenge upon the "enemies" of Jesus; rather, God vindicated the Holy Name by defeating treachery and death with resurrection and life.

Each of the five books of the Psalms completes its message with doxology, thus the conclusion of Book One is a song of praise. "Blessed be the LORD, the God of Israel, from everlasting to everlasting. Amen and Amen."

As You Read the New Testament

The Acts of the Apostles, Luke's well-told story of the early days of the church, follows the gospel that bears Luke's name. Luke's effort was a mammoth work by a brilliant theologian. Even Jewish scholars study his writings in order to try to discern some of the history of Judaism around the turn of the first century. Luke comes in a close second behind Paul as the most prolific author of our NT.

As you read the sermons in Acts, remember Luke said clearly that the stories he recorded were handed down to him by "eyewitnesses" (Luke 1). The sermons in Acts were composed from those oral traditions, they were words put into the mouths of the preachers. This is not a bad thing by any means; it simply reminds us that Scripture is not history according to our modern ideas of history. We read these stories with the eyes of faith—faith in the integrity and faithfulness of the authors and confidence that God is still speaking through these ancient words. Also remember the notion of "reading backwards" that we've explored before. Luke knew well the Hebrew Scriptures and weaves this story of Israel into the new fabric of Christ and the church. Watch for all the ways he does that, especially in the sermons of Paul and Peter.

Acts 15 relates the first church convention portraying leaders across geography and theology getting together to hash out a unified message. Some differences in perspective and emphasis were (and are) healthy and appropriate—the story is much too big to force it into one neat box. But some differences go too far and the church must discern together, and in tandem with the Holy Spirit, what is its basic orthodoxy. The church council we read about this week responded to a theological difference they judged to be dangerous. "Certain individuals came down from Judea and were teaching the brothers, 'Unless you are circumcised according to the custom of Moses, you cannot be saved'" (Acts 15:1). Recall we saw this same tension when we read Paul's letter to the Galatians.

As You Read the Gospel

Living in The Story takes us through the Gospel of John for a second cycle beginning this week. This time we will read more slowly so you can soak in the beauty of John's profound Christology and symbolic storytelling.

Reflection: *Faithful Women*

The voices of biblical woman are mostly muted, filtered through the voices of the male writers of the text. Even so, women of Scripture speak with their own power, albeit from the edges and the underside of power and privilege. The women of the Bible do not necessarily show us how women *ought* to behave; rather they tell us something about how women throughout history *have acted* within their time and place, from within their own particular circumstances.

These women are not to be used as simplistic templates shaped by our own modern Western standards of acceptable or unacceptable behavior, because, for the most part, the stories of Scripture reflect the patriarchal mores of the ancient Middle East and the Roman Empire. But also, of course, woven throughout these secular influences are the religious convictions of the people of Israel. The Israelites and the church did not (and do not) exist in a vacuum. Expectations and pressures from the surrounding culture are as powerful today as they were then, and too many of us stay unaware of the many ways our culture can influence our religious understandings and practice.

Feminist scholarship critiques and questions Scripture's patriarchal bias from a female perspective in light of the cultural realities of the time as well as the eternal ideals of justice and equity. These noble ideals have not yet fully come into being in our own human reality, and they certainly do not exist in most of Scripture. They are only hinted at, only dreamed about in the stories of the women preserved for us in our Bible.

I love these stories of faithful women woven in and through the stories of power and patriarchy. Again and again, *The Story* introduces us to women who were dismissed or dishonored by their society and then experienced startling reversals of amazing grace.

- Sarah—barren in her old age bore a son of promise (Gen 21).

- Hagar—used and abused by her masters, became the mother of a nation (Gen 21).

- Tamar—cheated out of a child by the deceptions of Jacob's family, exposed their hypocrisy by her own cunning. The Gospel of Matthew honors her by including her in the genealogy of Jesus (Gen 38; Matt 1:3).

- Shiphrah and Puah—midwives in Egypt defied a pharaoh and protected the lives of the male infants, including their own deliverer, Moses (Ex 1).

- Rahab—a foreigner, an enemy who protected the spies of Israel so that her family's life was spared in the battle. She too is included in Matthew's genealogy of Jesus (Josh 2; Matt 1:5).

- Deborah—led the tribes of Israel in battle and in wisdom (Judg 4).

- The Widow of Zarephath—a poor, gracious Gentile woman shared her last bit of oil and flour with a stranger (1 Kgs 17).

- Bathsheba—raped, impregnated, and made a widow by Israel's king David; she too, with her husband, are honored by Matthew in Jesus' genealogy as "the wife of Uriah" (2 Sam 11–12; Matt 1:6).

- Elizabeth—barren and post-menopausal, bore a son, the prophet John, who prepared the way for Messiah (Luke 1).

- Mary—young, poor, powerless, unmarried, but chosen nevertheless to become the mother of Jesus. Mary, like Hannah, sang a psalm of poetic prophecy praising God's startling reversals of grace (Luke 1 and 2).

"What God is doing is none of our business and beyond our control," my friend, Suzanne Stabile,[3] taught me. I don't particularly like that notion because I would much rather know *what* God is doing, *why* God is doing whatever it is, and *how long it will take*. But such knowing rarely (if ever) happens for us humans. There is something, though, that is most definitely our "business." Our *business* is our *calling*: our vocation, our ministry, our life, and our own story. Even when our lives seem out of our control, even when the chapters of our lives make unexpected plot twists, we can hold on to hope that God is working in and through us and we can trust that somehow or another, in God's mercy and mystery, our one little part will make a difference.

As women of faith living in the twenty-first century in the nations of the West, we have unique opportunity and special responsibility to step up to the fullness of our lives, to grow up into our full humanity. Those of us who enjoy some privilege and power, those of us who have found our own voice, must speak and stand and advocate for our sisters who continue to live with oppression, violence, and disrespect. When our feeble efforts of faith intersect God's infinite, immense faithfulness then we too can be about God's business—breaking the bows of the mighty and empowering the weak, lifting up the poor and challenging the rich, intersecting darkness with light, love, and hope, interrupting barrenness with abundance and grace, creating rich, diverse community.

So as we go about our living, we can ask ourselves, does our business look anything like God's work of surprising grace and God's way of startling reversals? I hope so. God is on the move doing all sorts of surprising things in our lives and in the lives of all kinds of people all around us. Will we be a part of *that* story?

---

3. Find out more about Suzanne Stabile's work teaching the Enneagram at Life in the Trinity Ministry @ https://www.lifeinthetrinityministry.com.

Week 26

Samuel

First Samuel 4–14
Psalm 11
Psalm 59
Psalm 61
Psalm 71
Acts 16–18
John 2–3

As You Read the Old Testament

READING SOME OF THESE ancient stories about Israel and the Ark of the Covenant makes me think of *Indiana Jones and the Raiders of the Lost Ark*. These old stories seem to engage in some of the same sort of magical thinking Hollywood has created about the power of this strange and holy relic. Remember our sacred scriptures are not verbatim words from God but rather the gathered and evolving wisdom of a community set in its own time and place.

Those of us of a certain age might notice this little event tucked away in 1 Samuel 7:12. "Then Samuel took a stone and set it up . . . and named it Ebenezer; for he said, 'Thus far the LORD has helped us.'" Sound familiar? You may have sung this puzzling little phrase, "Here I raise my Ebenezer, hither by thy help I've come," in a beloved church hymn.[1] I sang those words about "Ebenezer" for years before I learned what they meant and where they came from!

---

1. Robert Robinson, "Come Thou Fount of Every Blessing," 1758.

These chapters in First Samuel introduce us to the first king of Israel and give us the backstory of Saul and how he became king. I always find it poignant to read this explanation about why the people thought they needed a human king.

> But the people refused to listen to the voice of Samuel; they said, "No! but we are determined to have a king over us, so that we also may be like other nations, and that our king may govern us and go out before us and fight our battles (1 Sam 8:19).

"So that we may be like other nations." It makes me sad to hear similar sentiments lived out in some current day churches of the United States. How tempting it is to blend in with the pervasive culture of our society! It's all too easy us to confuse what it means to be the people of God with what it means to be an American. I cringe at the conflations everywhere around me.

As You Read the Psalms

Psalm 71 sings like a grandparent's prayer.

> O God, from my youth you have taught me and I still proclaim your wondrous deeds. So even to old age and gray hairs, O God, do not forsake me until I proclaim your might to the generations to come (71:17–18).
>
> Upon you I have leaned from my birth; it was you who took me from my mother's womb. My praise is continually of you (71:6).

Those of us who have earned some gray hairs come from a lifetime of experiences that shape our perspectives. We carry a long vision that allows us insights that were not possible when we were younger.

Father Richard Rohr[2] often talks about "the two halves of life" as a paradigm for growing older. During the first half of our lives, we build our sense of identity and security. During the second half, we have more time and some practical wisdom to interpret the lessons of life and discover some meaning and the purpose from those experiences. This is also the perspective of our psalmist: his life of trust allows him to stay grounded in the now as well as to hold onto hope for the future. May the faith of all us "gray hairs" also share such a witness to the coming generations.

2. Rohr, *Falling Upward*.

As you read, consider how cultural notions of "honor and shame" have been significant, complex values in many human societies throughout human history. The biblical concept of shame is much deeper than our Western notion of personal embarrassment or guilt. In his helpful little book exploring honor and shame throughout the Psalms, Jayson Georges says:

> When the righteous experience shame (either personally or corporately), this is a problem. Israel's shame violates the moral order established in the Sinai covenant—the faithful should be rewarded with blessings, favor, and honor . . . [3]

The shame a person or a nation endures is often considered to be unfair and unendurable.

Even today in some twenty-first century societies, a woman who has been assaulted (even through no fault of her own) is thought to have brought unforgiveable "shame" to a family or an entire village. Sometimes the "remedy" might be violence and annihilation of the attackers. Other times the solution may be violence against the victim who is an ever-present reminder of the community's shame. Throughout history, humans have attempted payback as balance and retribution, an "eye for an eye and a tooth for a tooth" kind of karmic justice. Within our skewed human perspective, this tit-for-tat violence is thought to restore honor.

Consider another example of an honor-shame culture at work much closer to home for American Christians. For most of our nation's history, white Christians have been a dominant force. During the twentieth century, Protestants reluctantly made room for Catholics to share some political and cultural influence; then later these Christians allowed some Jews to share in this societal power. As the twenty-first century dawned in the U.S., however, a wide variety of people from numerous ethnic, cultural, and religious backgrounds had begun to gain power—both as elected officials across the nation and as cultural influencers. The earlier dominance of white Christianity was diluted.

All Christians were forced to adapt to these cultural shifts, but white evangelicals, in particular, felt this loss of power and influence as a loss of "honor." Those who have felt this "shame" feel wronged and persecuted and have sometimes expressed their complaints in language similar to the psalmists. "My enemies speak concerning me, and those who watch for my life consult together. They say, 'Pursue and seize that person whom

3. Georges, *Psalms: An Honor-Shame Paraphrase*, 248.

God has forsaken, for there is no one to deliver'" (71:10–11). Unlike most of the psalmists, however, some of these Christians have turned to political "saviors" to rescue them from their cultural shame and restore their honor. This is always a mistake.

The psalmists' deep commitment to Covenant God allowed them to put their trust in divine justice and not in human vindication. Even if they wished for payback and shook their fists in protest, even while they complained about mistreatment, still the poets of Israel were patient to wait for divine right-making instead of enacting human revenge. And while they waited, they praised God.

> Salvation in the Psalms is not just forgiveness . . . but it also involves vindication of honor, restoration of status, deliverance from shame, and the humiliation of enemies . . .
>
> Psalms of praise glorify God for benevolence, patronage, faithfulness, covenant loyalty, favor and generosity as a trustworthy covenant partner.[4]

Any of us who wear the name of Christ constantly must recommit ourselves to the upside-down-and-right-side-up way of the cross. The human shame the Christ endured in persecution and crucifixion was transformed into cosmic honor, power, and glory in the resurrection. And so "we are not ashamed of the gospel, for it is the power of God . . ." (Rom 1:16–17).

As You Read the New Testament

> Paul stood in front of the Areopagus in Athens and said . . . "Since we are God's offspring, we ought not to think that the deity is like gold, or silver, or stone, an image formed by the art and imagination of mortals.
>
> "While God has overlooked the times of human ignorance, now he commands all people everywhere to repent, because God has fixed a day on which he will have the world judged in righteousness by a man whom he has appointed, and of this he has given assurance to all by raising him from the dead."
>
> When they heard of the resurrection of the dead, some scoffed; but others said, "We will hear you again about this" (Acts 17:22–32).

---

4. Georges, *Psalms,* loc. 136 of 814.

I'm not a bit surprised "some scoffed." We're talking Greece here where Plato's philosophical ideas had deeply influenced Paul's hearers. As a matter of fact, Plato's ideas have influenced western civilization throughout these many centuries and have even shaped Christian theology.

"Resurrection" wasn't a category in Platonic thought. There were, of course, plenty of stories about the gods who sometimes would interfere with death and bring someone back from Hades, but those were only stories, children's tales. These tales were nothing to found a faith on. This was nothing to build a life on.

Theologians and philosophers of Israel also had been contemplating the after life, and during the last few centuries before Christ, many had come to new understandings. Within Israel, there *was* a category of resurrection but, for them, resurrection was part of the final act of God that would bring all creation to completion; would bring all things to their appropriate end. Resurrection, in this Jewish way of thinking, was eschatological and apocalyptic. Resurrection was about the end of time.

Paul on the other hand, likely an educated man both in Jewish theology and Greek philosophy, was grasped with a whole new way of understanding God's mystery of life, death, and resurrected life in the death and resurrection of Jesus.

As You Read the Gospel

John (like the earlier Paul) makes meaning of the Christ through his resurrection faith. John's gospel is filled with "signs"—word pictures, symbolic acts, images, and pointers that give us a glimpse of something beyond our imagination. John's gospel points us to "life," and life is a huge issue for John.

> And the Word became flesh and dwelt among us . . . and in him was *life*, and the life was the light of all people . . . (1:4).
>
> For God so [thusly, in this way] loved the world, God gave the only Son, so that everyone who believes in him . . . may have eternal *life* (3:16).
>
> You search the scriptures because you think that in them you have eternal life; and it is they that testify on my behalf. Yet you refuse to come to me to have *life* (5:39–40).
>
> I came that you may have *life*, and have it abundantly (10:10).
>
> I am the bread of *life* (6:48).

I am way and truth and *life* (14:6).
I am resurrection and *life* (11:25).

Over and over and over, as you read again the Gospel of John during this *Living in The Story* cycle of weeks, you will see John's passion for life, real life, true life, resurrection life.

Reflection: *Resurrection—A Whole New Thing*

As you read John's gospel you can recognize John's "mono-vision." When I had my cataracts removed, the doctor implanted new lenses in my eyes so that one lens focuses on distance vision and the other lens focuses on near vision; my eyes see with mono-vision. It may sound odd, but it's not at all a "double-vision." Rather, my brain adjusts so that it sees my world in a unity of both near and far. My brain translates the perspectives from the two different lenses into one single, whole way of seeing: *mono-vision.* John's gospel is a little like that.

As we read these stories, we realize that John shows us *both* the earthly Jesus *and* the resurrected Christ at the same time. Everything the earthly Jesus of Nazareth did and said is to be seen and understood through the lens of the risen Christ. In John's theology, divine and human are inseparable.

I think that's a helpful approach. When we are tempted to dissect and separate body and spirit, mortal and immortal, sacred and profane, it is good to let Spirit's mono-vision show us the world in a whole new way. John's gospel, the stories of Luke-Acts, the writings and sermons of Paul all articulate the core Christian confession that resurrection is a new thing God has done in the cosmos.

I've really struggled to know how to talk about resurrection. Even though resurrection is foundational to the Christian confession, it's not easy to know what it is. Maybe it will help to talk a bit about what resurrection *is not.* For example, a few years ago, I was giving the children's sermon and (once again) struggling to know how to talk about Jesus' resurrection. I think I said something like "Jesus came back from the dead" and *whoa!* you should have seen the look on one little boy's face. "Jesus was a zombie?" No, Jesus is *not* a zombie and resurrection is not weird, spooky science fiction. But resurrection *is* unspeakable mystery, a new thing.

Neither does resurrection have anything to do with our normal cycles of nature. For example, year after year, the Easter lilies in my garden come back and bloom again. For months, it looks like they are dead, no sign of life; then, lo and behold, a green sprout pushes its way up from the dirt. And then, sure enough, bright white lilies burst from their buds. Then when winter comes, the plant dies and the bulb in the soil returns to its long sleep. Resurrection is *not* about cycles of dormancy and activity, sleeping and waking, winter and spring. No, resurrection happens *outside* of nature's normal cycles; it is a whole new thing.

One more thought. Resurrection doesn't have anything to do with our *human* nature. Plato's philosophies had shaped the thinking of Paul's hearers on the Areopagus of Athens so that for them, an immortal soul inhabited the body and slipped away to another dimension at the moment of death. But that's not what Paul is talking about when he talks about resurrection. "God raised him from the dead," Paul insisted. And they scoffed.

Whether or not one believes we humans are inhabited by an immortal soul doesn't have anything to do with resurrection, because resurrection is *not* about our human nature; resurrection is about the nature of God. Because God interrupted the normal cycles of living and dying, the Christian confession is that Jesus did not "come back" from the dead but rather Jesus the Christ was raised to another plane of existence. In resurrection, Jesus entered a whole new category of being. There has never been anything like this before.

Even though death has always been part of our human experience of life, the Christian hope is that our God is larger than life and stronger than death. Resurrection demonstrates that in this Christ—the one who has brought life, abundant life, life unending—God has defeated and is destroying death. Death is not the last word.

One final thing, resurrection is not just about what happens when we die. Remember what Paul said:

> Therefore we have been buried with him by baptism into death,
> so that, just as Christ was raised from the dead by the glory of
> the Father, so we too might walk in newness of life (Rm 6:4).

Not science fiction, not nature's faithful cycles, not our normal human nature; rather resurrection brings a whole new way of living. We are buried into Christ's death and raised to walk, to live, to exist in a whole new realm, a whole new plane of existence—right here, right now. Each of us, all of us who die to ourselves, who let go of life as we have defined it; all of us who allow God's resurrection power to change us and move us, to motivate and shape us—we too are brought into a whole new category of existence.

And thus we are able to see with new eyes, a kind of divine mono-vision where we understand we are both already-and-not-yet. We are both humans made in the image of God and new creations transformed into the image of Christ. We are both dead to ourselves and alive to God. Now that is something to ground a faith in. That is something to build a life on. This is a whole new thing. Thanks be to God!

Week 27

David

As You Read the Old Testament

THIS WEEK, WE BEGIN the David stories, some of our best children's stories. We read about the shepherd boy who used his slingshot to kill a lion and a bear when they attacked his flock, the pure hearted youth singing songs of praise with his harp, the bold young man taking down a giant with a single stone shot from his sling, and the discounted youngest child who was honored above his seven handsome brothers and anointed to be king of Israel.

Who remembers the children's song about a boy named David and the giant that came tumbling down?[1] When I was a girl, my Sunday school friends and I would spin like a slingshot—"round and round and round and round"—then come tumbling down together in a giggling heap. The stories about David in the Hebrew Scriptures sometimes sound like tall tales and there is good reason for that. The genre "tall tales" usually is based in history where real people and authentic flesh-and-blood figures are lionized as over-the-top heroes. For example, there is another

---

1. Arnott, "Only a Boy Named David."

David you may recall, another David of legend who was "born'd on a mountaintop in Tennessee . . . and kilt him a b'ar when he was only three." As a child, I loved singing this song as well.[2] As stories of these actual heroes' lives were told throughout the years, they became larger than life, and the legends around them grew. Looking back, it's not always easy to distinguish fact from embellishment.

Our biblical David, though, is much more than a children's book character. When we adults read these familiar stories anew as serious students of the Bible, we uncover all sorts of unfamiliar nuance.

As You Read the Psalms

Psalm 20 is categorized as a royal psalm, a liturgical blessing offered by the priests and the people on behalf of Israel's king. "May the LORD answer you in the day of trouble! May the name of the God of Jacob set you securely on high! May God send help from the sanctuary and support you from Zion!" As much as this psalm sings confidence in the monarch, though, it clearly places trust in God, the Lord of Israel, because in the psalmist's theology, it is God who is ultimately responsible for the king's successes.

Clinton McCann provides an interesting insight about this psalm.

> On one level, it is possible to hear Psalm 20 as nothing more than a piece of ancient Judean political propaganda—that is, God is on our side and God will give us the victory.
>
> It seems to be an ancient example of the kind of thinking that is so dangerous and frightening in our day; thinking that leads people to conclude that God sanctions whatever our nation does and to label our opponents as evil empires.
>
> On the other hand, it is possible to hear Psalm 20 quite differently building upon the insights that the primary actor in the psalm is God, not the king or the people.
>
> Keeping this in mind, we can hear in Psalm 20 the lesson that the people of any nation in some sense depend on their leaders, as well as the admonition that both the people and their leaders are to depend on God.

McCann then quotes theologian James Mayes:

2. Bruns and Blackburn, "Ballad of Davy Crockett."

As Scripture, the psalm teaches the church to pray for those who hold the power of office, because they, like us, are dependent on the Lord.

It warns against ever letting our dependence on their service turn into the trust we owe to God alone. It warns against allowing their fascination with military strength to make us support policies based on trust in military might. [3]

This perspective brings to mind the important insight of Dr. Martin Luther King Jr. "The church must be reminded that it is not the master or the servant of the state, but rather the conscience of the state. [The church] must be the guide and the critic of the state, and never its tool . . ."[4]

Every Sunday, during the Prayers of the People, Christians within the Anglican tradition pray for national leaders. In our community where I lived and worshiped in 2020, we prayed for "Donald our president, and the congress and courts of these United States . . . Guide the people of this land, and of all the nations, in the ways of justice and peace, that we may honor one another and serve the common good.[5] This year, in 2021, we pray for "Joseph our president." Praying for our leaders does not suggest we support everything they do or say. Rather, we are called to pray that our leaders will behave as God would desire, in the ways of justice and peace. Since *we* cannot force any of our leaders to behave in the ways of justice and peace, as people of faith it is logical, appropriate, and right for us to ask God's intervention and guidance in the hearts and actions of leaders across the globe.

"Some boast in chariots and some in horses but we will boast in the name of the LORD our God" (20:7). The name of God represents the presence and power, the identity and character of God. It is *this* name that gives us confidence to follow our leaders when they demonstrate the divine character. It is this name that gives us the courage to resist them when they do not. We must pray for our leaders but trust in our Lord.

As You Read the New Testament

In Acts, the first twelve chapters tell stories mostly about Peter while the remaining chapters shift their focus to Paul. Luke is careful to characterize

3. McCann Jr. "Psalms," 756.

4. Martin Luther King Jr., "A Knock at Midnight."

5. *Book of Common Prayer,* 388.

them both as equally significant leaders, describing their various ministries with some intriguing similarities. Notice how Luke frames each man's healing ministry.

> Yet more than ever believers were added to the Lord, great numbers of both men and women, so that they even carried out the sick into the streets, and laid them on cots and mats, in order that Peter's shadow might fall on some of them as he came by. A great number of people would also gather from the towns around Jerusalem, bringing the sick and those tormented by unclean spirits, and they were all cured (Acts 5:14–16).
>
> God did extraordinary miracles through Paul, so that when the handkerchiefs or aprons that had touched his skin were brought to the sick, their diseases left them, and the evil spirits came out of them (Acts 19:11–12).

This week we see Paul complete his third and last missionary journey and return to Jerusalem where he began the final chapters of his life and ministry. When he was arrested by Roman authorities and tried before several different Roman courts, he claimed Roman citizenship. Appealing his case to the highest court of the Empire, Paul was then transported to Rome. (Tradition says he was martyred there by the emperor Nero.)

As You Read the Gospel

I really like the Samaritan woman in John 4. I wish I knew her name. I like her spunk and her spirit. I like her questions. I like the way she stays engaged, letting the conversation always go deeper and wider. I like her courage. I say "courage" because it was not proper for a woman to speak to a strange man in a public place, and it was not typical for Samaritans and Jews to engage in social relationships. It also took courage for her to go tell the people in her village about this man she had met; it was risky for a woman with a tarnished reputation to bear witness to the Christ. What would people think!

In John and in Acts there are two significant stories to ponder this week, the woman of Samaria and the man Paul from Tarsus. Both these stories tell about people who moved from disbelief and cynicism to faith and trust. Two stories of people who turned from resisting to following; who—because of their passion for the Christ—found courage to let their lives be radically reoriented and reshaped by the Christ.

There are countless stories of faith like this. Again and again, across the ages, around the world, untold courageous people have let themselves be changed: their beliefs, their values, their priorities, their behaviors, their assumptions, their very lives. People who really encounter the living Christ *are really* changed.

Reflection: *This Takes Courage*

Here's another story about another courageous woman, Deb Richardson-Moore.[6] Deb was a seasoned journalist living in Greenville, South Carolina, but in order to learn how to write about religion more effectively for her newspaper, she decided to attend seminary. Little did she know what God had in store for her!

After graduating seminary, Deb was called to serve at the ecumenical Triune Mercy Center in inner city Greenville. She thought she already knew about the underbelly of her city but instead found she had no clue about the reality of homelessness throughout her community. Even though she had twenty-seven years of experience and had seen all kinds of things throughout her career, she quickly recognized that it is only God's mercy that can sustain a minister in ministry. She also realized it took the courage of an entire community to step up to the entrenched challenges that convoluted the lives of their neighbors. Like the woman from Samaria, powerful witness to the good news of Jesus Christ often comes in the brokenness of real people; all of us with all of our tarnished lives.

"Treasure in clay jars," Paul called it (2 Cor 4:7), where the light of God's presence shines through our cracks and testifies to an unreasonable, unpronounceable mercy. "Christ in you: the hope of glory," Colossians 1:27 promises.

The community of Triune Mercy Center shared a vision to minister to the homeless, the down and out, victims caught in the deadly spiral of addictions. But Mercy didn't want to be just a church for only the homeless; they wanted to be *church*. Church that is authentic community where rich and poor and black and white and hung over and sober could all embrace the weight of God's mercy that bound them together.

It hasn't been easy; it takes their courage every single day. Some of the board members left because they didn't like the direction the church was going. Some of the church members left because they didn't like a

---

6. Richardson-Moore, *Weight of Mercy.*

gospel that included "those" people. Some of the homeless and addicted left because they didn't like being held accountable. But Pastor Deb marvels at the people who came, and who keep coming. They come, Deb imagines, because they have never before seen the church living out the gospel in such tangible ways.

It's hard, messy, uncomfortable, and risky for a people to become this kind of church because there are no guarantees. It reminds me of the saying "courage is resistance to fear, the mastery of fear not an absence of fear."[7] Resistance and fearfulness are completely understandable in the face of change. We can be quaking in our boots, wondering how this is going to turn out; wondering what people might think; wondering if we are doing the right thing . . . wondering, fretting, worrying. But, even so, it is in those very quaking boots where we can take our stand for what we believe is right. We stand on the promises; we stand on Christ the Rock. And thereby we find the courage to continue to stand firm and move forward.

Lance Pape says of Jesus and his followers:

> The pioneer of cruciform faith did not find the trail he blazed to be "safe" in any conventional sense of the word.
>
> Those followers who have attempted most courageously to conform their lives to the identity disclosed through the narrative of his betrayal, arrest, and brutal murder at the hands of those threatened by his way of being in the world have consistently found that the abundant life he offers is not any kind of life they can secure for themselves.[8]

In his book, *The Scandal of Having Something to Say,* Dr. Pape explores the history of Christian preaching and theorizes that the decline of the church in our modern day has at least some connection to a sad reality of milk toast preaching. Pape agrees with Karl Barth that there is a key question people often ask when they come to worship: *Is this true?*

> Is it true, this talk of a loving and good God, who is more than one of the friendly idols whose rise is so easy to account for, and whose dominion is so brief?[9]

---

7. Attributed to Mark Twain

8. Pape, *Scandal,* 8.

9. Barth, "The Need and Promise of Christian Preaching," 108.

Pape affirms that seekers "want to know if the preacher has some-thing true to say—something more than the predictable aphorisms of the little gods of the age."[10]

If a preacher can't address the burning questions that seekers ask, then what's the point? But if, with courage, the preacher proclaims and the church embodies the surprising grace of the gospel of Jesus Christ, then, in the weight of God's mercy, amazing things can (and will!) hap-pen. People find hope and unexpected joy, grace surrounds, and love abounds when they are radically reoriented and reshaped by the Christ, the "homeless, crucified one." As Pape notes, since the American church is "in the late stages of cultural eviction anyway, the church may finally be ready to go willingly 'outside' (Heb 13:13) to the homeless, crucified one."

> Disabused of faith in our own words, we may be ready at last to make our preaching conform to his scandalous word and no other (1 Cor 2:2).[11]
>
> The startling prospect emerges that the . . . situation most proper and "native" to [Christian] preaching is perpetually one of audacity and jeopardy.[12]

Courage allows us to follow this Christ *with* audacity and *within* jeopardy, come what may. Courage allows us to be reoriented and re-shaped by *his* life and *his* way. Courage allows us to proclaim—and to become—God's radical and audacious gospel.

10. Pape, *Scandal*, 11.

11. Pape, *Scandal*, 9.

12. Pape, *Scandal*, 4.

Week 28
Signs and Symbols

First Samuel 21–31
Psalm 64
Psalm 88
Psalm 142
Acts 24–28
John 6

As You Read the Old Testament

THE STORY OF DAVID is central to the Jewish texts because David is the pivot of Jewish history. David is writ large in First and Second Samuel and in the books of the Chronicles. At first these were "no people," then they were a wandering, homeless people, and then a loosely knit tribal people. It was in David that Israel became a nation—a united kingdom with a monarch, a capital city, and a homeland. It was with David that Israel found respect among the nations and rest from their enemies. The David Years were, indeed, some of Israel's golden years.

As You Read the Psalms

The psalms speak the truth of lament that transcends nations and centuries. "I cry to the LORD . . . I make supplication . . . I pour out my complaint . . . no one cares for me" (Ps 142:1–4). Again and again, throughout the history of the world, people have suffered oppression and affliction.

Again and again, they have cried out for deliverance. Does God intervene in history? Does God care? This perennial question only faith can answer.

People of faith have dealt with that dilemma since the beginning of time and have forged their own answers on the anvils of their own experience. The stories of faith, faith-*less*-ness, and faith-*full*-ness within the Hebrew Christian Scriptures express this human drama. The psalms especially represent the gamut of responses to this multidimensional reality of living.

"The righteous will surround me for you will deal bountifully with me" (142:7). It is this hope that helps correct the earlier cry, "no one cares." When our cries join together with the cries of the oppressed, faith tells us that—in some unimaginable way—God will see, God will hear, God will know, and God will come (Ex 3:7–8). When our own work for justice joins together with the ministry of others who pursue righteousness, sometimes it is *we* who become the answer to the prayer of the oppressed.

As You Read the New Testament

These chapters conclude Luke's stories about the life and ministry of Paul as told in the Acts of the Apostles. As you read Paul's words related here, notice how faithful Paul remains to the core message of the gospel. Yes, he makes some legal arguments in his own defense, but mostly he takes every opportunity to speak kingdom truth and to speak truth to power. He finds words that just may pierce a hard heart and implant themselves like seeds in a fallow field. As a Christian preacher and apologist, Paul used words to point beyond themselves toward unseen realities.

As a preacher and a writer, my own gift, burden, and joy is to try to give language to mystery. I want to trust that, by God's grace, willing listeners may shift their perspectives and understandings (might even change their behavior!) My preaching professor, Lance Pape, says:

> The hope and the wager for the Christian preacher is that this language that comes to us in the Bible mediates a word that is God's true word for us and for God's church.
>
> It is the bold hope that, against all odds, we have been given something more to say than our own best human thoughts.[1]

---

1 Pape, *Scandal*, 56. This term "wager" comes from philosopher Paul Ricoeur and his original assertion that hermeneutical truth is a wager. See Ricoeur's *Symbolism of Evil*, 355.

I want to craft and release words that are more than my own human thoughts, believing that Spirit-breathed words can be breathed into life in someone else's life by the Spirit's mysterious power. Richard Lischer writes, "The preacher *makes* words, approximately fifteen-hundred of them on a Sunday morning, three-million in a career, and over the long haul of ministry, she speaks into existence an alternative world." [2]

How is it a preacher can "speak into existence an alternative world"? How does meaning grow in the space of a life that is womb and soil and potter's wheel? How can words spoken within a particular time/place/people spark an encounter with the Absolute? How does the presence of God take root in what (for all the world) looks like barren soil? How does the breath of God blow over the dark valleys of our lives, resurrecting hope, meaning, and a future? *It is all mystery.* The sermons, parables, poems, and visions of Scripture invite us into another world, another reality, into the infinite world of the God *beyond* history who has acted and continues to act *within* history. The world of the text invites us to see all our smaller human realities within the cosmic reality of the Eternal One.

Within the mystery of the biblical text and its proclamation, we can be configured and reconfigured according to this reality to which the text bears witness. And we are invited to invite others to share in this ever-new journey with us. It is journey to life and love and abundance. It is journey in mystery, hope, and joy.

As you read this week, note this little phrase of Paul's in chapter 24: "I cheerfully make my defense . . ." Again and again, we see Paul treated unjustly and even violently, but we never see him hopeless. Paul reminds us that God's faithfulness is not a magic wand making all our troubles disappear. God's love and our consequent peace do not come *after* the hardship, rather we are immersed in love and "peace that passes understanding" (Phil 4:7) within the very *midst* of our trials. This peace-that-doesn't-make-sense keeps us (like Paul) grounded and hopeful and faithful. The very real presence of such peace and love allows us continually and confidently to put our trust in God no matter our circumstance, to place our faith in the one who will never disappoint.

Also as you read, note Paul's description of the growing Jesus Movement as "the Way." Before the church became structure and institution, before it was tamed and domesticated, it was an ever-flowing, vibrant spring of life. May we seek to become people of *this* Way, the Way of the

---

2. Lischer, *End of Words*, 104.

Christ where Resurrection Life continues to be poured into every death, every darkness, and every dead end.

As You Read the Gospel

John's early chapters are sometimes referred to as the Book of Signs because in these stories the narrator designates Jesus' acts of wonders as signs (rather than miracles). A sign points to something. A sign signals something that is coming or symbolizes something unseen. And the signs that John highlights, the acts of wonder he describes delve into the core of Jesus' identity and the nature of the Christ. For John, the signs demonstrate the Creator's remarkable, hands-on intersection with creation. The signs suggest the mystery of God *being* present in the *being* of Jesus. *I Am*—John's Jesus tells us repeatedly.

I Am the Light of the world—spoken in the context of the healing of a blind man. *I Am the Resurrection and the Life*—spoken to Mary grieving the death of her brother, Lazarus. *I Am the Bread of Life*—spoken to those whose stomachs were filled with the multiplied loaves and fishes. John's brilliant and creative use of *figural* speech and metaphorical action weaves itself all through this profound gospel.

The opening prologue of *Logos* sets the tone so that we know this one who is *Word* will mystify and astound us. Then very quickly, in chapter 2, John has Jesus in the Temple, challenging the merchants and the moneychangers. Situating the Temple story here at the beginning introduces John's understanding that this one, Jesus, is now, figurally, the *new* Temple, the Living Temple where God's glory dwells. The Living Temple where heaven and earth meet. The Living Temple where redemption happens.

In the story of the cleansing of the Temple, John quotes Psalm 69 as if the eternal Word, the *Logos* was the speaker of the words of the psalmist: "Zeal for your house will consume me." Richard Hays explains:

> When John tells us that Jesus was "speaking of the Temple of his body," a light goes on: the Evangelist . . . is teaching his readers how to read.
>
> He is teaching us to read *figurally*, teaching us to read Scripture *retrospectively*, in light of the resurrection.

Only on such a reading does it make sense to see the Jerusalem Temple as prefiguring the truth now definitively embodied in the crucified and risen Jesus."[3]

Finding truth and meaning in Scripture *always* requires wisdom, reason, discernment, and the guidance of the Holy Spirit. This principle of learning how to read is always true for students of the NT, but it is especially true of the Gospel according to John.

As we post-Easter readers continue to be taught how to read; as we Enlightenment rationalists continue to rediscover figures and symbols and poetry; as we the church continue to embody the presence of the Holy in our own flawed way, the Gospel according to John is rich resource indeed.

Reflection: *Symbols in John's Gospel*

Years ago when my husband traveled across Turkey, the bus stopped near a little village off the beaten track. There was a small lake, clear and clean, with a stony bottom. And there was a shrine, marking the place as special, maybe even sacred in a long ago day. Locals think the shrine might have been built by the Hittite people; old, very, very old. But the shrine is not what impressed Jerry. Rather it was the natural spring that fed that little lake; the spring of water the shrine designates and celebrates as special and life giving, maybe even sacred. Water may well have been flowing from this spring for more than 4,000 years. Think of it—before Jesus, before King David, maybe even before Abraham—ever fresh, ever flowing water, giving life to a parched land and to a thirsty people.

We see images of water woven throughout the Gospel according to John. Here is Jesus at the annual Festival of Booths that included rituals of water, religious rites invoking God's blessing of water for the fall harvest. Jesus cries out, "Let anyone who is thirsty come to me and drink; for out of his heart shall flow rivers of living water" (7:38). Here is Jesus with the Samaritan woman at Jacob's well:

> Those who drink of the water that I give them will never be thirsty. The water I give will become in them a spring of water gushing up to eternal life (4:13–14).

3. Hays, *Reading Backwards*, 86.

When John's Jesus speaks of living water, we are immersed in a biblical sea of water-word pictures that portray *The Story* from Genesis all the way through to Revelation.

- The Spirit hovered over the waters of chaos. God separated the waters from the land, and it was good (Gen 1).

- The springs of the earth burst out of their bounds and chaos reigned once again until an ark of salvation rode the waves to safety and new beginnings (Gen 9).

- The waters of the Red Sea parted and God's people walked through the very center of the seas of chaos—out of slavery and into freedom (Ex 10).

- Water flowed abundantly from a rock to sustain the lives of God's wandering people (Ex 17; Deut 8).

- God is the Lord of all creation who walks on the water, who rules over that chaos and makes a pathway through the seas (Job 9:8; Ps 77:20; Isa 43:16).

- And this Jesus—the one sent from God, the one who brings God's presence to us—Jesus too is pictured as walking on the seas and calming the storms of chaos (Mark 6:45–52; Matt 14:22–33; John 6:16–21).

- One of these days, in *The Story* of stories, when creation is made complete with all its intended goodness, the seas of chaos will be no more. All creation will be gathered around "the river of the water of life, bright as crystal, flowing from the throne of God and of the Lamb" (Rev 22:1).

Scripture teems with rich images of earthy, tangible realities that point to the unimagined reality of God's way, of God's being. Throughout Scripture, symbols whisper, hint, glimpse, and suggest a reality that is so real we mortals cannot fathom it. Still we can have a sense of something beyond ourselves, in part, because the symbols are grounded in our own temporal reality, grounded in this world.

John's gospel in particular overflows with symbols, images, and signs that point beyond themselves to something beyond our human ability to speak or to know. John is a master at using the things we know to teach us something about what we cannot comprehend.

God is like light.
Spirit is like water.
Christ is like bread.

Christ is wine.
Spirit is wind.
God is life.

Jesus is Temple, Bread, Light, Life,
Shepherd, Door, Truth, Vine.
Jesus is Word.

John's gospel teems with symbols, images, and signs that deepen our awareness and widen our experience.

Words are not things; words are symbols. Words point to the things we want to describe. Words fitly spoken can conjure up a whole world of imagination and experience. All of Scripture can do this. All the words of Scripture can be understood as symbols that help create a space where we are invited to move beyond our small realities and encounter the one who is Real Reality.

Sometimes linguists and scholars talk about how Scripture "projects a world." This notion of "projecting a world" imagines that it is in the space between the world of the Bible and our own human experience where we make meaning; where we find that glimpse of Real Reality. Meaning doesn't so much happen *within* the Bible itself as much as it is found in the *intersection* between the words of the Bible and the embodied word of our real lives. Meaning is generated in the soil of human experiences, personal relationships, and social conditions: our ways of perceiving the world. It is here in this (often chaotic) mix that meaning true and transformative can be created by the living Word and the hovering Spirit.

The Gospel of John asks one primary question: *who is this Jesus?* Again and again, this way and that, John explores and probes this one question. Again and again, John reveals what he has come to believe is the key, this core truth: *Jesus is the one sent from God.* Jesus is the one who has come to reveal God, who embodied the Divine so that we embodied-beings can get a flesh-and-blood glimpse of what love and grace, what compassion and power actually look like in Real Reality.

When we faithful readers present ourselves and expose ourselves to the Scriptures, when we let our own stories intersect *The Story*, when we make ourselves available to the Spirit, we can claim with a certain audacity that God will come to us—not by our manipulations or our conjurings but rather in mystery, in grace, and in holy space.

God be Light to us. Christ be Bread to us. Spirit be Water to us. One God forever and ever, Amen.

Week 29

David's House

Second Samuel 1–10
First Chronicles 1–19
Psalm 56
Psalm 63
Psalm 115
Psalm 122
First Thessalonians
John 7–8

As You Read the Old Testament

SOME FOUR HUNDRED YEARS after David, the last king in David's line was executed by the Babylonians. Many of the people of Israel were marched across the Fertile Crescent as captives and plunder. Jerusalem was leveled and the Temple destroyed in 586 BCE. Once again God's people had no home, no land, no center, and in this crisis, there was a very real possibility that they would once again become no people.

Living in The Story has talked numerous times about this history, about how Exile was such a significant turning point for Israel. We've considered how Israel's oral histories were finally written and preserved onto scrolls, then how their defining stories were composed, gathered, and edited, and how, in Exile, Israel's scholars reflected on their meaning for a new time and a vastly changed circumstance. The Messianic Hope was birthed from the dark womb of Exile. Even though the dynasty of David would never again look like it did in their golden years, these people of faith and flexibility continued to dig into hope, hold on to faith, and stand on the promises.

Living in The Story adds First Chronicles to the reading cycles this week. The Chronicler probably composed his account of Israel's history as much as 500 years after the events took place. As you read, watch for differences between the ways different theological historians relate past events. (Or maybe "historical theologians" might be a better term.)

For example, while the writer of the Kings tells us some of the sad, sordid details in the life of David, the Chronicler does not. The Chronicles version of the history of the kings offers its own understanding of the significance of Israel's monarchy.

As You Read the Psalms

Psalm 56 acknowledges both the grittiness of life and the grace of God. The psalmist has "enemies" who constantly "stir up strife, lurk, and watch my steps." The Message paraphrased it this way: "they smear my reputation and huddle to plot my collapse. They gang up on me . . ." (Ps 56:5–6 MSG). This kind of conflict within our relationships can tear us apart and wear us down until we have no emotional energy left.

I've been there—feeling trampled, disrespected, disregarded. Have you? But in the midst of such grinding turmoil, the psalmist sees this grace: "You have kept count of my tossings; you put my tears in your bottle. Are they not in your record?" (56:8) I love this image! Each one of our tears gathered in a bottle and remembered-honored-redeemed by the Holy One.

The New International Version notes that the Hebrew word here refers to a wine skin. *God gathers our tears within a wine skin.* This image of wine skin makes me appreciate the thought all the more as I consider the bitter-sweetness of the Eucharist, the wine of communion that re-members/honors the blood of Christ. Tears and sweat, blood and water mingled into that which is redemptive and salvific. There is much to ponder here.

"In God (whose word I praise), in the LORD (whose word I praise), in God I trust. I am not afraid. What can a mere mortal do to me?" (56:10–11) This psalm teaches us something crucial about faith. It's not so much that we *have* faith. It's not so much that we *believe* certain propositions. It's not like the simplistic bumper sticker, "God said it; I believe it; that settles it." Rather biblical faith means *trusting* in the one who is trustworthy. It's about placing our faith in the one who is faithful, the one who keeps promises.

Theologian Clinton McCann lays out the question of the ancient psalmist and reframes it for us moderns.

> Psychologists and theologians alike tell us that we must believe in something. A perennial human question is not whether we shall trust but what or whom we shall trust.
>
> A persistent temptation, of course, is to trust ourselves, our abilities or achievements, our resources, as do the psalmist's opponents . . .[1]

McCann does not say we shouldn't have confidence in our abilities. Rather he encourages us to consider, who is the Creator of our abilities? What is the ground and foundation of our faith? "When I am afraid, I put my trust in you . . ." This "putting" is the active, intentional work we do as people of faith, constantly challenging ourselves to reorient ourselves toward the Source and Goal of our being. To consciously, intentionally, and repeatedly place our trust in one who is "for us," and beyond us, and with us.

"You have delivered my soul from death, and my feet from falling, so that I may walk before God in the light of life" (56:13). John's Jesus proclaims, "I am the light of the world. Whoever follows me will never walk in darkness but will have the light of life." *And the darkness cannot overcome it* (John 1:5). This Reality invites us, calls us, compels us to keep our own promises and to offer abundant thanks and praise to the God of all life.

As You Read the New Testament

First Thessalonians may well be our earliest NT document. Recall Luke's stories of Paul's second missionary journey as recorded in Acts 16 and 17. In this letter of First Thessalonians, Paul refers to some of the experiences he had while in Philippi, Thessalonica, and Athens.

Tales of conversion and conflict pepper the work of Paul as he expanded the message of Jesus across the Jewish Diaspora. Acts tells us that Paul's practice always was to preach first in whatever synagogue might house a congregation of Jews. His message that proclaimed Jesus as the Jewish Messiah sometimes was received with joy; oftentimes it was

1. McCann, "Psalms," 903.

rejected. With rebuff, Paul moved on to bring the good news of welcome to pagans and Gentiles. As you may imagine, expanding the perimeter of God's grace and including Gentiles in the community of Christ was a highly controversial endeavor.

Hardship can make a friendship all the deeper. Paul's clear affection for the Thessalonians reveals something of his pastor's heart.

> As you know and as God is our witness, we never came with words of flattery or with a pretext for greed; nor did we seek praise from mortals, whether from you or from others, though we might have made demands as apostles of Christ.
>
> But we were gentle among you, like a nurse tenderly caring for her own children. So deeply do we care for you that we are determined to share with you not only the gospel of God but also our own selves, because you have become very dear to us (1:5–8).

Paul's epistles offer us pastors an excellent example of servant leadership. They show all of us how to speak truth with courage, humility, love, and compassion.

As You Read the Gospel

John's Jesus is always both/and: both human and divine, both mortal and eternal, both limited and infinite. In their own ways, the other three gospels also tell the Christ story with this both/and perspective, but John weaves heaven and earth together in a unique and intriguing narrative.

John's Jesus can tell the future and reads people's minds. He is fully in charge of his own death, walking determinedly to the cross, the Good Shepherd "laying down his life" for his flock (10:11). Even so, the Gospel according to John most pointedly speaks of his humanity: this Jesus becomes tired and thirsty, this Jesus bleeds and dies like every other human who has ever been nailed to a cross.

John uses dualism, a kind of *double-entendre* to help communicate this both/and reality of John's Jesus. In the story of Nicodemus, for example, Jesus explains that one must be "born again/born from above." The Greek phrase means *both* either/or *and* both/and; Jesus and Nicodemus were using the same words but communicating different aspects of reality. Later in that same conversation, Jesus says he will be "lifted up," the meaning of which, we come to discover, is both lifted up on a cross and lifted up by God in exaltation. Responsible readers must always keep in mind this dual vision of the gospel storytellers in order to read appropriately. The Jesus of the gospels is always both Jesus of Nazareth and the exalted Christ.

Reflection: *David's House*

As we read the stories of David this week, we come across this little story in Second Samuel 7. Once you start unpacking it, it's surprising how many layers there are. David lives in a "house of cedar" (a palace) and proposes to build a "house" (a temple) for Yahweh. Temple building is one of the things kings do; yes, surely to honor God but also (maybe) to try to control God, to use God as a way to legitimate the king's power.

But then Nathan the prophet receives—and delivers to the king—an oracle from the Lord of hosts. Thus says the Lord, *"I have not asked for a house. I do not want a temple. I Am God on the move. I have tabernacled among you, moving about with the people of Israel wherever you have gone. But I will not be confined in your box, no matter how beautiful. I will not be limited by geography or architecture or politics. I am sovereign. I am free. I Am who I Am.*

"Do you think you can build me a house? No! I Am the one who will build you into a house, secure your reign and the kingdom forever. And I will be one who will never take my steadfast love away from you and all your descendants forever." Thus says the Lord.

It's a fascinating reversal. God took David from a pasture, raised him up to be king, and made him lord and savior of the people in the kingdom of Israel. David's house changed the course of Israel's history. David is the pivot.

Here's another layer. In the gospels, the Messianic hope was embodied in Jesus the Messiah. Christian theologians came to understand that God was doing a brand new thing in Jesus the Christ, the Son of David. In their theological reflections, Jesus is the one whom God took from a stable, raised up from a cross, and made to be Lord and Savior of all God's people in an ever-widening understanding of the kingdom of God. Jesus is the one of whom the angel in Luke said, "the Lord God will give to him the throne of his ancestor David . . . and of his kingdom there will be no end" (Luke 1:32–33). It is in Jesus that our hope is embodied; the promises of a faithful God have now become enfleshed.

First, the house of David was established for a newly formed nation. Then in Exile, the line of David provided hope for a promised Messiah. And then in the gospels, Jesus of Nazareth, Son of David, Messiah/Christ inaugurated a kingdom not marked by scepter and sword but rather revealed in broken bread, poured out wine, and an old rugged cross.

Now one more perspective, a final layer for us to consider. Recall the "church convention" described in Acts 15, a gathering of Jesus followers called to lead the infant community of Christ as they asked the ongoing *who are we?* question. When James the Elder spoke, he reminded the assembly of ancient promises envisioning a new future for God's people. He quoted the Scriptures and cited this prophetic word:

> After this I will return and I will rebuild the dwelling of David which has fallen.
>
> From its ruins I will rebuild it and I will set it up so that all other peoples may seek the Lord—even all the Gentiles over whom my name has been called.
>
> Thus says the Lord, who has been making these things known from long ago (Acts 15:12–18; see also Amos 9:11–12 and Isa 45:21).

In this last perspective, the "house of David" is the family made up of *all* people who seek the Lord.

There are plenty of other Scriptures that affirmed the exclusion of the Gentiles. But now—because of their experience with Jesus the Christ, now because of the wisdom brought to them by the Spirit of the Risen Christ—these Christian theologians saw persistent Scriptural hints that it has always been God's intention and action to enlarge Israel and expand the people of God.

Once again, faithful people of God reflected on Scripture's meaning for a new time and a vastly changed circumstance. And in their reflections, they recognized the good news that God has been including all kinds of unlikely people for a long time. James and the early church saw God's work among them here and now, in their time and place. And they said *Yes!* The house of David, the legacy of David, the people of God, the community of belonging doesn't look like it used to look—and that is exactly God's plan.

When we were children, we read the stories of David like children's stories but now, when we let these sacred stories intersect our own stories, we recognize how *The Story*, God's Story is rich with complexity and ambiguity. Now we can see how God's Story has always been moving, growing, becoming more than we ever could have imagined.

We are not children anymore. And yet, of course, we are. We are *all* God's children—growing together in God's family, living together in God's household, included in God's heritage, continuing the legacy of God's amazing grace.

We humans cannot build God a house. Instead, God is building *us* into a house, a home, a people, a family. I don't know about you, but I find this community of Christ to be a stunning reality, and I find myself asking along with David, *Who are we, oh God, that you have brought us this far! What is this people that you have made your dwelling among us so that all can find a home and become a family?* (see 2 Sam 7:18–29).

This is *The Story* of welcome, *The Story* in which "all means all." This is the paradox of grace: that God would come to dwell among such broken people in order to accomplish wholeness, unity, and harmony. Amazing grace, indeed.

Week 30

Confession

Second Samuel 11–24
First Chronicles 20–29
Psalm 32
Psalm 51
Psalm 93
Second Thessalonians
John 9–10

As You Read the Old Testament

IT WAS IN THE spring of the year when kings go off to war that David stayed in Jerusalem. It was in the cool of the evening when David paced on his high patio and looked down into his neighbors' garden that he spied a beautiful woman at her bath. It was in a moment of passion, made toxic by power and privilege, that David sent for the woman and had his way with her. It was in thoughtless carelessness that David discarded the woman he had abused; sent her home and forgot about her. It was in a time of panic that David heard she was pregnant, and it was in a tangled web of deceit that David sought to bring the husband home from the battlefront as a ploy to cover up his own wantonness. It was in desperation that David ordered the husband killed. It was in a pretense of compassion that he took the widow Bathsheba into his own home. And it was into this complacency of hubris that King David received the word of the Lord from the prophet Nathan.

There was a rich man with countless flocks and untold power and privilege (the prophet preached). *There was another man, a poor man, with only one little lamb that he loved like a daughter. One day, when preparing a banquet, instead of choosing a lamb from his own plentiful flock, the rich man took the lamb of the poor man. He killed the lamb and served it to his guests for dinner.*

The king was livid. It was in righteous indignation that he declared the appalling rich man should die. "You are the man, David!" Nathan stared him down. Finally it was in honesty and humility, in remorse and repentance that David fell to his knees and wept. "I am the man! Have mercy on me, O God!"

As You Read the Psalms

Psalm 32 celebrates grace. "Happy are those whose transgression is forgiven, whose sin is covered. Happy are those to whom the LORD imputes no iniquity and in whose spirit there is no deceit." See here the poetic rhythm that often characterizes the Psalms, a lovely coupling where two lines emphasize one another, both saying the same thing in different ways. "Forgiven" complements "covered," and "no iniquity" aligns with "no deceit." These are the people who find happiness, blessedness, and contentment in life.

But Psalm 32 also remembers sin. Even though we don't like to talk about sin, the reality of human sinfulness cannot be ignored. Sin presents us with huge social, psychological, and spiritual dilemmas because we humans almost never live up to our own ideals, much less to what God expects and desires for us. The psalmist captures this condition of "iniquity" and "deceit" with powerful imagery. "While I kept silence my body wasted away through my groaning all day long. For day and night your hand was heavy upon me; my strength was dried up as by the heat of summer" (32:3–4).

The psalmist's words poetically describe what the modern word "psychosomatic" names. Scientific understandings affirm that our psychic/ emotional self intertwines in deep ways with our physical body, our *soma*. In this case, both poetry and science affirm our human reality that we are connected and interconnected within the essence of our being in ways often beyond our comprehension.

"Confession is good for the soul," they say, and our psalmist would agree. "Then I acknowledged my sin to you and I did not hide my iniquity. I said, 'I will confess my transgressions to the LORD;' and you forgave the guilt of my sin" (32:5). The *Book of Common Prayer* offers this confession: "We have sinned against you in thought, word, and deed by what we have done and by what we have left undone. We have not loved you with our whole heart. We have not loved our neighbors as ourselves . . ." [1] Confession achieves a deep honesty with ourselves and with another that allows an unburdening of body *and* soul. Often there is a lightening of the spirit and a refreshment we can sense in our nerves, muscles, and blood pressure.

This psalmist has found enlightenment because of his experience and now, out of his own journey of sin and redemption, he seeks to shine a light for others who may struggle. "I will instruct you and teach you the way you should go. I will counsel you with my eye upon you" (32:8). Stories about redeemed sinners are inspiring, and so when we share even embarrassing or humiliating experiences with others who journey with us, we offer them humble grace. (Think of the powerful ministry of Alcoholics Anonymous.)

"So do not be like a mule, without understanding" (32:9). I have to smile at this metaphor because this pictures well our human stubbornness, our digging-our-heels-in arrogance. We all know someone like this. We all have been someone like this!

The apostle Paul quoted Psalm 32 in his treatise to the church at Rome. "David speaks of the blessedness of those to whom God reckons righteousness apart from works:

> Blessed are those whose iniquities are forgiven, and whose sins are covered; blessed is the one against whom the Lord will not reckon sin" (Rom 4; Ps 32:1–2).

"Righteousness" in this biblical understanding (both of the psalmist and of the apostle) does not refer to sin-*less*-ness but rather to *forgiven*-ness. The righteous one is she who has been "made right" by the grace of God.

Those who trust in the Lord are not perfect, sinless people. The righteous ones have not arrived, but, by God's grace, are on the journey. God's people are those who (over and over and over again!) put our trust in the grace, goodness, and forgiveness of the God of Grace who knows us completely and loves us anyway.

---

1. *Book of Common Prayer*, 360

As You Read the New Testament

Paul's first epistle to the Thessalonians suggests that the second coming of the Christ might happen within the lifetime of these first century Christians. The letter of Second Thessalonians continues this expectation and seeks to calm and clarify.

> As to the coming of our Lord Jesus Christ and our being gathered together to him, we beg you, brothers and sisters, not to be quickly shaken in mind or alarmed, either by spirit or by word or by letter, as though from us, to the effect that the day of the Lord is already here. Let no one deceive you in any way . . . (2:1–3).

False messiahs are nothing new. False prophets have been promulgating end times hysteria for centuries. People of the Christ must not be "alarmed" or "deceived."

As I write this in the early months of 2021, the first female vice-president in U.S. history has just been sworn into office. Within a few days of her taking office, fundamentalist frenzy labeled her "jezebel." It was a reference not only the historical character in First Kings, but more obviously to images in the Revelation; a bald attempt to foment apocalyptic fears about the end of the world. Every time a significant disaster occurs, some false prophet will profit from the horror, pronouncing divine judgment and proclaiming it to be "proof" that we are living in the last days and Jesus will be coming soon (so send me money!). With a kind of evil genius, false prophets twist Scripture (several of the misapplied verses come from these two letters to the Thessalonians) in order to deceive and alarm countless believers.

Yes, we are living in the last days, but this end time has been our human situation ever since Jesus of Nazareth proclaimed the "kingdom of heaven is at hand." The final act of God's coming reign began when the Risen Christ emerged from the tomb and ascended to the right hand of the heavenly throne. This age of the Christ has always been the beginning of the final eschatological consummation.

As we read these apocalyptic texts, we must take care to consider the genre and remember these works are highly symbolic and hyperbolic. Word pictures of "mighty angels in flaming fire, inflicting vengeance" and the "Lord himself, with a cry of command, with the archangel's call and with the sound of God's trumpet, descending from heaven" are just that: word pictures. But as *Living in The Story* emphasizes again and again, these descriptions are *true* even if they are not *literal*. Symbols, word pictures, and poetic hyperbole allow us to speak of realities that ever will be unspeakable with human words. They always will be unfathomable with our human understandings.

Apocalyptic literature may well confound our minds with their over-the-top descriptions. That's okay. What is important, though, is to let them open our hearts and point us toward unimaginable, indescribable truth.

As You Read the Gospel

You may know already that those little chapter and verse numbers were added to our Bibles many years after the authors wrote and the editors compiled the Scriptures. But what you may not know is that the NT writers penned their gospels and letters without any punctuation marks, spaces, or lowercase letters. When scholars read the Greek text, they do the best they can to translate and interpret where sentences and paragraphs ought to begin and end.

John 9:3–4 shows us how significant this challenge is. "Who sinned?" the disciples ask and Jesus answered, "Neither this man nor his parents sinned; he was born blind so that God's works might be revealed in him; we must work the works of him who sent me while it is day . . ." That's the way the translators of the NRSV place the punctuation marks (the markings, remember, that are not really there). I find it fascinating that, not only are the commas and periods not in the original Greek, the words "he was born blind" also are not there. So let's read these same words again, this time translated into English by Jamie Clark-Soles.

> Jesus answered: "Neither this man nor his parents sinned.
> [He was born blind]. (The brackets indicate that this sentence is not in the Greek text. If you choose to include it, you should do so only as a matter of fact statement. He was born blind. Stuff happens. Or, even better, just leave it out as it's not in the Greek text at all.)
> In order that God's works might be revealed in him, we must work the works of him who sent me while it is day."[2]

What a significant shift in meaning can happen when periods and commas are used one way or another!

2 Clark-Soles, *Reading John for Dear Life*, 48–50.

We all live in *The Story* that tells of blindness, brokenness, and sorrow, but we must never lose sight of a deeper truth: *The Story* of God's presence in the world also gives witness to the unfailing, unending work of light, redemption, and grace. Each of us individually and all of us together are called to participate in that divine work.

Reflection: *David's Undoing*

> Have mercy on me, O God, according to your steadfast love; according to your abundant mercy blot out my transgressions . . .
> Create in me a clean heart, O God, and put a new and right spirit within me.
> The sacrifice acceptable to God is a broken spirit; a broken and contrite heart, O God, you will not despise . . . (Ps 51).

The church traditionally understands that King David wrote this song of yearning and remorse after his great sin against Bathsheba and her husband Uriah. If you've been reading Second Samuel this past week, you've remembered this sad tale of David's fall and the consequent undoing of his family.

Mercy is all there is for times like these, mercy that can stare us down, that will expose our hubris, name our deadly acts, and challenge our sinful attitudes so that we may be restored to life. This is the only way, facing the darkness within so that we might find the light; naming our brokenness so that we might be healed. David cried out for mercy, compassion, and cleansing. So, of course, the God who is mercy, compassion, and steadfast love turned to David with that ever-amazing grace. With God nothing is unforgivable.

Even so, cycles were set into motion; Pandora's box had been opened. God doesn't wave a magic wand to eliminate the natural consequences of our actions. The prophet Nathan spoke the word of the Lord to David and promised God's unfailing faithfulness to make David and his descendants into a house, a legacy, a dynasty. It was a good word. But then Nathan was called to speak truth to power, to give another prophetic word to King David—a painful word but oh-so-needed for this one who had been blinded by power and privilege.

Remember the signature story of God's self-revelation, the stunning description of "the LORD, the LORD" that became a golden thread woven throughout the Hebrew Scriptures.

> A God merciful and gracious, slow to anger and abounding in steadfast love and faithfulness, keeping steadfast love for the thousandth generation, forgiving iniquity and transgression and sin,
>> yet by no means clearing the guilty but visiting the iniquity of the parents upon the children and the children's children to the third and the fourth generation (Ex 34:6–7).

This glorious description includes justice as well as forgiveness. It's an immensely challenging word that prompts me to ask, is it God who "visits" the iniquity of the parents upon their children? Or does God allow us to do that to ourselves?

It may be an unanswerable question, but I would say since we humans are so exceedingly adept at creating our own cycles of alienation and pain, maybe we are the ones who punish ourselves. This phrase from Exodus is used to describe how our own fallen human character and toxic behavior tends to reproduce itself in society's children and children's children. Abuse creates cycles of abuse until generations of people who are shaped and deformed by them don't know any other reality. Lies cultivate spirals of deception until the children and their children's children have forgotten (or have never known) that there is such a thing as truth. Disregard and disrespect, hatred and shame draw unsuspecting people into their orbit and thus alter their destinies.

These cycles of brokenness foster a systemic evil that is almost invisible to us because we are so used to it; this is our sad normal. In our particular society here in the U.S., there are so many varied forces that influence our thinking, that shape our values, forces beyond our understanding that trick us into seeing our world, seeing our neighbors, seeing ourselves with a skewed vision.

I often hear people say, "the God of the Old Testament is about judgment but the God of the New Testament is about grace." The ancient people of God would have puzzled over such a caricature of Yahweh, because the formulaic poetry of God as Creator and Liberator has always acknowledged the "steadfast love of the Lord to the thousandth generation . . ." (in other words, *forever*). This ancient biblical understanding also always recognized God's justice, "punishing iniquity to the third and fourth generation . . ." (in other words, judgment has its limits).

Law and grace, judgment and forgiveness, these have always been two sides of a coin, but notice two things. One, the judgment may well come from the natural consequences of the sin. Creator God (and we parents with our own children) often need only to wait for life to take its course so that people eventually will experience the effect of what they have set into motion. Actions have consequences. What goes around comes around.

But two, God promises the judgment can and will be curbed by grace. Within the formula, the punishment/consequences of our sinful choices may well affect our children and our children's children, but the positive consequence of God's eternal grace, forgiveness, and steadfast love dwarfs the time bound consequence of our sinfulness. The "sins of the fathers"—human cycles of self-destruction—may well carry on to third and fourth generations, but forgiveness stretches on to the "thousandth generation."

The Bathshebas and Uriahs of the world are all victims of the "sins of the fathers" that keep cycling through the generations. But the Davids of the world are victims too, caught in spirals of brokenness and therefore also in need of redemption and reconciliation. At some point, a people needs to stand up and say, *the cycle stops here.* From now on, we will choose to be a people of welcome and grace for all and—because of the welcome and grace God accomplished in Jesus Christ—we *can* do this. The "sins of the fathers" may last to the third and fourth generation, as Scriptures testifies, but thank God, divine mercy lasts to the thousandth generation, in other words, *forever.*

Week 31

Wisdom

Proverbs
Ecclesiastes
Song of Solomon
Psalm 14
Psalm 111
Psalm 112
James
John 11

THIS LOOKS LIKE A lot of reading but if you are able to take the time to consider all these works during one week, you will find wide and rich connections. Consider setting up some of these long readings in an audio Bible app so you can listen to a good reader read aloud.

As You Read the Old Testament

As you read Proverbs 8 again this week, recall the lovely image of Woman Wisdom calling out to humanity, enticing us to come, to learn, to walk in the way of Creator, the way of life. "Does not wisdom call; does not understanding raise her voice?"

> The LORD created me at the beginning of his work, the first of God's acts long ago . . .
>   When God established the heavens, I was there; when God drew a circle on the face of the deep and made firm the skies above; when God established the fountains of the deep and assigned to

the sea its limit . . . When God marked out the foundations of the earth, then I was beside him, like a master worker and I was daily God's delight, rejoicing always before him, rejoicing in his inhabited world and delighting in the human race (8:22–31).

As You Read the Psalms

All the psalms are part of Israel's Wisdom Tradition, but Psalms 111 and 112 are some that sing and eloquently that "the fear of the Lord is the beginning of wisdom." Fearing the Lord. Surrendering to the Inscrutable. Awed by the Awesome. While, biblically, the "fear of the Lord" generally means submission, allegiance, and obedience, this "fear" also suggests an appropriate heart-thumping, knee-knocking, spine-tingling response. The fear of the Lord comes from faith that trembles at the majesty and marvels at the mystery.

Clinton McCann offers practical help here as we humans seek to understand and embrace God's wisdom in our own lives.

> True knowledge—wisdom—is not grounded in ourselves but in God, and it involves the embrace of God's commitments and values. Thus wisdom will take concrete shape in righteousness, grace, and mercy (vv.3–4), and those who fear the Lord (Ps 112:1), therefore, will be "gracious, merciful, and righteous (Ps 112:4).[1]

God's wisdom takes concrete shape in God's compassionate upholding of all God's creation. Human wisdom takes concrete shape in acts of compassion as well.

"Great are the works of the LORD, studied by all who delight in them" (111:2). The psalmist also delights in those intentional times to study, ponder, discuss, and explore what all this means for God's people. As an old saying goes, "An hour of study is as an hour of prayer." Experiencing times of wonder and then pondering the wonder brings wisdom that goes beyond intellectual knowledge.

In Psalm 111, our poet bubbles with praise for God's great and wonderful works but especially with thanksgiving for God's covenant with Israel. Covenant is the anchor of Israel, salvation from slavery, protection through the wilderness, adoption at the mountain of fire and smoke, redemption from Exile. Even before Israel, God covenanted with Abraham,

---

1. McCann, "Psalms," 1134.

Isaac, and Jacob. Even before the patriarchs, God covenanted with Noah and all creation. All these "wonderful deeds" confirm God's faithfulness to covenant.

> The LORD is ever mindful of his covenant. God has shown his people the power of his works in giving them the heritage of the nations. The works of God's hands are faithful and just; all his precepts are trustworthy (111:6–7).

As God's people, we are called to trust these "trustworthy precepts." The work of God's people is to trust and obey.

Psalm 111 dovetails into Psalm 112. The editors of the psalter want us to see the same connection they saw between these two praise hymns. "Praise the LORD! Blessed are those who fear the Lord, who greatly delight in his commandments." The fear of the LORD brings wisdom, confidence, and joy.

As You Read the New Testament

The great reformer, Martin Luther, famously (or infamously) referred to James as "an epistle of straw . . . because it has nothing of the nature of the gospel about it."[2] To this day, some see the theology of James in opposition to the theology of Paul; this need not be. *Living in The Story* embraces theological variety as demonstrated throughout the Bible and does not shy away from ambiguities found within Scripture's many authors and long years of development. So the fact that James' and Paul's approaches to "faith and works" may not be completely uniform need not trouble us. Think of them as two sides of a coin.

"Faith without works is dead," James asserts. I think Paul would agree. "Faith is a verb," *Living in The Story* insists. Both James and Paul teach that faith is not synonymous with a system of beliefs, either confessed in creeds or in a list of propositional faith statements. Rather, authentic faith always must be multi-layered and many-sided: not just *what* we believe but *how* our beliefs move us to action.

As we read within the Wisdom Tradition this week, hear James' call. "If any of you is lacking in wisdom, ask God who gives to all generously and ungrudgingly, and it will be given you" (1:5). Notice how much emphasis

---

2. Luther, *Word and Sacrament*, 395–97.

James places on speech, how we talk to one another, how we use words for good or for ill. In this way, James echoes the wisdom of Luke's Jesus.

> The good person out of the good treasure of the heart produces good, and the evil person out of evil treasure produces evil; for it is out of the abundance of the heart that the mouth speaks (Luke 6:45).

Christians who purport to follow the one we claim is "the Word become flesh" would do well to pay much closer attention to all the ways we use words.

As You Read the Gospel

In week 2, we pondered John's reworking of the *Sophia/Wisdom* tradition as he interpreted the Christ event. John reread his own Scripture, recognized the Creating Wisdom of *Sophia,* and then rewrote the creation story to include the Creating Christ, the *Logos.* The concepts of Word and Wisdom, of *Logos* and *Sophia,* communicated a multilayered complex of meaning.

"If the Christian movement is anything," Walter Brueggemann says, "it is an ongoing interpretive reflection on the tradition . . ."[3] The Gospel of John, steeped in the Wisdom tradition, offers an "interpretive reflection" that ponders and celebrates unknowable mysteries that are being made known by God through Jesus the Christ. As Clinton McCann reminds, "For Christians, the one who perfectly embodied God's character and values also is professed as 'the wisdom of God' (1 Cor 1:24)."[4]

Jesus the Christ: the Wisdom of God embodied, incarnate. Jesus the Christ: truly God who has come to make God known, the one who has come to show us what love, grace, compassion, and fidelity actually look like and sound like and feel like. Jesus the Christ: truly human who has come to show us humans how to live in wisdom.

The Spirit of the Risen Christ, Spirit of Wisdom constantly teaching, guiding, surrounding, nudging, correcting, comforting, encouraging, and helping us become who we are created and called to be.

---

3. Brueggemann, *Theology of the Old Testament,* 690.
4. McCann, "Psalms," 1134.

Reflection: *The Way of Wisdom*

A few years ago, when my husband and I were reading to our second graders, they wanted to tell us about the newest word they had learned, "genre." Back when you and I were in the second grade, even if we didn't know the term "genre," we still knew there were different categories of the things we were reading. We knew the difference between comic books, history books, and biographies; we learned how fiction, nonfiction, and science fiction work.

The ability to discern between different genres comes in handy. For example, we know how important it is to notice the difference between objective news reporting and commentary or opinions; between science and poetry; between history with documentable facts and the stories that interpret and make meaning of facts. This is not to say that some genres are better than others, that some categories are necessarily "truer" than others, but it is to say that finding meaning and discerning what is true requires understanding a big picture, not just one small piece of reality.

Look at our music, for example. We wouldn't say that only classical music is "right" and country, rock, or bluegrass is "wrong." We see all those different genres of music as rich and interesting and beneficial as we seek to experience life more fully. All this variety makes us better and bigger as we share life together with all our different tastes and preferences.

In much the same way, we appreciate the numerous genres of Scripture. In this complex book we call the Bible, we come to realize that it is really more than one book; it is an entire library of books written by a variety of authors with a range of understandings over a number of centuries. As we've been reading the Bible this year, we've encountered numerous genres: poetry, prophecy, parables, narrative, apocalyptic (visions), and wisdom to name just a few. Considering these various genres of Scripture is an important way to read and reread our Bible. It's helpful to recognize how they work together to create understanding and reveal meaning.

As we read, we've also seen how a variety of perspectives, how various streams of thought come together to intersect and inform one another in the big picture of the Bible. For example, the narrative of Israel sometimes can be pretty raw, violent, and even hopeless when it describes a people stuck in generational cycles of broken humanity. But then other traditions inform and critique parts of Torah. Wisdom and the prophets offer the hope that humanity will not stay stuck; that God will not stay hidden but, in God's own time, will be faithful to intersect human history and accomplish the divine purposes for goodness and wholeness.

Here's another example. In our reading of Hebrews, we discovered how to reinterpret ancient understandings about the priestly system or the sacrificial system from the perspective of the Christ event. When we read the Bible and ask *what does this mean?* we learn to see the big picture of the writings within an overarching balance and counterbalance.

Wisdom is a tradition that stands in healthy tension with the covenantal narrative of the Law. When the Law offers "thou shalts" and "thou shalt nots" as the Word of the Lord delivered from the mountaintop and set in stone, Wisdom says *yes-and*; the "word is very near you, it is in your mouth and in your heart" (Deut 30:14). When the Law's Deuteronomic understandings say "you get what you deserve," Wisdom argues "*yes-but* . . . sometimes life doesn't work the way it's supposed to work."

When the Law thunders, "thus saith the Lord . . ." Wisdom hears the voice of God in the silences and in the still small voice, trusting that "when you turn to the right or when you turn to the left, your ears shall hear a word behind you saying, 'This is the way; walk in it.'" (Isa 30:21). When the Law reveals the will of God in the offering of the sacrifices, the duties of the priests, and the practices of the Temple, Wisdom also discovers the will of God in a mother's love, a father's devotion, and the faithfulness of a friend.

Within the sweep of the biblical story, all the various voices must always be heard and respected, but in our own time in particular, I think we modern church folks need to listen more carefully and more attentively to the voice of Wisdom. We need to pay attention because wisdom traditions offer the deep wisdom of lived experience. This is a kind of knowing that comes from doing, from actually living our lives with compassion and grace, with love and mercy. Lessons learned and truth discerned—this too is a way of knowing—not just "what the Bible says." The practical theology of our living helps us to discover something about the God who is; the God who creates, redeems, and sustains.

The Wisdom tradition of Israel is grounded in creation, and the Wisdom of creation teaches that all things are made for God's purposes and God's glory. All-that-is is good and is created to work together for good. All things are connected and interconnected, intimately woven together into a harmonic wholeness.

Wisdom teaches that even though we humans are an important and esteemed part of God's ultimate plan and purposes, we are not the center of this universe. Humans are one part of the whole, created in God's image, but always in process—ever being reshaped and recreated into the image of the one true God and the Creating Christ.

Week 32

Solomon

First Kings 1–11
Second Chronicles 1–9
Psalm 21
Psalm 45
Psalm 49
Psalm 72
First Timothy
John 12

As You Read the Old Testament

IT IS A SAD irony that the kingdom King David built was so short lived. David's heir, Solomon, followed his father's path of aggressive empire building, but then Solomon's own son saw the kingdom rent by civil war. The expansive land and legacy of David and Solomon dwindled into the small nation of Judah consisting of only two of the original twelve tribes. A look at Solomon is a look at the temptation to foolishness even for the wisest among us.

One of the most famous stories about the newly crowned king is the story of God's gift of wisdom as told in First Kings 3 where the Lord appeared to Solomon in a dream: "Ask what I should give you." The young Solomon answered with wise humility.

> You have shown great and steadfast love to your servant my
> father David, because he walked before you in faithfulness, in
> righteousness, and in uprightness of heart toward you; and you

have kept for him this great and steadfast love, and have given him a son to sit on his throne today.

And now, O LORD my God, you have made your servant king in place of my father David, although I am only a little child; I do not know how to go out or come in . . .

Give your servant therefore an understanding mind to govern your people, able to discern between good and evil; for who can govern this your great people? (3:6–9)

The new king began well. Humility is the foundation of greatness and it pleased the Lord that Solomon had asked for wise discernment. "I now do according to your word. Indeed I give you a wise and discerning mind . . . And I give you also what you have not asked, both riches and honor all your life; no other king shall compare with you. If you will walk in my ways, keeping my statutes and my commandments, as your father David walked, then I will lengthen your life" (3:10–14).

And God gave Solomon great wisdom, discernment, and breadth of understanding as vast as the sand on the seashore, so that Solomon's wisdom surpassed the wisdom of all the people of the east, and all the wisdom of Egypt.

He was wiser than anyone else and his fame spread throughout all the surrounding nations.

He composed three thousand proverbs, and his songs numbered a thousand and five. He would speak of trees, from the cedar that is in the Lebanon to the hyssop that grows in the wall; he would speak of animals, and birds, and reptiles, and fish.

People came from all the nations to hear the wisdom of Solomon; they came from all the kings of the earth who had heard of his wisdom (4:29–34).

One of Solomon's most famous visitors was the Queen of Sheba and, over the ages, this story has inspired legends and romantic tales. In Islamic literature the queen is known as *Bilqis* and (as the story goes) she converted from the worship of the sun god of her people to the worship of the one true God. In Persian folklore, she is considered the daughter of a Chinese king and a *peri*, a type of supernatural being. The story of the Queen of Sheba acquired special importance and impact within the Ethiopian tradition and history where she is referred to as *Makeda*; legend says she and Solomon produced a son who became the founder of the Ethiopian royal dynasty of emperors.

Solomon's Temple is yet another claim to fame for the king.

> Now the word of the LORD came to Solomon: "Concerning this
> house that you are building, if you will walk in my statutes, obey
> my ordinances, and keep all my commandments by walking in
> them, then I will establish my promise with you, which I made
> to your father David. I will dwell among the children of Israel,
> and will not forsake my people Israel" (6:11–13).

Recall how David wanted to build a house for God but the Lord turned the tables and instead promised to build David into a "house," a great legacy. In the story of Solomon, "house" again carries double meaning. Now, even as Solomon is building the physical structure he must also attend to the building of a legacy of faith and faithfulness. Yahweh laid the foundation for this House of David, but Solomon and his descendants were responsible to build upon that foundation by honoring, serving, and obeying God.

The king dedicated this magnificent temple in a great celebration. His prayer again shows humility and wisdom. "Will God indeed dwell on the earth? Even heaven and the highest heaven cannot contain you, much less this house that I have built!" (8:27)

The ancient nation of Israel saw its pinnacle with the reign of Solomon, but power corrupts, they say, and absolute power corrupts absolutely. The heady, expansive kingdom building of the great king Solomon began the cycle that ultimately led to the kingdom's demise; the crumbling happened within a generation. Solomon's son, Rehoboam, was shaped, not by his father's famous wisdom of the early years, but by the foolishness that infected and infiltrated Solomon's reign in the latter years. The enticements of money, sex, and power have turned the hearts—and the paths—of countless people throughout history, even the wisest among us.

As You Read the Psalms

Psalm 49 sings like the couplets of the Proverbs.

> Hear this, all you peoples; give ear, all inhabitants of the world,
> both low and high, rich and poor together.
>   My mouth shall speak wisdom; the meditation of my heart
> shall be understanding. I will incline my ear to a proverb . . .

This wisdom psalm reassures the faithful that God's way is the way of *true* wisdom. Human wealth and success may look like a wise course, but the psalmist has no doubt that—finally, ultimately, eschatologically—God's way is the only way that will endure.

The Psalms, Proverbs, Ecclesiastes, and Job all give insight into various approaches within the Wisdom Tradition. For example, the Proverbs are generally hopeful as opposed to the cynicism of Ecclesiastes. We also see a variety of understandings within the psalms: joy and lament, thanksgiving and warnings. Psalm 49 urges a persevering faith among believers.

> Why should I fear in times of trouble? When we look at the wise, they die; fool and dolt perish together and leave their wealth to others . . .
> Such is the fate of the foolhardy, the end of those who are pleased with their lot (49:13).

This psalmist speaks of *Sheol*, the shadowy place of the dead (not to be confused with our current notions of hell). The rich, he insists, take nothing with them to the grave and will make their home in *Sheol*, while the psalmist and the faithful ones will one day be "ransomed" from *Sheol* to be with God. The wealthy may be happy in this life, but rest assured, they will be stripped bare in the next life.

To us Christians this hints of resurrection, but we don't really know what the ancient poets believed about life after death. The NT suggests the Pharisees may had come to believe there was some sort of life beyond death but Sadducees scoffed at that notion; belief in an afterlife was not a settled issue in Israel. Through much of the Wisdom Literature, though, these hints stand out and keep us guessing. For example, Job's famous *bel canto* sings of a hope we hear echoed through the ages: "For I know that my Redeemer lives, and that at the last he will stand upon the earth; after my skin has been destroyed, then in my flesh I shall see God, whom I shall see on my side, and my eyes shall behold, and not another" (Job 19:25–27).

Wisdom teaches us that the world is not as it seems. No matter how things look in this life—finally, ultimately, eschatologically—*God's Way* is the way that will endure.

As You Read the New Testament

It took four years in seminary for me to achieve my Masters of Theology degree, and I needed every single day of those four years to find my way to a new understanding of Scripture. In nearly every class, with nearly every reading assignment, I learned something that challenged my old paradigm and rattled my heretofore settled theological world. One of the bigger shake-ups was learning that more than likely the apostle Paul did not write all the letters that carry his name. That they are written in Paul's name was an honor within the culture of the first century, a tribute to the weight of his influence and the significance of his ministry. Those whom Paul had taught and mentored continued his work of shaping the theology and practice of the churches he planted and nurtured throughout his life.

Biblical scholars make these kinds of determinations based on a variety of criteria: vocabulary, grammatical style, and/or theology. First Timothy gives us one clear clue to a shift in theology and practice that developed in the Pauline School's next generation of teachers. We find it in chapter 2.

> Let a woman learn in silence with full submission. I permit no woman to teach or to have authority over a man; she is to keep silent. For Adam was formed first, then Eve; and Adam was not deceived, but the woman was deceived and became a transgressor. Yet she will be saved through childbearing, provided they continue in faith and love and holiness, with modesty (2:8–15).

When we think about it, we realize this instruction does not sound like the egalitarian Paul we hear extolling the ministry of women in Romans 13 or arguing for the radical equality of those who are the "new creation" in Galatians 5.

Likely, as this new Jesus movement spread, it challenged some of the basic assumptions of a first-century, hierarchical culture, the "proper place" and function of women being one of those assumptions. In ancient Rome, as in many societies over human history, strong traditions of family structure defined relationships and provided familiar foundations that lent stability and continuity to a people. Anyone who challenged assumptions about the proper place of classes of people within that structure threatened to shake the very foundations of a society. Paul's teachings upended some of those traditions, and so it is not surprising that subsequent disciples may have toned down some of his expectations about the radical equality God has recreated within humanity by means of the cross. (More about this next week.)

As You Read the Gospel

In John, the story of Jesus' anointing is placed just after John relates the death and resurrection of Lazarus in chapter 11. This story of anointing by Lazarus' sister Mary is set not long before Jesus' passion, and so John's Jesus says explicitly that the anointing has to do with "the day of his burial." Note these details as you read:

- Mary's anointing happened in their hometown of Bethany.

- The anointing oil was pure nard, "a costly perfume."

- Mary anointed Jesus' feet and wiped them with her hair, a provocatively intimate act.

- The anointing triggered the indignation of Judas Iscariot and propels the narrative towards his act of betrayal.

Reflection: *The Women Who Anointed Jesus*

I title this reflection "the women" (plural) because of the four ways the four gospels tell four stories about Jesus' anointing. We considered the way John tells the story of Mary above. Now let's see what Matthew, Mark, and Luke say about this intriguing event.

Luke's story about Mary and Martha is not an anointing story. Recall Luke's Jesus gently chided Martha for her "worries and distractions" while the master affirmed Mary "sitting at his feet and listening" and reassured them that such a choice "will not be taken away from her" (10:38–42).

Luke's anointing story is in chapter 7 and makes no connection to Mary of Bethany. Instead, this woman was a sinner who entered the home of Simon the Pharisee. The setting was not specified but the story does not seem to happen in Bethany. The unnamed woman brought an alabaster jar of ointment, and the ointment was mixed with the anointing of her own tears. She too dried his feet with her hair, but she also kissed Jesus' feet—even more intimate than in John's story.

Luke revealed to us the thoughts of Jesus' host: "If this man were a prophet, he would know what kind of woman this is, a sinner" (Luke is the only one who refers to the woman as a sinner). Jesus perceives Simon's private ponderings, and this prompts a parable about a creditor who forgives his debtors. "So who would love more?" Jesus asked Simon, "The one forgiven a large debt or the one forgiven a small debt?"

(7:41–43). As parables always do, the answer creates more questions: is it the woman labeled "sinner" or the judgmental man in this story who has the "greater debt?" Luke ends the story with Jesus' words of forgiveness and blessing to the woman, "Your sins are forgiven. Your faith has saved you; go in peace."

Unlike the other three gospels, Luke placed this story early in the ministry of Jesus and followed it with a description of other women disciples who accompanied Jesus and provided for him as he traveled and taught.

In Mark's story, an unnamed woman came to the house of Simon to anoint Jesus' feet, but here Simon is "the leper." This story is set in Bethany, near the end of Jesus' ministry, and this woman brought "an alabaster jar of very costly ointment of nard" and anointed Jesus' head.

Mark does not name Judas as the indignant one but rather "some who were there" complained about the wastefulness of the expensive ointment. Jesus explicitly connected her anointing to his own burial. And then these famous words of grace by Jesus:

> Truly I tell you, wherever the good news is proclaimed in the whole world, what she has done will be told in remembrance of her (Mark 14:3–9).

Matthew's version follows Mark quite carefully. A woman from Bethany came to the house of Simon the leper "with an alabaster jar of very costly ointment" to anoint Jesus' head. The ones who decried "the waste" were Jesus' own disciples. Jesus scolded the naysayers saying, "Why do you trouble the woman? She has performed a good service for me." And again, Matthew's Jesus made the connection between this anointing and his own burial. Then Jesus repeated the blessing found in Mark verbatim: "Wherever the good news is proclaimed in the whole world, what she has done will be told in remembrance of her" (Matt 26:6–13). Matthew (following Mark) immediately segued into the story of Judas' intent to betray Jesus.

Our *Living in The Story* effort often reveals these kinds of differences as we read through the Bible. Please note that different versions of the same story are not to be taken as contradictions; they are not inconsistencies that need to be reconciled. Nor are they examples of different location viewpoints, for example, four people standing on four corners describing the same accident (a popular explanation). Or the old tale of the blind men describing an elephant from their different positions: trunk, legs, body, or tail. Instead of this kind of logical approach, the four gospels reveal *theo*-logical differences and varied understandings offered by thoughtful, serious students of Scripture pondering the eternal mystery of the Christ event. I compare these theological perspectives to the church experience in our own day. Consider the range of theological and christological understandings among Roman Catholics, Southern Baptists, United Methodists, or Pentecostals, for example. The range is wide and quite reasonable.

Please don't let the variations of these stories confuse you. Although solidly grounded in authentic history, remember that the gospel writers are less concerned about historical facts and more concerned to make meaning of the world changing Christ event. A good Bible student will challenge herself to read the ancient text within its own historical, social, and theological contexts and let it stand there, not forcing the texts into our own modern boxes of understanding.

One more thing. Please notice that none of these women—and particularly not the "sinner" of Luke's gospel—is named as Mary Magdalene. One of the (many!) sad things about Christian history is the way some of these stories were manipulated as they were handed down. Pope Gregory the Great bears much responsibility for the maligning of Mary's story when, in 591 CE, he preached a homily that conflated Mary of Magdala with Mary of Bethany, the woman described in Luke 7. There is absolutely no biblical or historical evidence that Mary Magdalene was a reformed prostitute.

Week 33
Elijah

First Kings 12–22
Second Chronicles 10–23
Psalm 7
Psalm 42
Psalm 50
Psalm 52
Second Timothy
John 13

As You Read the Old Testament

A BRIGHT ELIJAH THREAD weaves throughout the Scriptures. Elijah's story begins during a time when Israel's story had become a sad history of rebellion and civil war. The united kingdom of David and Solomon had fractured into two separate nations: the northern kingdom of Israel and the southern kingdom of Judah. In First Kings 16, the storyteller says, "Now Ahab son of Omri reigned over Israel in Samaria twenty-two years. And Ahab did evil in the sight of the LORD more than all who were before him" (16:29–30). Ahab was breaking bad and his queen Jezebel may have been even worse; Elijah was the prophet God sent to stand against them and challenge their wickedness. It was a thankless, dangerous job, and King Ahab disdained Elijah as the "troubler of Israel."

Usually Elijah's courage was remarkable. For example, there was the time when Elijah confronted King Ahab with the news of a coming famine, a drought pronounced as punishment for the evil doings of the faithless king (1 Kgs 17). Then there was the time when Jezebel had their neighbor, Naboth, murdered so she could take over his vineyard and present it to Ahab as a gift. Elijah railed against such injustice (1 Kgs 21).

There also was the time when Elijah orchestrated a battle of the gods on Mount Carmel (1 Kgs 18). When the one true God sent fire to consume the offering, lick up the water, and burn the stones to ashes, the false prophets were humiliated and executed, sending Jezebel over the top with rage. She swore to have Elijah assassinated. So Elijah fled from the murderous queen and escaped to a cave on the top of Mt. Horeb.

Here is where the bright Elijah thread weaves into the story of Moses. Tradition has it that Mt. Sinai and Mt. Horeb are the same mysterious mountain—a numinous space, a thin place of intersection between heaven and earth. As the story goes, when Moses was on the mountain, he heard the voice of God in fire and cloud, in rumblings, thunderings, and quakings. In contrast, when Elijah met God on the mountain, this time God was present in the silence.

As You Read the Psalms

Our psalmist in Psalm 7 stands boldly before the Lord his God and proclaims his righteousness. He prays for vindication, for God to keep the promise of protection, and to rescue him in the face of unjust persecution.

> O LORD my God, if I have done this, if there is wrong in my hands, if I have repaid my ally with harm or plundered my foe without cause, then let the enemy pursue and overtake me . . . (7:3–5).
> Awake, O my God, you have appointed a judgment . . . O let the evil of the wicked come to an end, but establish the righteous, you who test the minds and hearts, O righteous God (7:6–8).

Many of the psalms confess sin and acknowledge God's right to judge and punish. Many other prayers call out rampant injustice and petition God to remain faithful to covenant by protecting the righteous and hindering those who practice unrighteousness.

The yearning of the poet is that God's own righteousness will be vindicated in the earth. He prays that "the wicked" will come to know beyond any doubt that God's righteousness and integrity *will* triumph and reign throughout the world.

> See how they conceive evil, are pregnant with mischief, and
> bring forth lies.
> They make a pit, digging it out, and fall into the hole that
> they have made. Their mischief returns upon their own heads,
> and on their own heads their violence descends (7:14–16).

Look here at the images of conception, pregnancy, and delivery where the poet describes how wickedness progresses from thought to plan to deed. Also see the karmic wisdom of the psalmist: "they fall into the hole they have made." The psalmist realizes that judgment is not his responsibility and he counts on God and the cosmos to make appropriate payback.

Many of the psalms are eschatological, that is, they trust in an ultimate judgment and vindication, and they articulate a hope that is much larger than the reality of their current circumstances. "Awake, O my God, you have appointed a judgment . . . O let the evil of the wicked come to an end" (7:9). Whatever that judgment actually, ultimately may look like, here is the constant hope of all us people of faith, a final end to evil and violence and the final triumph of God's *shalom*.

As You Read the New Testament

This *Living in The Story* project appreciates the refreshing reevaluation first century theologians applied to *The Story* of God's redemptive work on behalf of all creation but note that, during the same time Paul and the other NT authors were writing, a number of other "gospels" circulated as well. Many years later, when the church as a whole maneuvered the process of canonizing writings into the new Christian Scriptures, only Matthew, Mark, Luke, and John made the cut. The wider church acknowledged that there is more than one way to tell the story of the Christ event at the same time they affirmed that not every way is authentic. Hear this warning from the author of Second Timothy 2.

> I solemnly urge you: proclaim the message; be persistent wheth-
> er the time is favorable or unfavorable; convince, rebuke, and
> encourage, with the utmost patience in teaching.
> For the time is coming when people will not put up with
> sound doctrine, but having itching ears, they will accumulate for
> themselves teachers to suit their own desires, and will turn away
> from listening to the truth and wander away to myths (4:1–5).

As you read these second generation epistles, appreciate their faithfulness to the ministry of Paul, even as you understand how theological developments within our human movements always will be more or less faithful to *The Story* of God's work in the world.

> As for you, continue in what you have learned and firmly believed, knowing from whom you learned it, and how from childhood you have known the sacred writings that are able to instruct you for salvation through faith in Christ Jesus.
>
> All scripture is inspired by God and is useful for teaching, for reproof, for correction, and for training in righteousness, so that everyone who belongs to God may be proficient, equipped for every good work (3:14–17).

I believe every generation that lives in *The Story* has opportunity to begin anew, and to reexamine approaches and assumptions of those who have come before us. As we read, we see how our own Scriptures demonstrate this ongoing process of reconsidering, rethinking, and rereading in its endless search for truth. The vibrant, dynamic kingdom of God is never settled; nor should we be. More chapters of *The Story* are yet to be written.

As You Read the Gospel

Centuries after the ancient stories about Elijah were penned, NT theologians read and reread their Holy Scriptures and interpreted the meaning and tradition of Elijah based on their encounter with the Risen Christ. In the three synoptic gospels, John the Baptist is seen as the one who continued the bright thread of Elijah's ministry. For example, Luke tells of the angel Gabriel announcing John's birth to his father Zechariah. "With the spirit and power of Elijah, [John] will go before [Messiah] . . . Even before his birth he will be filled with the Holy Spirit. He will turn many of the people of Israel to the Lord their God, to make ready a people prepared for the Lord" (1:13–17).

The three synoptic gospels also place Elijah and John the Baptist within the decisive conversation of the meaning of Jesus. "Jesus . . . asked his disciples, 'Who do people say that the Son of Man is?' And they said, 'Some say John the Baptist, but others say Elijah . . . ' Jesus said to them, 'But who do you say that I am?' and Simon Peter answered, 'You are the Messiah, the Son of the living God'" (Matt 16:13–20; see also Mark 8:29 and Luke 9:20).

In Luke's famous scene of Jesus preaching in Nazareth, Jesus' commissioning sermon as he began his ministry, Jesus observed that prophets are rarely welcome in their hometowns. And then Jesus really riled his hearers. "'There were many widows in Israel in the time of Elijah, when there was a severe famine over the land; yet Elijah was sent to none of them except to a widow at Zarephath in Sidon' . . . When they heard this, all in the synagogue were filled with rage" (Luke 4:24–28). These listeners hated hearing that a foreign widow was the only one with whom Elijah found true welcome and sanctuary.

All three synoptic gospels tell the story of Jesus' transfiguration, a pivotal NT event involving Moses and Elijah on yet another mystical mountaintop. The Mount of Transfiguration is not so much geographical as it is theological—or maybe traditional, since the transfiguration proclaims Jesus the Christ stands squarely in the same tradition as Moses and Elijah. However, this vision of transfiguration insists that the Christ surpasses both these great prophets of Israel.

After the transfiguration, Mark and Matthew continue to weave the bright thread as they make this Elijah/John the Baptizer connection. "The disciples asked Jesus, 'Why do the scribes say that Elijah must come first?' He said to them, 'Elijah is indeed coming first to restore all things. How then is it written about the Son of Man, that he is to go through many sufferings and be treated with contempt? But I tell you that Elijah has come, and they did to him whatever they pleased, as it is written about him'" (Mark 9:9–13. See also Matt 17:10–12).

Again, much as the mountains of Sinai, Horeb, and Transfiguration are more theological than geographical, so the timing of Jesus' death takes on theological significance for John. Recall how John the Baptizer announced Jesus as "the Lamb of God" in John 1:36. Now consider this gospel's way of seeing the Lamb of God sacrificed as the perfect Passover Lamb. John's gospel does not describe last supper that is carried over into the Christian tradition as the Eucharist (some of us think the sign of Christ feeding the multitude serves this purpose in John). Rather, John's "last supper" recites the story of Jesus washing the disciples' feet (continued in the Christian tradition as Maundy Thursday).

Since we are talking about Elijah this week, we should note that at every Seder (Passover) meal to this day, our Jewish siblings set a place at the table for Elijah and leave the door open so that, at the appointed time, Elijah may once again "calm the wrath of God and . . . turn the hearts of parents to their children and restore the tribes of Jacob" (Sirach 48:10).

Reflection: *What Are You Doing Here, Elijah?*

I don't know about you, but conflict and confrontation wear me out. I can't imagine how it was to be Martin Luther King Jr. How did he find the stamina to continue his work when the vast power of the status quo resisted everything he did, opposed everything he stood for, despised everything he was? I can't imagine how it was to be the ancient prophet, Elijah. Day in and day out, Elijah brazenly confronted powerful and dangerous people because of their abuse and misuse of authority. Elijah went up against some of the worst offenders of human rights and common decency in ancient Israel.

Elijah knew well the personality disorders of unfaithful unscrupulous leaders. Even in our day there are politicians who manipulate people and turn us against each other in an effort to control their opponents and enthrone themselves as false saviors. Even in our day there are abusers and misusers, wolves in sheep's clothing, who are quite adept at using the cloak of religion to lead people into the worship of false gods of self-sufficiency, self-centeredness, and self-preservation.

Any prophet who speaks truth to power, who stands with the needy Zarephath widows, who speaks out for the swindled Naboths, who advocates for the powerless and the voiceless—these prophets engage in risky (and exhausting) business. Such public prophetic work can stretch us almost beyond our limits. So it doesn't surprise us that here in First Kings we find a story about a disillusioned, discouraged, and drained Elijah running for his life. He is ready to be done with this wearisome prophet business.

> The word of the LORD came to him, saying, "What are you doing here, Elijah?"
>
> Elijah answered, "I have been very zealous for the LORD, the God of hosts; for the Israelites have forsaken your covenant, thrown down your altars, and killed your prophets with the sword. I alone am left, and they are seeking my life, to take it away."
>
> The LORD said, "Go out and stand on the mountain before the LORD, for the LORD is about to pass by."
>
> Now there was a great wind, so strong that it was splitting mountains and breaking rocks in pieces before the LORD, but the LORD was not in the wind; and after the wind an earthquake, but the LORD was not in the earthquake; and after the earthquake a fire, but the LORD was not in the fire; and after the fire a sound of sheer silence.

> When Elijah heard it, he wrapped his face in his mantle and went out and stood at the entrance of the cave. Then there came a voice to him that said, "What are you doing here, Elijah?" (19:9–13)

As a minister I've experienced my share of conflict. People come to pastors with stories of conflict in their jobs or in their families. Pastors walk with people through dark valleys of brokenness, addiction, pain, or death. And no matter what we ministers do, within our churches or in our communities, we surely will be criticized and chastised by someone or another. It's easy for any of us who do such work to wonder *what the heck am I doing here!*

In my own work as a minister, I know I haven't done near enough standing up to the "principalities and powers" of this age, the powers of darkness that keep people blind, the cycles of poverty that keep people enslaved, the damage of abuse that assaults the most vulnerable among us. Even though I haven't done as much as many others, still Elijah's weariness resonates with me when I find myself wanting to escape to a cave on a mountaintop and whine like Elijah.

As I've pondered how to persevere when discouragement and apathy sneak into my soul, I've thought of two things I can do. *One thing I know about myself is that I need to believe I'm doing something that matters*, that my work is important and that I can make a difference for someone somewhere. Maybe this is true of you as well. Similarly, I know this also is true of church. If we truly are the church of Jesus Christ, then we *must* be about doing what's important, what is big and life giving and lasting. If we really are people of the Christ, then that means we have died with Christ, we are new creatures created in the image of Christ, we are living our lives for God *and* living our lives for others.

It is so easy to get all wrapped up in ourselves. It's so tempting to make our own desires, opinions, and preferences into idols and to place ourselves at the center of our universe. How much better if we would spend ourselves on behalf of another? If we would invest ourselves in God's purposes in the world? If we could stand with the widows and advocate for the children and challenge the abuse of the oppressed and dispossessed? Then at least, when we're exhausted, we know it's for a good cause. At least then, when we're weary, we know we've made a difference somewhere; we know we've left behind a legacy of courageous caring and bold living.

So one thing we can do to fight against discouragement is to be active. *Another thing we can do to work against discouragement is to be still.* When Elijah met God on the mountain, God was not in the wind, the earthquake, or the fire; God was in the silence. I find this to be true very often. Many times it is in stillness and waiting that we discover the small voice, the whisper, the clarification, and the affirmation of the Holy.

If we are filled up with the whirlwind call of the world, then we can't hear the voice of the Divine. If we listen to the rumblings of the voices that accuse, scold, and criticize, then we can't hear the voice of the Divine. If we let the fires of fear and anxiety burn us and turn us, then we can't hear the voice of the Divine.

I think many times when we hear the voice of the Holy, it will call us both to "be still and know that *I Am* God" (Ps 46) and it will challenge us to ask ourselves, "What am I still doing here?" It's all in the balance. Be still, listen, wait, rest. And then get up, get out of yourself, be on your way, do *something*. Shine light in darkness, bring hope to despair, stand firm against injustice. Be on your way loving one another just as Christ has loved us.

Be still and know my love, says the Lord. *Be active and show my love*, says the Lord. *That's* what we are doing here.

Week 34
Elisha

Second Kings 1–16
Second Chronicles 24–28
Psalm 12
Psalm 78
Psalm 79
Titus
John 14–16

As You Read the Old Testament

I HAVE A FRIEND who just about lost faith in the Bible when he first heard the tale of Elisha being taunted by this gang of disrespectful boys. "In the name of the LORD" (2 Kings 2 says), Elisha cursed those rude, foolish boys so that two she-bears came out of the forest and attacked them. The Sunday school teacher insisted this story was literally true and demonstrated God's will. "They should have watched their words and been kind, shouldn't they? There were consequences for being disrespectful." My friend nearly lost his temper, almost lost his faith. "I just don't believe that," this thoughtful, practical boy argued back to his teacher.

What on earth is this weird story doing in our Holy Scriptures anyway? Here is just one of many examples why it's important to understand the genres of Scripture, some of the different kinds of parables, fables, and history-like stories that are a part of our Scriptures. This is one of the reasons I took on this read-and-blog-through-the-Bible project in the first place: to try to help us all make theological sense of the stories we find within *The Story* (yes, even the nonsensical ones!) This friend's confusion (and his teacher's) reminds us why it's critical to understand what kind of book the Bible is. And what kind of book the Bible is not.

These *Living in The Story* essays talk a lot about how to read and reread, how to interpret and reinterpret Scripture. I hope you can tell the Bible is precious to me. I hope you can see how much I respect its power to reveal truth about who we are as humans; how much I believe that God continues to speak a current word through these odd and ancient words. I believe the Bible is true. But then we still have these stories that are just flat weird. What can it mean that this story about the she-bears can be "true?"

My first bit of advice is don't try to force things to make sense (things in Scripture as well as things in life). My favorite seminary professor helped me with this: "When you don't understand something, just put it on a shelf in your mind. Don't try to force it to make sense. Give it time." You have no idea how important that advice has been to me over the years so I pass on his wisdom hoping it will be helpful to you as well.

Throughout history, faithful people of God have interpreted Scripture in many ways. In our modern era, especially since the Enlightenment, there have been several different hermeneutical methods, i.e., various ways to interpret Scripture and try to make sense of it. For a while in our modern Western world, a "liberal way" was to de-mythologize the Bible and to understand its truths as *only* spiritual, moral, or ethical. This technique rejected the supernatural and scorned any notion of miracles. In that approach, "making sense" meant it had to make sense according to current scientific understandings and modern ways of reasoning.

On the other hand, a "conservative way" was a sort of backlash against this academic, liberal approach. This fundamentalist, conservative way insisted every word of Scripture was the literal word of God. If there were inconsistencies in the Bible, it was because of human error in the scribal transmissions and translations over the years, this approach argues. The Bible must be "inerrant" and in this hermeneutic, "true" had to mean factually, historically, and scientifically accurate.

Ironically, both these approaches try to judge the veracity of the Bible based on modern scientific method. Liberals dismissed Moses' parting of the Red Sea because (of course) that couldn't really happen in our world of natural laws and gravity. Some explained it away by theorizing that Israel passed through the Sea of Reeds at a particularly shallow crossing. Conservatives wanted to prove that Noah really built an ark and populated it with pairs of every known animal, even dinosaurs! The Noah's Ark Park in Kentucky attempts to use science to prove how all the animals could have fit on the boat and survived.

Both liberals and conservatives in these scenarios completely misunderstand the concept of "truth" as we find it in the Bible. The ancients who wrote these documents did not operate within our modern understanding of science, they did not conceive of history in the same way we do, they did not write their stories in line with Enlightenment standards of rationality. The ancients were storytellers.

Story is how we humans probe the truth of our existence, it's how we discover and discern what is real and true about our shared humanity. Story is a time-honored way to make sense of who we are as humans, where we come from, why we're here, and what is the meaning of life; it's a way to watch for intersections with the Holy. As my theologian husband wisely said:

> Sometimes folk tales have been incorporated into the text of the Bible. No one ever thought or intended that these folk tales should be taken as factual.
>
> They're morality fables: a talking snake, a talking donkey, a great fish that swallows and then spits out a man unharmed, rude boys getting their come-uppance from two mama bears, two thousand pigs rushing headlong over a cliff because a demon named Legion has been sent into them (don't you know the people who first heard this tale chuckled at the similarity of the pigs to the occupying legions of their hated Roman oppressors?).

Different genres are embedded within the various stories in the texts making up the Bible, and these stories bear witness to a people's living faith in a living God. They are human stories, one and all.

Within the ancients' understanding, heaven and earth were separated by only a breath, by a veil, a whisper: thin places all around. There were no categories called "supernatural" and "natural," rather everything existed and functioned within the overlap of heaven and earth, of gods and mortals. The gods sent or withheld rain, caused the crops to grow, and held human life in their power. When the gods were pleased, the harvest was bountiful. When they were angry, the gods sent punishment of floods and earthquakes, disease and pestilence.

It should be no surprise that ancient Israel shared many of these cultural assumptions and interpreted their lives in light of these pervasive cultural understandings. Even as they developed their monotheistic theology of one God, they continued to believe that the experiences of their lives were connected to the Holy through a thin veil.

If she-bears came out of the woods and mauled children, then God must have sent them. If a flood or a drought devastated an area, then God must have been angry. Religious communities never have had a shortage of people who think they have God all figured out. To this day, people hurt our ears with their scapegoating. "Some particular kind of people sinned some particular kind of sin and that's why this hurricane or tornado or epidemic roared through New Orleans or Indonesia or wherever."

Sometimes this is a way of thinking, believing, and explaining the world that attempts to honor the power and sovereignty of God—often a noble effort, but grossly inadequate. Because woven into *The Story* is our own human story of self-justification, self-protection, and self-gratification. With all that brokenness comes a kind of karmic reality: many times actions *do* create natural consequences. We often reap what we sow. Air pressure and water temperature cause hurricanes. Sometimes bears kill children. Everything that happens is not God's will or God's doing.

Faithful believers can believe in Creator's overarching interconnection with creation without believing God personally manufactures tailor-made consequences for every action. We can believe in Creator's supreme power at the same time we believe in the human power of choice. We can believe in Creator's overarching movement for reconciliation and ultimate justice within creation all the while enduring the reality of injustice prevalent in our world. And we can trust that all our stories (no matter how weird) can still be used by the Creator of *The Story* to offer hope: to point to and bear witness to God.

As You Read the Psalms

In the marvelous Psalm 78, the psalmist sings a poetic history of God's people in Israel and seeks to tell their story to future generations. "I will open my mouth in a parable; I will utter dark sayings from of old, things that we have heard and known, that our ancestors have told us. We will not hide them from their children; we will tell the glorious deeds of the LORD to the coming generation; and his might and the wonders God has done" (78:2–4). Similarly, Deuteronomy commands: "Teach your children . . ." (Deut 6:4–9). Scripture reminds how crucial it is to share our faith with the next generations.

In the United States, during the tumultuous 1960s, young people in our churches wondered what was the meaning of all the chaos going on in our world, and they wondered how people of faith should respond. Protests, marches, riots, and assassinations challenged this nation to our core, and young people looked to the church for guidance as they pondered how faith should answer the challenges of war and injustice.

In many ways, in many churches, we failed them. And we lost them. Hundreds and thousands of youth in the sixties completely gave up on church because they didn't find the values of institutional religion to be relevant to their real lives. Now, more than fifty years later, we see a gaping hole. The youth of my generation who came to see faith as irrelevant now have children and grandchildren of their own, and these later generations, in large part, were never even introduced to faith.

Current demographic categories for faith in America have added the "Nones" and the "Dones:" people who have given up on religion. A nation of people that thought of itself as a "Christian nation," that once assumed wide spread faith commitment, now sees an increasing percentage of Americans who are committed to secular values rather than being shaped by values of religious faith.

For the generation of Jews after Babylon who were committed to salvaging their ancient faith, passion to tell and retell the story of Israel to their children and grandchildren would have been a priority, because Exile showed them how faith is always only one generation away from extinction. But training next generations in rules and rituals or in doctrine and dogma is useless unless the foundation of faith is authentic relationship. Faith in a relationship is so much more than a belief system; rather this faith trusts and obeys in a Living God who is in real relationship with real people.

Psalm 78 acknowledges the rightness of God's judgment but still celebrates the Divine Grace that continues to draw God's people back into covenant relationship. This is *The Story* of God in relationship with God's people throughout the ages—amazing grace, persistent (sometimes painful) redemption, and surprising faithfulness. Clinton McCann says:

> To be sure, Psalm 78 is a reminder that knowledge does not guarantee faithfulness, but it insists that knowing the story is the foundation for faith and hope and life.

The church in recent years and throughout its history has often been so self-absorbed and preoccupied with institutional maintenance that it has forgotten what God has done.

It has failed to tell the old, old story that is so full of new possibilities for responding with gratitude and service to God's persistent and amazing grace.[1]

We who are the twenty-first century church must pay attention and understand that indoctrination is not the same as handing down the faith. Our own children and grandchildren must see and hear authentic witness from us. They must hear us confess our mistakes and foolishness as well as experience our journeys of faithfulness, no matter how flawed and tentative they may be. We, and they, are ongoing chapters in this remarkable story of grace. *The Story* contains our stories too.

As You Read the New Testament

In the letter of Paul to Titus (likely penned by a disciple of the apostle), we see some strong admonitions given to church leaders: "silence . . . rebellious people, idle talkers, and deceivers." We hear instructions to "rebuke sharply" those who are "detestable and disobedient." According to this pastoral letter, pastors should "avoid stupid controversies . . . for they are unprofitable and worthless. After a first and second admonition, have nothing more to do with anyone who causes divisions . . ." (3:9–11).

I grieve the ongoing reality of conflict and division that exists within the body of Christ to this day. And I sympathize with the difficult work pastors must do as they seek to find precarious balance in their responsibility to confront false beliefs in service to faithful teaching. Some critics claim that naming divisiveness is divisive in itself. Pastors walk a fine line; wisdom, love, and humility must always be crucial characteristics in the pastors we choose to follow.

As You Read the Gospel

These chapters in John continue the final teachings of Jesus to his followers just before the passion of his crucifixion and death. You may have heard some of these words read at funerals because they offer comfort

---

1. McCann, "Psalms," 993.

and eschatological hope for those of us who must continue living after someone we love has died.

Note especially how John's Jesus describes the coming *Advocate*. Consider teachings you have heard or experiences you have had in modern Christianity about the Holy Spirit and compare those with John's understanding of Spirit's presence and purpose. "The Spirit of Truth" is one of John's names. "The Spirit of the Risen Christ" is how I often describe the power and presence breathed upon the disciples by the Resurrected Christ in John 20. "You know him, because he abides with you, and he will be in you. I will not leave you orphaned (John 14:18). Spirit's presence with us guarantees to us that we belong and we are not "orphans."

Reflection: *Open Our Eyes, Lord*

My favorite Elisha story comes from the sixth chapter of Second Kings. I think you will enjoy it too—especially when you read the story with all its playful ironies.

As an enemy army ringed the hills above the town, Elisha's servant must have frozen in his tracks when he looked up and saw the horses and chariots of the king of Aram in full battle gear. Elisha's calm assurances sounded odd, maybe even naive. "Do not be afraid; there are more with us than there are with them." In spite of Elisha's confidence, the servant could see they were badly outnumbered.

Then the prophet prayed God would open the eyes of the servant. Yes, there was this one obvious reality, but Elisha was able to see beyond to another different but very real reality. "So the LORD opened the eyes of the servant, and he saw. The mountain was full of horses and chariots of fire all around Elisha" (6:17). *God opened his eyes and he saw.* I love that!

Even as Elisha prayed for insightful vision for the servant, Elisha asked for the enemy soldiers to become sightless. So those who thought they could see were blinded and those who yearned to see beyond this physical reality were enlightened. Sometimes "seeing is believing" and sometimes "believing is seeing." Elisha's story teaches us that this kind of real vision is not at all naive; it is a gift from God.

Google the name "Antoinette Tuff" and find a powerful story about another faithful visionary. On August 20, 2013, Antoinette Tuff faced a would-be shooter at an elementary school. When Ms. Tuff looked at this angry young man in this very scary situation, she saw something most people would not/could not see: she saw him as a lost, hurting, but beloved child of God. Because she saw his pain and fear, she offered him compassion and love, something he had seen too little of in his troubled life. The young man put down his weapon and surrendered to police. Not one person was hurt.

By God's grace, Antoinette developed a kind of "double vision." She saw the danger right in front of her and at the same time she saw hope. This woman of faith had eyes wide open to the reality of the pain, eyes opened to her own call to share in that pain, and eyes open to the ever surprising presence and work of God. It is this kind of vision that can ground us within the solid, absolutely Real Reality of the Eternal One even when everything around us is fluid, fearful, and fleeting.

How do we mortals learn how to see our lives and the lives of others from such a perspective? By opening ourselves to God's presence, opening our minds to God's work in the world, and opening our hearts to the presence of God in the lives of others. It is this orientation that allows God to open eyes to new visions of reality, to see new possibilities and opportunities. In my experience and in the story about Elisha's vision, when we open ourselves to God, what God may open to us is often beyond our imagining; beyond our wildest expectations.

Week 35

Self-Destruction

Second Kings 17–25
Second Chronicles 29–36
Isaiah 36–39
Psalm 44
Psalm 87
Psalm 89
Psalm 92
Jude
John 17

As You Read the Old Testament

I HAVE A RABBI friend who says it's impossible to know what Judaism was like before the Exile because during those several decades of captivity in Babylon, God's people were changed forever. Rabbi Jeffrey points out that all the gathered writings we have today were written, compiled, and edited from the perspective of that dark experience and those deep transformations.

The Northern Kingdom of Israel was besieged, then conquered and scattered by the Assyrians around 722 BCE. The Southern Kingdom of Judah was besieged and conquered and carried into captivity by the Babylonians in 586 BCE. Remember that our *Living in The Story* readings this week offer a hindsight perspective. As they relate the pivotal historical events that forever changed Israel as a people, these texts tell their story not in a current moment, but rather through the long angle lens of exile and return.

The people of Judah (now taking back the name Israel) had returned to their homeland and learned some valuable lessons. "We did this to ourselves," is the bottom line of their self-analysis, a self-reflection in the story line we read through the Kings, the Chronicles, and the prophet Isaiah. Remember all this is history within a theological perspective.

> The king of Assyria invaded all the land . . . he carried the Israelites away and he placed them in the cities of the Medes.
>
> This occurred because the people of Israel had sinned against the LORD their God, who had brought them up out of the land of Egypt from under the hand of Pharaoh king of Egypt and they had worshiped other gods . . .
>
> Yet the LORD had warned Israel and Judah by every prophet and every seer, saying: "Turn from your evil ways and keep my commandments . . ."
>
> But they would not listen; they were stubborn, as their ancestors had been . . . They despised the covenant . . . and rejected the commandments . . .
>
> So the LORD rejected all the descendants of Israel; he punished them and gave them into the hand of plunderers, until they had been banished from his presence (2 Kgs 17).

King Hezekiah had led Judah in real reform for twenty-nine years, after which his son, Manasseh, led his people into spiritual and economic decline for fifty-five years. Then King Josiah brought revival and renewal so that the nation prospered for thirty-one years before King Zedekiah watched helplessly as the armies of the powerful King Nebuchadnezzar ushered in Judah's last days. The army breached the walls of Jerusalem, plundered the Temple, and executed the king's family before putting him in chains and marching him and his people across the Fertile Crescent.

> How long, O LORD? Will you hide yourself forever?
> Where is your steadfast love of old, your faithfulness which by you swore to David? But now you have spurned and rejected him. Have you renounced the covenant with your people? (Ps 89)

It's a story of a sad, slow spiral of self-destruction as this people of Creator God persisted in creating their own gods in their own image, as they resisted loving their God with heart, soul, and might. "We did this to ourselves" is the theological reflection of the later writers who preserved the lessons learned and passed on these tragic stories of loss.

As You Read the Psalms

Psalm 89 begins with praise and confidence but ends with lament and confusion. Our poet lays a solid, irrefutable groundwork as he confronts Yahweh: *This is what you have said. This is what you have done.* The psalmist is counting on the character of Israel's God to come through for them once again as they languish in exile.

He uses the word "faithfulness" eight times throughout this psalm staking his own reputation on the trustworthiness of Covenant God. God's mighty acts within creation help him make his case.

> Who is as mighty as you, O LORD? Your faithfulness surrounds you.
> You rule the raging of the sea; when its waves rise, you still them. You crushed [the chaos monster] Rahab like a carcass; you scattered your enemies with your mighty arm.
> The heavens are yours, the earth also is yours; the world and all that is in it—you have founded them (89:8–11).

This is glorious cosmic poetry. Once again, the poet's theme repeats: "Righteousness and justice are the foundation of your throne; steadfast love and faithfulness go before you." The poet-theologian reminds the Creator, "This is who you are! This is what you do!" Then he moves on to proclaim God's mighty acts on behalf of the nation of Israel and to remind God of the covenant promises sworn to Israel's kings.

> You spoke in a vision to your faithful one, and said: "I have found my servant David and I have anointed him with my holy oil. My hand shall always remain with him . . .
> "Forever I will keep my steadfast love for him, and my covenant with him will stand firm. I will establish his line forever and his throne as long as the heavens endure" (89:19–29).

As the story in the books of Samuel goes, the Lord actually resisted Israel's clamor for a king when they wanted to be like the other nations; they whined and noodled Samuel until God gave in. (Lesson: be careful what you ask for!) In their original relationship, God was this people's only Savior, Benefactor, Creator, Redeemer, Sustainer, and King. But evidently an invisible king was not enough, the people yearned for gilded pomp and circumstance, someone they could see and hear, someone whose physical presence would represent the presence of God among them and unto the nations.

In their clamoring, they were fairly warned. The prophet Samuel resisted and persisted, but finally God gave the people what they wanted. And, as so often happens, they got more than they bargained for.

> If [David's] children forsake my law and do not walk according to my ordinances . . . If they violate my statutes and do not keep my commandments . . . Then I will punish their transgression with the rod and their iniquity with scourges.
> But I will not remove from him my steadfast love, or be false to my faithfulness. I will not violate my covenant . . . (89:30–34).

It was a big *if.* "History may not repeat itself but it often rhymes,"[1] because we all know all too well that kings do not remain faithful and people do not keep promises. The poet admits this sad reality and acknowledges that the Lord has every right to punish them.

But (he questions) has God gone too far? "Now, though, you have spurned and rejected your anointed . . . You have renounced the covenant with your servant: defiled his crown in the dust and laid his strongholds in ruins . . . You have cut short the days of his youth and have covered him with shame" (89:38–45). Notice how, in this context, "your anointed" suggests *all* of Israel. The king served as representative for and from the Lord, but the king also stood as summary for the people. It is not just the king the poet grieves; it is all Israel that suffers, and it seems that in the psalmist's mind, it is the Lord God who actively created this calamity.

In Psalm 89, the poet laments the end of the Davidic dynasty, the ravaging of their Promised Land, the devastation of Jerusalem and Solomon's Temple, and so (he reasons), God has broken the promises. Notice the biblical variation of theology we can see this week. While the poet-theologian of Psalm 89 challenges God for unfaithfulness, other Hebrew theologians understood the calamity as the inevitable consequence of Israel's unfaithfulness. *We did this to ourselves.*

A typical pattern within the Psalms is for the poets to start off with complaint and then finish with a hopeful *nevertheless.* Psalm 89 surprises in that it begins with a deep foundation of praise but then finishes with a mighty complaint that God is breaking covenant by not living up to promises. It's a serious charge. Still, this kind of human-divine grappling is what lament is all about. When life turns us upside-down-and-inside-out, God's people very often speak honestly the pain and confusion of

---

1. Quote attributed to Mark Twain.

our hearts. This is what solid relationship looks like when we speak our deepest truth and trust that the other will keep loving us anyway.

Psalm 89 ends abruptly with doxology. "Blessed be the LORD forever. Amen and Amen." Sometimes there is nothing more to say.

As You Read the New Testament

To this day, Jews hold on to hope that a Messianic Age is yet to come in their future. *Olam ha-ba* means 'the world to come' and many Jews believe this will be a time of peace with a blessed absence of war and hatred. For Christians, however, the promise of Messiah was fulfilled in Jesus the Christ. NT theologians read Psalm 89 and saw God's promises made real and embodied in the Crucified and Risen Christ as the "firstborn," as the "highest king of the earth," as one seated on a throne that now is established "as long as the heavens endure."

Eschatological faith holds onto this confidence even as we confess the already-and-not-yet nature of this current age of Messiah, even today when the world around us crumbles in chaos. We may complain bitterly at the brokenness that often breaks us but still we, like our psalmist, keep standing on the foundation of faith in this God who rules raging seas and whose faithfulness is forever.

As You Read the Gospel

Throughout history, the caustic exchanges John's gospel describes between Jesus and "the Jews" have been misused to justify antisemitism. We have seen John's Jesus speak harshly and accusingly to "the Jews" as if there were an ethnic and religious difference between them, but of course that was not true; all the main characters in the story are Jewish.

So we must understand how John's telling is multilayered, a story about Jesus of Nazareth sparring with the Temple leaders *at the same time* John alludes to the situation of Jesus' Jewish disciples who (a generation later) were being ousted from their synagogues because of their Messianic faith. There was a deep rift in this painful family feud and the bitterness of excommunication becomes obvious as John tells his story.

Next week we will read John's version of Jesus' passion, and the betrayal of "the Jews" is gut wrenching. Whenever we listen in to these stories, we modern Christian readers need to remember some important hermeneutical guidelines.

- The stories are set in another time and place.
- The stories articulate tensions between opposing factions within the same ethnic and religious family.
- The stories express the deep pain of those who had suffered damaged relationship with their family, their friends, and their religious community.

People who misapply the internal conflict of this complex family group to justify their own prejudices misunderstand how this particular story is also our universal human story. When we hear the mob crying out "crucify him," we must listen to the many ways we all tend to sacrifice goodness on the altar of self-centeredness. When God's people in John's story proclaim, "we have no king but Caesar," people of faith must recognize our own faithless complicity and idolatry.

Honoring our joint Scriptures, acknowledging our common heritage, recognizing our mutual connection to Creator can support respectful relationship between Jews and Christians. Acknowledging the deep and painful truths we find in *The Story* can spur humility and gratitude among the entire human family.

Reflection: *The Final Days*

Reading these stories of the last days of Israel, Judah, and Jerusalem is sad reading indeed, maybe because it sounds familiar. Back in the 1930s, the rich grasslands of the American mid-West were transformed into a Dust Bowl. It's heart breaking to see the photographs of that stark, brown world. At the same time, Wall Street was collapsing and sending shock waves throughout every Main Street in the United States. Amid the multiple crises with joblessness, homelessness, and food scarcity, many people may have wondered if these were our last days as a nation.

It is always difficult for any people who are in the middle of traumatic events to be able to recognize all the causes and to discern a way forward. It isn't until we get some distance from a crisis that we can learn the life lessons these events can offer. So it wasn't until later (with a good deal of hindsight and broader perspective) that the United States was able to admit a painful truth about these tragedies: "we did this to ourselves."

But then again, hindsight isn't always 20/20. I don't know about you, but when I look back at many of the challenges and choices in my own life, I still do not know if I did the right thing. Even so, like the people of Israel telling and reflecting on their story, there are always lessons to be learned. A broader perspective will grow in our awareness when we give some things some time.

When the desperate captives from Jerusalem found themselves languishing in Babylon, they came to the realization that this was their time. They could be lost to history as were the ten lost tribes of Israel, or they could turn, repent, and reinvent themselves. So it was in the time of Exile that the Jews finally became a monotheistic people and began to worship *only* the one true God, to have no other gods.

Because of the Exile, Hebrew stories were shaped into the written witness of the journey of this people of God. They told their story—the good, the bad, and the ugly—so that maybe other generations might learn the lessons of their own mistakes. The story they told became their Holy Scriptures, a sacred witness so that other generations might know the faithfulness of the God who is God alone.

During this *Living in The Story* project, we encounter the big picture of God's stubborn grace within the sweep of human history. We don't dismiss and diminish the trauma that can come to us and to others, but we can see those experiences within the larger cycles of living. What those cycles can show us is that every time there is a last-days event, something new can be born. We too remember good, bad, and ugly experiences of our own lives so that we also can recognize newly born grace.

When the U.S. looks back and remembers the bloody battles between brothers during the Civil War, does that mean we have finished learning the lessons we need to learn about working through strong differences of opinion? Clearly not. When we look back and remember the turmoil and the dreams of the Civil Rights Movement, does that mean we have finished learning the lessons we need to learn about treating all people with equity? Evidently not. When America looks back and remembers that bright blue day on September 11 when the Twin Towers fell, does that mean we have finished learning the lessons we need to learn about humility and forgiveness? Obviously not.

But one very important lesson I hope we *are* learning is that all those cycles of light and darkness, all those cycles of living and dying are shot through with grace. In all our last-days events, something new can always be born. Newness is the Christian Hope, the Gospel, the confidence we have as people of the Christ.

Because of what God has done in Jesus Christ, there is life in every dying. No matter the predictable cycles of living and dying, in Jesus Christ, God has created a new cycle of life that overlays everything else. Because of what God accomplished in the Christ, there is now a new reality that will one day completely overpower the regular cycles of death. In Christ, God has brought a whole new thing into existence, life never ending that begins right here, right now. It is because of the life, death, and raised again life of Jesus Christ that we can find the courage to die to ourselves, to give ourselves over to the eternal life and love of the one who is our beginning and our end.

Death is still inevitable in this mortal life we share, but the question is not *when will we die?* The question must be *how shall we live?* We can participate in the downward spirals of self-centeredness and self-destruction or we can step up to the challenges of the reforms and renewals of the faithful Hezekiahs God surely will keep sending our way. We can give in to the downward spiral of hopelessness and despair or we can share in the revivals of all our various Josiahs. The question is not, are we in our last days? But rather, *what will we do with the days we have?* The question is, *will we live in hope?* Or not?

I'm not a predictor of the future but I can say this with some confidence: if history continues long enough, the United States of America will see her last days. Denominations and congregations will see their last days. You and I certainly will see our last days. But these reflections about our days need not be filled with anxiety and despair. Whether we do it to ourselves, creating our own painful crises, or whether tragedy and challenge not of our making come to us, either way hindsight helps us remember that in every hard experience of living, in every last day of dying, something new will be born.

Either way we can stand with confidence in the big picture of God's stubborn grace within the sweep of human history. God has done a new thing in Jesus Christ, God is ever doing a new thing in the church and in the world, and—no matter what—God will do some surprising new thing in us. Count on it.

Week 36

Laments

Lamentations
Jeremiah 1–4
Isaiah 1–12
Psalm 137
Psalm 138
Psalm 141
Philemon
John 18–19

As You Read the Old Testament

WE HAVE FINISHED UP the history-like narrative in the Kings and the
Chronicles that describes the downfall of the northern kingdom of Israel
and then the southern kingdom of Judah. Next we will engage the prophetic
tradition and hear the Word of the Lord from the mouths of the prophets.

The story of Israel has now taken us to Exile in Babylon. *Where is
God?* they surely asked. Yes, maybe we did do this to ourselves on one
level, but still—what about God's faithfulness. What about God's promises? What about the covenant?

Living in The Story aligns the gut-wrenching Psalm 137 with the laments of Isaiah, Jeremiah, and Lamentations because it is so breathtakingly
honest. Psalm 137 cries out the full-throated grief of Israel in their devastation. This requiem gives language to the unspeakable pain of any parent
whose children have been raped or enslaved, tormented or murdered. I

can't imagine the loss of so many people across the ages. Laments give voice to the universality of human tragedy; they help us to be human.

As You Read the Psalms

Psalm 137 breaks our hearts. It also is one of the only laments that breaks the pattern. Because the pain is so deep, it never finds its way back to praise. In Psalm 137, there is no *nevertheless*.

> On the willows we hung our harps . . . for our captors asked us
> for songs, and our tormentors asked for mirth, saying, "Sing us
> one of the songs of Zion!" How could we sing the LORD's song
> in a foreign land? (137:1–2)

Jerusalem's destruction is complete. The walls are toppled, the Temple is razed, the last of David's kingly descendants are executed, and God's people are either slaughtered or marched across the Fertile Crescent to Babylon. All they have now are their memories.

"If I forget you, O Jerusalem, let my right hand wither! Let my tongue cling to the roof of my mouth if I do not remember you, if I do not set Jerusalem above my highest joy" (137:5–6). Some of the memories picture the shining Temple on the hill of Zion, sparkling in the light of the morning sun.

More recent memories see blood running in the streets and betrayal—the painful treachery of their neighbor nations. "Remember, O LORD, against the Edomites the day of Jerusalem's fall, how they said: 'Tear it down! Tear it down! Down to its foundations!'" (137:7) And then this gut wrenching cry for vengeance:

> O daughter Babylon, you devastator! Happy shall they be who
> pay you back what you have done to us!
>   Happy shall they be who take your little ones and dash
> them against the rock! (137:8–9)

Parents of Israel watched this happen to their own beloved children, so for them, what would justice look like? Very often for us wounded humans, justice looks like vengeance.

It is difficult to read this troubling prayer, but I think it is helpful to read these words with correct emphasis on the words "your" and "them": "Happy will they be who take *your* little ones and dash *them* against the rock [like *you* did to *our* little ones]." The psalmist seeks God's justice but also hopes divine judgment will satisfy his need for human vengeance. Then he leaves it in God's hand because that's what prayer does. On one level, prayer may seek to change God's mind and move God to action, but mostly prayer is *letting go and letting God*. Mostly prayer is for the pray-er.

As You Read the New Testament

This little letter from Paul to Philemon concerning the fate of the enslaved Onesimus is a touching insight into the pastor side of the apostle Paul. "Though I am bold enough in Christ to command you to do your duty, yet I would rather appeal to you on the basis of love—and I, Paul, do this as an old man, and now also as a prisoner of Christ Jesus" (1:8–9). Paul advocated for the slave's freedom even as he suffered his own lack of freedom in prison.

> Perhaps this is the reason he was separated from you for a while, so that you might have him back forever, no longer as a slave but more than a slave, a beloved brother . . . (1:15–16).

It is a sad reality about Christianity in America that every major denomination split over the issue of human enslavement before, during, or just after the Civil War. Imagine how different the history of the church in America might have been if American Christians had taken seriously the teachings and example of Paul in his letter to Philemon.

As You Read the Gospel

As you read again the story of the passion of Christ as told by John, pause to notice Jesus' mother. (John never names Jesus' mother. If we only had this gospel, we would not have known her name was Mary.)

> Meanwhile, standing near the cross of Jesus were his mother, and his mother's sister, Mary the wife of Clopas, and Mary Magdalene.
> When Jesus saw his mother and the disciple whom he loved standing beside her, he said to his mother, "Woman, here is your son." Then he said to the disciple, "Here is your mother." And from that hour the disciple took her into his own home (19:25–27).

Yet another mother watching her child sacrificed by the evil of the world: their heads bashed against rocks, their bodies riddled by bullets, swinging from lynching trees, herded into gas chambers, sold for sex.

Sometimes I think we speak too easily our belief that Jesus is truly-human-and-truly-divine. What does this mean? If Jesus of Nazareth were truly human, then he would have faced his death like all of us must—with the sure knowledge that when humans die, they stay dead, with the understanding that death is the ultimate enemy of life. Even so, this very human Jesus believed anyway, he trusted anyway, he counted on God's faithfulness in spite of the sureness of death.

As you read John's passion, imagine the community of John, seventy years after Jesus, still grappling with the unfathomable reality that their long awaited Messiah had been crucified as a criminal. Why did this happen? What does this shameful reality mean? Thank goodness their faithful efforts produced these rich and complex gospels that continue to invite us to our own grappling.

Reflection: *Where Was God?!*

A friend of mine wrote to me after the horrific tragedy at Sandy Hook Elementary School. Just before Christmas 2012, a young man walked into a classroom full of first graders and riddled their little bodies with high caliber bullets until they were unrecognizable. "Where was God?!" he asked. I suspect lots of people continue to ask that hard question as violence around the globe continues to skyrocket. I made a stab at an answer but I don't think he was satisfied with it. How could he be? I wasn't satisfied myself.

Another friend and I sat at lunch just after her husband was sent off to prison for ten years. She asked pretty much the same question, and I made a stab once again: "God is with you. God weeps with you. God will never leave you." It sounded pious and pastoral but it didn't help much on that afternoon of grief and anger. "But why didn't God *do* something!?" she protested.

Ah! There's the rub! Anyone who asks that question is in good company because it's an age-old struggle, articulated especially throughout the Psalms. "My God, my God! Why have you forsaken me! I am poured out like water; my heart is like wax . . ." (Ps 22).

> I cry by day, but you do not answer; I cry by night, but find no
> rest . . . (Ps 74).
> > Why do you hold back your hand . . . ? Rise up, O LORD!
> O God, lift up your hand! Do not forget the oppressed! (Ps 10)

Theodicy is what we call this dilemma whenever we claim God is all-powerful, all-knowing, and all-loving, but then we also have to acknowledge that evil and suffering continue to exist within this world. If God is really powerful, if God is truly loving, then why doesn't God *do* something? These unanswerable questions have challenged the faith of countless people across the ages.

Psalm 137 is a gut wrenching complaint. Might this be a psalm for the Sandy Hook parents? For survivors of the Holocaust? For mothers in Somalia or Myanmar? How does a parent live after such death? I don't know. Gut-wrenching anger takes time before grief can evolve into something more balanced. Eventually, through many (many!) painful days and nights, this process of grief may transform hopelessness into hope. Grief can transform trauma into advocacy and courageous efforts for justice.

Grieving with those who grieve is uncomfortable work. We must admit we can't fix anything, we can't make anything better, and there are no magic words. I pray I will never judge another person's grief and presume to tell them how they should navigate such sorrow and suffering. I pray I will never be guilty of mouthing facile platitudes and spouting easy answers to someone who is in the midst of unspeakable pain.

I have learned better than to tell someone they shouldn't feel such anger or rage or revenge. People feel what they feel. Feelings are neither right nor wrong, because they come from our deepest, most honest places. And I have learned that our emotions must be expressed—even in all their raw honesty—or else they will turn into poison and eat us alive. Or else they will turn into a lasting woundedness that will keep on wounding everyone around us.

So we wait without judgment and allow our own grief and anger to be real while we "weep with those who weep." We endure the discomfort and confusion inherent in tragedy (especially senseless tragedy) and continue to trust in the God whose "mercies are new every morning" (Lam 3:22–24). We learn to watch and wait for whatever tiny graces may come to soften the grief, for any flickering light that surely will shine in every darkness. We endure until the memories finally begin to bring less agony and more comfort. We push through until our need to make sense evolves into a need to make a difference.

Asking hard questions of God, arguing with God, even shaking a fist at God are not acts of faithlessness, rather this kind of honest struggle is an expression of deep living faith. Ponder the honest faithfulness we experience with the psalmists, with the prophets, or with Job. See this same kind of faithfulness in Jesus: "My God, why have *you* forsaken me!" Where was God when Jesus was nailed upon that cross?

There have been numerous attempts to answer this question throughout Christian history. Numerous theologies and Christologies have tried to make sense and make meaning, but please recognize these are various attempts and theories for understanding, because there is no one way to think about the meaning of the cross. There is no one explanation that is the "right" answer. None of us knows the mysteries of God, and so we do the best we can to grapple with unanswerable questions: Where was God? Why didn't God *do* something?

Here is part of my own effort to make meaning: Jesus the Christ *is* God "doing something." It was in the Christ that God entered into human suffering. It was in the Christ that God experienced our pain, our confusion, and the dilemmas of our faith. It was in the Christ that the Eternal God tasted forsakenness and death. Christ *is* what God has done. "It was God in Christ, reconciling the world to himself . . ." (Paul explains in 2 Cor 5:19).

I'm thinking "where is God" is not the right question anyway. I'm thinking the better question is: *where are we?*

Isaiah calls God's people to seek justice, rescue the oppressed, defend the orphan, plead for the widow; so *where are we* in that holy work? When God's children are used and abused, when God's beloved are sick or lonely or afraid, when God's lost ones are angry and hurting and confused, *where are we?* As people of the Christ, are we willing to enter into the suffering of others, to hear their cries and kiss their tears? As the community of Christ, as the hands and feet of Christ, are we willing to touch the untouchables, bless the children, and walk right into the messy middle of the pain of the world?

It's hard. Oh, so hard. It will break your heart. But it will answer the question: *where is God?* Here we are, right here. If we are willing to move out of our comfort zones to get our hands dirty and our hearts broken; willing to touch the untouchables and welcome the despised; willing to enter into pain and suffering and to love with reckless abandon. *Here we are; send us.*

Week 37

Isaiah

Isaiah 13–39
Psalm 77
Psalm 130
Psalm 131
Revelation 1
John 20

As You Read the Old Testament

THE BOOK OF ISAIAH is a tremendous work, long and meaty, full of fascinating prose and brilliant poetry. Isaiah shaped the entire theology of Israel during a critical turning point of their history. As they looked back at their experience of Exile, Jewish theologians sought to understand what had gone wrong within their covenant relationship with Israel's God; they sought to learn from their mistakes and forge a new future with hope and faithfulness. Especially notice the descriptions of the Suffering Servant in Isaiah 52:13—53:12; for the ancients and for rabbis today, these painful words described Israel.

Isaiah is quoted or referenced numerous times throughout the New Testament. Within the pages of Isaiah, NT theologians discovered profound insights helping them make sense and understand the one whom they proclaimed to be Christ, God's Messiah. For example, Christian theologians expand and apply the depiction of the Suffering Servant to Jesus. (See the excursus, "Isaiah for Christians" below.)

Isaiah's oracles of divine warning and judgment against the nations sound alien to us moderns. These were actual political states that existed in history, but remember the Word of the Lord that comes to us in Scripture does much more than recite history. Our reading challenges us to attend to what this prophetic word meant to the people of Isaiah's time in order to give that meaning a proper hearing. But then, as we continue to ponder, we step again into our own time and listen for the Word of the Lord that might be speaking to *us*. Which warnings sound like they could be spoken to our own nation or the church of our own day? Which promises reassure you to hope and urge you to perseverance and faithfulness?

As You Read the Psalms

Psalm 77 reads like the diary of anyone who has ever suffered unspeakable pain. "I cry aloud that God may hear me . . ."

> In the day of my trouble I seek the LORD; in the night my hand
> is stretched out without wearying.
> My soul refuses to be comforted. I think of God, and I
> moan. I meditate, and my spirit faints. I am so troubled that I
> cannot speak (77:1–4).

This dark night of the soul *is* speechless. There are no words that can communicate deep trauma and grief. Like Job, sitting in silence in the ashes for seven days, sometimes there is nothing to say.

And then, after the *silence* (as is true of all the laments of the psalms), comes the *challenge*. For Israel, God is the Covenant God, the one who has promised to keep promises. So *where is God now?!* the poet cries. "Has God's steadfast love ceased forever? Are God's promises at an end for all time? Has God forgotten to be gracious and in anger shut up his compassion?" (77:8–9)

But then—after the *silence*, and after the *challenge*—this psalmist turns to *memory*. Even in the midst of the current despair, his spirit's searchings produce memories of another time when God's faithfulness was actual and visible. Remembering is a strategy. Memory is a move of hope for the psalmist and a reminder to the Lord.

> I will call to mind the deeds of the LORD; I will remember your
> wonders of old. I will meditate on all your work, and muse on
> your mighty deeds.

> You are the God who works wonders; you have displayed
> your might among the people and with your strong arm you
> redeemed your people . . . (77:11–15).

Our psalmist is tapping into communal memory that continues
among this people of God to this day: *what happened to our ancestors,
happened to us.*

The poetry of Psalm 77 sings the praise of Creator who commanded
creation to participate in redemption and justice.

> When the waters saw you, O God, they were afraid; the very
> deep trembled.
>   The clouds poured out water; the skies thundered; your ar-
> rows flashed on every side. The crash of your thunder was in the
> whirlwind; your lightnings lit up the world; the earth trembled
> and shook.
>   Your way was through the sea, your path is through the
> mighty waters—yet your footprints were unseen (77:16–19).

The psalmist sings praise of the Shepherd who guided wanderers
to a new home, a Promised Land. "You led your people like a flock by
the hand of Moses and Aaron." And here is where our grieving poet in
Exile ends his prayer. This Creator-Redeemer-Sustainer God did mighty
work before on behalf of the people. Will God intervene and once again
redeem Israel and rescue them from Babylon?

The poet begins with lament and ends with memory. The psalmist offers this confidence of remembrance both for Israel and for Israel's
God: *covenant cannot, must not, will not fail.*

As You Read the New Testament

If at all possible, read (or listen to) the entire Revelation in one sitting
because the Letter to the Seven Churches was meant to be read aloud
as an experience of worship. Reading the Revelation in this way helps
generate an overarching sense of the spirals of reality: good and evil, light
and darkness, hope and despair.

It's like a symphony; you feel it even if you can't read music. It's
like an opera; you get the story even if you can't speak Italian. It's like
a radio drama; we can "see" what's happening with only the sounds of
the words in our ears. This is our holy imagination at work. We give
ourselves permission to make sense and understand something that is

deeper than logic, something like this revelation—a fantastic work of prophetic imagination.

The Letter to the Seven Churches is a pastoral letter from John revealing his vision from the Risen and Reigning Christ. The vision was given to this prophet in order to encourage discouraged, confused Christians and to reassure them of God's sovereignty and care. John wrote as a pastor encouraging his people. And he wrote as a prophet reminding them that the unseen, one true God truly *is* the sovereign lord over all of history—no matter what the Emperor claimed. John wrote to call people to faithful hope.

John's letter describing his vision speaks in another language that is hard for us to understand, the language of dreams and apocalyptic visions. From the time of Isaiah and Jeremiah, on to the time of Daniel, and throughout the period between the testaments, numerous prophets wrote in the apocalyptic style; it was a familiar language for John and the people of his day. John's reader/hearers got it. We? Not so much.

But plenty of Christians throughout history and even in our own day *would* get this. Oppressed people identify with these descriptions of mistreatment and brutality. Persecuted people pray for God's judgment upon the evil they experience. People suffering injustice yearn for God's justice and so here in John's vision, these people hear a word of hope. Christians in Nazi Germany, in the killing fields of Cambodia, in Stalin's Gulag, in modern day China—countless people of faith have experienced what John's community experienced.

John's vision pulls back the curtain of the heavens and reveals the workings of holy judgment upon the empires of the earth on behalf of God's beloved people. As M. Eugene Boring summarizes:

> The last "book" of the Bible is a pastoral letter to Christians in Asia in the late first century who were confronted with a critical religiopolitical situation, from a Christian prophet who wrote in apocalyptic language and imagery.
>
> Like the Bible in general, there is some difficulty in understanding Revelation, but it can and should be understood, for it has enormous influence in religion, history, and culture and has an urgently needed message for the contemporary church.[1]

---

1. Boring, *Revelation*, 1.

As You Read the Gospel

John 20 is one of my favorite chapters in the entire Bible. These encounters with the Resurrected Christ are rich with layers of meaning and mystical insights. Mary Magdalene does not recognize the Risen Jesus, not because her human eyes were filled with tears, but because such perception never comes from human understanding. Epiphany is always gift and divine grace. Thomas meets the limits of human logic when he finally meets the risen Christ. The disciples' "Pentecost" experience in the gospel of John comes with Christ's breath breathed upon them, con-spiring ("breathing together") and inspiring disciples to go forth and change the world. In this chapter, we meet the ever living, Crucified and Resurrected Christ marked now with sacramental scars that forever meld humanity with divinity.

In this powerful chapter, we hear clearly John's thesis statement defining the purpose and goal of his powerful gospel.

> Now Jesus did many other signs in the presence of his disciples, which are not written in this book. But these are written so that you may come to believe that Jesus is the Messiah, the Son of God, and that through believing you may have life in his name (20:30–31).

Take time to read slowly, thoughtfully, and prayerfully. Take time to ponder and breathe in the profound beauty. Read chapter 20 more than once if you can.

Reflection: *The Call of Prophets*

The prophetic tradition of Israel challenged arrogance, privilege, and oppression while calling God's people back to faithfulness.

> How the faithful city has become a whore!
> She that was full of justice, righteousness lodged in her—
> but now murderers!
> Your princes are rebels and companions of thieves.
> Everyone loves a bribe and runs after gifts.
> They do not defend the orphan and the widow's cause does
> not come before them (Isa 1).
> The haughty eyes of people shall be brought low,
> and the pride of everyone shall be humbled;
> and the LORD alone will be exalted on that day.

> For the LORD of hosts has a day
> against all that is proud and lofty,
> against all that is lifted up and high (Isa 2).
> The LORD rises to argue his case; he stands to judge the
> peoples.
> The LORD enters into judgment with the elders and princes
> of his people:
> It is you who have devoured the vineyard;
> the spoil of the poor is in your houses.
> What do you mean by crushing my people, by grinding the
> face of the poor? says the LORD God of hosts (Isa 3).

The prophetic tradition of Israel called God's people to faithfulness, but also to hope. Yes, God's covenant promises included consequences for unfaithfulness, but the unending covenant also assured God's amazing grace.

Excursus: *Isaiah for Christians*

The scroll of Isaiah had become Israel's sacred Scripture by the time of Jesus, and so Christian theologians searched and researched their own Hebrew scriptures in order to glimpse the mystery of *who is God?* and *who is this Jesus?* Now the writings of these wise writers have become our own sacred Scripture as Spirit leads us Christians also to ponder—and to participate in—the fathomless mystery.

When we stand with Jesus in his hometown synagogue and watch him ask for the scroll of Isaiah, when we hear him announce his ministry with the prophet's own words, we too are invited to share in this mission.

> The spirit of the Lord God is upon me, because the Lord has
> anointed me.
> God has sent me to bring good news to the oppressed,
> to bind up the brokenhearted,
> to proclaim liberty to the captives,
> and release to the prisoners . . . (Luke 4; Isa 61).

When we hear Jesus' parable of the vineyard, we experience a fresh interpretation of Isaiah's song for a new day.

> Let me sing for my beloved my love-song concerning his vine-
> yard: My beloved had a vineyard on a very fertile hill . . . (Mark
> 12; Luke 20; Isa 5).

When we read Paul's celebration of the gospel in his letter to the Romans, we understand here is yet another insight to the hope of Isaiah.

> How beautiful upon the mountains are the feet of the messenger who announces peace,
>> who brings good news, who announces salvation,
>> who says to Zion: "Your God reigns!" (Rom 10; Isa 52).

During the Church year, in the annual season of Advent and Christmas, we recall Isaiah as we sing, "Joy to the world, the Lord is come!"

> For unto us a child is born . . . to us a son given and authority rests upon his shoulders.
>> He is named Wonderful Counselor, Mighty God, Everlasting Father, Prince of Peace (Isa 9).

When we hear Handel's magnificent *Messiah*, we listen again to Isaiah's promises.

> Comfort ye, comfort ye, my people, saith your God. Speak comfort to Jerusalem, and cry unto her: that her warfare is accomplished, that her iniquity is pardoned.
>> The voice of him that crieth in the wilderness: Prepare ye the way of the LORD. Make straight in the desert a highway for our God (Isa 40 KJV).

When we travel through the forty days of Lent, Isaiah travels with us pondering the sacrificial life of God's Suffering Servant.

> Surely he has borne our infirmities and carried our diseases; yet we accounted him stricken, struck down by God, and afflicted.
>> But he was wounded for *our* transgressions, crushed for *our* iniquities; upon *him* was the punishment that made *us* whole, and by his bruises, *we* are healed.
>> All we like sheep have gone astray; we have all turned to our own way, and the LORD has laid on him the iniquity of *us* all (Isa 53 emphasis mine).

The book of Isaiah is a vastly significant work both within Judaism and Christianity. As serious Bible students and faithful seekers of truth, it is well worth our time to read this hefty book at least once a year.

Week 38

Revelation

Isaiah 40–55
Psalm 73
Psalm 74
Psalm 120
Revelation 2–3
John 21

As You Read the Old Testament

SCHOLARS NOTE THREE MAJOR and distinctive writings within the one book that carries the name Isaiah. First Isaiah (chapters 1–39) seems to have been penned by Isaiah of Jerusalem during its last days. The narrative overflows with startling visions of the Divine, challenges the sins of the nation of Judah, and warns of dire consequences.

Second Isaiah (chapters 40–55) may have been written during the years of Exile in Babylon. There are no new visions but the writer is an inspired interpreter of First Isaiah. Here is some of the most soaring poetry in all of Scripture, maybe in all of literature, holding out hope in the midst of hopelessness.

Third Isaiah (chapters 56–66) sounds like it was recorded after the exiles returned home to rebuild their devastated land. The words encourage the weary people and hope for the return of Yahweh's shining glory to the Second Temple.

As You Read the Psalms

Across the globe, across the ages, the rich getting richer while the poor get poorer has been a terrible truth for most of the people on the planet. Even here in the United States, we are seeing the demise of the middle class and a significant rise in poverty. Psalm 73 reads like a commentary on today's world.

The problem is not simply that some people are rich and others are poor. It's not that rich people are "bad" and poor people are "good." The problem is the self-righteousness and indifference that prosperity can create within the wealthy and the deep inequities that can diminish and devalue poor people. Our psalmist saw this first hand.

> I was envious of the arrogant; I saw the prosperity of the wicked. For they have no pain; their bodies are sound and sleek. They are not in trouble as others are; they are not plagued like other people.
>
> Therefore pride is their necklace; violence covers them like a garment. Their eyes swell out with fatness; their hearts overflow with follies.
>
> They scoff and speak with malice; loftily they threaten oppression. They set their mouths against heaven, and their tongues range over the earth (73:3–9).

The oppression of the rich over the poor is as old as humankind itself. But what is even more baffling to me is the approval these oligarchs often receive from the very people they crush and burden with their practices and policies. "The people turn and praise them and find no fault in them" (73:10).

What is that about? How is it that those who are oppressed sometimes make excuses for their oppressor? That the vulnerable believe power brokers will do what is right and best? How does that make sense? Maybe it doesn't make sense, not in any framework we can imagine, anyway. "When I thought how to understand this, it seemed to me a wearisome task until I went into the sanctuary of God; then I perceived their end" (73:16–17). The psalmist helps us enlarge our imagination to a bigger picture, into a cosmic scale, in order to consider our lives within the eternal, eschatological frame of reference. "Truly you set them in slippery places; you make them fall to ruin. How they are destroyed in a moment, swept away utterly by terrors!" (73:18–19)

In Luke 16, Jesus told a parable about a poor man named Lazarus who begged for handouts while he sat homeless outside the home of a rich man. The cosmic, divine justice in the story is either comforting or chilling depending on where we see ourselves in the story. When Jesus taught the truths of the upside-down-inside-out beatitudes, poverty like the psalmist describes may have been at the front of his mind. "Blessed are the poor . . ." Luke 6 says. "Blessed are the poor in spirit . . ." Matthew 5 softens a bit. God's truth upends our human truths and the truth of God's eternal right-making often can be seen only with the eyes of faith.

Faith allows us to wait and watch for God without bitterness and envy. Faith allows us to grasp some inkling of God's work of *shalom* within the universe. Faith motivates us to work on behalf of God's justice. "But for me it is good to be near God; I have made the LORD God my refuge—to tell of all your works" (73:28).

As You Read the New Testament

"Bizarre" is a pretty good word to describe the book of Revelation. In this vision, we see images of four horsemen of the apocalypse, seven bowls of wrath, tormented sinners crying out from a lake of fire, the satan bound for a thousand years, and then the final battle of Armageddon. "Bizarre" is also a good word to describe many of the interpretations of the book of Revelation that have been offered over the years. There is some deeply flawed theology out there—I'm sure you've noticed.

For one entire semester in seminary, I dug into the Revelation, translating the Greek text and probing the apocryphal theology. What did this pastoral letter mean to the seven churches of Asia who first received it at the end of the first century? And what can it mean for us now in the twenty-first century? Finding that bridge of appropriate interpretation across time and culture is no simple task.

The overarching story of the OT is the story of liberation—slaves rescued from Egypt and exiles redeemed from Babylon. Now a people occupied and oppressed by the empire of Rome are yearning once again for rescue. John taps into this basic story of liberation as he describes his vision of judgment and hope.

Whenever we ask *what did it mean?* we need to look at the time and place of the writing. Most of Scripture (and this letter in particular) was written from the perspective of the bottom of society, people experiencing oppression, occupation, and powerlessness. John's vision reveals holy redemption on behalf of victims of the Roman Empire.

Many of us who live today in first world nations experience the world from the top rather than from the bottom. Those of us who live in places of privilege, power, and prestige find it hard to comprehend what life is like for the "least of these" living on the underside of our social hierarchies. So one reason we have trouble reading the book of Revelation is because of our privilege; when we don't share the perspective of underprivileged people, we struggle to understand their struggles.

But there is another reason why we might have trouble reading the Revelation. M. Eugene Boring says:

> The chief difficulty in understanding Revelation may be neither historical nor conceptual but a matter of the heart.
>
> Biblical prophets offer a vision of reality which conflicts with the natural inclinations of the human will and its values (1 Cor 2:6–16). This is powerfully illustrated by John's vision of self-sacrificing love, the Slaughtered Lamb as representing the ultimate power of the universe (5:1–4), which not only goes against the grain of our cultural and conceptual understanding, but also conflicts with our commonsense will to power.

This goes against our grain, indeed! We humans are about self-preservation, self-satisfaction, and self-determination while the prophetic word of John is about dying to self and living in *witness*, living as *martyrs* for the kingdom and the reign of God.

The one who is "faithful" is one who rejects the self-centeredness of our bent-in-upon-ourselves human nature and becomes recreated and reborn as self-giving and self-sacrificing, a spiritual reorientation that gives witness to the way of the Christ. But it always and forever will "go against the grain" of the way of empires. Boring continues, "Revelation makes a claim on the reader, a claim we may not want to hear. This native resistance to the call to discipleship may be the ultimate barrier to understanding the message of Revelation."[1]

What is envisioned in this beautiful and bizarre writing is that the Sovereign God—Alpha-and-Omega-Beginning-and-End—is on the throne and in control. What is seen through our imagination is that the Risen Christ/the Slaughtered Lamb now lives forever and ever. What is confirmed is that the Spirit is alive and well and still speaking to and within the churches. What must be heard by every reader/listener and

---

1. Boring, *Revelation*, 46.

Christ follower is that our command and call is to live as faithful witnesses to this Very Real Reality.

As You Read the Gospel

The fascinating epilogue found in John 21 redeems Peter after his three-fold denial of Jesus because here we find him pledging his love to Jesus in three intentional statements. What is curious, though, is the nuance we find in the Greek: "Do you love me. Do you *agape* me?" Jesus asks the first two times. "Yes, Lord, I love you," Peter answers. "I *phileo* you." Much has been written about this intriguing exchange of love commitment.[2]

We discussed elsewhere how John's gospel tells fewer stories while delving deeper into meaning. In its epilogue, the Gospel of John says clearly that it has left out a lot. "But there are also many other things that Jesus did; if every one of them were written down, I suppose that the world itself could not contain the books that would be written" (21:25). *The Story* is larger than any of us can fathom; it goes on forever.

Reflection: *Living in Apocalypse*

The Story of the human race has cycled through numerous apocalyptic ages throughout our history and when we are there, it feels like the end of the world. Our current *Living in The Story* texts lead us readers into Exile with Israel; their previous world has ended and things will never be the same. At the same time, we encounter the experience of first century Christians after the destruction of the Temple and the defeat of Jerusalem; their world also had come to an end. During both these epochal ages, Judaism and Christianity evolved into something completely different. Something old died and something new emerged. A new creation was birthed into the world.

This image of birthing is helpful as we consider how to respond to apocalyptic times. When everything we know, everything we are is in transition, it can feel as if the whole earth is in labor. As I wrote during the traumatic summer of 2020, our world was embroiled in tumult with a deadly global pandemic, threats of economic collapse, climate crises, constant war, rising violence, ethnic conflicts, class divides, and waves of

2. If you want to ponder this more deeply, I recommend C.S. Lewis' fine little book, *The Four Loves*.

authoritarianism. As I struggled to understand this societal chaos, I kept reminding myself, as bad as all this is, this is not the worst things have ever been. And I wondered, are we also in labor? Will something completely different be birthed into the world as we make our way through this painful birth canal?

During the first several years of my adult life, I worked as a labor and delivery nurse. Fresh out of nursing school with no children of my own, I coached and encouraged mothers through labor. The experience deepened me and opened me up to the mysteries of life and death as I had never known them before. As a pastor, I saw myself as a kind of midwife, coaching and encouraging those who found themselves in some turmoil or another. All of us have been there, and most of us recognize how trauma and crisis provide fertile ground for growth.

As a matter of fact (according to the popular example), the Chinese character for "crisis" brings together the two symbols for "danger" and "opportunity;" both realities are present but it is up to us to choose our response. We can give in to the dangers with confusion and panic, or we can focus, breathe, and push through that which is beyond our control. I believe we need more wise spiritual midwives helping us through these hard times. I believe more of us need to *become* wise spiritual midwives: grounded, calm, and focused.

If I am right—that we are living in apocalypse in the twenty-first century—then how do we live faithfully? How do we align ourselves with the faith of our fathers and mothers? How do we see beyond the crisis in order to focus our vision on new possibilities? How do we make peace with the reality that our own eyes may not see the new thing; maybe it will be our children's grandchildren who will be the beneficiaries of our faith and faithfulness.

I have no easy answers. But like Isaiah and Jeremiah who cast their long-range vision of redemption even in the midst of destruction, like John who revealed the hopeful picture of God's presence and governance at work behind the scenes, I too want to midwife hope. I want to stay grounded and focused, to remember to breathe, and to help my sisters and brothers push through all that is currently out of our control. To wait and to work for whatever the next new thing may be.

Week 39

Prophets' Imagination

Isaiah 56–66
Psalms 133, 134, 135, 136
Psalm 121
Revelation 4–6
Mark 1

As You Read the Old Testament

DURING WEEK 39 OF *Living in The Story*, we complete the massive work of Isaiah the prophet. We have referred to these final chapters as Third Isaiah because of a shift in its style and themes. There is no absolute clarity or scholarly agreement about the author, origins, and timing of this section, but the richness of its prophetic encouragement continues to spark hope for God's people.

As you read, watch for the emphasis on worship as Isaiah projects a future when social divisions, physical differences, and cultic exclusions will be replaced with the unity and harmony of true worship. For example, foreigners and eunuchs (prohibited from participation with the community's worship under the Law) one day will enjoy full inclusion.

> All who keep the Sabbath, and do not profane it, and hold fast my covenant—these I will bring to my holy mountain, and make them joyful in my house of prayer; their burnt offerings and their sacrifices will be accepted on my altar; for my house shall be called a house of prayer for all peoples.

Thus says the LORD God, who gathers the outcasts of Israel: "I will gather others to them besides those already gathered" (Isa 56:6–8).

NT theologians brought forward this "gathering of outcasts" promise as they pondered the meaning of Jesus Christ and his ministry of
grace and inclusion.

In contrast to right worship, Third Isaiah continues warnings about
the dire consequences of "wrong" worship: the dangers of idols, hubris,
and injustice. "Why do we fast, but you do not see? Why humble ourselves, but you do not notice?" The God of Isaiah and Israel answers:

Look, you serve your own interest on your fast day, and oppress
all your workers. Look, you fast only to quarrel and to fight and
to strike with a wicked fist. Such fasting as you do today will not
make your voice heard on high . . .

Is not this the fast that I choose: to loose the bonds of injustice, to undo the thongs of the yoke, to let the oppressed go free,
and to break every yoke?

Is it not to share your bread with the hungry, and bring
the homeless poor into your house; when you see the naked, to
cover them, and not to hide yourself from your own kin?

Then your light shall break forth like the dawn, and your
healing shall spring up quickly; your vindicator shall go before
you, the glory of the LORD shall be your rear guard (Isa 58:3–8).

For Isaiah, as for many other prophets, worship is not simply piety;
rather worship is the full practice of compassion and service in a faithful life.

Third Isaiah provides the source for Jesus' famous sermon text at
the beginning of his ministry. "The spirit of the Lord God is upon me,
because the LORD has anointed me; he has sent me to bring good news to
the oppressed, to bind up the brokenhearted, to proclaim liberty to the
captives, and release to the prisoners; to proclaim the year of the LORD's
favor, and the day of vengeance of our God . . ." (Isa 61:1–4). Notice Luke's
edit as he tells this story in Luke 4:16–19; he left off the threat of vengeance and ended Jesus' reading of the Isaiah scroll with a word of hope.
In Luke's understanding, Jesus is sent to "proclaim the year of the LORD's
favor." Jubilee! Good news indeed.

As You Read the Psalms

The beautiful and beloved Psalm 121 offers deep comfort and assurance. "I will lift up mine eyes unto the hills, from whence cometh my help. My help cometh from the LORD, which made heaven and earth" (121:1–2 KJV).

Psalm 121 is part of the *Songs of Ascent* collection. Remembering the Lord who travels with them on the way to Temple continues as a powerful metaphor for the God who travels with us every step of the way in all our life's journeys. "He will not suffer thy foot to be moved: he that keepeth thee will not slumber. Behold, he that keepeth Israel shall neither slumber nor sleep." (121:3–4 KJV).

When I was a girl, our church sang a favorite hymn of the old-timers: "There's an eye watching you; there's an all seeing eye watching you . . ."[1] It gave me the willies as I imagined a huge, judgmental divine eyeball watching my every move, just waiting for me to make a mistake.

Fortunately I outgrew this childish theology but unfortunately this notion gets stuck in the belief system of some Christians who persist in their belief of a vindictive God quick to judge and punish instead of the biblical God "merciful and gracious, slow to anger, and abounding in steadfast love and faithfulness" (Exodus 34 et al). I want to think the old-timers who sang along with me took comfort in the image of God's wakefulness and constant presence much as Israel must have taken comfort as they regularly recited and sang Psalm 121. "The LORD is thy keeper . . . The LORD shall preserve thy going out and thy coming in from this time forth, and even for evermore." (121:5–8 KJV).

The poetry of this psalm is gorgeous. As short and powerful as it is, Psalm 121 might be right up there with Psalm 23 as one incorporated into the memories of people of faith for all these centuries. It is easily memorized and invites recitation as one is settling into sleep or trying to find one's footing in a difficult situation.

As you read Psalm 136 this week, notice how it functions as a kind of call and response song, a great teaching tool for pilgrims as they recall Israel's story and God's faithfulness.

---

1. J. M. Henson, (1887–1972).

As You Read the New Testament

In this one letter, this Revelation, John makes over 500 allusions to OT biblical images as he describes what the Risen Christ had revealed to him. The Revelation rereads the Hebrew prophets as the text brings a new but familiar prophetic vision forward from ancient days into the first century. Note just one example brought forward from Third Isaiah.

> The sun shall no longer be your light by day, nor for brightness shall the moon give light to you by night; but the LORD will be your everlasting light, and your God will be your glory (Isa 60:19).

Compare Isaiah's hope with the hope of John:

> And the city has no need of sun or moon to shine on it, for the glory of God is its light, and its lamp is the Lamb. The nations will walk by its light, and the kings of the earth will bring their glory into it (Rev 21:23–24).

What does the Revelation reveal about the church? Here is what John wrote: "I looked and there was a great multitude that no one could count, from every nation, from all tribes and peoples and languages, standing before the throne and before the Lamb, robed in white . . ." (7:9–10). *This* is the church of Jesus Christ, a people larger than any of our human boundaries, tribes, or other distinctions. *This* is the authentic church to which we bear witness.

As You Read the Gospel

Most scholars believe Mark invented the gospel genre and provided the basic framework that both Matthew and Luke followed twenty years later. Mark's story is direct, quick, and on the move. Mark's Jesus is bold, controversial, and focused.

Notice that Mark begins the story of Jesus with an incomplete sentence: "The beginning of the good news of Jesus Christ, the Son of God." His opening line seems to function as a title, and his succinct opening sets the story of Jesus firmly midstream in the story of Israel.

When Jesus was baptized, Mark says, a voice spoke from heaven, "You are my Son, the Beloved; with you I am well pleased" (1:9–11). "Out of Egypt I called my son," the God of Hosea proclaimed centuries before (11:1) signifying Israel as the first to be called a beloved son of the Most

High. So what did it mean for Mark and his Christian community to say that this Jesus is "the Son of God?"

For Mark, "son" is a category of being. When Mark uses this word to refer to Jesus, he's not suggesting that Jesus is the next generation of God, like we think of our sons and daughters. Nor is it a term that designates gender. Rather, son in this context means one who belongs to a particular type, a particular category. Jesus comes from the classification "God." Jesus exists within the category of being "divine." For Mark, Jesus as "Son of God" suggests that Jesus is truly God.

But Mark's Jesus is of another category as well, because throughout his gospel, Mark also speaks of Jesus as "Son of Man." Jesus comes from the classification "human" and exists within the category of "mortal." For Mark, Jesus as "Son of Man" suggests that Jesus is truly human. Mark's Jesus throughout this narrative is always both/and. Mark's Christology understands him to be *both* fully human *and* fully divine.

Reflection: *The Prophets' Imagination*

Unpacking the prophets' imagination is especially helpful as our *Living in The Story* readings lead us through both the works of the OT prophets and the Revelation of John in our NT. Prophets persistently challenge status quo, counter conventional wisdom, and cast alternative visions.

Walter Brueggemann's classic book, *The Prophetic Imagination*, reminds readers that Torah needs the prophets to name both the human brokenness and the divine remedies. Every society in every age needs prophets who will speak truth to all us stumbling ordinary people as well as speak truth to power.

The great Jewish scholar Rabbi Abraham Joshua Heschel described the nature and function of the prophets.

> The prophet is a poet. His experience is one known to the poets. What the poets know as poetic inspiration, the prophets call divine revelation . . . The inspiration of the artist is what is meant by "the hand of the Lord which rests upon the prophet."
>
> Like a poet, [the prophet] is endowed with sensibility, enthusiasm, and tenderness, and above all, with a way of thinking imaginatively. Prophecy is the product of poetic imagination. Prophecy is poetry, and in poetry everything is possible, [such

as] for the trees to celebrate a birthday, and for God to speak to [humans].[2]

Kelly Brown Douglas explored the prophetic work of Martin Luther King Jr. and especially noted the imaginative vision Dr. King cast in his iconic "I Have a Dream" speech.

> A moral imagination is grounded in the absolute belief that the world can be better. A moral imagination envisions Isaiah's "new heaven and new earth," where the "wolf and the lamb shall feed together," and trusts that it will be made real (Isaiah 65).
>
> What is certain, a moral imagination disrupts the notion that the world *as it is* reflects God's intentions . . . [It] is nothing other than the hope of black faith. Such hope trusts that the arc of God's universe does in fact bend toward justice.[3]

The imaginative ministry of prophets continues to challenge inequities and injustices that harm and hold back God's beloved. Brueggemann calls the imagination "prophetic," Heschel sees this imagination as "poetic," and Douglas terms it "moral." All these aspects describe how prophetic work imagines, envisions, and dreams alternative realities that allow for human flourishing.

Brueggemann says it this way: "Prophetic speech is so daring as to specify concrete places where the presence, purpose, and reality of God's 'otherness' make decisive inroads on the human process in either friendly or hostile ways. It names the places where intrusion, gift, ambiguity, and newness are present, and it gives to those happenings the name of holiness, either holy graciousness or holy judgment."[4]

While we moderns debate whether God "intrudes" into human affairs or not, the prophets assume God *has, does,* and *ever will* break into our worldly reality in order to inject a healthy dose of heavenly reality: Real Reality. This divine corrective recognizes our human bent-ness and offers realignment with Real Truth. The prophetic voice proclaims newness and liberation. Brueggemann again:

> The prophetic tradition of Israel is the offspring of both the narrative that tells of the "newness" bestowed on Abraham and Sarah and the Mosaic event of liberation.

---

2. Heschel, *The Prophets*, 367–68

3. Douglas, *Stand Your Ground*, 225, 226.

4. Brueggemann, *Texts That Linger*, 36.

In Israel there arose a series of human speakers—prophets—who were emboldened by holiness and who conceived of scenarios of possibility that "the rulers of this age" had declared to be impossible.

On the one hand, these prophets dared to envision a terrible impossibility, namely that God's own people would answer for their cynical, willful disobedience and come to a suffering end.

On the other hand, these prophets dared to imagine a totally new beginning, whereby God would re-form God's people in exile so as to create (as there had not been before) a people after God's own heart.

These prophets dared to speak of "plucking up and tearing down, of planting and building." They dared to speak what their contemporaries regarded as either craziness (cf. Hosea 9:7) or treason (cf. Jeremiah 38:4).

They dared to voice what imperial power had nullified and fate had settled. And in their speaking, they worked a newness.[5]

The biblical prophets were not future tellers, as some literalist theologies suggest (though the prophets might envision a projection of the future). Nor were the prophets simply social justice advocates, as some liberal theologies suggest. Prophets, from within their divine orientation and keen ability to hear the Holy, can "work a newness" in the midst of our earthly orientation. That is, their words of "holy graciousness or holy judgment" can work newness within those who have eyes to see and ears to hear.

History mostly is written by the winners where "might makes right." That topside perspective is not the only way to tell a story, because *God's Story* is most always inside-out-and-upside-down from the way we humans prefer to tell our stories. *The Story* offers new possibilities, even impossible possibilities. Brueggemann makes the connection between the OT prophetic tradition and the NT understanding of Jesus.

It is through this tradition of new possibilities that the early church understood Jesus. In him, it saw wonders worked and impossibilities enacted . . .

It seems clear that lying at the foundation of the church is the claim that Jesus is a full embodiment of the prophetic tradition of the Old Testament. Jesus speaks and enacts the holy word of God in ways that "pluck up and tear down," that "plant and build."

5. Brueggemann, *Like Fire in the Bones*, 77.

It is equally clear that the church's discernment and story of Jesus do not stop with this characteristically Jewish understanding. The church has gone further, to confess that Jesus is not only an *utterer* of the word but is himself the *uttered* word.[6]

Hear that again. Jesus—not only an *utterer* of the word but himself the *uttered* word. Jesus—"the Word made flesh" (John 1:14).

---

6. Brueggemann, *Like Fire in the Bones*, 78, italics in the original.

Week 40

The Psalms

Jeremiah 5–24
Psalm 62
Psalm 70
Psalm 108
Revelation 7–9
Mark 2

As You Read the Old Testament

JEREMIAH, LIKE ISAIAH, IS a massive literary work. Five of these lengthy books are referred to as the Major Prophets: Isaiah, Jeremiah, Lamentations, Ezekiel, and Daniel. The Minor Prophets are shorter, though nonetheless significant.

The prophetic tradition of Israel was a current word to the people of God in a time of apostasy or distress—both a word of warning and a word of hope. Note, though, how often Jeremiah recites the tragic words "but they would not listen." Hearing, listening, and obeying are constant themes throughout Scripture, a theme continued by Jesus. "Let anyone with ears to hear, listen!" (Mark 4:9). When I wrote these words in 2020, it was yet another time of grave distress: global pandemic, ongoing epidemics of bigotry and oppression, blatant campaigns of disinformation. These ancient words of Jeremiah seem a current word for our own time.

> From prophet to priest everyone deals falsely. They have treated
> the wound of my people carelessly, saying, "Peace, peace," when
> there is no peace . . . (Jer 6)

They have grown strong in the land for falsehood, and not for truth; they have taught their tongues to speak lies . . . (Jer 9)

Thus says the LORD: Do not let the wise boast in their wisdom, do not let the mighty boast in their might, do not let the wealthy boast in their wealth; but let those who boast boast in this, that they understand and know me, that I am the LORD; I act with steadfast love, justice, and righteousness in the earth, for in these things I delight, says the LORD (Jer 9).

As Simon and Garfunkel taught my generation, "the words of the prophets are written on the subway walls."[1] Every age needs the courage and imagination of prophets. Benedictine Sister Joan Chittister observes:

These prophetic people, people just like us, simple and sincere, eager and inspired—these sheep herders like Amos and small-business people like Hosea, these simple country farmers or priests like Jeremiah, these thinkers and writers and dreamers like Isaiah and Ezekiel, these struggling lovers and suffering witnesses like Micah, these brave and independent judges and leaders, like Deborah and Miriam, made no small choices.

They chose courage. They chose the expansion of the soul. They chose to stake their lives on what must be rather than stake their comfort, their security, the direction of their lives, on what was.

It is that steadfast, unyielding, courageous commitment to the eternal Will of God for Creation—whatever the cost to themselves—that is the prophetic tradition. It sustains the eternal Word of God while the world spins around it, making God's Word—Love—the center, the axle, the standard of everything the faithful do in the midst of the storm of change that engulfs us as we go.[2]

Let those who have ears to hear, listen.

As You Read the Psalms

Much as there are five books of Torah, five books of Wisdom, and five books of the Major Prophets, the 150 psalms of the Book of Psalms also are organized into five books. The prayers and hymns of Israel that sang their faith were gathered, edited, and organized into the Psalter that Jews

1. Simon, *The Sounds of Silence*, 1964.
2. Chittister, *The Time Is Now*, 17–18.

and Christians still use to this day. The arrangement of hymns seems to speak to the cycles of our lives with the poetry of our faith.

One thing we all know about life: it is messy. Sometimes we feel overwhelmed with goodness and beauty and our hearts overflow with gratitude and thanksgiving. Other times, when we are overwhelmed with sorrow, pain, and injustice, our broken hearts cry out in complaint and lament. Such was the experience of Israel as well. From the Golden Age of David and Solomon, into the long painful spiral of unfaithfulness, through the desolation of the Exile, then back to the devastated land and the hard work of rebuilding, the Psalms cycled through the highs and lows of the life of Israel.

In this process, the poems express the wide range of emotions within the human experience, not only in Israel's story but in all our stories. What I think is particularly wonderful is that even the bitterest cry of a broken heart almost always cycles back around to praise.

But understand, "praise" doesn't mean "happy." The psalmists didn't always thank God *for* the situation in which they found themselves, circumstances of sin or betrayal or injustice. Rather they praised God *in the midst* of that circumstance. Yes, sometimes the Psalms admit the situation is terrible, unfair, and unjust, and therefore we feel angry, fearful, alone, and confused. *And yet* . . . You are God. You are holy. *Even so* . . . I will choose to put my trust in you. *Nevertheless* . . . I will entrust myself to you. *Against all reason* . . . I will praise you.

I will praise God *because* . . . "You, O LORD, are a God merciful and gracious, slow to anger and abounding in steadfast love and faithfulness" (Ps 86:15). I will praise God *because* "righteousness and justice are the foundation of your throne and steadfast love and faithfulness go before you" (Ps 89:14). *Because* . . . "the earth is full of your steadfast love" (Ps 33:5). *Because* . . . "by day the LORD commands steadfast love, and at night God's song is with me" (Ps 42:8).

Praise is subversive and countercultural, an act of faith that flies in the face of conventional wisdom. Praise says—no matter what is going on in my life or in my family's life or in the church or in my nation or in the world—*nevertheless*, I will proclaim that God is on the throne. We will watch for God's presence. We will wait for God's movement. We will trust in God's faithfulness. *No matter what—we will practice praise.* "The Lord sits enthroned upon the praises of his people" (Ps 22:3).

These remarkable hymns testify it is not only we humans who praise; Psalm 148 suggests the Creator is enthroned upon the praises of all creation.

"Praise him, sun and moon. Praise him, all you shining stars! Praise him, fire and hail, snow and frost. Praise him, mountains and hills, wild animals and cattle." Can you hear it? Rain, both wild and gentle, singing Creator's song. Trees dancing and rustling with the music of the Creator. The majestic roaring of the beasts and the contented humming of the herds praising the Creator. "Make a joyful noise to God, all the earth! All the earth worships you! They sing praises to your name" (Ps 66:1–4).

As You Read the New Testament

Over several decades around the turn of the first century, one crisis after another rocked the world of those who lived in the time of John's Revelation: famines, earthquakes, and volcanoes (Vesuvius was one); wars and rumors of war, political intrigues, rebellions, and coups—not to mention the brutal destruction of Jerusalem. John wrote this letter to the seven churches in a time of complex cultural, political, and religious challenges. While pagans sought to come to terms with such chaos through philosophy, religion, or superstition, Christians pondered what it meant to claim that God was sovereign and that Jesus was God's anointed king in such a cataclysmic world.

Here also was a time when Christians were beginning to gain attention and sometimes disapproval from their pagan neighbors. These unusual people called "Christians" were accused of being atheists because they said they worshiped God, but there was no image or statue that anyone could see. They were accused of being cannibals because they admitted to eating the body and blood of this one they called the Christ. They were accused of being traitors because they refused to acknowledge the emperor as "lord" and claimed instead only Jesus Christ is Lord.

John mentions one martyr who has died, and John fully expects a large-scale persecution to break out upon his fellow Christians around Ephesus, Smyrna, and Thyatira. In many ways it must have seemed like the end of the world; actually that is what John may have believed. Many of the NT writers seemed to expect Jesus to return at any time. "The time is near," John warns, as if the cosmos were in labor, experiencing birth pangs of a new something coming very soon.

As You Read the Gospel

Mark 2 tells a story about a paralyzed man, stuck, helpless, lifeless, but fortunate to have a community of friends who cared, companions willing to be inconvenienced, willing to look foolish, willing to risk. So the friends carried hope for the man; and then they literally carried him to the one who can really make a difference in a life. Maybe they couldn't repair the entire world, but they did what they could, they did it together, and it made a huge difference for one precious soul.

As you read these little stories Mark tells, notice that many of them are resurrection stories. Again and again, we meet someone who is laid low—and then they meet Jesus. It is in this Jesus encounter that they meet God's grace, God's forgiveness, God's healing, God's kindness, God's own life. And they are raised to a new life: resurrection. Each one of these stories is the gospel in miniature, good news made tangible, the gospel enfleshed in one person after another. We once were lost and now we're found. We once were blind and now we see. We once were sick and now we're whole. We once were dead and now we live. The good news goes on and on.

Reflection: *Stars and Mitochondria*

One of my favorite authors is Madeline L'Engle, a person of deep faith and soaring imagination. Her most famous book is probably *A Wrinkle in Time*, but this little story comes from its sequel, *A Wind in the Door*.[3]

Meg is the central character in this series of stories; she's a moody but courageous teenager who desperately worries about her little brother, Charles Wallace. It seems that something is seriously amiss within his mitochondria and the crisis looks as though it could be fatal. When Meg meets a cherubim in the back meadow, she learns they have been chosen to travel inside Charles Wallace's body, deep into his cells in order to find out what is wrong. What they find is that the mitochondria have forgotten the song of the cosmos; his mitochondria have lost touch with the stars and have stopped singing.

It's a powerful image. We humans, made of stardust, connected to the stars. We creatures of the creation created with the song of the Creator knit within our very cells. So when Meg and the cherubim call these

3. L'Engle, *A Wind in the Door*.

disconnected cells back to their core purpose—when they remember the song—the cosmos is set right and the galaxy that is Charles Wallace becomes whole again.

I love the notion that we are created to be people of praise, that praise is our core purpose, woven into our very cells. I love the idea that all creation is empowered to sing the song of the Creator in unity and in harmony. I continue to hold onto hope that the church will come to understand our core purpose and to truly become people of praise, embodying this cosmic song in our flesh and in our bones.

And I hope we will continue to find all sorts of ways to sing God's song of praise with joy and confidence into the cacophony of our world.

Week 41

Jeremiah

Jeremiah 25–39
Psalm 3
Psalm 26
Psalm 148
Revelation 10–11
Mark 3

As You Read the Old Testament

AGAIN AND AGAIN, JEREMIAH reminds his people of God's covenant and calls them back to faithfulness. As you read, recall that it is always *God's* covenant—divinely initiated and sustained—to which God's people had agreed. Remember the story of God's covenant with Abraham and the odd (to us) vision of the animals slaughtered with the torch passing through the severed pieces (Gen 15). It was an ancient ritual, a startling physical reminder of commitment to an agreement. Jeremiah recalls this ritual as he challenges the nation's infidelity.

> And those who transgressed my covenant and did not keep the terms of the covenant that they made before me, I will make like the calf when they cut it in two and passed between its parts: the officials of Judah, the officials of Jerusalem, the eunuchs, the priests, and all the people of the land who passed between the parts of the calf (Jer 34:18).

When Israel broke the divine covenant, Jeremiah proclaimed the Lord's righteous anger. But since this is *God's* covenant sustained by God's authority, "the word of the LORD that came to Jeremiah" proclaimed a word of hope as often as it threatened judgment. Justice is God's foundation but compassion is God's essence. "Surely I know the plans I have for you . . . plans for your welfare and not for harm, to give you a future with hope" (Jer 29:11).

As you read the book of Jeremiah and other biblical writings, remember that the word proclaimed by the prophets, the stories recalled by the narrators, and the witness offered by the faithful storytellers of Scripture is a word for the *community* of God. Sometimes we moderns tend to read the Bible as if it is a personal letter written just to me. Consider the lovely verse above, which is a favorite of many faithful Christians, and consider how the meaning shifts if we take that promise as assurance of some specific divine plan for an individual in contrast to its meaning for a hopeful future for a *community* of God's people. We Western individualists would do well to critique our self-centeredness and continue to grow in our practice of community.

As You Read the Psalms

Psalm 3 offers a powerful demonstration of faith functioning without sight. We should know that faith never comes with clear vision or guarantees, but even so, how often do we want reassurance of favorable outcomes *before* we allow ourselves to trust? It is oh so easy to let feelings of anxiety and fear overwhelm our intellect instead of finding the delicate balance between our head, heart, and gut. Feelings serve as signals; they alert us that something very real is roiling deep within. Even so our minds, our thinking, our cognitive abilities must provide counterweight to our feelings. Whole, healthy humans seek to keep head and heart in good balance.

This is what we see in our psalmist, he counters his feelings of despair with his affirmations of faith. "You, O LORD, are a shield around me, my glory; the one who lifts up my head . . . I am not afraid of ten thousands of people who have set themselves against me all around" (3:3–6). Our psalmist proclaims the unseen reality of his Lord. He names God as Shield and Sustainer even as he struggles with the reality of tormenting foes. His faith allows him to look his troubles in the face and say, "I am not afraid of you!"

Courage is fear that has said its prayers.[1] Living our lives with courage, facing the various kinds of foes that rise against us, holding onto faith and hope doesn't mean our knees aren't knocking and our palms aren't sweating. But courage does mean we can step up to the challenges of our lives in spite of our fears. Courage keeps fear from paralyzing us. Courage coupled with faith means we step into the Shield and lean into the Sustainer.

Now, finally, the psalmist's prayer moves to the petition. Tucked away in the lament of his reality and his commitment to trust anyway is this one request for God's intervention. "Rise up! Deliver me!" But with this cry for deliverance comes an expectation of vengeance. "Strike all my enemies on the cheek and break the teeth of the wicked" (3:7).

This psalmist sings his belief (and the understanding of many people of faith) that vengeance is the same as justice. I beg to differ. I know I often don't understand God's ways of justice, judgment, and setting the world to rights, but the psalmist shows us—whatever our need, whatever our heart, whatever our request—we can offer any concern honestly, freely, and confidently to the God who is Shield and Sustainer.

It is not up to us to exact revenge, and we may not always be able to execute justice. Whatever his feelings and emotions may tell him to do, the psalmist makes the choice to leave his dilemma in the Lord's just and capable hands. Whatever God decides to do about all the complexities of any trying situation, that is God's place, God's prerogative—because God is God and we are not.

Psalm 3 ends with beatitude, the pronouncement of blessing and, in this case, blessing even in the midst of turmoil and trauma. As in the beatitudes found in Matthew and Luke, God's blessing doesn't wait until our physical circumstances are resolved. God's blessing blossoms best in the dark, rich soil of our very complex, very real lives. "Blessed are the poor for theirs is the kingdom of heaven" (Luke 6:20). Amazing grace!

As You Read the New Testament

Remember our discussion about "genre" and recall there is a wide variety of literature in this library we call the Bible, i.e., poetry, narrative, histories, and prophetic writings. Apocalyptic literature is one of those categories.

1. Quote attributed to Dorothy Bernard

I think we thoroughgoing Western rationalists have particular difficulty understanding apocalyptic writings because we have been shaped by a very different way of thinking—an evaluation process that is logical and concrete. It sometimes is hard for us to let go of that rationality in order to let our imaginations run free.

This is one reason literalist interpretations of this book are off base because readers cannot take these fantastical word pictures and pound them into concrete images. One can't take these numbers and reduce them to some sort of math when they were meant to paint a broad, impressionist work of art. The images and pictures are intended to elicit feelings and emotions more than logical explanations. This letter to the seven churches does that best with dramatic, oral readings. Or even with dramatic music. You may recognize this call of praise that is offered by heavenly voices as it has become amplified in the powerful "Hallelujah Chorus" of Handel's *Messiah*. "The kingdom of the world has become the kingdom of our Lord and of his Messiah, and he will reign forever and ever."[2]

The song of the elders celebrates this eschatological achievement.

> Then the twenty-four elders who sit on their thrones before God fell on their faces and worshiped God, singing:
> "We give you thanks, Lord God Almighty, who are and who were, for you have taken your great power and begun to reign.
> The nations raged but your wrath has come and the time for judging the dead, for rewarding your servants, the prophets and saints and all who fear your name, both small and great, and for destroying those who destroy the earth" (Rev 11:16–18).

Creator's divine wrath is poured out upon all that which destroys the beloved creation.

As You Read the Gospel

This little story in Mark 3:1–6 continues the controversy described in chapter 2: who has authority here? Who interprets the traditions? Who speaks for God? Mark's Jesus has made it clear, ". . . the Son of Man is lord even of the Sabbath" (2:27–28). It is Jesus who speaks for God.

Notice Mark's christological understanding of "Son of Man" as Jesus encounters the man with the damaged hand in a synagogue on a Sabbath day. No one else in the story even speaks while Jesus forces the issue, calls

---

2. George Frideric Handel, 1741. See Revelation 11:15.

forth the startled man, and challenges the stubborn onlookers. "Is it lawful . . . to save someone's life, or to destroy it?" It's a simple question even for the most pious Sabbath keepers: save life, of course. But Jesus waits for affirmation of the man's life that never comes. They will not assent to Jesus' authority because their minds are made up; their hearts are hard.

The "heart" (*kardia*) in the Greek concept is not so much about emotion as it is the center of the will. Sometimes in the biblical tradition, Scripture suggests a "hardened heart" is a function of Creator's sovereignty over creation (for example, the way the Exodus story portrays Yahweh as occasionally hardening the pharaoh's heart, cf. Exod 8:15 and 4:22). But more often the biblical stories describe "hardening" as human willfulness: a refusal to see, to hear, and to understand.

In the biblical story, it is this stubbornness that often evokes God's wrath. Mark's Jesus stands here as one who is truly human—feeling emotions of anger and grief. And, also, at the same time, as one who is truly divine—expressing divine wrath and righteous anger. M. Eugene Boring explains:

> Jesus . . . responds with a combination of wrath and sorrow, expressing not only the emotion of a truly human being, but the dialectic of the divine wrath and compassion. He can unilaterally heal a withered hand, but not a hard heart.[3]

Mark's Jesus shows us the heart/*kardia* of God.

Reflection: *Righteous Anger*

When I was in seminary, I wrote papers on Martin Luther and John Calvin, influential Reformation theologians from the 1500s. They both spoke strongly about God's wrath, God's righteous anger because of human sinfulness. "In a marvelous and divine way, [God] loved us even when [God] hated us . . ." John Calvin said.[4] The Reformers did not seek to foster a sense of shame or hopelessness; rather they sought to emphasize the enormity of human estrangement from God in order to demonstrate the immensity of the grace of God available in Jesus Christ. They wanted us to see ourselves and our situation honestly so we truly can appreciate the

---

3. Boring, *Mark*, 95.

4. Calvin, *Institutes, vol. 2*, 16.4.

proffered salvation, the healing and the wholeness God has accomplished on our behalf.

Unfortunately, many of us who are heirs of the Reformation tend to misunderstand the Reformers. Instead of immersing ourselves in the grace, we wallow in the guilt. Instead of embracing God's embrace, we focus on God's judgment and punishment. I suspect we humans always have tended to cultivate the negatives much more than we have allowed the positives to shape us.

So I ask, is God for us or against us? *Yes!* I say. God is for us! But, also *Yes!* God is against wickedness, evil, and death. God opposes anything that is at work within us or around us to destroy this good creation.

Here is where the righteous anger comes in, God's justified wrath against the creeping death that so easily deludes, diminishes, and damages us humans. God would heal that living death within us. God's righteous anger would destroy that which destroys the beloved. God's wrath would purge creation of these deadly thorns and thistles so that Creator's creation is finally restored to beauty, wholeness, and *shalom*. This is our eschatological hope.

But here, now, in the world we actually inhabit, we continue to see brokenness wherever self-righteousness, self-deception, hubris, and apathy run rampant. Jeremiah's indictment of the politics of his day makes me ponder the politics of our own time. These prophetic proclamations against religious leaders who subvert politics (and/or against political leaders who subvert religion) could be chronicled almost verbatim in our own day and age. Why can't our political leaders realize they are responsible to care for (and to care about) the widow, the orphan, the alien, and the poor; our neighbors who continually live one crisis away from disaster? And why can't the church hold our political leaders accountable to this kind of compassionate servant leadership?

I believe such brokenness within community demands righteous anger *and* soft hearts. And make no mistake: tender hearts *do* break. As the heart of Jesus broke in the presence of hard heartedness and as the heart of God breaks for the pain of the world, may this divine character of passion destroy any lingering apathy within us and allow compassion to thrive instead.

Some of us may be called to be prophets within this death-dealing culture. We may be called to publically proclaim prophetic wrath for the creeping death that damages our own society. Such a calling will move us out of our comfort zones because such a ministry will conflict sharply with the self-righteous fury of the status quo. But, if we are called, we can be confident that God will accomplish God's will within us. Sometimes a little righteous anger is good for all of us.

Week 42

Hope

Jeremiah 40–52
Psalms 124, 125, 127
Revelation 12–15
Mark 4–5

As You Read the Old Testament

THE JEWS OF THE Exile for whom Isaiah and Jeremiah wrote lived far from their homes as captives in Babylon. Every family had lost someone in the war, and the memories of destruction and defeat continued to break their hearts.

Years of prophetic warnings became reality for God's people, but, because they are God's people, the prophets continued also to offer hope; hope grounded in relationship with the trustworthy God whose essence and character is marked by faithful, steadfast love. As the Lord told Jeremiah, "As for you, have no fear, my servant Jacob, says the LORD, for I am with you. I will make an end of all the nations among which I have banished you, but I will not make an end of you!" (Jer 46:27–28)

Jeremiah 46 begins the record of the judgment upon the nations for the ways they have oppressed God's people, Israel. Even though God sometimes uses the nations to punish Israel, Jeremiah believes, they too will one day suffer judgment for their mistreatment of God's beloved.

As You Read the Psalms

Imagine pilgrims on their way to Jerusalem. Imagine the gradual gathering of more and more travelers joining together as the roads drew closer to the Holy City, and then the final ascent up the hill of Zion where the Temple shone bright in the morning sun. Imagine the joy, the wonder, and the deep sense of community these pilgrims must have experienced. Now imagine them singing these *Songs of Ascent* as they ascended toward Jerusalem, their shining city on a hill.

Ancient editors grouped the hymns into this collection near the close of Book Five. These psalms are short, easily memorized, and often characterized by a call-and-response participation. They sing of personal faith or family life or national pride. Their pilgrim faith assumes God as the Source and Center of all.

Pilgrims traveled to Jerusalem for three holy feasts each year, twice in the spring and once in the fall.

> Three times a year all your males shall appear before the LORD your God at the place that he will choose: at the festival of unleavened bread, at the festival of weeks, and at the festival of booths.
> They shall not appear before the LORD empty-handed; all shall give as they are able, according to the blessing of the LORD your God that he has given you (Deut 16:16–17).

Spring brought the most holy celebration of Passover, the remembrance of their rescue from slavery in Egypt. Seven weeks later, the celebration of First Fruits reminded them of the grace of living in a settled homeland. Fall brought *Sukkot*, a reenactment of their wilderness wanderings that brought back vivid recollections of the Lord's meticulous faithfulness.

The pilgrims' anticipation of these high holy days was amplified by sharing together these traveling psalms. Clinton McCann considers the purpose of the ancient editors as they formed this collection of hymns.

> This collection was likely used by ordinary persons on the way to or on arrival at Jerusalem. The juxtaposition of psalms reflecting the daily concerns with those reflecting national concerns (Psalm 123—126; 130—132; 134) makes sense in the context of festal celebrations, where individuals and families from all over would have been brought together by loyalties that transcended the personal and familial. [1]

1. McCann, "Psalms," 1176.

Modern day Jews—sans the Temple, priesthood, and sacrificial system—continue to celebrate several of these ancient feasts with notable theological and national enlargements. Along with the biblical feasts, numerous other holy days have developed over the centuries, festal celebrations "where individuals and families from all over [are] brought together by loyalties that transcend the personal and familial." Time honored traditions and purposes find fresh expression in new generations, thus accomplishing the hopes of pilgrims sung across many ages.

As You Read the New Testament

The Christians of Asia to whom John wrote lived with constant anxiety within the Roman Empire. Confessing Jesus Christ as Lord (instead of pledging allegiance to the emperor as "lord") labeled them as traitors and subversives. We've heard of the atrocities of Nero and other emperors who harassed Christians with economic persecutions, torture, and even death when they would not deny their faith in Jesus.

In the middle of so much uncertainty, the Revelation of John pulls back the curtain of the heavens in confident reassurance that death is not the end of the story; that martyrdom is actually victory. John pictures the final culmination of the covenant promises of God and offers a glimpse of the day when all creation will be restored to wholeness and goodness, the day when hope will become ultimate reality.

As You Read the Gospel

Mark's gospel is both simple *and* complex. It is clear *and* filled with ambiguity. It's straightforward *and* multilayered. Like every good story, Mark's gospel stays with you and won't let you go. One of the parts of the story that lingers is the way Mark's Jesus is misunderstood by nearly everyone at almost every turn. *Who is this?* the characters in Mark's story ask again and again.

We who are listening in to the story, however, we who are watching from the audience get to overhear the narrator set the stage. We hear the storyteller telling us more clearly about this Jesus who is Son of God, Son of Man. Unlike John the baptizer and the other disciples, we readers can hear the voice that Jesus heard, the voice that split the heavens: "You are my Son, my Beloved" (1:11). Most of the other characters in the story

Mark tells don't have that clarity, that divine perspective. But the demons seem to; they called Jesus of Nazareth the "Holy One of God" (1:24). The pagan centurion seemed to understand; he confessed the crucified Jesus as "Son of God" (15:39).

Scholars believe the reason that no one else *got* Jesus throughout the entire gospel is because of Mark's use of a rhetorical device we call the Messianic Secret.[2] As Mark contemplates the mystery of the Truly-Human-Truly-Divine One, he employs a literary approach that communicates his theology that the truth of who Jesus is can only be understood from this side of the cross.

Jesus as Messiah/Christ—anointed and appointed by God to reveal God and to inaugurate the kingdom of God—is known only in the way of the cross. Jesus as Son of Man/Son of God—truly-human-and-truly-divine—is known only in his resurrection. Any effort to *get* Jesus by way of logic and reason, by any means other than trust (and by entrusting ourselves to the Way of Christ) is inadequate. As you read, consider Mark's wisdom in telling the story through this paradigm of the Messianic Secret.

The chapters in Mark 4–5 are packed with stories of hope. The kingdom parables continue to spark a kind of subversive hopefulness that often contrasts sharply with the seen reality of social, economic, and political realities. Mark's brilliant storytelling embeds one story of hope and healing within another: a sick girl—twelve years old—is dying while a woman—sick for twelve years—has been isolated and alone. A man, a father, an influential religious leader on the one hand and a lonely, lowly woman on the other, each reaches out to Jesus with extravagant hope and both experience a kind of resurrection.

Reflection: *Holding on to Hope*

A friend of mine showed me pictures of his visit to Auschwitz. The scenes are chilling, gut wrenching. So many powerful, profound stories of Holocaust survivors cause my heart to ache. How did they hold on to hope in such a time?

Sometimes I feel discouraged and powerless. Some days I feel almost completely hope-less; I can hardly bear to hear the daily news.

- Horrible stories from war zones;

2. Wrede, *The Messianic Secret*.

- Mind boggling stories from disaster areas;

- Outrageous stories about political and corporate corruption;

- Heart breaking stories about gun violence, police violence, domestic violence;

- Discouraging stories about too many of my friends right here in my own community who, every single day of their life, walk a tightrope between well-being and disaster.

How do any of us hold on to hope when everything around us seems so hopeless?

A few years ago, one of my seminary professors, Dr. Andrew Lester, wrote an important book about hope. Dr. Lester teaches that lived hope is first grounded in reality, then oriented toward possibility, and finally made possible within community. Hope is deeply connected to reality.

When hope is grounded in reality our eyes are wide open. We name our situations honestly and we recognize the challenges clearly. Hope doesn't see the world through rose-colored glasses; it is not wishful thinking. Hope knows full well how hard this is. But hope also sees a larger reality, a bigger picture than that which is visible to our human eyes. Christian hope counts on an invisible reality that exists because of God's existence; a reality that has come into existence through the work of God in the life and work of Jesus Christ.

This hope is real to people of the Christ—as real as it gets. Even when our observable reality appears to be hopeless, hope taps into the unseen reality of God's presence in the world, God's movement in our lives. We can look honestly at the facts of our situation and say *and yet*. We can look clear-eyed at all the evidence and say *nevertheless*. We trust that something else is true besides just our circumstances; something else is real besides the obvious. We can see the bigger picture of what God has done and what God is doing. Christian hope is grounded in the reality of the present and is oriented to the possibilities of the future.

People of faith always have been oriented towards the future. Faith means moving toward something we cannot see; stepping out on a path when we don't know where it will lead; heading in a direction that may seem completely irrational and unreasonable. People who trust can live with this kind of confidence because people of faith are deeply and irrevocably people of hope.

And where does such hope come from? Lester says, "The foundation of hope in the Judeo-Christian tradition is rooted in the character
of God, the Creator and Redeemer of the universe."[3] Because of hope,
we believe that the God who creates, redeems, and sustains is primarily
characterized by love: *agape*. Since both creation and incarnation reveal
the nature of this self-giving love, we trust that Jesus Christ is the visible
expression of God's faithfulness. This confidence gives us reason to hope
for the *not-yet-ness* of our future.

When we look toward our future, when our future stories are
shaped and fashioned with faith, hope, and love then—no matter what
comes our way—we can live our lives with deep, unshakable peace. We
can see the movement of God in our lives and in the world, and we can
confidently stand on the promises of a future with hope.

Lived hope is grounded in reality, is oriented toward possibility, and
is made possible within community. As a matter of fact, Dr. Lester says
hope *cannot* be lived in isolation; it is community that creates and nur-
tures faith. He calls it "contagious hope"—a spark of hope that generates
a spontaneous combustion of hope within an entire community.

But there is a flip side. Sometimes an infectious *hope-less-ness* takes
hold within a community. Sometimes a people will despair over their
current circumstances, cannot imagine an alternative, become so fixated
by their past that they become closed off to the future. One good antidote
for that kind of gloom is for even a few faithful people to keep themselves
grounded in the reality of God's past and present work of faithfulness and
to keep themselves oriented to God's future with hope. Just a few faithful
people living with hope can spark contagious hope and incite joyful generosity within a larger community. Just a few faithful people can thwart
an epidemic of infectious hopelessness.

The prophetic word of Jeremiah promised a new covenant—God's
way written not on tablets of stone but written on the human heart. God's
promise to forgive sin, to restore *shalom*, to be known—truly known,
intimately known. This ancient and new covenant of hope is the foundation for Christian faith. Christians see the life and death and resurrected-
eternal life of Jesus Christ as God's embodied promise. Christ *is* the new
covenant in this our new future with hope.

There is much to be discouraged about in our current world. If (as
Dr. Lester says) we begin by naming our reality then we have to admit

---

3. Lester, *Hope*, 65.

things quite often are quite depressing. It is all too easy to despair, to feel hopeless and powerless in these troubled days. Lester encourages us to name all that, but not to stay there. Rather we must move on to imagine future possibilities; we must plant ourselves in hope's rich soil. We best do this in community because we are a people who hold on to each other as we hold on to hope. Together, we become a people who hope for each other as we imagine future possibilities.

Impossible possibilities is a constant theme throughout *The Story*. When we are grounded in faith and hope; when we are shaped by God's character of self-giving love; when we can glimpse God's bigger picture; when we are living in *God's Story*—then we can imagine all sorts of impossible possibilities and we can remind each other to hold on to the one who holds on to us.

Week 43
Ezekiel

Ezekiel
Psalm 83
Psalm 139
Revelation 16–18
Mark 6

As You Read the Old Testament

READING ALL OF EZEKIEL in one week may seem daunting, but it's very doable. You might use this guide to help you zip through some of the sections and then slow down to appreciate other portions with its fascinating apocalyptic poetry.

The prophet-priest Ezekiel was in Babylon with an early wave of exiles deported from their homeland as a part of King Nebuchadnezzar II's "brain drain" in 597 BCE.

> In the thirtieth year, in the fourth month, on the fifth day of the month, as I was among the exiles by the river Chebar, the heavens were opened, and I saw visions of God.
>
> On the fifth day of the month (it was the fifth year of the exile of King Jehoiachin), the word of the LORD came to the priest Ezekiel son of Buzi, in the land of the Chaldeans by the river Chebar; and the hand of the LORD was on him there (1:1–3).

Chapters 1–5: Visions of winged creatures darting to and fro like lightening, each with four faces (human, lion, ox, and eagle), each with four wings, and each accompanied by a wheel within a wheel rimmed with eyes all around. Visions of a scroll, eaten and tasting like honey. Object lessons embodied by Ezekiel warning of impending judgments. Ezekiel's visions spark our imagination and cultivate our curiosity; they bring us to wonder.

Chapters 6–24: Harsh indictments and startling promises of destruction; prophecies against Israel and Jerusalem charged with high crimes of breaking covenant. "The word of the LORD came to me: 'O mortal, set your face . . . and prophesy . . .'" (6:1).

Chapters 25–33: Proclamations against the nations. Notice how Yahweh complains about the nations' mistreatment of Israel. "Then you shall know that I am the LORD" are the powerful words that follow almost every one of these declarations.

Chapter 34 rails against sham shepherds in Israel while promising rescue and restoration of the flock of God's people.

> I myself will be the shepherd of my sheep, and I will make them lie down, says the LORD God. I will seek the lost, and I will bring back the strayed, and I will bind up the injured, and I will strengthen the weak, but the fat and the strong I will destroy. I will feed them with justice (34:15–16).
>
> I will set up over them one shepherd, my servant David, and he shall feed them: he shall feed them and be their shepherd (34:23).

Then the famous and enigmatic chapter 37: "The hand of the LORD came upon me. He brought me out by the spirit of the LORD and set me down in the middle of a valley; it was full of bones. He led me all around them; there were very many lying in the valley, and they were very dry. And God said to me, 'Mortal/son of man, can these bones live?'" (37:1–3)

Chapters 40–48 envision a new Temple, an alternative future renewed with hope. "As the glory of the LORD entered the temple by the gate facing east, the spirit lifted me up, and brought me into the inner court; and the glory of the LORD filled the temple" (43:4–5). "And the name of the city from that time on shall be: *The LORD is There*" (48:35).

Note the prophet and "the word of the Lord" gave no hope that the people and land of Ezekiel's day would be spared from destruction. The time of judgment had come and it was irrevocable. OT Scholar Katheryn Pfisterer Darr says:

> First, Ezekiel asserts Yahweh's unparalleled sovereignty over history and the nations. His worldview is utterly theocentric. God

is at work in the world, controlling nations and events according to God's own plan.

Second, that plan includes the destruction of Judah. Ezekiel insists that the approaching devastation is the doing, not the undoing, of Israel's God . . .

Third, Ezekiel insists that God's punishments are just . . .[1]

The hope offered was given for future generations who, on the other side of Exile, had opportunity to become a more faithful people than their ancestors had been.

As You Read the Psalms

Psalm 139 is one of my favorites. I have a strong memory of a time when I was overwhelmed with self-doubt and a negative self-image. When I got to verse 14 and read these beautiful words, I wept: "I praise you, for I am fearfully and wonderfully made. Wonderful are your works; I know that very well." During those miserable days, I certainly did not feel like a "wonderful work," but the psalmist helped turn my insecurity into humble confidence. Even with all my flaws and failures, the poem helps me *know* I too am a wonderful work of the Creator.

"Where can I go from your spirit? Or where can I flee from your presence? . . . If I take the wings of the morning and settle at the farthest limits of the sea—even there your hand shall lead me; your right hand shall hold me fast" (139:7–10). Sometimes some people talk as if the world is divided into sacred and secular, holy and profane, but that is not the understanding of this poet. Instead, Creator-Redeemer-Sustainer fills every nook and cranny of creation and saturates all the world with holiness. There is no place where God is not.

Psalm 139 continues with a celebration of life's mystery.

> It was you who formed my inward parts; you knit me together in my mother's womb; I praise you, for I am fearfully and wonderfully made (139:13–14).

Remember this is *poetry*, not physiology or anatomy. If talking points about the science of when life begins influence your reading here, please set them aside; instead simply relish the beautiful mystery of life of which the poet sings. God's people have always had (will always have)

---

1. Darr, "Ezekiel," 1085.

different understandings about life's beginnings and endings. Life is mystery and only Creator holds the full mystery. The rest of us do the best we can holding all life as sacred and not desecrating any life for any reason—human, plant, or animal.

This poetry about being "woven in the depths of the earth" and about a "book" that preordains our days is deeply true but not literal. Consider also that our poet may be speaking of something much larger than an individual life; he may well be celebrating the creation and the very existence of Israel. From "nothingness" (from slavery), God knitted together a people and created/formed a beloved "son." Within God's "book" (covenant) is life and wisdom for the living of every day.

"How weighty to me are your thoughts, O God! How vast is the sum of them! I try to count them—they are more than the sand." Then there is this odd, dark interlude:

> O that you would kill the wicked and that the bloodthirsty would depart from me—those who speak of you maliciously and lift themselves up against you for evil! Do I not hate those who hate you, O LORD? (139:17–21)

When Psalm 139 is read in church settings, these jarring words are usually left unsaid. Some scholars theorize a later editor added them to the original poet's words; that may be. Nonetheless I think we must take the poet (or the editor) seriously and consider what this imprecatory prayer might have meant to him.

We have seen the pattern repeated throughout the psalms where the pray-ers ask God to curse the wicked, to punish evildoers, to pay back wrongs. This may be personal, but within the tradition of Israel, it is more likely to be communal. The poets speak for all God's people.

When the entire beloved community is threatened, disrespected, and damaged, the reputation of Israel's *God* is at stake. These startling prayers are the psalmists' efforts to motivate God to act righteously in the face of unrighteousness and to put the world back into its proper balance.

The prayers are also eschatological, that is, the pray-ers are counting on God's ultimate justice to one day bring all encompassing *shalom* to all God's creation.

The psalm's conclusion is a bold prayer, a way for the poet to declare unambiguously *I am on the Lord's side.* "Search me, O God, and know my heart; test me and know my thoughts. See if there is any wicked way in me and lead me in the way everlasting" (139:23–24). Such intimate, honest knowledge is our salvation. Oh that the church of today would open ourselves to such holy, refining, redeeming knowledge; to this divine searching, knowing, and leading!

As You Read the New Testament

Seven angels wield seven bowls filled with the wrath of God. The great whore rides upon a scarlet beast with seven heads, which are seven mountains. The woman is clothed in purple and scarlet, drunk with the blood of the saints: *Babylon the great, the mother of whores.* "This calls for a mind that has wisdom," the angel warns (17:4–9). Indeed, I say!

The pastoral letter of John's apocalyptic vision was written to the seven churches of Asia around 95 CE, at least twenty years past the Roman-Jewish War of 60–70 when Rome had vanquished Jerusalem and devastated the Second Temple. Hearkening back to the devastation of the First Temple by the Babylonian Empire, John (along with other Jewish and Christian writers) used "Babylon" as an obvious symbol for the Roman Empire.

As you read Revelation alongside Ezekiel, ponder the sturdy thread that connects these two prophets across the centuries. Whereas Ezekiel envisioned a restored temple, the final part of John's vision says, "I saw no temple in the city, for its temple is the Lord God the Almighty and the Lamb" (21:22).

Whereas Ezekiel blasted Israel with a litany of her sins, John comforts God's people with prophetic reassurance of God's faithful presence with them and ultimate victory on their behalf.

> I saw another angel coming down from heaven, having great authority; and the earth was made bright with his splendor. He called out with a mighty voice: "Fallen, fallen is Babylon the great!" (Rev 18:1–2)

The final fall of Rome would not happen for another 350 years, thus reminding us of the truth articulated by Martin Luther King Jr. "The arc of the moral universe is long, but it bends towards justice."

As You Read the Gospel

There is this little gem of a story in Mark 6 about Jesus returning to his hometown. Jesus addressed the synagogue and began to teach, but very quickly, the congregation took offense.

> Then Jesus said to them, "Prophets are not without honor, except in their hometown, and among their own kin, and in their own house." And he could do no deed of power there, except that he laid his hands on a few sick people and cured them. And he was amazed at their unbelief (6:4–6).

As Mark tells the story, even Jesus' own intimates struggled to understand who he was and what he was about; the miracles and signs only seemed to confound them more. After five thousand people were fed with five loaves and two fish, after Jesus walked across the sea to join them in their storm-tossed boat, "they were utterly astounded for they did not understand about the loaves, but their hearts were hardened" (6:52). Hardened, dulled, veiled—in Mark's understanding, faith is much more than logic, reasoning, or rational assent. Rather, we are *faith*-full when we open ourselves to God's ever-coming kingdom as gift, miracle, and revelation. Our faithful response to God's presence and work is bound up in God's own faithfulness and grace.

Chapter 6 also tells the story of the NT prophet, John the Baptizer, martyred by King Herod. Those who dare speak prophetic truth to power—this John, along with John of Patmos, Ezekiel, and so many others—have always suffered pushback, and even violence, from the powers and kingdoms of this world.

Reflection: *Visions, Parables, and Poetry*

Centuries after the devastation of Ezekiel's beloved community, Mark's Christians endured the assault of Rome within that same land. Once again, the city was leveled and the Temple destroyed. Jesus' followers in the troubled days of Mark and John of Patmos remembered the promise that the Risen Christ would come again (*now would be a good time*, they must have been thinking). But, no, difficult times dragged on and on.

Hearing again the stories of Jesus, remembering how he taught that things come to fullness in their time, hoping again in the God whose ways may be hidden but who is ever at work in the most ordinary events of our lives—would these first century Christians have ears to hear and eyes to see this grace? Would they, too, hold on to hope?

> The whole house of Israel says: "Our bones are dried up, and our hope is lost; we are cut off completely."
> But you shall know that I am the LORD, when I . . . bring you up . . . O my people. I will put my spirit within you, and you shall live . . . Then you shall know that I, the LORD, have spoken; I will act (Ezek 37).

Surely the words and the experiences of their ancestor Ezekiel in exile helped early Christians hold on to hope.

These stories of Scripture tell us truth, truth about who we are as humans and who we are as God's people—formed, re-formed, and constantly transformed. They point us beyond what we see with our eyes in the here and now, and they project alternate realities, different possibilities, other visions of what is and what may be. The storytellers, poets, and visionaries among us play a crucial role; they help us make meaning. They help us see.

Plato had his philosophies and Einstein had his formulas, but it is storytelling and poetry that is the way of Scripture. Adam and Eve, Noah and the ark, Jonah and the great fish, dry bone valleys—all these stories help us grasp a truth that is larger and deeper than facts, that is much more than history. These stories of Scripture are not meant to be parsed as literal events, rather, they are intended to be *discovered* and *experienced* as deeply true by our deeper ways of knowing.

The stories of Scripture not only tell us something about who we are, where we've come from, and where we're going, they also give us glimpses of truth about the God who is the Author and Goal of *The Story*, the one overarching story of which all our little stories are a part. The visionaries of Scripture help us envision the possibilities of our lives. They help us hear the whispers of heaven and the cry of our neighbor. They help us name what is real.

The eschatological hope of this apocalyptic poetry has echoed again and again throughout human history. African American slaves who tilled the sandy soil of the South often sang spirituals drawn from images of the prophets: *"Dem bones, dem bones gonna rise again! Now hear the word of the Lord!"* Can you imagine how dry the bones of these weary people must have felt? How hopeless their lives must have seemed? Even in our own day, too many of our Black sisters and brothers continue to live their lives in too many dry bone valleys.

Oppressed and marginalized people continue to hold onto the hope expressed by prophets like Ezekiel and John, the stories of Scripture seeping into their bones, finding connection in their joints, breathing in and out across generations until something new is finally brought to life. This ancient vision from Ezekiel continues to speak to the beleaguered faithful in every age, offering courage to endure the present as well as finding hope that points to the future: *"these bones gonna rise again!"* Maybe not now, maybe not soon or even in our own time and place—but someday! The promise is sure!

Week 44

Daniel

Daniel
Psalm 57
Psalm 58
Psalm 60
Revelation 19–20
Mark 7–8

As You Read the Old Testament

THE FIRST SIX CHAPTERS of the book of Daniel contain a collection of short stories from the Hebrew exile, stories about Daniel and his friends, Azariah, Mishael, and Hananiah. (Those of us who heard these stories growing up may be more familiar with the names Shadrach, Meshach, and Abednego, slave names given to them in Babylon.) These several short stories function much like novellas, as we saw in the books of Esther and Jonah. Try to make time this week to read the entire book of Daniel in one sitting.

I love all these Daniel stories but especially the one about the fiery furnace. Hananiah, Mishael, and Azariah were present at the dedication of a gigantic statue of King Nebuchadnezzar when the drums began to roll and the flutes began to play, when all the people were commanded to bow down and worship the image. But of course—good Jews that they were, Hebrews who had learned their lesson and had become thoroughly monotheistic—these three worshipers of the one true God would not bow down to another.

Nebuchadnezzar was furious. His face contorted with rage, he spewed threats and stoked the fires of the immense furnace. I love their reply. "If our God whom we serve is able to deliver us from the furnace of blazing fire and out of your hand, O king, let him deliver us. But if not, be it known that we will still not serve your gods and we will not worship the golden statue" (3:16–18). Their conviction reminds us of Queen Esther. Our God *can* deliver, but if not, all right then: *if I perish, I perish.*

In that day, in this kind of empire, to defy a king was a death sentence, and so the three courageous men were bound and driven into the fiery furnace. But instead of incineration, when the king looked closer, he saw them strolling within the blazing fire. Not only were they walking instead of burnt to a crisp, but a fourth man could be seen strolling in the fire with them. "One like a Son of God," the storyteller marvels.

> "Did not we cast three men bound into the midst of the fire?"
> They answered and said unto the king: "True, O king."
> He answered and said: "Lo, I see four men loose, walking in the midst of the fire, and they have no hurt; and the form of the fourth is like the Son of God" (Dan 3:24–25 KJV).

(*Living in The Story* usually quotes from the NRSV, which translates the original language as "the fourth has the appearance of a god." Here is another reminder that there is no such thing as reading without interpretation. Every translation is an interpretation.)

Fiery furnaces or lions' dens—people of faith don't go through hard times because we haven't been good enough or faithful enough. *No!* As often as not, our obedience to God's way, our faithfulness to God's values are the very things that place us in opposition to the values of the world. It is exactly *because* we try to do what is right that we often find ourselves embroiled in some controversy. So be it. Like Daniel, like Hananiah, Meshael, and Azariah we will not define ourselves according to what other people think is right. And we must not let fear decide our path. "One like a Son of God" walks with us.

As You Read the Psalms

Although the traditional setting of Psalm 57 places it during the time of David's trials, we can see Daniel in the poet's cries of complaint and praise. "Be merciful to me, O God, for in you my soul takes refuge . . . I lie down among lions that greedily devour human prey; their teeth are spears and arrows, their tongues sharp swords . . ." See the double meaning here: adversaries like lions and their accusing words like swords. Adversaries like beasts that lie in wait and plot destruction.

How do any of us respond to such threats and challenges? Like Daniel and like the psalmist, people of faith will orient themselves toward the Creator-Redeemer-Sustainer of all-that-is. "I cry to God Most High, to God who fulfills his purpose for me (57:2)."

This profession that God "fulfills" our life's purpose does not mean God dictates every decision we make and every step we take. Rather Psalm 57 suggests that God holds overarching meaning for us, the one who is our beginning and our end sustains our big picture plan. Such a belief comforts us because we can trust that Creator is in everything— dark and light, danger and safety, terror and beauty. Faith leads us to trust that God Most High holds all things and is weaving everything together in ways we will never understand.

As You Read the New Testament

Just as the apocalyptic visions of Daniel reminded Israel in Exile that God's people were not abandoned, so the Revelation offered hope to beleaguered Christians under Roman occupation. No matter the long, weary years of oppression, the prophets reassure, God is at work in the world.

"The man clothed in linen . . . raised his right hand and his left hand toward heaven. And I heard him swear by the one who lives forever that it would be for a time, two times, and half a time, and that when the shattering of the power of the holy people comes to an end, all these things would be accomplished" (Dan 12:7). Closely following Daniel, Revelation encourages John's generation that all times are in God's hands.

> But the woman was given the two wings of the great eagle, so that she could fly from the serpent into the wilderness, to her place where she is nourished for a time, and times, and half a time (Rev 12:14).

Prophets across the ages have reminded God's people that history continues to move toward God's ultimate consummation of peace.

> He said, "Go your way, Daniel, for the words are to remain secret and sealed until the time of the end" (Dan 12:9).
> And he said to me, "Do not seal up the words of the prophecy of this book, for the time is near" (Rev 22:10).

The Revelation affirms that the beginning of the end has begun. When everything all around is chaos, when the world seems overcome with beasts and dragons, the message of apocalyptic literature gives insight into the present darkness and glimpses into the future. Thus the core message of the Revelation is: Faithful God is working faithfully for the goodness and *shalom* of all creation, therefore remain faithful even unto death. The Creator and Completer, the Alpha and Omega, the Beginning and the End is on the throne. Death is not the end of the story.

You and I may have a hard time imagining the oppression of people of faith across the ages and across the globe because we modern Christians (especially we white American Christians) live with much privilege in our time and place. For those of us ensconced in privilege, it's a good exercise for us to learn to read these texts through the lens of our oppressed sisters and brothers. After all, we remember the Bible was written *by* people on the bottom of society *for* people on the bottom—that's why the gospel is such good news to all those who are oppressed and marginalized. But then again, even those of us who live comfortable lives also experience pain, grief, hopelessness, confusion, and uncertainty. So yes, of course, the gospel is good news for everyone.

As You Read the Gospel

Mark 8 serves as a hinge in this gospel and the Messianic Secret is wound extremely tight as Mark portrays (at the same time) *both* the earthly Jesus traveling the way of the cross *and* the Crucified-Risen Christ exemplifying the eternal way of the cosmos: "those who lose their life for God's sake . . . will save it."

Jesus affirms that he is, in fact, Messiah and elaborates on its meaning. "The Son of Man must undergo great suffering, and be rejected by the elders, the chief priests, and the scribes, and be killed, and after three days rise again" (8:31). Then he calls all his disciples to "deny themselves and take up their cross and follow . . . For those who want to save their life will lose it, and those who lose their life for my sake, and for the sake of the gospel, will save it" (8:34–35). Much as Peter took issue with this startling way of Messiah, so we too resist such a way. This way of salvation feels upside-down to us self-centered humans but, as we have seen again and again throughout the Scriptures, this inside-out-and-right-side-up way is God's eternal way. Any attempt to circumvent that way of cosmic wisdom treads the way of fools. "Get behind me, satan," commands the Truly-Human-Truly-Divine One. Do not set your mind on human things, rather orient your mind toward divine things.

There is an odd little story in Mark 7 that challenges us as we try to make sense of *who is this Jesus?* and *who are we?* I really like this woman who argued with Jesus.

> A woman whose little daughter had an unclean spirit immediately heard about [Jesus], and she came and bowed down at his feet. Now the woman was a Gentile [and] she begged him to cast the demon out of her daughter.
>
> [Jesus] said to her, "Let the children be fed first, for it is not fair to take the children's food and throw it to the dogs."
>
> But she answered him, "Sir, even the dogs under the table eat the children's crumbs" (7:24–30).

Of all the characters in Mark's gospel, this woman is one of the few who catches a glimpse of the coming together of Jews and Gentiles living in harmony and wholeness within the reign of God.

Even in the face of Jesus' provocative pushback that it is the Jews who are God's "children," she is bold to argue, "Yes, but." Even God's "crumbs" provide more than enough grace for outsiders and more than enough kindness for strangers. Even crumbs of God's mercy are more than enough for one little Gentile child. It is the gospel she proclaims.

The authors of the Book of Common Prayer[1] understood the function of this story in the Gospel of Mark: it reassures faithful Jewish Christians that Jesus fully welcomes their Gentile brothers and sisters into the fellowship of the church, and it gently cautions us Gentile Christians against arrogance toward our Jewish brothers and sisters. They were here first. We are grafted into the vine.[2]

Mark says it was "because of her saying" that the woman's daughter was healed. This "saying," this *logos* (the Greek word), this word of the gospel is the good news of God's saving grace to *all* people.

Like a mama bear protecting her children, this woman who argued with Jesus is *our* mother too; all us Gentiles are her children. In the pattern of the psalmists who argued that God must keep faith and live up to

---

1. *Book of Common Prayer,* Rite 1, 337: "We do not presume to come to this thy Table, O merciful Lord, trusting in our own righteousness, but in thy manifold and great mercies. We are not worthy so much as to gather up the crumbs under thy Table. But thou are the same Lord whose property is always to have mercy . . ."

2. See Paul's discussion in Romans 11.

the covenant, so she insisted, if the gospel truly is good news, then it must be lived out truly.

Reflection: *In The Lions' Den*

Have you ever been in a den of lions? You are sitting at your dining room table with bills piled high. There's another stack of letters too: the eviction notice, the termination date, the warning that they will soon repossess the car; you're surrounded with troubles that are tearing you apart. You are at the bedside of your loved one. The door opens and in walks the doctor, the charge nurse, and the chaplain; you know life is about to close in on you. You are in a church meeting when people who love each other start clawing and tearing at one another. You can't believe your ears. What could possibly be so important that Christian friends would devour each other? You wish an angel would shut all their mouths.

Whatever the particular lions' dens that have threatened you over the course of your life, whatever the details, we all can say we've been there, done that. And I'm guessing on the other side of all these troubles, many of us might say—like Daniel, like Hananiah, Meshael, and Azariah—"God saved me." God hasn't saved us in the same way our storyteller describes, but somehow, in some mystery, we knew we were not alone and we got through some kind of impossible situation by sheer grace.

It is in these kinds of experiences that we knew we found strength beyond our own strength, wisdom beyond our own wisdom, endurance that we never could have imagined. And we know God was somehow in it all, walking with us, carrying us, leading us, nudging us, and protecting us.

Malala Yousafzai reminds me of these bold believers in the story of Daniel. Malala was eleven years old when the Taliban in her Pakistani hometown began to threaten the girls who dared go to school. These fanatics insisted girls should stay in their place and work in the home; they believed formal education for women was unnecessary, even dangerous for their vision of society. Malala disagreed and began to say so publicly. "Why should I wait for someone else to speak up for me?" she asked. "I need to stand up for myself." She did, and speaking up made her into a target.

Malala had thought about the possibility of attack since threats and warnings were everywhere. She imagined herself facing a terrorist, wondering what she would do. "Maybe I'd take off my shoes and hit him. But then I'd think—if I did that, there would be no difference between me and the terrorist." So Malala made a plan. She would say to her attacker, "Listen to me. What you are doing is wrong. Every girl ought to be able to go to school. OK, shoot me . . ."[3]

Malala was fifteen when the Taliban invaded her school bus and shot her in the face. Malala survived and courageously fought her way back to her bold, outspoken life. Then, on her sixteenth birthday in 2013, Malala Yousafzai addressed the United Nations General Assembly. In 2104, she was awarded the Nobel Peace Prize. Like Daniel, like Hananiah, Meshael, and Azariah, Malala would not define herself according to what other people think is right; Malala would not let fear decide her path.

Like Daniel, like Esther and even Malala, we also can see how Jesus' authority comes from a much different source than the kings and tyrants of the age; Jesus' power comes from self-giving and self-sacrifice. The gospel announces the unreasonable love of God poured into the cross of Jesus Christ and proclaims the unstoppable love of God breathing life into death. Like the Christ whose name we wear, like the God whose image we bear, like the Spirit whose call we hear, the church is a people who give ourselves away. Within the gospel is the power to create (even in us self-centered humans) a passion to surrender our own rights and privileges on behalf of others.

Such mysterious power can be quite intimidating to some people, because God's power does not seek to conquer and control, rather the power of God is power to save, heal, and reconcile. The power of love was the message Jesus preached. But Jesus did more than *proclaim* the message. Jesus did more than *commit* himself to the message; Jesus the Christ *is* the message, the good news that the one true God is King, Sovereign, and Lord of all creation.

When Jesus was placed in his own den of death, when the stone rolled over the opening and all hope was gone, it was Jesus' faith and self-sacrifice that created space for God to do an audacious and faithful thing. From the crucible of Jesus' obedience and self-giving, God caused death to birth life, and hope was born for all of us. The cross is the very heart of the gospel.

3. Yousafzai, *I Am Malala*, 4.

Week 45
Ezra

Ezra
Haggai
Zechariah
Psalm 17
Psalm 67
Revelation 21–22
Mark 9–10

As You Read the Old Testament

EZRA AND NEHEMIAH ARE short books, around a dozen chapters each. Most likely they were originally one literary work so this may explain why some of the chronology confuses scholars who try to reconstruct the Ezra-Nehemiah story within history. Dating events in post-exilic Israel begins with dating the kings of the east alluded to these stories. Notice how many kings are mentioned: Cyrus the Great (539–30 BCE), King Darius (522–486), King Ahasuerus (486–65), and King Artaxerxes (465–25), all rulers in history to whom we can apply some reliable dates.

(By the way, you may recognize the name Ahasuerus mentioned in the Esther story, which "happened in the days of Ahasuerus, the same Ahasuerus who ruled over one hundred twenty-seven provinces from India to Ethiopia" (Esth 1:1). This is a reminder that not all Jews returned to their homeland. Jews of the Diaspora made new homes in nations across the known world.)

Ezra was a scribe, trained in the meticulous production and repro-duction of manuscripts, thus scribes were widely respected as learned and knowledgeable people. Ezra's account of the restoration history be-gins with King Cyrus, the Persian monarch who had conquered Babylon's empire. In the language of faith (not simple history), Ezra asserts that the Lord God put it into the king's heart to restore the Jewish people to their homeland. So around the middle of the sixth century BCE, Cyrus returned treasures that had been plundered from Solomon's Temple, outfitted the travelers with supplies, and encouraged Persian citizens to contribute financially to their quest as the first wave of exiles returned to their homeland.

Zerubbabel rises as the wise and trustworthy political leader who partnered with Jeshua, a priest from the tribe of Levi. (I love these names! Zer-RUB-bubble is such a fun name to say. It means "seed of Babylon." The name Jeshua may sound familiar. "Joshua" is its other version but when we come into the NT, this name becomes "Jesus." As you read, watch for descriptions of Jeshua's ministry and character. Messianic allu-sions are hard to miss.)

The early exiles engaged the hard work of resettling Jerusalem and rebuilding the Temple. This Second Temple was dedicated ca. 516 BCE, just about seventy years after the Jews had been removed from Israel, a timeframe that had been proclaimed by the prophets. (See Jer 25:11–12 and 29:10; Dan 9:2.)

Ezra returned to Jerusalem about fifty-eight years after the Temple was rebuilt (mid-fifth century BCE). His particular challenge was to rees-tablish proper Temple worship and instruct the people in the Law and its requirements for life and piety. Nehemiah probably arrived in Jerusalem about a dozen years after Ezra with the task was of rebuilding the walls around the city and reestablishing Jerusalem's civil society.

As you read Zechariah, note how the first eight chapters flow with a narrative style, while chapters 9–14 record a catalogue of oracles from the Lord of Hosts, most of them "regarding the nations that plundered you: 'Truly, one who touches you touches the apple of my eye'" (Zech 2:8).

The book that carries Zechariah's name begins with the story of Zechariah's divine call. "On the twenty-fourth day of the eleventh month, the month of Shebat, in the second year of Darius, the word of the LORD came to the prophet Zechariah . . ." Descriptions of Zechariah's prophetic visions follow—visions of horses, blacksmiths, and chariots. There are angels, the satan, and the high priest, Joshua/Jeshua, competing for influence among the people of Israel. And then, filling everything, "the eyes of the LORD, which range through the whole earth" (4:10). Zechariah envisions a renewed Temple where God's glory may once again dwell—visions that are much more eschatological than historical.

Plenty of dire warnings punctuate Zechariah's message, but for the most part, he offers encouragement and hope for post-exilic Israel, restoration and redemption—"not by might, nor by power, but by my spirit, says the LORD" (Zech 4:6).

As You Read the Psalms

Picture someone's face beaming upon their beloved, eyes sparkling, mouth curved into a huge smile of enjoyment at the very presence of the one they love. Several of the psalms repeat this charming metaphor, which first was given to Israel in the context of the dedication of the tabernacle.

> The LORD spoke to Moses, saying: Speak to Aaron and his sons, saying: Thus you shall bless the Israelites, you shall say to them:
> "The LORD bless you and keep you. The LORD make his face to shine upon you, and be gracious to you; the LORD lift up his countenance upon you, and give you peace" (Num 6:22–26).

I see this blessing in my husband's face when he basks in the beauty of our grandchildren. I often see it in my husband's eyes when he looks at me. What amazing grace to be so adored, so deeply blessed by such shining love! Psalm 67 confidently asks for this divine love, grace, and blessing. "May God be gracious to us and bless us and make his face to shine upon us . . ." But notice the context; the poet seeks this blessing upon God's people so that God's people may become a blessing to the nations—"that your way may be known upon earth, your saving power among all nations."

> Let the nations be glad and sing for joy, for you judge the peoples with equity and guide the nations upon earth (67:1–4).

The psalmist hearkens back to God's promise to father Abraham, "I will make of you a great nation, and I will bless you, and make your name great, so that you will be a blessing. I will bless those who bless you . . . and in you all the families of the earth shall be blessed" (Gen 12:1–3).

"Blessing" must never be taken as an end in itself. God's grace always is given so that it may be given again. Grace not shared is insufficient grace. Our calling, our vocation as people of faith is to become vessels, conduits of blessing to everyone we meet. To give what we have received and pay it forward, to share what God has graciously shared with us.

Consider again the image of a delighted face beaming. In the presence of open-hearted human love we are able to glimpse the shining face of God's love. We humans find ourselves blossoming and blooming in the sunshine of such gracious acceptance. Once the church grasps the amazing grace of God's loving acceptance toward us, our life task from then on is to offer that acceptance to others.

As You Read the New Testament

You may have noticed that mainline preachers mostly avoid the Revelation of Jesus to John. This is unfortunate on so many levels. My NT professor at seminary helped me see that some of the current weirdness surrounding interpretations of the Revelation is partly the fault of the mainline church. Instead of progressive Christian teachers offering solid theological reflection on this apocalyptic text, we too often have failed to teach and preach from the book and thus we created a vacuum—a vacuum within which all sorts of odd interpretations of the vision have incubated in American Christianity in the past decades.

While this apocalyptic text has been much misappropriated by modern day faux prophets, the rest of the church has missed its message of hope. The Revelation is a vision of hope offering courage to Christians living under the thumb of oppressive governments and under the disapproval of unbelieving societies.

The original readers recognized the symbolism and understood the message without much trouble, because our first century sisters and brothers were steeped in this genre of apocalyptic visions. They would have been quick to interpret the metaphors. For us, the images seem bizarre, startling, and violent; quite strange to our modern sensibilities. But maybe they shouldn't be so strange. We too are familiar with stories of fire breathing dragons and spectacular battles between good and evil. We know something about the devastations of earthquakes, fires, and floods. We see violence and hate and hubris all the time. Every once in a while, we even experience the sun turning dark!

It's always tricky to do faithful biblical interpretation that reaches across the ages from the first century to the twenty-first century; even so appropriate interpretation is vital practice for today's church. So here is an important interpretive principle: *the Revelation was not written to us.* This vision was revealed to John as a timely message for particular congregations in a particular circumstance of history. It was a word for them in their unique situation.

But then again, of course, Scripture *is* written for us. Most faithful students of the Bible have experienced the mystery of being addressed by the Word of God through the words of Scripture. Sometimes we find a message that is exactly the word we need to hear at a particular circumstance of our own lives. As you read the Bible, always stay open to that mystery.

As You Read the Gospel

Mark's gospel tells us truth—deep and profound truth—but it tells this indescribable truth in simple stories. We don't know if all these stories happened in history the way Mark tells them; probably not. Mark's way is a theological story telling. He assumes the flesh and blood reality of the man Jesus of Nazareth, but his gospel ponders what it *means* that heaven has now intersected earth and changed everything in the life, death, and resurrection of Jesus. It is *meaning* that is significant within the gospel of Mark (and with all the biblical writers). *Who is God? Who are we? Why does this matter? What does this mean?*

Later Christians will grapple with this truly-human-truly-divine mystery and attempt to distill it into creedal statements. Later Christians will let its theological nuance divide them into camps. Later Christians will try to come up with neat explanations that contain wide truth in well-defined boxes. But Mark is wise enough to recognize how indescribable this mystery actually is, so when Mark seeks to describe the truly-human-truly-divine conundrum, he does it with story. As he writes his gospel and tells *The Story* in his own way, Mark's Jesus shows us who God is. And Mark's Jesus teaches us who we are; who we are meant to be. [1]

Reflection: *All Things New*

> Then I saw a new heaven and a new earth, for the first heaven
> and the first earth had passed away, and the sea was no more.

---

1. M. Eugene Boring's little book *Truly Human Truly Divine* is an excellent look at this mystery. I highly recommend it.

> And I saw the holy city, the new Jerusalem, coming down out of heaven from God, prepared as a bride adorned for her husband.
>
> And I heard a loud voice from the throne saying, "See, the home of God is among mortals. He will dwell with them as their God; they will be his people and God himself will be with them; God will wipe every tear from their eyes. Death will be no more. Mourning and crying and pain will be no more, for the first things have passed away."
>
> And the one who was seated on the throne said, "See: I am making all things new."
>
> Then he said to me, "I am the Alpha and the Omega, the beginning and the end. Those who conquer will inherit these things, and I will be their God and they will be my children" (Rev 21:1–7).

This glorious passage is used often at funerals as families gather around a loved one's casket to hear comforting words that point to a hopeful future, words that whisper "reunion."

Revelation 21 offers a final vision of creation's eschatological future. It's a glorious picture of hope as we hold on to faith that the Creator is bringing all-that-is to a good and perfect consummation. The Revelation pictures Creator as the Alpha and the Omega, the Beginning and the End, the First and the Last. God who is All-in-All is bringing into being a new heaven and a new earth, "a new Jerusalem" coming down from heaven. (Consider how important this image would be for Christians of John's time who had experienced the destruction of the beloved Jerusalem.) In the walls of this heavenly city, there are twelve gates that are twelve pearls. And the gates are always open.

I have a confession to make. I cheated on the above Scripture passage. The part we read at the first is beautiful, hopeful, and joyful. But the very next sentence that I didn't quote says this:

> As for the cowardly, the faithless, the polluted, the murderers, the fornicators, the sorcerers, the idolaters, and all liars, their place will be in the lake that burns with fire and sulfur, which is the second death (21:8).

Startling, isn't it? But again, unsettling language is a key aspect of apocalyptic literature. In this dualistic genre, there is only good and evil, right and wrong, light and darkness. There is no grey, no middle ground. For John, faith must make no compromise.

But what stands out for me is the promise that God is making *all* things new, so that even the faithless and cowardly can be made new. What impresses me is the image of the holy city with all its gates flung wide open, so that even those polluted by deception and infidelity can be redeemed, renewed, and invited in. What amazes me is the message of welcome and hope for anyone who is willing to come, to turn, to enter, and to be made new.

Any church that catches a glimpse of this vision has opportunity to align itself with this cosmic, heavenly reality that Alpha and Omega is bringing into existence. We Christians have fresh chances to shape our own kingdom-life into the contours of the reign of God, to cultivate communities that hunger and thirst for newness. To be a people who do not give in to fear and faithlessness but who live into courage and commitment. To offer the witness of good news, to *be* the good news for our neighbors who struggle with uncertainty and hopelessness. To make sure the doors of our own hearts stay wide open for everyone because we believe in the promise of the one who makes everything new.

May we too trust in the Spirit who ever conceives and births new life within us and among us. May we continue to open ourselves to eternal newness.

Week 46

Nehemiah

Nehemiah
Psalm 13
Psalm 68
Psalm 147
Philippians
Mark 11–12

As You Read the Old Testament

In Nehemiah's Memoir, he says he served as cupbearer for King Artaxerxes I (465–25) and lived in the capitol city of the Persian Empire. He described his distress when he received word about his fellow Jews in Jerusalem.

> The survivors there in the province who escaped captivity are in great trouble and shame; the wall of Jerusalem is broken down, and its gates have been destroyed by fire.
> When I heard these words I sat down and wept and mourned for days, fasting and praying before the God of heaven (1:3–4).

Nehemiah petitioned the king and was appointed governor of Judah with authority to rebuild the walls and bring order to the city. (The "cupbearer," as attested throughout centuries of history and legend, was generally a favored, trusted, youthful official. Also notice Nehemiah's impressive political savvy as he negotiated for the king's support. This skill served him well as he managed both external and internal conflict in Jerusalem.)

The key event of the Ezra-Nehemiah story is found in Nehemiah 8 where it describes reading the Law to the assembled community. The priest, Ezra, read "from early morning until midday, in the presence of the men and the women and those who could understand; and the ears of all the people were attentive to the book of the law" (Neh 8:3).

The readings of "the law" came from the Pentateuch, but we can only guess which passages Ezra might have chosen to read to the people. As Ezra read for these long hours, the text says the priests and the Levites "helped the people to understand the law . . . So they read from the book, from the law of God, with interpretation. They gave the sense, so that the people understood the reading" (Neh 8:7–8).

We *Living in The Story* readers know something about this, don't we? All us seekers need guidance as we try to make sense, as we ask our ongoing question: *What does this mean?* Imagine how these questions must have overwhelmed this people as they listened to the words of their Scripture, maybe for the very first time, "for all the people wept when they heard the words of the law."

> Nehemiah, who was the governor, and Ezra the priest and scribe . . . said to all the people, "This day is holy to the LORD your God; do not mourn or weep."
>
> Then he said to them, "Go your way, eat the fat and drink sweet wine and send portions of them to those for whom nothing is prepared, for this day is holy to our LORD; and do not be grieved, for the joy of the LORD is your strength" (8:9–10).

The Hebrew word for "hearing" is *shema*, but this word always connotes a two-fold response: hearing *and* obeying. The post-exilic people of God still had a long way to go as they continued to listen and learn, as they continued to trust and obey. The Jewish people continued to re-invent themselves for four more centuries, becoming the people we read about in the NT. The Temple changed as well, undergoing numerous renovations, rescues, and revivals as one empire after another occupied the Jewish homeland and made its mark on their culture. Nevertheless, this covenant people of God had discovered some crucial answers to their core questions *Who is God?* and *Who are we?*

> Hear, O Israel: The LORD is our God, the LORD alone. You shall love the LORD your God with all your heart, and with all your soul, and with all your might (Deut 6:4–5).

The labyrinthine way Father Abraham began continues for his descendants—all his offspring, both physical and spiritual. May we all hear and obey as we continue our own journeys deeper into the heart of God, the one who is Lord alone.

As You Read the Psalms

Psalm 147 overflows with thanksgiving for the Lord of the cosmos who is abundant in power with understanding beyond measure. "Praise the LORD! How good it is to sing praises to our God for God is gracious! A song of praise is fitting . . ."

Within the context of *Living in The Story*, we consider Psalm 147 at the same time we see the remnant of exiles returning home. Even as they encountered a devastated Temple, land, and city, still they chose to sing of the grace of Yahweh who once again kept covenant with Israel.

> The LORD builds up Jerusalem and gathers the outcasts of Israel. God heals the brokenhearted and binds up their wounds (147:2–3).
>
> Praise the LORD, O Jerusalem! Praise your God, O Zion! For he strengthens the bars of your gates and blesses your children within you. God grants peace within your borders and fills you with the finest of wheat (147:13–14).
>
> The LORD declares his word to Jacob, his statutes and ordinances to Israel. God has not dealt thus with any other nation . . . (147:19–20).

Here is a song of praise and thanksgiving worthy of the celebrations described in the Memoir of Nehemiah.

But this psalm reaches far beyond the borders of Israel. Here also is a universal song of praise, a cosmic hymn celebrating the Creator-Redeemer-Sustainer of *all* creation who:

> determines the number of the stars and gives to all of them their names;
>
> covers the heavens with clouds, prepares rain for the earth and makes grass grow on the hills;
>
> gives to the animals their food and to the young ravens when they cry;
>
> gives snow like wool and scatters frost like ashes (who can stand before his cold?)

Then he sends out his word, and melts them; he makes his wind blow, and the waters flow.

Do you hear our poet alluding to the creation stories in Genesis?

Fast forward now to Christians living in the first century, and consider how Psalm 147 would have offered eschatological hope to these believers who also had endured the devastation of their homeland and holy Temple. Within the faith and theology of Christians, the ancient confidence becomes even more personal and intimate—God's "Word became flesh and dwelt among us" (John 1:14). As from the founding of the cosmos, God's Wind-Breath-Spirit continues to birth life.

Like a poem, like a painting, like a sculpture, like a symphony, creation reveals something true and real about the one who creates. I love this prayer from the *Book of Common Prayer*: "Give us all a reverence for the earth as your own creation that we may use its resources rightly in the service of others and to your honor and glory."[1] It dovetails nicely with the prayer and praise from this psalmist.

As You Read the New Testament

As Nehemiah and Ezra reassured the people of God that "the joy of the LORD is our strength," so the apostle Paul wrote to the people of Christ in Philippi.

> Rejoice in the Lord always; again I will say, Rejoice. Let your gentleness be known to everyone. The Lord is near. Do not worry about anything, but in everything by prayer and supplication with thanksgiving let your requests be made known to God.
> And the peace of God, which surpasses all understanding, will guard your hearts and your minds in Christ Jesus (Phil 4:4–7).

Paul's letter to the Philippians overflows with gratitude for a community of believers who seemed to be doing things right. This is the only letter Paul wrote that doesn't include criticisms, corrections, or admonishments, instead his pastor's heart swells with pride on behalf of these "brothers and sisters, whom I love and long for, my joy and crown . . . my beloved" (4:1).

Spend extra time this week with the powerful hymn in chapter 2. Most Bibles offset verses 6–11 into the shape of a poem because most

---

1. *Book of Common Prayer*, 388.

scholars believe these words came from a liturgical hymn dating back to the earliest days of the church. It may have been a baptismal liturgy reciting the faith of the first believers.

We sometimes refer to this as a poetic example of "U-shaped Christology" because of the way it begins with Christ in heaven, bends down into life on earth, then even further into the grave, and finally rises back up to heaven in triumph over death. Notice how this *Christology* is powerful *theology*; Christ "emptied himself," "humbled himself," "became obedient." It is *God* who is the Primary Actor in this cosmic picture. Ponder what this hymn might mean for you as you seek to "let the same mind be in you that was in Christ Jesus . . ."

As You Read the Gospel

The Gospel of Mark is a great read. From the prophet's opening call to prepare the way of God, to the voice splitting the heavens and declaring favor on the beloved Son, to the message of Jesus proclaiming the good news that the kingdom of God has come near, all the way to the open-ended, uncomfortable close of the Gospel according to Mark (16:8)—it's all just the *beginning* of the good news, Mark tells us.

But all the gospel evangelists also give witness to the backlash that inevitably comes whenever the good news is announced. This word of the kingdom, this pronouncement that God's kingdom is come near will provoke resistance because of a fundamental clash of kingdoms. Much as the psalmists teach about the "two ways," so the gospels demonstrate how we humans keep trying to build our own "kingdoms," our own power structures of hierarchy and self-sufficiency. We humans keep trying to make our own way.

The kingdom of God, on the other hand, is not appropriated by our feeble human efforts. The kingdom of God is not a matter of formulas or philosophies or scientific proofs, it's not a matter of our accomplishments or abilities. Rather, the kingdom of heaven comes to us outside our control. The kingdom is not ours to create but rather it is *God's* work and movement in the world.

That said, Mark tells a little story in chapter 12 about Jesus' conversation with a wise scribe who affirmed the good and true way of loving God with heart, soul, mind, and strength, coupled with loving one's neighbor as oneself. The scribe's wisdom lies in his realization that our proper human response is to orient ourselves toward God's kingdom, to accept the movement of God and participate in the mystery.

"When Jesus saw that he answered wisely, he said to him, 'You are not far from the kingdom of God'" (Mark 12:34).

One of my favorite things to do in my local community is to read to second graders once a week. These children are lively and lovely and bright. Once, at the end of a school year, they made thank you cards in which they had created acrostic greetings. Here is one little girl's thank you.

T = terrific reading
H = happy
A = an angel
N = nice
K = knowledgeable (didn't I say they are bright!)
Y = yummy cupcakes for our party
O = oriented to heaven
U = understanding

"Oriented to heaven." That's it, isn't it? Not pie-in-the-sky-by-and-by-heaven but rather God's-kingdom-come-on-earth-as-it-is-in-heaven heaven. Not God's heavenly banquet one of these days, but everyone— here and now—all welcome at the Table of the Christ.

God's people must ever stay oriented to the ever-coming, welcoming kingdom of God and keep participating in the mystery of Spirit's movement, always becoming the good news of the Christ for everyone we encounter. Yes, this way inevitably will provoke backlash, but walking in this way, we will never be far from the kingdom.

Reflection: *The Joy of the Lord is Our Strength*

Opposition, even violent conflict, has characterized the experience of the Jewish people throughout many centuries. Crusades and pogroms, *Kristallnacht* and Holocaust, private and public terrors—the history of the Jews continues to be woven with too many dark threads.

Rebuilding a life takes a lifetime of work. As I wrote this in 2020, sisters and brothers across the globe were faced with the deep challenges of rebuilding: one hurricane after another devastated parts of several coasts; raging fires destroyed forests, homes, and businesses throughout the west; earthquakes shook the foundations of Mexico; wars and violence in Syria, Central America, across the Middle East and Africa continued to drive people from their homelands, exiled refugees living lives of chaotic uncertainty; rampant pandemic raged with untold death.

Nehemiah and Ezra worked together alongside many persistently faithful Jews in the midst of hardship and persecution. Even with so many challenges, Ezra and Nehemiah remind us not to wait until everything is perfect. In the midst of imperfect circumstances, people of faith and hope can still find joy and "peace that passes understanding" (Phil 4:7).

Pleasant circumstances may bring us a measure of happiness that can last for a while, but it is the joy of the Lord that gives us strength to endure.

Week 47

Minor Prophets

Hosea
Amos
Obadiah
Nahum
Psalm 126
Psalm 128
Psalm 129
Colossians
Mark 13–14

DON'T BE OVERWHELMED WITH this reading list. Reading one of the Minor Prophets each day is very doable.

As You Read the Old Testament

> The word of the Lord that came to Hosea son of Beeri, in the days of Kings Uzziah, Jotham, Ahaz, and Hezekiah of Judah, and in the days of King Jeroboam son of Joash of Israel (Hosea 1).
>
> The words of Amos, who was among the shepherds of Tekoa, which he saw concerning Israel in the days of King Uzziah of Judah and in the days of King Jeroboam son of Joash of Israel (Amos 1).

Hosea and Amos prophesied to God's people both in Israel ("Ephraim") and in Judah during a time of settled prosperity. Even so, all the warning signs were clear to anyone with eyes to see. The nations were "sowing the wind" with their overconfidence and unfaithfulness, and Hosea promised they would "reap the whirlwind" (Hosea 8:7).

Amos also warned several surrounding nations of God's ultimate judgment because of their mistreatment of God's chosen people, while both Amos and Obadiah spoke a particular word of condemnation against Judah-Jacob's distant kin, Edom-Esau. "On that day, says the LORD, I will destroy the wise out of Edom, and understanding out of Mount Esau."

> You should not have gloated over your brother on the day of
> his misfortune; you should not have rejoiced over the people of
> Judah on the day of their ruin (Obad 1:12).

Nahum's pronouncement uttered Yahweh's denunciation of Nineveh, capital of Assyria. Even as God had used Assyria (and Babylon) as a tool in the divine hand to accomplish the divine will, still these nations stood in judgment because of the harm they had done to God's chosen ones. "As you have done, it shall be done to you; your deeds shall return on your own head" (Obad 1:15).

As You Read the Psalms

In the imagination of Israel, Zion was the divine King's ultimate dwelling place, the holy throne situated in the highest heavens, thus everything built in the Temple signified and symbolized these invisible heavenly realities. Even though Israel often used the words "Zion" and "Jerusalem" interchangeably, the city and the Temple were always and only physical metaphors that pointed to the spiritual unseen-ness of God's presence in the heavenly Zion.

Notice how many of these short, joyful *Songs of Ascent* reflect (what Walter Bruggemann calls) a New Orientation.[1] The years of Babylonian Exile radically altered Israel and realigned their orientation to their God in profound ways.

This shift in orientation after the Exile redefined the importance of the land, fostered a renewed reverence for Jerusalem and the Temple, and reinforced their commitment to pass on their faith to coming generations. This realignment reminded the people of the fragile blessing

1 Brueggemann, *The Message of the Psalms*, 19–23.

of posterity—too many of their children had been lost in the war and the deportation—but gave them opportunity to cultivate faith within the next generations in order to ensure the nation's future. In the Psalms for this week, join in the celebration of our children so that we too may recommit ourselves to hold them precious and to share the stories of our faith with our children and grandchildren.

As You Read the New Testament

Whenever I read Colossians, I think of the Psalms. Listen to this psalm of praise from the writer to the Colossians. Consider how it echoes songs of praise and wonder from Israel's psalter.

> Christ is the image of the invisible God, the firstborn of all creation. For in him all things in heaven and on earth were created, things visible and invisible, whether thrones or dominions or rulers or powers—all things have been created through him and for him.
>
> He himself is before all things, and in him all things hold together. He is the head of the body, the church; he is the beginning, the firstborn from the dead, so that he might come to have first place in everything.
>
> For in the Christ all the fullness of God was pleased to dwell, and through him God was pleased to reconcile all things to himself, whether on earth or in heaven, by making peace through the blood of his cross (1:15–20).

There it is: the song of the cosmos incarnated in Jesus the Christ, the song of praise to the Creator binding all creation together. There it is: the gospel. May our lives also *become* this song, *enflesh* this poem, and *incarnate* God's praise.

As You Read the Gospel

When we read carefully, we discover that the synoptic gospels (Mark, Luke, and Matthew) lay out the Jesus story within a period of about a year with Jesus celebrating Passover only once. John, however, describes three different trips to Jerusalem for three different Passovers. Thus began the tradition that Jesus' earthly ministry lasted three years.

This week we read again Mark's story of the anointing of Jesus' feet. As you read, note this one little phrase repeated in three of the four gospels: "You always have the poor with you . . ." (John 12:8, Mark 14:7, Matt 26:11). I sometimes hear some Christians quote these words of Jesus as a way to argue that our society is justified in its acceptance of poverty and homelessness. Some people use these words to sanction a status quo of poverty, arguing that poverty is inevitable, part of the natural order, an unsolvable reality. Some even claim that Jesus' words prove that poverty is God's will—a bizarre perspective.

Part of this understanding comes from a long tradition that has roots in a perverse prosperity gospel. As this reasoning goes, "God helps those who help themselves" and thus a person's poverty only "proves" they are lazy with a lack of character while a person's wealth "proves" they have been divinely blessed. In American Christianity, we often hear the argument that charity must be private and personal, that helping the poor should be the responsibility of the church and of individuals, but not of the government.

This approach dismisses the reality that societal structures and governmental policies often are responsible for creating and perpetuating poverty. The approach that focuses only on individual charity downplays the power and responsibility of community. Scripture's perspective always assumes community, whereas our modern way of reading it with a bias toward individual rights and privileges has done deep damage to the authentic message of the Bible.

The woman in the story in Mark 14 is poor and yet her gift to Jesus is an opulent gesture. Conventional wisdom (within the biblical stories and in our current day) may label it wasteful, foolish, senseless, but in God's economy, abundant amazing grace is never wasteful. The women who anointed Jesus poured out their offering with reckless abandon and sanctified the moment with their lavish love, honoring Jesus with daring extravagance.

This is the kind of giving that creates grace; this is the kind of giving to which we are called. Our gifts given to God—and then given to others in Christ's name—should reflect something of God's own opulent, extravagant way of giving. In the giving of such grace, we mustn't presume to judge the worthiness of another. We don't control how our gift will be received by another and we can't know how our gift will be used by others. As givers in the way of Christ, we simply are called to give, to offer grace in abundance—just as God does.

As you read Mark this week, note how these chapters set the stage for Jesus' final hours which begin on "the first day of Unleavened Bread, when the Passover lamb is sacrificed . . ." (14:12).

Reflection: *Repairing the World*

Our Jewish siblings have long been committed to *tikkun olam*—"repair of the world." *Tikkun olam* is a value of Judaism that calls for God's faithful people to be intentional about performing caring acts that can help mend the frayed fabric of our shared life: acts of personal charity, acts of social advocacy for the homeless, hurting, and hungry, as well as actions that protect and preserve our environment.

The prophetic call throughout history is to do justice for the widow, for the orphan, for the poor, for the exploited, for the neglected, for the stranger, for the vulnerable. *This* is the call of the word of the Lord. *These* are biblical values. How has the Christian church not heard and lived into that calling for far too often? We have become so bent in on ourselves that we forget the whole reason for our existence is to love our God and to love our neighbor.

This call to justice and mercy, the challenge of *tikkun olam*, is rooted in the Hebrew prophets: Micah and Joel, Amos, Isaiah, and Jeremiah. This call resounds again in the life and ministry of Jesus the Christ. Because of the generosity and self-giving of Jesus the Christ, because of the faithfulness of the God who is Life itself, death is becoming undone. Because of the gospel, the brokenness of humanity is becoming whole, the lost are being found, the pain is being healed, the sin is being forgiven, and the world is being repaired.

But the work must be recreated and renewed in every generation. Those of us who are people of the good news of Jesus Christ don't have to remain paralyzed over the brokenness of our world, we can choose to enter into the pain of our neighbors, we can work to remove whatever barriers keep them from wholeness, and we can help bring them to the one who heals and repairs. We can make a difference.

In his book, *The Liberating Path of the Hebrew Prophets*, Nahum Ward-Lev speaks to all of us when he says:

> While most of us are not yet prophets, we also know the pres-
> ence of a great love, a love that includes the entire world. Awak-
> ened by that love, we too are aggrieved in the face of human

oppression. A voice within us calls out, "This is wrong and cannot stand." We yearn for a world in which all can flourish. Fueled by our own particular yearning, we occasionally entertain visions for how some small part of our world can be liberated into greater possibility.[2]

I know you know this little story. It's been around for years but it's worth repeating. A child stood at the seashore where thousands of starfish had been stranded on the sand and were slowly dying. The child picked them up one by one and tossed them back into the waves.

A man came along, someone who had seen a lot of life, was seasoned and experienced and therefore a touch cynical. "What are you doing?" he asked the child.

"I'm saving the starfish," she replied.

The man watched as she picked up another and tossed it into the sea. He watched some more as she picked up one, two, three more starfish. But there were thousands and there was no way one little girl could save them all. "Why do you keep on doing this?" the man asked. "Don't you know you can't possibly save them all? There is no way you can make a difference for so many starfish."

The girl stopped, thought for a minute, then picked up one more starfish and flung it into the water. "It made a difference for that one," she said.

Each one of us doing what we can where we are with what we have: *tikkun olam.* All of us together—willing to be inconvenienced, to risk, even to look foolish, odd, or unusual to those around us—making a difference.

2. Ward-Lev, *The Liberating Path of the Hebrew Prophets*, 4–5, 11.

Week 48

Final Reflections

Joel
Micah
Habakkuk
Zephaniah
Malachi
Psalm 102
Psalm 145
Psalm 150
Ephesians
Mark 15–16

OUR *FINAL* WEEK! YOU DID IT!

As You Read the Old Testament

The prophet Micah asks, *What does God require in order for us to be pleasing, to be acceptable? What does God want from us anyway?*

This sounds like the perennial questions we have been asking ourselves this year: *Who is God?* and *who are we?* Then Micah answers his own question. Just this: "do justice, love kindness, walk humbly with your God" (Mic 6:8). Seems simple enough, doesn't it? So why do we humans have such a hard time doing justice, being kind, and living our lives with humility and reverence? What is so bent within us that these three simple things trip us up over and over again?

Remember it was Martin Luther who defined sin as "the self bent in upon itself." There is a bent-ness inherent about us humans and a bent-ness that permeates the entire world. Consequently we create societies that are curved in on themselves. We create a world that is very often unjust, unkind, and arrogant so that countless people are damaged every single day by society's injustices, mean spiritedness, and hubris. I believe each of us is called, in some way or another, to continue the prophetic ministry seen in the ancient prophets and embodied in the prophetic life of the Christ, speaking truth to power and standing with the poor, oppressed, and the vulnerable.

As You Read the Psalms

Through this year of *Living in The Story*, we have listened closely as numerous previous generations have offered their witness to us in our own generation. "One generation shall laud your works to another, and shall declare your mighty acts . . ." (Ps 145). Their witness of faith sometimes wept from the depths and sometimes sang from the heights—just as our own lives give witness. And through the Psalms, we have joined with all creation to give thanks and praise to Creator. "All your works shall give thanks to you, O Lord."

As we all continue to live in *The Story* into our own future, may we all continue to share our stories—and *The Story*—with the generations that are coming after us.

As You Read the New Testament

This is your second time to read Ephesians. Think of this as a bonus gift of powerful poetic prose and soaring theology.

The Ephesian writer proclaims a gospel of radical grace that sows life-giving kingdom seeds in the soil of any heart ready to receive it. "For [Christ] is our peace; in his flesh he has made both groups into one and has broken down the dividing wall, that is, the hostility between us" (2:14). Even his introductory statement to the prevailing family code of his first-century society, if taken seriously, would turn every human relationship on its head: "Be subject to one another out of reverence for Christ" (5:21). The ongoing challenge to the church of Jesus Christ is to grow more and more adept at living God's way within our culture instead of letting the culture of this world tame God's radically inclusive kingdom.

Ephesians 6 is where we find the lively image of "the whole armor of God." The belt of truth, the breastplate of righteousness, the gospel of peace, the shield of faith, the helmet of salvation, and "the sword of the Spirit, which is the word of God." Notice that all this armor is defensive, not offensive.

Some Christians have a nasty reputation for going on the offense and wielding the Bible like a sledgehammer. But consider a couple of things here. First, "the word of God" is not synonymous with the Bible. Remember, for the Ephesian writer, his only "Bible" was the Hebrew Scripture, not the leather-bound, type-set-in-stone Bible we have on our bookshelves. For NT authors, the prophetic and pastoral word of the Lord was discerned through diligent prayer and faithful listening to the Spirit living and acting through the community of faith. Second, "the word of God, the sword of the Spirit," functioned more like a scalpel than a hammer. The author of Hebrews said it well:

> Indeed, the word of God is living and active, sharper than any two-edged sword, piercing until it divides soul from spirit, joints from marrow; it is able to judge the thoughts and intentions of the heart. And before him no creature is hidden, but all are naked and laid bare to the eyes of the one to whom we must render an account (Heb 4:12–13).

Consider the "sword," the "word," to be less like the words of a book (no matter how precious) and more like the living "Word made flesh, dwelling among us" (John 1). It is only this Word who is capable of slicing through our self-deceptions and piercing the hardness of our hearts. It is only this Word who is capable of doing battle "against the rulers, against the authorities, against the cosmic powers of this present darkness, against the spiritual forces of evil in the heavenly places." According to Ephesians, our assignment as mortals within this cosmic battle is to "withstand," to "stand firm," and to pray. Spirit is our defense and prayer is our offense.

As You Read the Gospel

Several years ago, a master performer, Alec McCowen, created a powerful recitation and one-man presentation of the entire Gospel of Mark. I highly recommend it. (You can find it on YouTube.)[1]

As you read the final chapter of Mark, notice how your Bible frames the ending. Most translations place the second half of verse 8 into brackets, because scholars doubt that Mark's original version included these words. We call this the short ending. Verses 9–20 also are bracketed for the same reason; we call this the long ending—most likely added to the Gospel of Mark by a later editor.

If verses 8b–20 were not from the hand of Mark, consider the odd ending of this gospel: "So [the women] went out and fled from the tomb, for terror and amazement had seized them; and they said nothing to anyone, for they were afraid." *The End.* What might such an ending mean?

I have come to agree with those who think Mark intended this abrupt ending to his gospel, this open-ended ending as a way to communicate his conviction that *The Story* is not over. As Mark's gospel transitions from the story of the crucified Jesus to the mystery of the resurrected Christ, we readers realize we are no longer observers sitting in Mark's audience, because Mark has written *us* into *The Story*. We have become participants in the good news of Jesus Christ, Son of God and Son of Man. It is *we* who are challenged to "go and tell," to be witnesses of the invisible, inscrutable reality of the risen Christ.

Just as Mark began his gospel within *The Overarching Story* that has been unfolding for eons, so he finishes his chapter with the full awareness that *The Story* will continue.

So now it is our turn. How will we write our chapters in the ongoing, overarching story of love and grace? Write it well, my friends.

Final Reflection: *The Word of the Lord. Thanks be to God.*

> In the beginning . . . God said: *Let there be light.* And there was light. (Gen 1).

---

1. Alec McCowen gave his first solo performance of St. Mark's Gospel (King James Version) in 1977 in a tiny church basement in Newcastle, England. Mr. McCowen, who recited the entire text of the Gospel from memory in this presentation, was nominated for a Tony Award in 1979.

> The heavens are telling the glory of God; the firmament proclaims God's handiwork. There is no speech; there are no words; and yet—their voice goes out throughout the earth, their words to the end of the world (Ps 19).
>
> Where were you when I laid the foundations of the earth ... Where were you when all the morning stars sang together ... (Job 38).

Sometimes the poetry of Scripture gives me chill bumps. There is such beauty and mystery in these words, they draw me in and fill me up. I smile. I wonder. I weep. I furrow my brow and scratch my head. I argue. I wait. I watch. I listen.

Scripture is a vast ocean. We can sail the seas of Scripture and rock gently in its waves one day, then hold on for dear life the next. Sometimes its waters are crystal clear and we see into depths we never imagined. Sometimes its ocean roils red or stretches out before us in unimaginable greens, blues, and greys. Some people don their snorkel gear and plunge in deeper; there are wonders to be found beneath the surface. Some people strap on air tanks and dive to the depths; there is always more to learn.

If you have been reading through the Bible with *Living in The Story* over the past forty-eight weeks, maybe you have experienced Scripture with fresh eyes. I hope you learned something new through your reading. I hope you caught a glimpse of its inexhaustible mysteries.

Throughout this project, I have tried to write about these Scriptures in a way that helps us make a bit more sense of this strange and wonderful book. Just maybe, through this experience, all of us are learning to listen and to see more clearly. Maybe all of us are doing a better job of asking-seeking-knocking.

Before I retired, when I was preaching regularly on Sundays, after reading aloud the words of Scripture the lector would pronounce the "Word of the Lord," and we hearers dutifully responded "Thanks be to God." But what does it mean to say that this Bible is the "Word of the Lord?"

When I would stand in the pulpit, I would pray the same prayer Sunday after Sunday: "You have spoken to us once and for all in Jesus Christ and you continue to speak in these Holy Scriptures. Speak to us now, we pray . . ."[2] When I would read the text for the sermon, I would begin by saying: "Listen now for the Word of the Lord in this the Holy Scripture." So you might ask what I mean when say this Bible is the "Word

---

2. Prayer adapted from my mentor and friend, Gene Boring.

of the Lord?" You might ask what it is I believe about this book we call the Holy Bible. Why do I call it "holy?"

Followers of the one true God, over several millennia, have given witness to their experience with God. The Bible is the record of that changing understanding and testimony to the variety of ways God's people have found meaning and tried to live their lives with faith in the one who is beyond our knowing, the one beyond our grasping, the One-Who-Is.

Sometimes the stories record great unfaithfulness (yes, that is our sad human history). Sometimes the stories show misunderstandings and sometimes, great wisdom (yes, we humans are both wise and foolish). Sometimes the stories tell of remarkable courage and goodness (yes, humans have a way of rising above adversity and responding to the challenges of life with tenacious faith and stubborn hope).

Over the years, these writings have offered faithful witness to a people's relationship with the God of their understanding. And so, over the years, these writings have become our sacred Scriptures, the "Holy" Bible giving witness to the holiness of living in the presence of a holy God.

The Old Testament together with the New Testament are the Scriptures of the Christian Church. So, I believe, in order for the church to be "Christian," it must engage the Christian Scriptures. By "engage" I mean read, study, learn from, argue with, protest about, be shaped by, be challenged with, be spoken to, and changed by this Holy Bible.

But the Scriptures are not only the witness of human beings. Somehow, also, in some mystery, again and again, the God of all creation speaks in and through these human words. "Speak to us now we pray, that we may know you." Don't ask me to explain that.

I'm grateful I have learned to trust it without being able to explain it. I trust it because I see evidence of God's presence in our lives and in the world, and that evidence supports my confidence. I trust it because I see how the Word of the Lord has created a people who are bound together over countless ages, who are connected despite the differences that seek to divide us. I trust it because deep honest logic can see something deeply true about the witness of Scripture, but also because (as the mystics teach us) people of faith are able to see with our "third eye"—people of faith see beyond logic.

We can perceive God's ever new presence, God's call to new beginnings, and God's will and way for us today even through these ancient, culture-bound, human words of Scripture. Evidence, experience, tradition, reason, community, intuitive knowing—they all come together to allow us to trust that somehow, in some mystery, again and again, the God of all creation speaks in and through these human words.

So when I say "the Word of the Lord; thanks be to God," I am giving witness that I believe God is still speaking. I give witness that the witness of Scripture can speak authentically in every age about who we are as humans and about who God is as God.

But of course, that "speaking" is not exhaustive. All words are limited and limiting, and the words of the Bible are no exception. There are just so many ways words can represent reality and all ways are always inadequate. Human words are not things; rather words are symbols and pointers pointing beyond themselves to something else. The words of the OT point to, direct us toward something in their future, while the words of the NT point to, direct us toward something in their past.

And what is this "thing" the words of Scripture point to? What is the point of this book we call the Bible? "In the beginning was the Word . . . and the Word became flesh and dwelt among us . . . and this Word is light and life to all people" (John 1). Scripture points to Christ—the crux, the hinge of history—*the* Word of the Lord.

But again, Scripture is not "just" history. Scripture also points forward toward the ultimate future of all creation brought together in unity and harmony in this Christ. Whether someone knows that or not, claims it or not, I believe God has spoken once and for all in Jesus Christ. And in Jesus Christ, God has spoken love and grace and welcome for *all*. In this divine self-revelation, God has been unveiled, has emerged from the fire and cloud, has stepped out of the whirlwind, and said, *I Am.*

I Am . . . swaddled in a manger in a cattle stall; working with a calloused hand and a carpenter's saw; reaching out to the lost and forsaken; embracing the children; feeding the hungry; healing the sick; washing dirty feet; hanging on a cross; reigning and redeeming all creation within its ultimate *shalom*. This is who *I Am*. This is what love looks like and sounds like and acts like.

And so now here with this final *Living in The Story* essay, "I pray that we may have the power to comprehend . . . the breadth and length and height and depth of love, and to know the love of Christ that is beyond knowing . . ." (Eph 3)

The Word of the Lord.

Thanks be to God.

Amen.

Bibliography

Arnott, Arthur Smith. "Only a Boy Named David." London: Salvationist Publishing, 1931.

Barth, Karl. *The Doctrine of Reconciliation*, 2/4. In Church Dogmatics, vol. 4. Edited by G.W. Bromily and T.F. Torrance. Translated by G.W. Bromily. London: T&T Clark, 1958, paperback, 2004.

———. *The Epistle to the Romans*. 6th ed. Translated by Edwyn C. Hoskyns. London: Oxford University Press, 1968.

———. "The Need and Promise of Christian Preaching." In *The Word of God and the Word of Man*. Translated by Douglas Horton. Gloucester, MA: Peter Smith, 1978.

Bolle, Kees W. "The Nature, Functions, and Types of Myth." *Britannica*. www.britannica.com/topic/myth.

Boring, M. Eugene and Fred B. Craddock. *The People's New Testament Commentary*. Louisville: Westminster John Knox, 2004.

Boring, M. Eugene. "The Book of Matthew." In *The New Interpreter's Bible: A Commentary in Twelve Volumes*, vol. 8. Nashville: Abingdon, 1995.

———. *First Peter*. Abingdon New Testament Commentary. Nashville: Abingdon, 1999.

———. *An Introduction to the New Testament*. Louisville: Westminster John Knox, 2012.

———. *Mark: A Commentary*. New Testament Library. Louisville: Westminster John Knox, 2006.

———. *Revelation*. Interpretation: a Bible Commentary for Teaching and Preaching. Louisville: John Knox, 1989.

———. *Truly Human Truly Divine: Christological Language and the Gospel Form*. St. Louis, Mo: CBP Press, 1984.

Brueggemann, Walter. *An Introduction to the Old Testament: The Canon and Christian Imagination*. Louisville: Westminster John Knox, 2003.

———. *Like Fire in the Bones*. Minneapolis: Fortress, 2006.

———. *The Message of the Psalms: A Theological Commentary*. Minneapolis: Augsburg, 1984.

———. *The Prophetic Imagination*. Minneapolis: Fortress, 1978.

———. *Texts That Linger Words That Explode*. Minneapolis: Fortress, 2000.

Bruns, George and Tom Blackburn. "Ballad of Davy Crockett." New York: Cadence, 1954.

Calvin, John. *Institutes of the Christian Religion*, vol. 2. In Library of Christian Classics. Edited by John T. McNeill. Translated by Ford Lewis Battles. Louisville: Westminster John Knox, 1960.

Charpentier, Etienne. *How to Read the Bible: Two Volumes in One*. Translated by John Bowden. New York: Gramercy Books, 1981.

Chittister, Joan. *The Time Is Now: A Call to Uncommon Courage*. New York: Convergent Books, 2019.

Clark-Soles, Jaime. *Reading John for Dear Life: A Spiritual Walk with the Fourth Gospel*. Louisville: Westminster John Knox, 2016. Kindle.

Craven, Toni. *The Book of Psalms*. Collegeville, MN: Liturgical Press, 1992.

Darr, Katheryn Pfisterer. "The Book of Ezekiel." In *The New Interpreter's Bible: A Commentary in Twelve Volumes*, vol. 6. Nashville: Abingdon, 2001.

Dear, John. "Gustavo Gutierrez and the Preferential Option for the Poor." *The National Catholic Reporter*. Kansas City: National Catholic Reporter (November 2011). https://www.ncronline.org/blogs/road-peace/gustavo-gutierrez-and-preferential-option-poor.

Douglas, Kelly Brown. *Stand Your Ground: Black Bodies and the Justice of God*. Maryknoll, NY: Orbis, 2015.

Fretheim, Terence E. "The Book of Genesis." In *The New Interpreter's Bible: A Commentary in Twelve Volumes*, vol. 1. Nashville: Abingdon, 1994.

Georges, Jayson. *Psalms: An Honor-Shame Paraphrase of 15 Psalms*. Timē Press, 2017. Kindle.

Hambrick-Stowe, Charles E. "Ruth and the New Abraham, Esther the New Moses." In *Christian Century* (December 1983) 1130–134.

Handel, George Frideric. *Messiah: An Oratorio*. London: 1741.

Hays, Richard B. *First Corinthians*. Interpretation: a Bible Commentary for Teaching and Preaching. Louisville: Westminster John Knox, 1997.

———. *Reading Backwards: Figural Christology and the Fourfold Gospel Witness*. Waco: Baylor University Press, 2014.

Heschel, Abraham J. *The Prophets*. New York: Harper and Row, 1962.

Hughes, Richard T. *Myths America Lives By*. Chicago: University of Illinois Press, 2003.

Johnson, James Weldon. "The Creation." In *God's Trombones*. New York: Viking, 1927.

King, Martin Luther Jr. "A Knock at Midnight." At Mt. Zion Baptist Church. Cincinnati, Ohio, (June 1967). https://kinginstitute.stanford.edu/king-papers/documents/knock-midnight.

L'Engle, Madeline. *A Wind in the Door*. New York: Farrar, Straus and Giroux, 1973.

Lester, Andrew D. *Hope in Pastoral Care and Counseling*. Louisville: Westminster John Knox, 1995.

Levine, Amy-Jill. *The Misunderstood Jew: The Church and the Scandal of the Jewish Jesus*. San Francisco: HarperSanFrancisco, 2006.

Lewis, Alan E. *Between Cross and Resurrection: A Theology of Holy Saturday*. Grand Rapids: Eerdmans, 2001.

Lewis, C.S. *The Four Loves*. New York: Harcourt Brace Jovanovich, 1960.

Lincoln, Abraham. Second Inaugural Address. April 10, 1865. Transcribed and annotated by the Lincoln Studies Center, Knox College, Galesburg, Illinois. https://www.ourdocuments.gov/doc.php?flash=false&doc=38&page=transcript.

Lischer, Richard. *The End of Words: The Language of Reconciliation in a Culture of Violence*. Grand Rapids: Eerdmans, 2005.

Luther, Martin. *Word and Sacrament I*. In Luther's Works, vol. 35. Philadelphia: Fortress, 1960.

McCann, J. Clinton Jr. "The Book of Psalms." In *The New Interpreter's Bible: A Commentary in Twelve Volumes*, vol. 4. Nashville: Abingdon, 1996.

McCowen, Sir Alec. *St. Mark's Gospel*. Oklahoma City: Daystar Foundation and Library, 2003.

McLaren, Brian D. *Faith After Doubt: Why Your Beliefs Stopped Working and What to Do About It*. New York: St. Martin's, 2021.

————. *We Make the Road by Walking: A Year-Long Quest for Spiritual Formation, Reorientation, and Activation*. New York: Jericho Books, 2014.

Miles, Sara. *Take This Bread: A Radical Conversion*. New York: Ballentine, 2007.

Moltmann, Jürgen. *The Crucified God*. Minneapolis: Fortress, 1993.

Pape, Lance B. *The Scandal of Having Something to Say: Ricoeur and the Possibility of Postliberal Preaching*. Waco: Baylor University Press, 2013.

————. Unpublished lecture. Ministers' Workshop at First Christian Church. Tyler TX, March 2015.

Phelps-Roper, Megan. *Unfollow: A Journey from Hatred to Hope, leaving the Westboro Baptist Church*. New York: Farrar, Straus and Giroux, 2019.

Richardson-Moore, Deb. *The Weight of Mercy: A Novice Pastor on the City Streets*. Grand Rapids: Monarch Books, 2012.

Ricoeur, Paul. *The Symbolism of Evil*. New York: Harper and Row, 1967.

Rohr, Richard. *Falling Upward: A Spirituality for the Two Halves of Life*. San Francisco: Jossey-Bass, 2013.

————. *Things Hidden: Scripture as Spirituality*. Cincinnati: St. Anthony Messenger, 2008.

————. *The Wisdom Pattern: Order, Chaos, Reorder*. Cincinnati: Franciscan Media, 2020.

Simon, Paul. *The Sounds of Silence*. Performed by Paul Simon and Art Garfunkel. Produced by Bob Johnston. New York: Columbia Records 9629, 1965.

Stabile, Suzanne. Unpublished lecture. Ministers' Week at Brite Divinity School. Fort Worth TX, February 2010.

Taylor, Barbara Brown. *Speaking of Sin: The Lost Language of Salvation*. Cambridge MA: Cowley Publications, 2000.

Thiselton, Anthony C. *New Horizons in Hermeneutics: The Theory and Practice of Transforming Biblical Reading*. Grand Rapids: Zondervan, 1992.

Tillich, Paul. "You Are Accepted." In *The Shaking of the Foundations*. Eugene, OR: Wipf and Stock, 1948.

Toulouse, Mark. *God in Public: Four Ways American Christianity and Public Life Relate*. Louisville: Westminster John Knox, 2006.

Trible, Phyllis. *Texts of Terror: Literary-Feminist Readings of Biblical Narratives*. Philadelphia: Fortress, 1984.

Ward-Lev, Nahum. *The Liberating Path of the Hebrew Prophets: Then and Now*. Maryknoll, NY: Orbis Books, 2019.

Watts, Isaac. *The Psalms of David Imitated in the Language of the New Testament*. 2nd ed. London: John Clark and Richard Ford, 1722.

Willimon, William H. *Pastor: The Theology and Practice of Ordained Ministry*. Nashville: Abingdon, 2002.

Wrede, William. *The Messianic Secret*. Translated by J. C. G. Greig. London: James Clark, 1971.

Yousafzai, Malala. *I Am Malala: The Girl Who Stood Up for Education and Was Shot by the Taliban*. London: Orion Publishing Group, 2013.